The Boer War

The Boer War

DENIS JUDD
&
KEITH SURRIDGE

JOHN MURRAY
Albemarle Street, London

A catalogue record for this book is available from the British Library

ISBN 0-7195-5585 X

Typeset in 12.25/13.5 Garamond MT by
Servis Filmsetting Ltd, Manchester

Printed and bound in Great Britain by
Butler and Tanner Ltd, Frome and London

Contents

Contents

Illustrations

The authors and publishers would like to thank the following for permission to reproduce illustrations: Plate 1, National Portrait Gallery, London; 2, 6, 8, 11, 12, 13 and 32, Anglo-Boer War Museum, Bloemfontein; 3, 4, 5, 7, 9, 10, 14, 15, 17, 18, 19, 20, 21, 22, 23, 24, 25, 26, 27, 28, 29, 30, and 31, Macmillan Collection, University of Cape Town Library; 16, Foreign and Commonwealth Office Library; 33 and 34, Mary Evans Picture Library.

Acknowledgements

We are indebted, predictably enough, to many institutions and people for their help during the research and preparation of the book. For the use of documents in their care, we would like to thank Birmingham University Library; the Bodleian Library and the Warden and Fellows of New College, Oxford; the University of Cape Town; the library and archives of the Ladysmith Museum; the Manuscripts Department of the British Library; the Marquess of Salisbury; Royal Pavilion Libraries and Museums (Hove Reference Library); the National Army Museum, Chelsea; and the Controller of Her Majesty's Stationery Office for permission to use Crown copyright documents held in the Public Record Office, Kew. In the Preface we mention the many individuals to whom we are grateful for their assistance in bringing this book to fruition.

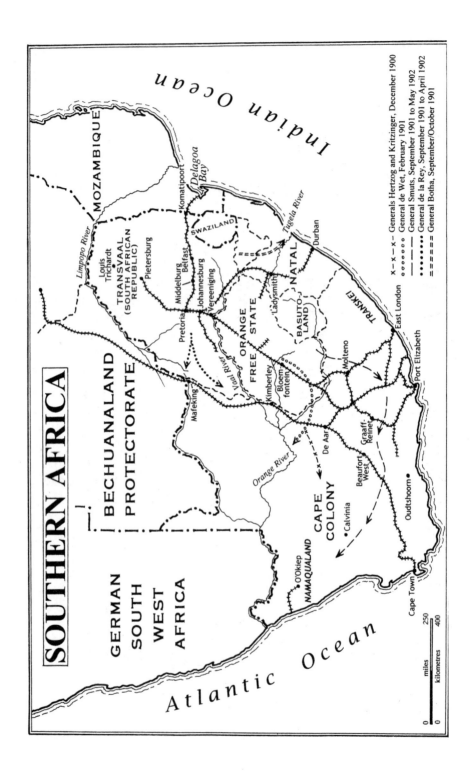

SOUTHERN AFRICA

Indian Ocean

Atlantic Ocean

MOZAMBIQUE

GERMAN SOUTH WEST AFRICA

BECHUANALAND PROTECTORATE

TRANSVAAL (SOUTH AFRICAN REPUBLIC)

SWAZILAND

NATAL

ORANGE FREE STATE

BASUTOLAND

CAPE COLONY

TRANSKEI

NAMAQUALAND

Limpopo River
Vaal River
Orange River
Tugela River

Louis Trichardt
Pietersburg
Middelburg
Belfast
Komatipoort
Delagoa Bay
Johannesburg
Pretoria
Vereeniging
Ladysmith
Durban
Mafeking
Kimberley
Bloemfontein
Molteno
East London
Graaff-Reinet
De Aar
Beaufort West
Port Elizabeth
Calvinia
O'Okiep
Oudtshoorn
Cape Town

x–x–x– Generals Hertzog and Kritzinger, December 1900
ooooooo General de Wet, February 1901
·········· General Smuts, September 1901 to May 1902
—·—·— General de la Rey, September 1901 to April 1902
======= General Botha, September/October 1901

miles   0   250
kilometres 0   400

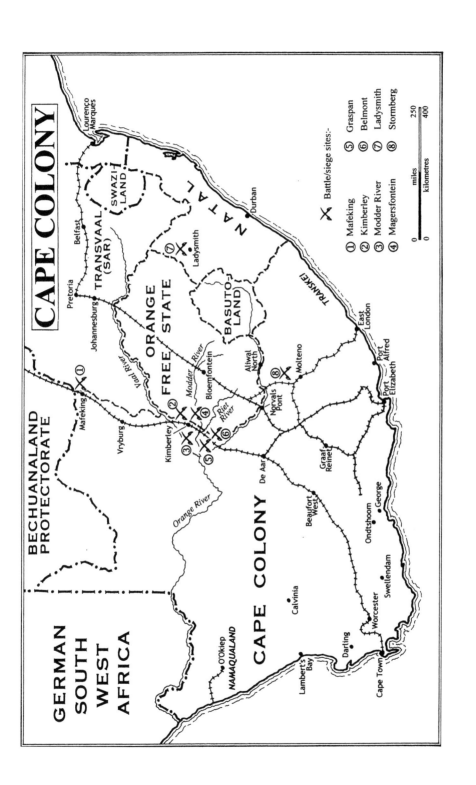

CAPE COLONY

GERMAN SOUTH WEST AFRICA

BECHUANALAND PROTECTORATE

Lourenço Marques

TRANSVAAL (SAR)

SWAZI-LAND

NATAL

Belfast

Pretoria

Johannesburg

ORANGE FREE STATE

Ladysmith

Durban

BASUTO-LAND

Modder River

Bloemfontein

Rict River

Aliwal North

Molteno

Vryburg

Mafeking

Kimberley

Norvals Pont

East London

Port Alfred

Port Elizabeth

TRANSKEI

Vaal River

Graaf Reinet

George

De Aar

Beaufort West

Ondtshoorn

Orange River

Calvinia

Worcester

Swellendam

O'Okiep

NAMAQUALAND

Lambert's Bay

Darling

Cape Town

CAPE COLONY

Battle/siege sites:-

① Mafeking ⑤ Graspan
② Kimberley ⑥ Belmont
③ Modder River ⑦ Ladysmith
④ Magersfontein ⑧ Stormberg

miles   250
0
kilometres 400
0

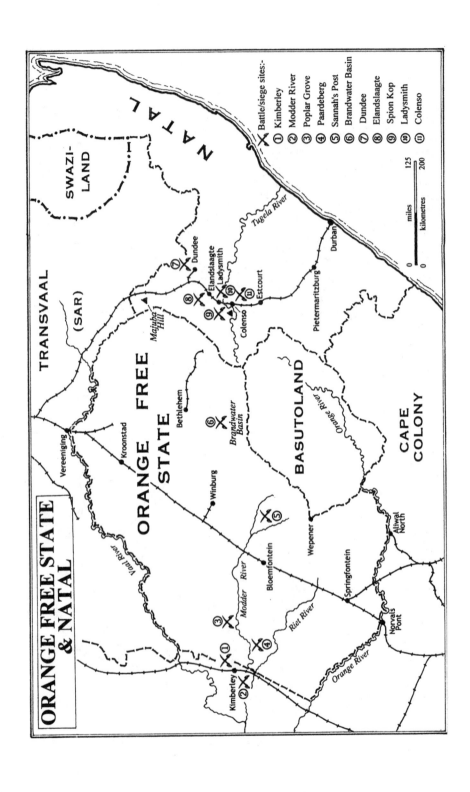

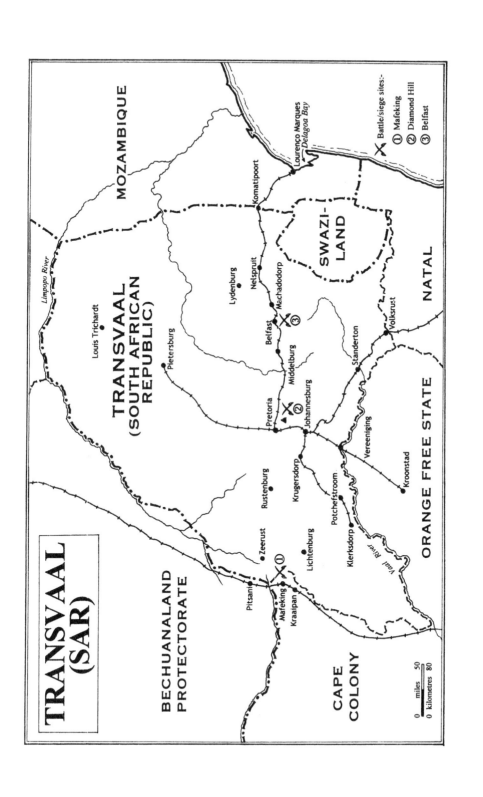

TRANSVAAL (SAR)

MOZAMBIQUE

SWAZI-LAND

TRANSVAAL (SOUTH AFRICAN REPUBLIC)

NATAL

BECHUANALAND PROTECTORATE

CAPE COLONY

ORANGE FREE STATE

Battle/siege sites:-
① Mafeking
② Diamond Hill
③ Belfast

Limpopo River

Louis Trichardt

Lourenço Marques
Delagoa Bay

Komatipoort

Lydenburg

Nelspruit

Michadodorp

Pietersburg

Belfast

Middelburg

Volksrust

Standerton

Pretoria

Johannesburg

Vereeniging

Kroonstad

Rustenburg

Krugersdorp

Potchefstroom

Zeerust

Lichtenburg

Klerksdorp

Vaal River

Pitsani

Mafeking

Kraaipan

0   miles   50
0 kilometres 80

Preface

This book is a cooperative venture – a successful and creative one we hope – arising out of the academic and professional interaction of the two authors and their shared areas of research interest. We are each responsible for certain sections of the text, but have also made amendments and suggestions, sometimes substantial ones, to each other's work. We have worked closely together throughout the writing of the book. More importantly, perhaps, we have been able to work harmoniously and happily on a project that is dear to our hearts and central to our academic interests. We sincerely hope that our readers will be satisfied with the final product.

Essentially, we have tried to examine and clarify certain aspects of the conflict – confusion, ambivalence, surprising alignments and realignments, misrepresentation, 'spin doctoring', double standards and the great residual mass of mythology attaching to the war – that have traditionally been either ignored or misunderstood. We have also presented a substantial section describing the military campaign.

In writing this new history of the Boer War we have inevitably read and profited from the works of many scholars and writers; our warm thanks go to them all. Many of them are acknowledged in the end-notes – though at the publisher's request we have tried to keep these notes to a minimum. Anyone wishing for more details about the books consulted will find this information in the bibliography. The same applies to the primary material used; readers who want to know more should consult the abbreviations page and the bibliography.

Denis Judd has found various conversations with fellow scholars, draft chapters for books, and a number of conference paper presentations, very useful in the preparation of this book. He would especially like to mention Professor Bill Nasson, Professor Albert Grundlingh, Dr Iain Smith, Dr Jacqueline Beaumont, Dr Donal Lowry, Dr Amanda Nelson, Dr Jeremy Krikler, Dr Bernard Mbenga, Dr Bala Chandramohan, Professor Shula Marks, Tim Jeal, Dr André Odendaal, Philip Sellars and Dr Christopher Heywood.

We would like to thank Grant McIntyre at John Murray for his belief in the book, for his enthusiasm, for his patience as the project unfolded, and for his thoughtful and scrupulous editing. Gail Pirkis has also been an editorial rock: combining discretion with clarity, and sympathy with firmness. Caroline Westmore has helped us in many ways, and always with considerable kindness and efficiency. Our South African copy editor Douglas van der Horst has been a great help. Many thanks to Barry Liknaitzky for his invaluable picture research.

Denis Judd is particularly grateful for the sabbatical leave and research relief granted to him by the University of North London. He also remembers with great affection his tramps over Boer War battlefields under the expert guidance of John Snyman. Lesley Hart, keeper of the historical archives deposited at the University of Cape Town, and Cornia de Villiers of the Ladysmith Museum and its archives, were especially helpful. Both he and Keith Surridge are greatly indebted throughout to the good sense and creative advice of Bruce Hunter of David Higham Associates.

Finally we would like to give especial thanks to everyone – our families, friends and colleagues – who have had to come to terms with our frequently distracted and preoccupied states while working on this book. We hope that, for all of you, it has been worth waiting for.

Denis Judd and Keith Surridge
London, 2001

Introduction:
An Irrepressible Conflict?

THE BOER WAR of 1899–1902 was Britain's last great expansionist imperial war. Its events both symbolised Britain's unique imperial status and, simultaneously, exposed embarrassing and potentially crippling weaknesses at the heart of her military machine. The final victory seemed to mark the climax of Britain's late-nineteenth century process of imperial expansion, but it also coincided with, and helped to produce, a conspicuously more sober and introspective approach to Empire and overseas commitments – the result perhaps of the reverses, frustrations and defeats so honestly acknowledged at the war's end in Rudyard Kipling's celebrated and cautionary poem 'No End of a Lesson'.[1]

Like so many wars, the Boer War promoted legends, convenient national myths and a wide variety of half-truths. It consolidated patriotic sentiment at home and also led to bitter internal disputes, within political parties and the media and among the public at large. It was marked by great acts of heroism and self-sacrifice, both individual and collective, but was also, on closer examination, shot through with scandal, corruption and malpractice. It provoked widespread hostility overseas, where a variety of foreign states, many of them imperial rivals of the British, expressed misgivings over Britain's conduct – misgivings that were often most vehemently expressed by the policy-makers and leaders of public opinion in those states. But the war also led to the active participation of a number of foreign volunteers who fought for the Boers within the late-nineteenth century equivalent of the International Brigade of the Spanish Civil War.

Indeed, one of the characteristics of the war was its capacity to produce confusion and ambivalence and to highlight the complexities found within both the group and the individual in relation to loyalty, motive and even identity. This is not unusual, of course, in any number of confrontations, whether or not they proceed to the point of war. In South Africa, however, the conflict had many of the qualities of a civil war. Naturally, once the war began, both sides chose to dwell on the failings and perceived wrongdoings of their opponents; much was made of differences, real or imagined; and, in an acting out of one of the major but fundamental characteristics of conflict, all manner of sins and crimes were projected onto the enemy, both to vilify them as the strange, threatening 'other', and in the process to purge and purify those who hurled the accusations. Despite this propaganda war of vilification and abuse, it is plain that, for all their proclaimed differences and dislikes, Afrikaans-speaking and English-speaking South Africans were often bound together in subtle and complex ways.

They shared the same environment and often faced the same struggles with drought, cattle disease and the vagaries of the climate and the land. They had many common causes, even if some of them were understated and unacknowledged. Chief among these was the need to keep adequate control of the black majority, and indeed of all 'non-Europeans', and thus to ensure not only their own physical and personal safety but also the success of their various businesses, trades and occupations. Frequently the two groups met at social gatherings, at sporting events, at festivals and fairs. Sometimes they intermarried. Within the Afrikaner elite a significant proportion of young men were sent to Britain for their higher education, often to the universities of Cambridge or Oxford. The demands of a colonial society – and in many ways a rough-and-ready frontier society – meant that reliance upon neighbourly goodwill and assistance often took priority over entrenched or instinctive political, religious or 'national' differences.

In the last resort, moreover, the English-speakers and Afrikaners were both equally committed to the maintenance of a white supremacist South Africa. Even though there were some significant differences in emphasis and ideology when it came to their treatment and perception of the black majority, this should not obscure the fundamentally solid, essentially racist and exclusionist common ground on which both cultures rested.

As a result of this sharing of an overwhelmingly self-interested set of assumptions and hopes for the future regarding relations between whites and blacks, one of the intriguing and paradoxical themes of the confrontation that led to the outbreak of war in October 1899, and of the negotiations that resulted in the peace settlement of May 1902, was the search for compromise rather than an implacable, instinctive hostility.

There is no doubt that strenuous attempts were made to find some way of avoiding war during 1899 and even earlier; well before the final peace there had been other, abortive peace negotiations; and the final Peace of Vereeniging was a remarkably inclusive treaty that sought to minimise the impact of the defeat of the Boer republics and to begin at once the task of binding up the nation's, or at least the white nation's, wounds. Most significant of all perhaps was the decision in May 1902 to abandon the political aspirations of black and brown South Africans for the sake of the white man's peace. As a consequence, the future franchise in the Transvaal and the Orange Free State – and from 1910 in the Union of South Africa – was ruthlessly to exclude non-whites from the electoral process.

Despite these complexities and ambiguities, however, and the search for compromise that had attended the descent into war, at the outbreak of hostilities the British public were simply told by the government that the war was an unavoidable necessity and was being fought primarily to protect the Uitlanders of the Transvaal, most of whom were British citizens, from the tyranny of the Afrikaner government under Paul Kruger. The significance of the economic, financial and strategic implications of the confrontation in South Africa were either underplayed or virtually ignored in the propaganda war that preceded the real conflict. Equally simplistically, the Afrikaners of the Transvaal and the Orange Free State, as well as many of their fellow-Afrikaners in the Cape and even Natal, were convinced that a deep-laid and diabolical plot to strip them of their independence and to subordinate them once and for all to imperial rule had been hatched by the British government in close concert with capitalist forces within South Africa, of which Cecil Rhodes was the most vehement and ostentatious representative.

It was therefore understandable that some British liberals and radicals were convinced that the war was simply being fought on behalf of, and at the behest of, national and international capitalism, among whose ranks the manipulative, often 'faceless' financiers of the golden city Johannesburg – 'Jewburg' as anti-Semites described it – were playing a significant role. Such misgivings were reinforced dramatically as the war progressed, and as protracted Boer resistance compelled the British forces to resort to the 'methods of barbarism' so strongly denounced by many British liberals, radicals and socialists, and which included the burning of Afrikaner farms, the eviction of much of the Afrikaner civilian rural population, and the wholesale deaths in the deeply hated and bitterly controversial concentration camps.[2]

Critics of the war also argued that the origins and progress of the conflict clearly demonstrated all that was wrong with British imperialism. They pointed out the apparent contradiction between Britain, the self-proclaimed 'mother of democracy', forcing a war upon two minor, independent states, the Transvaal and the Orange Free State, and chiefly for the purpose of incorporating the booming, gold-based economy of the Transvaal within the British imperial and capitalist systems.

Not only was there a wide range of domestic opinion – conveniently and often inaccurately labelled as 'pro-Boer' – that opposed the war, either out of principle or on account of the methods employed by Britain, but some British citizens actually fought on the other side – most notably the volunteers in the Irish unit commonly described as 'MacBride's Brigade'. Indeed, after a while, as some Afrikaners noted with pleasure, Irish fighters in the field became difficult to tell apart from their Boer comrades in arms.[3]

That Irishmen should have fought on both sides was, perhaps, predictable. Far more surprising is the fact that some other English-speaking South Africans actually fought for the Boers. A striking example of this can be found by examining the composition of the commando unit formed at Heidelberg, a town some twenty miles south-east of Johannesburg in the Transvaal. Here, as men rallied to the Boer cause in October 1899, sixteen men with British surnames joined them; they included Thomas and George Loversage, Thomas Taylor, Benjamin Russell, Charles Cothill and David Anderson. For good measure, two Russian Jews, Morris Levin and Paul Minski, also volunteered to fight alongside their Afrikaner compatriots.[4]

Elsewhere in the imperial system, a surprising number of British subjects were either sympathetic to the Afrikaner cause or indifferent to Britain's success. Australian citizens of Irish origin were unlikely to be fervent supporters of a power that they associated with political oppression and a cynical disregard for generations of Ireland's rural poor. French-Canadians had a long tradition of at best ambivalence, and at worst downright hostility to the British Empire. Indian nationalists included a growing number who were beginning to show a militancy that envisaged India throwing off British rule and pursuing the goal of self-government, perhaps even outside of the Empire.

As the war progressed a considerable number of British citizens chose to be identified with the pro-Boer side, or to be conspicuously impartial in their responses to the conflict. The example of two British women is enlightening. Emily Hobhouse, coming from a sheltered but deeply liberal English background, emerged as the formidable and vociferous critic of the scandals of the British concentration camps in which so many Afrikaner women and children were to die. She wore Kitchener's description of her as 'that bloody woman' as a badge of honour. Mary Kingsley, a fiercely independent, single, middle-aged woman, and the doughty explorer of West and Central Africa, though committed to the imperial ideal, refused to dress up like female British patriots in 'a cockylora hat and khaki small clothes', and instead went off to South Africa as a nurse. But, characteristically, she chose to nurse Boer prisoners of war, exulting in the 'killing work ... All this work here, the stench, the enemas, the bed-pans, the blood is my world.'[5] It was indeed 'killing work' and Mary died of enteric fever caught from her 'enemy' patients in June 1900.

The war was not therefore quite as straightforward in its delineation of who were allies and who were enemies as the contemporary 'official' version insisted. In fact, as we shall see, there was no uniformity of response to the war from among the white citizens of the British Empire. Similarly, if one peers beneath the surface of things, there was considerable confusion as to who might be perceived as a 'typical' Boer.

More than this, there was a good deal of sympathy for the Boers among the British officer class sent to wage war against them in South Africa. A Captain Montmorency of the 21st Lancers wrote: 'In my opinion, the cause of the Dutch Burghers was a just one and I regarded the Boers as men fighting for their hearths against greedy, foreign aggressors.' Equally, some British officers disliked the idea of fighting for the safely distanced capitalists of the Rand and the City of London. 'I am afraid', complained Captain C. Ballard of the Norfolk Regiment, 'we are fighting chiefly for the benefit of a lot of money grubbing German Jews.'

As an illustration of the complexities of the Afrikaner identity, at the war's outset two-thirds of the European population of the self-governing colony of the Cape was Afrikaans-speaking rather than English-speaking; many of these stayed loyal to the British Crown. Also, towards the end of the war, so many Boers had joined the imperial side, including the National Scouts, that General Louis Botha was ironically to remark that unless peace was made very soon 'it may be that the Afrikaners against us will outnumber our own men'.

Equally ironic was the fact that by the end of the war several of the more successful and resolute Boer commanders had acquired heroic status in the eyes of some of the British public. Nor was the British publishing industry slow to seize the opportunity of some handsome profits, and, not long after the fighting was over, the memoirs of erst-while implacable foes of the British Empire, even men like the *bitter-einders* ('bitter enders') Christiaan de Wet and Deneys Reitz, were being published in London and eagerly purchased.

As if this was not confusing enough, the identities and experiences of many of the most resolute leaders of the Boer forces were entangled with the culture and history of Britain and with the British people. The Cape-born Jan Smuts had gained a double first at Cambridge, been called to the Bar in London, and, although married to a reliable Afrikaner vrou, later, had as a lifelong intimate and confidante a British woman, Margaret Clark, whom he met during a visit to England in 1905 and who was the granddaughter of the great Radical British statesman John Bright. J.B.M. Hertzog was born in Wellington, Cape Colony, and the initials J.B. stood for James Barry – not the purest of Afrikaner first names. Louis Botha, whose birthplace was Greytown in sturdily Anglophile British-settled Natal, was married to an English speaking-wife, Annie. A *bittereinder* commando member such as Deneys Reitz was connected by marriage to a 'liberal' pro-British leader, the Cambridge-educated W.P. Schreiner, who became Prime Minister of the Cape Colony in 1898 and had close links with many Afrikaner communities. Even the archetypal Boer leader Paul Kruger, so savagely caricatured by

British cartoonists, was not without his English-speaking connections: while President of the Transvaal he was very close to the Rand entrepreneurs and gold millionaires Joseph Robinson and Sammy Marks. It was Marks who not only put Kruger's uncertain financial affairs onto a firm and prosperous footing but also introduced him to many English-speaking luminaries – H.M. Stanley, for instance, in 1897.[6] Many more examples of complex, cross-cultural, Anglo-Afrikaner interactions could be produced.

Naturally enough, many of these finer points of interpretation and analysis were swept aside in the rush to war. Patriotic Britons were convinced, or at least convinced themselves with a little help from the government's propaganda machine, that the war was both necessary and just, and simple to justify. There is little doubt that the majority of citizens of the United Kingdom, as well as of the white-dominated self-governing colonies, felt – certainly at the outset – that the conflict was virtually a crusade to rescue and liberate the Uitlanders, the allegedly ill-used, mainly English-speaking population of the Transvaal, from the repression of the Kruger regime. By ensuring that the English-speakers of the Transvaal would be protected by the might of British power, the British Empire seemed to be demonstrating that, as Palmerston had argued so eloquently during the highly-charged Don Pacifico debate of June 1850, Her Majesty's Government had a:

> sense of duty which has led us to think ourselves bound to afford protection to our fellow subjects abroad and … as the Roman, in days of old, held himself free from indignity, when he could say 'Civis Romanus sum'; so also a British subject, in whatever land he may be, shall feel confident that the watchful eye and the strong arm of England will protect him against injustice and wrong.[7]

Opinions among contemporaries as to why the war occurred were manifold and often freely expressed. Sir Arthur Conan Doyle, creator of Sherlock Holmes, and a war correspondent in South Africa, needed no subtle and obscure clues to come to a judgement, though, naturally, some investigating was necessary:

> There might seem to be some connection between the barrenness and worthlessness of a surface and the value of what lies beneath it … the bare slopes of the Witwatersrand … are the lids which cover [one of] the great

7

treasure chests of the world ... it was only in 1886 that it was realised that the deposits ... are of a very extraordinary and valuable nature ... the peculiarity of the Rand mines lies in the fact [that] throughout this 'blanket' formation the metal is so uniformly distributed that the enterprise can claim a certainty which is not usually associated with the industry. It is quarrying rather than mining. Add to this that the reefs which were originally worked as outcrops have now been traced to enormous depths, and present the same features as those at the surface.[8]

In a word, an abundance of gold was the cause. The future Labour Prime Minister Ramsay MacDonald expressed another opinion. Having spent some time in South Africa at the war's end, MacDonald felt that:

The war was between two races each inspired by different historical origins, and taking different views on several important questions, each unwilling to acknowledge the supremacy of the other, both dragged by the Jameson Raid out of that frame of mind which would have enabled them to live in harmonious cooperation, both the victims of the chopping and changing in English policy from 1806 onwards.

I do not say that caused the war. If I thought that, I should consider that the war was inevitable, an idea which my investigations on the spot have convinced me is infantile. But what we must now understand is, that the Johannesburg [Uitlander] agitation and policy revived the dying racial antagonisms; that the war when it came, was a race war and cannot be explained on any other grounds ...

The Briton does not trust the Boer and the Boer does not trust the Briton. To the Briton the Boer has a circuitous character. If he can discover a twist in the road he will take it ... In the game of political bargaining the Englishman is no match for the Dutch ...

Thus it is that amongst the English one meets with a kind of feverish desire to secure dominance, irritated by a clouded fear that it is beyond their reach.[9]

From the Afrikaner side, Deneys Reitz, who fought through the war and left South Africa for Madagascar at its end as one of the 'irreconcilables', and who was not only very well connected in the Orange Free State but, as we have seen, related by marriage to the Cape Prime Minister W.P. Schreiner, both agreed and disagreed with MacDonald:

Our small country [the Orange Free State] was a model one ... nor, until after the Jameson Raid of 1895, was there any bad blood between the Dutch and the English. We had no railways, and the noise of the outside world reached us but faintly ... Looking back, I think war was inevitable. I have no doubt that the British Government had made up its mind to force the issue, and was the chief culprit, but the Transvaalers were also spoiling for a fight, and, from what I saw in Pretoria during the few weeks that preceded the ultimatum, I feel sure that the Boers would in any case have insisted on a rupture.[10]

Jan Smuts, a future Prime Minister of South Africa and British Field Marshal, and a glittering model of a new breed of worldly, pragmatic, sophisticated young Afrikaners who would one day inherit the future 'greater South Africa', and come to a fruitful accommodation with the British Empire, viewed the prospect of war with a mixture of disbelief and defiance:

If England should venture into the ring with Afrikanerdom without a formally good excuse, her cause in South Africa would be finished ... Our volk throughout South Africa must be baptised with the baptism of blood and fire before they can be admitted among the great peoples of the world ... Either we shall be exterminated or we shall fight our way out ... and when I think of the great fighting qualities that our people possess, I cannot see why we should be exterminated.[11]

Despite the rival claims and perceptions of those who contemplated the conflict, or those who went on to have increasing misgivings over its conduct as well as its origins, the Boer War was widely perceived by contemporaries as an event of paramount importance in British and imperial history. One of the reasons for this was simply that it had been preceded by a period of deepening crisis in South Africa, and that once it began it proved to be a far larger undertaking, and also far costlier, in terms of both the loss of lives and expenditure, than many had anticipated at the outset. It also provided a series of embarrassments and traumas deriving mainly from the unexpected and decisive Boer victories in the early stages of the conflict.

As if this was not bad enough, the war was subjected to the intense scrutiny of the rapidly expanding new media in Britain and beyond. There were black and white moving films shown to the enthralled, packed audiences of the newly built cinemas. Some of these films also included dramatic reconstructions of alleged Boer atrocities directed at British personnel. A typical example of such fare is a short film showing a British nurse tending a wounded Afrikaner who is shamming, and who subsequently assaults her, necessitating her rescue by some of the 'brave British boys in khaki'.

Possibly more powerful was the impact of the freshly established and increasingly sensationalist popular press, of which the *Daily Mail* was the most potent example. These widely read and increasingly influential newspapers could be sneered at as 'written by office boys for office boys',[12] but they presented the events and issues of the war in a vivid, readable form, and were able to engage both the minds and the emotions of the reader. Fiercely competing for circulation as the century drew to its close, the popular press was now a new estate of the realm and accordingly conscious of its weight and appeal. From the point of view of these newspapers, the war in South Africa was manna from heaven, a marvellous vehicle for the promotion of the new journalism and for commercial spin-offs. The dramas, triumphs and disasters of the conflict could command the steady attention of a reading public that, though generally literate, could also be easily distracted from issues of national or international importance.

Apart from the attention of an increasingly powerful and popular press, the war in South Africa also provoked considerable and intense scrutiny because it seemed to belong to a different category from the smaller-scale and less dramatically presented wars of imperial conflict and containment that had characterised the second half of the nineteenth century – the 'little wars' that had been part and parcel of the 'Pax Britannica', the policy of global policing carried out by Britain. Moreover, apart from the 1880–1 Anglo-Transvaal War, that brisk and dramatic precursor of the much larger conflict of 1899–1902, it was the only war that Britain waged against opponents of European origin since the 1854–6 hostilities in the Crimea. Perhaps as a result, the fighting seemed to be a more genuine test of the nation and the Empire's character than yet another campaign against inadequately armed indigenous peoples – such as the Mahdists (or Dervishes) during Kitchener's successful Sudan campaign, which was completed the year before the outbreak of the Boer War.[13]

The South African War of 1899–1902, popularly known as the

Boer War, was invested with an enormous amount of contemporary symbolism and meaning. The British government, and the majority of the citizens of the self-governing colonies, as well as countless others throughout the dependent Empire, supported the war, which was, as we have already seen, presented by patriotic propaganda as almost a crusade to rescue the underprivileged and ill-used English-speaking population of the Transvaal. In South Africa, the budding apostle of non-violence and the future leader of Indian nationalism, Mohandas Gandhi, even organised an ambulance team to assist the imperial armies, believing that the Empire's citizens had obligations as well as privileges deriving from membership of the British Empire.

Rudyard Kipling, shrewd and best-selling bard of Empire, demonstrated once more his gift for articulating the essence of a crisis as well as its more uncomfortable dilemmas, when he wrote at the outset of the war:

> When you've shouted 'Rule Britannia,' when you've sung
>   'God Save the Queen,'
> When you're finished killing Kruger with your mouth,
> Will you kindly drop a shilling in my little tambourine
> For a gentleman in Khaki ordered South?
> He's an absent-minded beggar, and his weaknesses are great –
> But we and Paul must take him as we find him –
> He's out on active service, wiping something off a slate –
> And he's left a lot of little things behind him![14]

As the conflict developed and became more protracted, and especially when the British forces proved inept at finishing off Afrikaner resistance during the period of the guerrilla war from 1900 to 1902, as farm burning increased and the newly established concentration camps filled up with Boer civilians, the outcry against the conflict reached new heights. It was then that Sir Henry Campbell-Bannerman, the leader of the Liberal party from 1898, courageously and subtly asked the potentially lethal question, 'When is a war not a war?' and provided the following answer: 'When it is carried on by methods of barbarism in South Africa.'[15]

Equally controversial, although less well publicised, were the accusations of the campaigning journalist W.T. Stead that British troops had raped Boer women – especially during the guerrilla stage of the conflict. Even though Stead was less explicit than he might have been, his meaning was plain enough when he described in a pamphlet:

> the smoke of the burning farmstead ... the cries of the terrified children [and] in the darkness we hear the sobbing of the outraged woman in the midst of her orphaned children ... It may be said ... that such horrible and shameful incidents are inseparable from letting loose 250,000 troops among a population of scattered and helpless women ... [No one] would allow their servant girl to remain out all night on a public common in England in time of profound peace in the company of a score of soldiers. Why, then, should they suppose that when the same men are released from all the restraints of civilisation, and sent forth to burn, destroy and loot at their own sweet will and pleasure, they will suddenly undergo a complete transformation as to scrupulously respect the wives and daughters of the enemy.[16]

It was claimed at the time, and has been claimed subsequently, that the Boer War was a highly significant watershed in the history and evolution of the British Empire; that its context, agenda and prosecution marked it out from other imperial conflicts, and imbued it with portent and substance. The campaign, it was argued, proved conclusively that imperial expansion could not always be had on the cheap; moreover, there was no guarantee that the process of imperial conquest would provide a glorious or edifying spectacle. It was also asserted that, coming after the crude excesses of late-nineteenth century jingoistic imperialism, the fiascos of the Boer War obliged the British people to return, with a proper sense of puritanical guilt, to nobler and more restrained and traditional imperial pursuits.

Perhaps the war in South Africa made such an impact upon contemporary opinion, and has excited such interest ever since, for altogether more straightforward reasons. For one thing, as we have seen, it was a far bigger and more protracted affair than had been imagined at the beginning. The scale of its embarrassments and traumas were not merely shocking in themselves, and likely further to undermine national self-esteem, but were also subject to the intense scrutiny and vivid journalism of the newly established popular press. As it was only the second war of any duration that Britain had fought against opponents of European origin during the 100 years from 1815 to 1914, it was seen as a truer test of the nation's mettle than victories over poorly armed indigenous people.

The final reason for the perceived significance of the war probably owed more to the Christian calendar than to more complex and deep-seated causes. The conflict began less than three months before the end of the nineteenth century. Popular speculation about what the new century would hold for Britain and the Empire had been widespread as the old century drew to its close. When the twentieth century opened with further demonstrations of British military impotence, culminating in the humiliation of Spion Kop, the worst fears of the pessimists were realised and the hopes of optimists dashed. Crudely put, the answer to the question 'what does the future hold for Britain?' was: disaster and humiliation.

These embarrassments led some to see the Boer War as a dramatic, make-or-break episode in British history. Was the conflict simply the last throes of the old imperial expansionist order which had apparently served Britain so well during her long nineteenth century experience of global supremacy, or would it prove that, as a new century began, the foundations of the old order were inadequate and that Britain was poorly placed to maintain her industrial, naval and imperial supremacy into the twentieth century? As the end of the nineteenth century approached, the impression of the world running out of space and of Britain running out of time was subtly, and sometimes powerfully, reinforced. The Boer War, in its origins and in its unravelling, played into these and similar morbid fantasies and anxieties.

The impression of time running out was enhanced by the obvious frailty and old age of the great royal totem, Queen Victoria. Nor was this all: Gladstone died in 1898 and, as the nineteenth century ended, the Conservative and Unionist Prime Minister, Lord Salisbury, who had shared the political hegemony with the great Liberal leader for the last quarter of the century, was also increasingly frail. When the old Queen died in January 1901 with the Boer War still dragging on, the public mood became noticeably depressed, and the leader writers of a great national newspaper like *The Times* produced sober assessments of Britain's prospects couched in pessimistic and anxious terminology.[17] It was as if the stuffing had been rudely knocked out of British self-confidence by the not untimely death of a sovereign who, for all her robust support for her fighting men in South Africa, had hardly provided the inspirational leadership of a renaissance prince. Nor could the failure of British forces to 'finish off' their ridiculously outnumbered foes have much helped the national mood.

The Boer War, therefore, came to be viewed as a climactic event in British imperial history, and, at least at its outset, was perceived as a conflict that would neatly bring to a close a lengthy period of imperial aggrandisement, expansion and consolidation. The actual experience of the war was, at the very least, ambiguous. The conflict provided no neat and tidy conclusion to the nineteenth century, but, instead, a messy and uncertain beginning to the twentieth. The hopes of optimists were dashed, and the fears of pessimists were realised.

For those who took a more realistic, balanced view, what the war demonstrated was that Britain needed urgently to begin a process of reassessment and reform, in order to ensure that the nation and the Empire would be able to face the unfolding of the new century with at least a modicum of self-confidence. It is no coincidence that the conflict overlapped with, and in many ways stimulated, what came to be described as the 'Quest for National Efficiency'. In the flurry of reforms which were precipitated by the Boer War, and which marked its aftermath, can be seen an important component in the reassessment of Britain's military, naval, foreign policy and imperial priorities which so clearly marked the Edwardian age from 1901 to 1914.[18] In that sense, for all its messiness, confusion and disappointment, the Boer War was to provide an invaluable service to Britain's policy makers and opinion formers.

Part I

The Background to the War

I

British Rule, Confrontation and Compromise, 1815–1886

THE CONFUSION IN which the British found themselves in the Transvaal and indeed throughout the whole of South Africa in the early 1880s, after their embarrassing defeat in 1881 at the battle of Majuba Hill – which effectively enabled the Transvaal to regain its independence in the war of 1880–1 – was a telling and cautionary illustration of the difficulties and hazards that very rapidly seemed an inevitable and chronic part of Britain's involvement in the region following the formal annexation of the Cape of Good Hope in 1814.

The cardinal reason why Britain had retained control of the Cape, which it had taken from the Dutch during the French Revolutionary and Napoleonic Wars, was that before 1869 and the opening of the Suez Canal, the only feasible sea route to India and the Far East was round the Cape. The acquisition of the maritime facilities of Cape Town, and the development of Simonstown as an increasingly important Royal Navy base, did not mean, however, that Britain's role in the area was simply strategic. Although policy makers in London would ideally have wished to avoid involvement with the Cape's hinterland, a number of factors and processes dragged Britain into an increasingly complicated, and for a considerable time, unrewarding and unprofitable entanglement with the whole of South Africa.[1]

This happened partly because of the inexorable and pressing demands of the imperial frontier. Once they had become the new rulers of the Cape, the British had been obliged to take on the responsibility of governing, or at the very least controlling, the 'Cape Dutch', the Afrikaans-speaking European settlers, numbering some 27,000 in 1815. Whether they liked it or not, the British imperial authorities were also brought into direct and unavoidable confrontation with the various African tribespeople of southern Africa, as well as assuming responsibility for the Cape coloured population – a people who were mostly the result of two centuries of interracial sexual activity between the dominant white settlers and either local black women or females from among the descendants of slaves earlier brought to the Cape from the Dutch East India Company's possessions in the East Indies.

The British administration of the Cape would undoubtedly have been more tranquil and easy if it had to deal predominantly with fixed local populations and stable patterns of commerce and trade. South Africa, however, was in some important respects frontier territory – often, when it came down to it, the equivalent to an American Wild West at the southern tip of Africa. Historically groups of white settlers had tended to push, according to their needs and ambitions, to the north, while various black tribes were also on the move. The Afrikaner political propaganda machine, especially after the establishment of apartheid in 1948, was used to asserting that as white settlers moved north, black tribespeople moving south met them head-on.

This was a partial truth. Overall, population movements throughout the region were not a simple matter of groups of people from the north colliding with groups migrating from the south. To fulfil their subsistence, economic, political and military needs, a wide variety of people within South Africa moved north, south, east, and west to wherever there was better grazing, free available land, and the chance to shake off persecutors or rulers – whether they were dominating rival tribes or the newly installed British imperial authorities.

Within this context, the Afrikaners of the Cape were simply another African tribe, although a white one and possessing great power. They were, moreover, sustained by a coherent and fundamentally inflexible ideology. The Afrikaner people were derived from several different nationalities – Dutch, Flemish, and German, with a strong and influential contingent of exiled French Huguenots. They shared an adherence to Calvinist principles and an intense dislike of overriding government authority. Seeing themselves as a racially pure elect in a black continent, and accustomed to decades of neglect by the Netherlands government, they overwhelmingly considered themselves to be the makers of their own destiny. In response, the British administrators of the Cape, who came like the British missionaries and settlers from a social and cultural environment strikingly at odds with the rough and isolated life of the hinterland, were disinclined simply to let the Afrikaner settlers do as they wished.

Some twenty years after the final establishment of British control in the Cape in 1814, relations between the Afrikaner *volk* and the imperial authorities had been stretched to breaking point. Fundamental to this disaffection was the Afrikaner conviction that the British were mounting both an overt and a covert assault on their privileges and position. It is clear that British administrators, and certainly the British settlers, had no ambitions to overthrow the Afrikaner people and to promote the black African tribes in their place. The humanitarian standards of the imperial administration, however, and the liberal impulses of the British evangelical missions, could easily be seen by the Afrikaners as a concerted threat to a set of convictions of nearly two centuries' standing.

The irony was that neither British administrators nor British missionaries had a markedly separate political agenda for South Africa. Although often sensitive to the differing identities of local people, the British colonial empire was also governed according to certain common policies; these could not be waived simply to placate a few thousand Afrikaner farmers on the other side of the world. It was, however, the case that British missionaries often subscribed to a less dogmatic analysis of racial differences than the Calvinist, Dutch Reformed Church of the Afrikaners. The anxiety about their position at the apex of Cape society resulted in a distressingly predictable cycle of Afrikaner paranoia, attended by exaggerated fears and wild misconceptions. On this analysis, British rule frequently seemed to be wilfully and deliberately out of touch with Afrikaner sensibilities and, worse still, to be irredeemably biased towards the blacks.

A further problem was that Britain seemed determined to limit Afrikaner expansion to the north. There were obvious enough reasons for this. Like all colonial subjects, if the Afrikaners could be contained it would be easier to tax and administer them. If, however, they were allowed to shake off imperial control, their continued expansion to the north and east would inevitably bring clashes with the African tribes there and so disturb, perhaps for an impossibly long time, the peace and stability that the British so strongly desired for the Cape Colony.

Inevitably, perhaps, the Afrikaners saw things very differently. They claimed that the scourges of drought and cattle disease made the regular acquisition of new grazing lands an imperative. They pointed to their history of almost continuous frontier clashes with African tribespeople, conflicts that centred primarily on the possession of land and cattle. The 'Kaffir War' of 1834–5, though merely one of a long sequence, was attended by more than the usual measure of bloodshed, farm burning and cattle slaughter. As a result, the fighting stimulated further white settler movement into safer and more peaceful regions to the north.

In 1833 the abolition of slavery throughout the British Empire was an even more fundamental blow to Afrikaner tradition and susceptibilities. In fact, comparatively few Afrikaner farmers owned slaves. Their lifestyle, however, did depend heavily upon the dirt cheap labour of farm hands and domestic servants, many of whom worked in exchange for produce or the use of a piece of land, rather than for wages. In this context, the abolition of slavery seemed to provide the clearest indication that the British were hell-bent on the subversion of the Afrikaner way of doing things in the Cape. As if this was not bad enough, many Afrikaners felt insulted by what they saw as inadequate British compensation, both for the freed slaves and for material losses incurred during the 1834–5 'Kaffir War'.[2]

In a response common among European settler communities far from home, especially those facing unpalatable changes and beset by threatening indigenous communities, feverish Afrikaner imaginations were soon feasting on fantasies of the British administration handing over vast tracts of available land to blacks, sponsoring mixed race marriages and even forcibly imposing Roman Catholicism on the devoutly Calvinist Boer population. These threats were perceived as merely the worst excesses of a deliberate programme of Anglicisation which had made English the official language in 1827, had brought about the scrapping of the Dutch military system, and had introduced some elements of the British legal structure.

Starting in 1834, one of the defining and climactic events of Afrikaner history took place. Known in Afrikaner folklore and mythology, and in numerous South African history lessons, as the Great Trek, the migration of some 14,000 Boers across the Orange River to lands to the east and the north indisputably changed the course of South African history. The Great Trek was essentially an act of civil rebellion, the rejection of a government whose policies seemed at variance with the self-interest of the trekkers. In their covered ox wagons, frequently accompanied by their black servants and labourers, thousands of Afrikaner families struck off into the wilderness hoping for better days, better land and, above all, wishing to break free from British rule, or indeed from the rule of any distant, centralising power.[3]

The intensity of Afrikaner hostility towards the perceived drift towards racial equality can be seen in the words of Anna Steenkamp, a sister of the Voortrekker leader Piet Retief, when she asserted that the Afrikaners trekked because of:

> the shameful and unjust proceedings with reference to the freedom of our slaves – and yet it is not their freedom that drove us to such lengths, as their being placed on an equal footing with Christians, contrary to the laws of God, and the natural distinction of race and religion, so that it was intolerable for any decent Christian to bow down beneath such a yoke; wherefore we rather withdrew in order to preserve our doctrines in purity.[4]

In essence the Great Trek was equivalent to the seventeenth century migration of political and religious dissenters across the Atlantic, or to the flow of discontented, destitute and ambitious settlers to Australasia at the same period during the nineteenth century. Interestingly, by no means all of the Afrikaner population of the Cape left on the trek, and despite the British government-sponsored landing of some 5,000 English-speaking settlers at Albany in the eastern Cape in 1820, the Afrikaans-speaking section of the European population in the colony continued to comprise at least two-thirds of the whole white community well into the second half of the twentieth century – with all the political and social complexities and cross-currents that this involved.

The British did their best to tidy up in the aftermath of the Great Trek. They were not prepared to see an Afrikaner republic established on the Natal coast and in 1843 they annexed the territory, as a consequence driving the majority of Boer settlers inland, where many of them ended up in what became known as the Transvaal. Having denied the Voortrekkers access to the coast on the Indian Ocean, the British authorities now had to decide what policies to adopt toward the various Afrikaner settlements in what, after a process of amalgamation and takeover, became known as the Orange Free State and the Transvaal.

In a pragmatic, and to some extent tolerant, decision, Britain decided to let the trekkers get on with it. It is necessary to understand that at this time, and arguably for at least another half century, the Afrikaners were not a homogeneous, united people. There were, for instance, several small Boer republics established across the Vaal River as a consequence of the Great Trek and subsequent migrations, including Vryheid, Zoutpansberg and Lydenburg. The separate republics were quite often at odds with each other, even to the point of military conflict. Indeed, early in 1857, forces from the Transvaal, led by Marthinus Pretorius, actually invaded the Orange Free State in an unsuccessful attempt to bring about a forcible union between the Afrikaner republics – an ironic precursor of subsequent British imperial efforts to engineer a South African federation.

It is not difficult to see why the imperial government, in the years following the Great Trek and its subsidiary migrations, was not eager to assert control over the newly settled territories. They calculated, quite understandably as they perceived the situation, that the various ramshackle structures would simply fall apart, destroyed by the aggression of black tribespeople and undermined by their own obscurantist ideologies, backward pastoral economic practices and chronic bankruptcy.

There was, however, a properly structured constitutional and political settlement in the aftermath of the Great Trek, the British government eventually negotiating separate agreements with the two main Afrikaner republics. In 1852 the Sand River Convention recognised the independence of the 15,000 Transvaalers. Two years later, the Bloemfontein Convention acknowledged the sovereignty of the Orange Free State. Both treaties dealt with one of the major causes of British anxiety resulting from the great Afrikaner migration when they laid down guarantees for the security and integrity of the northern frontiers of the two major Boer republics. As a result of their undertaking not to push even further north, thus provoking clashes with African tribes, the Afrikaner people of the Transvaal and the Orange Free State were granted a free hand in their internal affairs. In particular, they now had complete control over the black tribespeople within their borders. Although it is not easy to see what Britain would have been able to do in practice to intervene in the republics' internal administration, even if they had wished to do so, the settlements of the early 1850s were a plain indication of the British desire to live and let live – certainly it gives the lie to the notion that the imperial authorities were steadfastly dedicated to the wholesale emancipation of South Africa's black people.[5]

The political and constitutional settlements of the 1850s can be seen primarily as an exercise in co-existence, or at least relevant to the co-existence of Afrikaans-speaking and English-speaking whites. For Britain, struggling to make sense of its new responsibilities in South Africa, it was also a comparatively low-risk, low-cost policy. Until 1870, the region – in effect a sub-continent – seemed, in comparison to other areas of European settlement, unprofitable and unduly troublesome. Neither capital nor British immigrants were drawn to southern Africa in any substantial quantity. Economically, the returns seemed poor, and the physical environment unreliable: there were severe droughts that put erratic pressure on agriculture, a generally impoverished soil, and the disruptions caused by cattle disease and plagues of locusts. In South Africa, the great staple products and crops so central to the expanding colonial economies of Canada, Australia and New Zealand, namely timber, wheat, wool, coffee, sugar and tobacco, all failed adequately to establish themselves. Of these staples, South African wool was the most successful, and by 1862 twenty-five million pounds were being exported annually, but the quality of the region's wool, particularly that produced in the Transvaal, was among the poorest grades in the British market.

Until at least the 1860s, South Africa's docking and maritime facilities, even those of Cape Town, were underdeveloped, which limited the opportunities for trade as well as employment for British immigrants. One result was that English-speaking migration to South Africa remained disappointingly low until the 1870s, even compared with some of the least attractive destinations for British immigration, such as the Australian colonies and New Zealand. On top of these difficulties there was also the intractable nature of much of the Afrikaans-speaking population and the chronic prospect of armed conflict with various African tribespeople over land-grazing rights, water supplies and cattle. No wonder English-speaking immigrants preferred the United States and Canada for so much of the nineteenth century.

Within the territories that were directly ruled by Britain in South

Africa – first the Cape and, after 1843, Natal – the constitutional developments that characterised other British colonies of settlement also took place. In 1854 a new parliament met in Cape Town; interestingly, both parliamentary houses were elective and thus in advance of similar constitutional practice in Britain and in the colonies of European settlement in Australia or Canada. Equally interesting was the fact that the Cape franchise was open to those of all races, although the financial qualification for voting rights was sufficiently high to disenfranchise the vast majority of Cape coloureds and the overwhelming majority of blacks. Indeed, it was technically possible for a non-European to sit as a member of the Cape legislature, but the stark fact was that during the entire life of the Cape parliament, from 1854 to 1910, none actually did so.

In Natal, which was a separate British colony, constitutional developments lagged several decades behind those of the Cape, but they nevertheless followed the same pattern. The Natal constitution, like that of the Cape, although theoretically 'colour-blind', set the financial qualification for voting so high that very few non-Europeans managed to register. Thus the franchise arrangements in both the Cape and Natal allowed for the possibility that black or coloured people could become voters; in practice, however, the self-interest of whites, anxious to maintain their political supremacy, meant that the concession had little substance. In the Afrikaner republics to the north, there was no such posturing, pussy-footing liberalism. Voting in the Transvaal and the Orange Free State was strictly reserved for those of European descent.

Although the South African economy seemed lacking in promise, and despite the obduracy of the Afrikaner people, especially those in the newly established republics, some mid-Victorian British statesmen still cherished the hope of engineering a federal solution to the awkward interaction of the various groups in the region. During his governorship, beginning in 1854, Sir George Grey, much admired for his recent and outstandingly successful administration in New Zealand, tried his best to bring about a federation of the different provinces in the area. The British government, however, ultimately shied from the possible expense and the almost predictable difficulties involved in the enterprise. When Grey left the Cape in 1861 to resume the governorship of New Zealand, the federation issue was apparently dead and buried.

Amid this upheaval and manoeuvring, life in South Africa for the European settler communities – whether Afrikaans-speaking or English-speaking – was a strange and sometimes melodramatic mixture of solid certainty and high risk. The beautiful whitewashed Cape-Dutch farmhouses of the western Cape were unashamedly symbols of prosperity and social standing. These gabled edifices, often comprising three or four wings, were cool, self-sufficient buildings, which, with their outhouses and servants' quarters, had a good deal in common with the planters' mansions of the contemporary American Deep South. They also had much in common as the focal points of an agricultural system employing large numbers of blacks and, by implication, serving as fortresses of white supremacy. Further afield, the humbler farms of the Free State or the Transvaal were equally sturdy outposts of European colonisation.

Within the white settler communities, hospitality for fellow-Europeans was as a rule generous, and the sheltering of travellers the hallmark of what was still very much a pioneer society. Especially among the Afrikaners, the bonds of family were exceptionally strong, and neighbours generally cherished. In these ways, the authority of scattered, sparsely populated white settlements was maintained. Typically the Afrikaner family relied heavily upon the authority of the Bible and of the Dutch Reformed Church and its pastor. When illness struck, colonial medicine was primitive and generally based on ignorance and superstition. Homoeopathy, herbal preparations and sometimes ludicrously 'unscientific' remedies, some of which were learned from the tribespeople, were often the only available medicines.

In the developing towns, especially those of the Cape, but also gradually in settlements like Durban, Bloemfontein and Pretoria, there was at least a veneer of European civilisation. As European South Africa became established, theatres, music halls, and libraries sprang up. Organised sport developed, and if the Afrikaners vehemently rejected British egalitarian and racial theories, they eagerly embraced the British sports of rugby and, rather later in the day, cricket.

By 1870 the European settler minority in southern Africa was firmly rooted, if divided among itself. The British calculation was that growing commercial and economic interchange between the different communities would soften the hard edges of political separatism and that a voluntary federation would ensue. On the most optimistic assessment, this meant that a natural evolutionary process would bring about the gradual and inevitable unification of South Africa, in which the richer, more populous and British-controlled Cape Colony would dominate, and within which the Afrikaner people would be painlessly absorbed. It was an analysis that had earlier been enthusiastically applied to the French-speaking minority in Canada after the establishment of the Canadian Union in 1840.

As it happened, there were two serious potential obstacles to this gradualist and fair-weather philosophy. One of these was predictable, indeed virtually inevitable, in view of the nature of white supremacy and need: namely, serious, perhaps long-term, trouble with the black tribespeople. The second obstacle in the path of the gradual, peaceful and inevitable assertion of British supremacy was, as it turned out, much more difficult to imagine and to plan for. This was the discovery, beginning in 1867, of such substantial deposits of diamonds and subsequently of gold, that, in the wry judgement of one Afrikaner historian, F.S. Malan, in the end catastrophe overtook the two republics 'in the form of fabulous riches'.[6]

The leisurely calculations of British imperial policy makers certainly began to unravel in 1869 with the discovery of diamonds at Kimberley. Since Kimberley was situated in the territory of Griqualand West, the control of which was disputed between Britain and the Orange Free State, this discovery and the subsequent 'diamond rush' created a new and difficult situation within a region that was already chronically on the brink of conflict. The immediate crisis was eventually resolved in 1876 when the British government bought out the Free State's claims for £90,000. Centred on what later became the 'Big Hole' at Kimberley, the diamond fields boomed, enabling a few individuals to make their personal fortunes, among them an odd, sickly and querulous young man called Cecil Rhodes. Once Kimberley had been incorporated into the Cape Colony, and the principal mines developed under British control, it is evident that a new optimism, enriched by the mineral discoveries, marked British attitudes towards South Africa.

As had so often been the case in other areas transformed through the discovery of precious minerals, the Cape Colony enjoyed some immediate benefits from the rapidly developing diamond mining industry centred on Kimberley. The revenue generated by the diamond strike freed the Cape from its reliance upon funding from an often tight-fisted British government at Westminster. Partly as a result, full responsible government, so often the reward for economic self-sufficiency as well as political maturity, was granted in 1872.[7]

Fortuitously, the rapid development of the diamond mining industry occurred during a difficult period in the economic fortunes of the Cape. A number of agricultural exports had suffered as a result of their exposure to the market forces of the relatively new free-trade environment of the British Empire. Many Cape farmers' problems were exacerbated by a series of natural disasters, including drought and the devastating cattle scourge rinderpest that affected much of southern Africa after 1869. At the same time, cheap loans were proving more difficult to raise, in what was in effect colonial frontier territory, via the cautiously orthodox finance houses of Britain. This in turn generated a demand amongst both English-speaking and Afrikaans-speaking people for the establishment of 'country banks', which were seen as being more in tune with local needs. Another problem was that the comparatively high wages paid to workers in the diamond-mining industry tended further to depress the labour market on farms and estates.

Inevitably, perhaps, British policy makers paid less attention to the problems of South African agriculture than to the immediate and profitable consequences of the diamond discoveries. There were optimistic assessments that other valuable mineral deposits would soon be unearthed. As a result, imperial policy towards South Africa was dramatically transformed. The old game of waiting for the Boer republics to fall like ripe plums into Britannia's lap was abandoned. It is striking that during the 1870s there were four British-backed attempts to achieve a confederation of the South African colonies, an initiative that also mostly included a determined courtship of the Afrikaner republics.

The drive for federation failed for a number of reasons. To begin with, local white settler opinion, even in the two British colonies, could not be won over in sufficient quantity. Even the most persuasive and persistent of British confederators, Lord Carnarvon, Colonial Secretary in the mid-1870s, failed to convince enough doubters. (Perhaps this, as well as his capacity to fuss, had something to do with Disraeli's mocking nickname for him, 'Twitters'.) The European colonists certainly wanted better communications and more unified and coherent policies toward land and labour, but not at the price of surrendering local autonomy. Many Cape colonists resented the notion that their relatively prosperous economy would almost certainly be obliged to bear, or at any rate subsidise, the financial burdens of their more impoverished neighbours. Many of the Cape Afrikaners, moreover, feared federation as simply the re-assertion of imperial control through other means.

Lord Carnarvon's federating agenda, added to his determination and drive, did, however, lead to the unexpectedly easy annexation of the Transvaal in 1877. Subsequently, the medium-term British calculation was that the Orange Free State, with its far more intimate economic and commercial relationship with the Cape, would be obliged to join a federation in due course. The problem of the Transvaal was far more tricky. This republic was the flagship of Afrikaner separatism, and was, moreover, the homeland – in effect the last refuge – of all those Boers who from the 1830s had trekked as far as they could to escape British imperial control. This bunker mentality was to prove, at least in the short to medium term, almost impossible to deal with.

The anticipated Afrikaner resistance to British control or interference was, however, blunted by the fact that the rural economy of the Transvaal was in dire straits by 1877. When Carnarvon's agent, Theophilus Shepstone, arrived in Pretoria to negotiate with the Transvaal leadership, he found the treasury almost empty and the government, under President Burgers, surprisingly prepared to consider the advantages of annexation.

In April 1877, with comparatively little opposition, the Transvaal was formally annexed to the British Crown. It was, on any analysis, a spectacular advance for British policy, and appeared to run full in the face of seventy years of Anglo-Afrikaner antipathy and disengagement.[8]

On closer scrutiny, however, the deal that Britain offered to the Transvaalers was essentially straightforward and in the short term advantageous. The Transvaal's administration would be put upon a sound financial footing, steps to increase revenue and implement a substantial degree of local autonomy would be speedily taken, and, of great immediate concern, the imperial armies would rid the northern and eastern regions of South Africa of the menace of the independent and aggressive Zulu kingdom in Natal, for good it was hoped.

In 1879 the newly arrived Governor of the Cape, Sir Bartle Frere, eager to break the Zulu threat once and for all, engineered the outbreak of war with the issuing of an aggressive and uncompromising ultimatum to the Zulu King, Cetshwayo. The Anglo-Zulu War of 1879 provided Afrikaners, not merely in the Transvaal but throughout southern Africa, with considerable, if partly perverse, satisfaction. First, there was the early, totally unexpected and humiliating defeat of British troops by the Zulu impis at the battle of Isandlwana. Second, and more paradoxical, was the final crushing British victory at the battle of Ulundi, a triumph which appeared to break Zulu power forever. The victory at Ulundi, however, also removed at a stroke the most persuasive of Britain's justifications for the annexation of the Transvaal – the protection of its European citizens from black aggression.[9] It was a development not lost upon those Transvaalers who increasingly resented British rule and wanted it ended.

The annexation of the Transvaal and the Anglo-Zulu War had taken place during the premiership of Benjamin Disraeli, from 1874 to 1880. While in office, Disraeli – hoping to restore the political fortunes of the Conservative party after the long post free-trade ascendancy of the Liberals precipitated by the Tory party split over the repeal of the Corn Laws in 1846 – had pursued a policy of imperial aggrandisement in the conviction that a close association of the party with Empire and with imperialism would triumphantly serve that purpose.

Disraeli's imperial initiatives included the acquisition of the Khedive of Egypt's Suez Canal Company shares, the annexation of the Transvaal, the precipitation of the Anglo-Zulu War and the invasion of Afghanistan. Lord Carnarvon's drive, as Colonial Secretary, and the enthusiastic cooperation of various imperial 'men on the spot', had given the package its cutting edge. An added bonus was the warm approval of Queen Victoria, still resolutely mourning the death of the Prince Consort and all too ready both to be flattered by her new Prime Minister's attentions and to see in his policies the fulfilment of her own patriotic and imperial prejudices.

Hardly had Disraeli ascended the greasy pole of British politics, however, than events caused him to slither down once more. In the general election of 1880, Gladstone and the Liberals were returned to power with a substantial majority. Gladstone, moreover, had campaigned, at least to some extent, on the rejection of the immorality and selfish nationalism that he perceived as part and parcel of Disraeli's foreign and imperial policies. Once in office, however, Gladstone's political choices were seriously limited by what was practically achievable, and also by the need to keep his divided and quarrelsome cabinet as united as possible.

Despite the rhetoric of electioneering and Gladstone's bid to occupy the moral high ground, it soon became evident, particularly in regard to South Africa, that both Conservative and Liberal administrations in practice followed a policy of bipartisanship. In June 1880, within a few weeks of winning the general election, the new Prime Minister met a Transvaal delegation headed by the subtle and intransigent Paul Kruger, ex-Vice-President of the fallen republic, and announced in an astonishing volte face: 'Our judgement is that the Queen cannot be advised to relinquish her sovereignty over the Transvaal.'[10]

For most Transvaalers this dramatic switch was seen, not as the predictable result of an opposition party assuming office and discovering that government forced on them policies they had hitherto criticised, but as an act of Gladstonian treachery and hypocrisy. As a result, it proved to be a breaking point. On 15 December 1880 the first shots were fired in the Transvaal's uprising against British rule. The unforeseen and shaming British defeat by the Transvaalers at Majuba Hill in January 1881 destroyed the possibility that, somehow, mainly through a show of force, the Gladstone government could retain control of the territory.

At the Pretoria Convention, the Anglo-Boer conference that took place in the immediate aftermath of the battle of Majuba, the independence of the Transvaal was formally restored. After their military defeat, the British had no realistic option but to withdraw from such hostile territory. The problem was to be that this agreement was partly renegotiated before it was finalised at the London Convention in 1884.

As it finally turned out, the settlement was blurred and confused in one significant respect. The Pretoria Convention of 1881 had contained a clear reference to 'the suzerainty of Her Majesty', perhaps a concession made by the Afrikaners because they were anxious to bring an immediate end to British military operations, ineffective though they had proved to be, in the republic. This crucial and loaded phrase was, however, deleted in the final agreement of 1884,[11] seriously weakening Britain's hand in any future dispute with the Transvaal.

The London Convention included the agreement that Britain should have oversight of future treaties between the Transvaal and any other nation (except the Orange Free State), and with African tribes to the east and the west. But the wider issue of British suzerainty remained obscure. The upshot was that the Transvaal, led after 1883 by the tough and wily Paul Kruger, denied that suzerainty existed, while the British government refused to acknowledge this claim. Perhaps none of this would have mattered much if the economic and demographic circumstances of the region had remained reasonably static. In the event the broad, uneasy and essentially unresolved question of Anglo-Transvaal relations, and the more specific and potentially explosive issue of British suzerainty, were to be revived in dramatic circumstances after 1886.

2

The Descent to War, 1886–1899

THE DISCOVERY IN 1886 of the huge gold deposits on the Witwatersrand, in the republic of the Transvaal – officially known as the South African Republic – changed the political and economic climate in the most dramatic and, as it turned out, irreversible fashion. The 1886 gold strike led to a sequence of events that evolved into a lengthy crisis and, in the last resort, precipitated the war of 1899–1902.

As a result, war in South Africa became increasingly unavoidable, especially from the mid-1890s. Up to that point, and particularly after the Transvaal had regained its independence in 1881, it was still possible to believe in the long-term strategy of waiting for the Transvaal, and the less prosperous Orange Free State, to be drawn into a unified South Africa dominated by British business interests and British political practice.

At first the 1886 discovery in the Transvaal of the very substantial gold deposits on the Witwatersrand reef seemed to confirm this analysis. Certainly the development did much to encourage those who hoped for, and indeed counted on, the eventual absorption of the awkward republic into a British dominated South Africa. As tens of thousands of fortune-hunting foreigners, most of whom claimed British citizenship, migrated to the gold mines of the Transvaal it seemed that that country's identity would be changed permanently and in Britain's favour. Within a decade these predominantly English-speaking immigrants, backed and empowered not only by their technological and workplace skills but also by the investment of capital from overseas as well as from within South Africa, had established a thriving industrial economy centred on the rapidly developing infant city of Johannesburg.

Observers in the area and elsewhere were soon calculating that the foreign migrants, described by the Afrikaners as Uitlanders – or outsiders – outnumbered the Afrikaners of the Transvaal. The fact that the reckoning was wrong, and more of a propaganda device than a piece of rational demography, proved to be irrelevant. On the widely accepted contemporary analysis, the influx of Uitlanders promised to hand British imperial policy an easy, probably bloodless victory through the inevitable transformation of the Transvaal into a community dominated by its English-speaking citizens. Understandably, the Transvaal government led by Paul Kruger was determined to avoid this fate. Although the administration persistently refused to admit the Uitlanders *en masse* to full citizenship, it did not seem feasible that these delaying tactics would be effective for long in the face of the unbridled power of the economic and capitalist revolution gripping the Transvaal.

Probably by 1894, and certainly by 1895, however, any optimistic assessments that the South African Republic would somehow implode and collapse internally, or simply wither away and become easy imperial pickings as the result of inexorable demographic change and economic transformation, were becoming unsustainable.

There were several reasons for this. Among them was the plain fact that the gold deposits on the Rand were shown to be the largest in the world and capable of profitable production for at least another hundred years. Although shallow-level or outcrop mining played a significant part in the Rand's development, it was soon evident that deep-level mining would be the predominant method by which the gold ore was extracted; as a result, both the technological and labour costs of the process increased sharply. The price of gold, however, was fixed in the world markets. It was not possible simply to meet increased costs by hiking up the price of the precious mineral.

Consequently, the great deep-level gold-mining companies of the Rand needed a government in the Transvaal that was sensitive to the needs of the industry and willing fully to cooperate in its development. One of the most powerful and vociferous of the gold magnates, Cecil Rhodes, backed by deep-level mining companies such as Wernher, Beit and Co., claimed that if the gold industry had the full support of a sympathetic local regime, then mining costs could be cut by at least six shillings (thirty new pence) on every ton of earth dug up, thus saving the industry over £2,500,000 each year. Rhodes also wanted the Kruger government to permit a large increase in the recruitment of black labour; this, together with a ruthless policy of wage cutting, he argued, would improve productivity.

Predictably, though perhaps short-sightedly, the Kruger government, mostly obscurantist, and fundamentally fearful and resentful of the changes being brought about in the Transvaal through immigration and industrialisation, was only minimally cooperative. President Kruger was certainly encouraged in his resistance to the demands of Rhodes and his supporters by the fact that five of the ten leading mining companies, including Lewis and Marks, and Joseph Robinson's company, tended to back him in the confrontation. Interestingly this split in the mining hierarchy was chiefly, although not entirely, the product of different economic and hence political needs. The deep-level mining companies were most urgently in need of a more sympathetic approach by the regime, and hence more radical in their political agendas and more bitterly opposed to the Kruger government; those still substantially committed to outcrop mining methods were more supportive.[1]

This schism not only gave substance to Rhodes's assertion that it was the economics of deep-level mining that made the overthrow of Kruger's republic essential, but it also goes a long way to explain the confused, half-hearted Uitlander response to the Jameson Raid at the end of 1895. Failing to cash in on this split, and perhaps not caring enough to take action, the Kruger administration continued to levy heavy taxes on Transvaal industry, like that imposed on the sale of dynamite, and to extract all that they could out of monopolies.

Caught between the powerfully articulated demands of much of the gold mining industry and the obduracy of the Transvaal government, statesmen and industrialists, both in South Africa and in Britain, began to despair of a peaceful and, as they saw it, 'sensible' resolution of the growing conflict of interests between the Kruger government and outside and inside pressure groups. Worse still, the anticipated process of attrition through the demographic changes created by English-speaking immigration was in any event being neatly thwarted by the Transvaal government's refusal to extend full citizenship and voting rights to the Uitlanders.

A further complication was the fact that imperial Germany

seemed determined to involve itself in Transvaal affairs and to act as a champion of the Kruger regime. By 1895 over 5,000 Germans were living in the Transvaal and formed a substantial, well-to-do, and generally pro-Kruger, community. German mining enterprises were being established and German investment was soon in excess of 300,000,000 marks. Although it is difficult, given Germany's lack of anything approaching British sea power, to imagine how an effective military threat to the exercise of Britain's interests could have been mounted by the Berlin government, the German colony of South West Africa was in close proximity to the Cape and could in theory have provided a base for harassing British military operations in the region.

By the mid-1890s, the comfortable British Colonial Office assumption that a 'peaceful commercial annexation of the country [the Transvaal]' would result from the irresistible progress of British enterprise, technology and migration, seemed increasingly ill-founded. Indeed, the balance of power in South Africa seemed to be shifting inexorably and permanently away from the Cape to the increasingly prosperous and powerful Transvaal.

Suddenly the South African future seemed destined to be dominated by a revitalised Afrikanerdom, centred in the Transvaal, and sustained by the continuing exploitation and development of the Rand's economy. It was a spectre that increasingly troubled the newly established British Unionist government under Lord Salisbury. With the shrewd and ruthless imperialist Joseph Chamberlain appointed Colonial Secretary in July 1895, the direction of Colonial Office policy was now switched to a course that was designed to resolve the South African crisis one way or the other in the very near future.

Once more, the generalised feeling that time was running out for Britain was given a specific edge in this increasingly valuable and potentially extremely prosperous region. Few British statesmen put the position more plainly than Lord Selborne, Chamberlain's Under Secretary of State at the Colonial Office, and like him a Liberal Unionist, when he wrote:

In a generation the South African Republic [the Transvaal] will by its wealth and population dominate S. Africa. S. African politics must revolve around the Transvaal, which will be the only possible market for the agricultural produce or the manufacture of Cape Colony and Natal.

> The commercial attraction of the Transvaal will be so great that a Union of the African states with it will be absolutely necessary for their prosperous existence.[2]

Lord Selborne's pessimism, or rather realism, expressed in the autumn of 1896, had been partly provoked by two other recent developments. The first of these was the realisation that Cecil Rhodes's 'drive to the north', which had only recently resulted in the opening up of Rhodesia, was not going to redress the geopolitical balance in South Africa. There were no great precious mineral deposits in the Rhodesias, despite the subsequent development of copper mining in the north, and Rhodes's assertion that 'The gist of the South African question lies in the extension of the Cape to the Zambezi' had been proved disastrously wrong. In 1896 the terrifying Ndebele and Shona rebellions against white rule in Southern Rhodesia seemed further confirmation that the territory's future was, at best uncertain and potentially costly, and at worst bleak, compared with that of the Transvaal.

It was, however, another armed uprising, and this time a white one, in the mid-1890s that seemed, once and for all, to wreck every hope of a peaceful resolution of the 'Transvaal problem'. This was the Jameson Raid. There is no doubt that Cecil Rhodes was the inspiration behind the Jameson Raid. By 1895, and probably earlier, he had become convinced that, for British interests to thrive throughout the whole of South Africa, and for his commercial and political ambitions to flourish with them, the South African Republic would have to be destroyed, almost inevitably by force.[3]

This was a perfectly rational assessment, and Rhodes was not alone in making it. What is significant, and typical of his energy and his capacity to tackle great projects, is the fact that he felt compelled to do something practical about it. His determination to topple the Kruger regime through armed intervention also arose from his unbridled ambition and from his remarkable success hitherto as a maker of history.

Rhodes's fabulous wealth had enabled him to put flesh upon the bones of his imperial and expansionist fantasies. The multi-millionaire and conqueror of the Rhodesias had no need to shy at mounting a coup aimed at the destruction of an apparently moribund and obstructive Transvaal government, even though such an enterprise would almost certainly mean the end of his premiership of the Cape Colony where he depended upon moderate Cape Afrikaner support to sustain him in office. Perhaps Rhodes also had the feeling that he was running out of time. Indeed, by 1902 he was dead; certainly by 1895 he had run out of patience.

Rhodes's plans for the subordination of the Transvaal were well laid and not at all unrealistic. From the Rand, sufficient Uitlanders gave assurances that they would arm and organise themselves and, at the appropriate time, rise in rebellion. Indeed many proceeded to set up small, local groups in order to acquire weapons and to train in their use. It was planned that the uprising would be supported by an armed expedition into the Transvaal, composed of detachments of the British South African Police force, which was in effect Rhodes's private army for maintaining control of the Rhodesias.

The conspirators knew that they would raise a storm of international protest, but calculated that foreign indignation and complaint would be unable to prevent the coup. Within South Africa there seemed to be many cards stacked in their favour. Rhodes, as we have seen, was Prime Minister of the Cape, and in alliance with the moderate Cape Afrikaner Bond party led by Jan Hofmeyr. Natal, dominated by its English-speaking settler population, would support the enterprise. It would, moreover, be possible to present the intervention in quasi-humanitarian terms, claiming that the coup was necessary to guarantee the Uitlanders their British birthright of free and equal citizenship. The propaganda war was there to be won.

It is clear that Rhodes also felt confident that the British government would support him in his attempt to overthrow Kruger's republic. This was not merely the result of his overweening self-confidence and ability to get his way on the world stage. He had already made discreet overtures to the Liberal government led by the Liberal imperialist Lord Rosebery, before it fell from power in the summer of 1895, and had not been discouraged in his plans.

Far more significantly the formation of Lord Salisbury's Unionist government, a coalition of Conservatives and Liberal Unionists, in July 1895, seemed even more propitious. The new Colonial Secretary, Joseph Chamberlain, a man of clear-cut strategic aims and impatient with delay, shared Rhodes's desire to be rid of the Kruger regime, although naturally he was obliged to act more discreetly than the lumbering, multi-millionaire 'colossus'. It is now plain as a pikestaff that Chamberlain connived at Rhodes's plan for an invasion of the Transvaal, was privy to the planned Uitlander uprising, and did all he could to promote the venture by ceding the Pitsani strip, part of the Bechuanaland Protectorate, to the British South Africa Company, as a convenient base from which to launch the attack.

The Jameson Raid began on 31 December 1895. Its main thrust was the invasion of the Transvaal, undertaken by troopers of the British South African Police force based in the Rhodesias, and led by Rhodes's confidante Dr Leander Starr Jameson. 'Dr Jim' had enjoyed the affection and trust of the 'colossus' ever since he had attended Neville Pickering, Rhodes's greatly loved young companion, on his deathbed. Probably Jameson was not the right man for the job of leading the Raid. In some ways as impetuous as Rhodes himself, Jameson seems to have jumped the gun and to have decided to make an end of waiting with an abrupt and, as it turned out, hopelessly premature armed intervention.

Catastrophe overtook the Raid, despite its powerful backers and the relatively careful preparations. The Uitlanders of Johannesburg and the Rand were meant to rise in rebellion and link up with Jameson's invading troopers. Indeed the raid was designed to galvanise all those who disliked the Kruger regime for whatever reason. Significantly, the senior British administrator in the region, the High Commissioner for South Africa and Governor of the Cape, Sir Hercules Robinson (who was incidentally a shareholder in Rhodes's British South Africa Company), boarded a train bound for the Transvaal, planning to step into the clamour and confusion that would have resulted from the overthrow of the Kruger government and to act as a mediator, although, in the circumstances, a decidedly partial one.

The hope had been that the speed of the military operation and success of the coup would leave the international community breathless and nullify their hostility. In any event, it was difficult to see what any foreign power that wished to support the Transvaal government could do about it in practice, even if, like imperial Germany, they had a stake in the region.

None of this worked out as Rhodes and his supporters had planned. The Uitlander uprising was a half-cocked affair, seeming to confirm the views of a number of British statesmen, on both sides of the political divide, that Mammon not Queen Victoria was the true idol of Johannesburg. Dr Jameson's dashing invasion force was routed, speedily rounded up by Afrikaner commandos, and, dusty and dejected, handed over to the British authorities for trial.

The Jameson Raid was a humiliating flop. The event, but especially its failure, was a staggering reverse for Rhodes's 'forward' policy in South Africa. In its immediate aftermath, Rhodes was a deflated, broken man, accusing his old comrade 'Dr Jim' of 'upsetting his applecart', and even – such is friendship between thieves – sending him instructions in Pretoria gaol to take the whole blame for the fiasco.[4]

Inevitably nemesis soon overtook Rhodes. He was forced to resign as Prime Minister of the Cape, his alliance with Hofmeyr's Afrikaner Bond predictably in ruins. Afrikaner opinion throughout South Africa, which Rhodes had tried so hard to woo or at least subvert, rallied to Kruger and his beleaguered government. Within the Transvaal – where, ironically, moderate, anti-Kruger factions had hitherto been optimistic of winning the imminent presidential election – Afrikaner opposition was temporarily silenced. The Orange Free State was drawn closer to its northern sister republic. In the Cape, many of the Afrikaans-speaking people, who accounted for two-thirds of the white population, were encouraged to feel more strongly than ever their ties of kinship with the Afrikaners of the two republics. The German Kaiser, Wilhelm II, sent Kruger a telegram of strident and provocative congratulation – to Britain's embarrassment, though in the end to no great practical effect.

Within the United Kingdom, liberal opinion was outraged at the aggression, and an inquiry was called for. A Select Committee of the House of Commons was set up, though it took time to call before it a wide range of witnesses, who mostly had to be brought from South Africa to give evidence. Even when it eventually got under way, the enquiry was handled, or, as some thought mishandled, so as to cover the traces of the Jameson plotters. Certainly it seems clear that the British establishment closed ranks. Liberal members of the Committee pulled their punches, anxious not to reveal their complicity in the early planning stages of the Raid. Unionist members, with Chamberlain breathing down their necks, were unlikely to rock the boat of party and of Empire.

Brought before the Committee of Inquiry, an unrepentant Rhodes treated its members with breathtaking insolence, even remarking to the Liberal Leader of the Opposition, Sir William Harcourt, 'Nobody is going to name a country after you.' Chamberlain, widely suspected of plotting with Rhodes, was confident that the inquiry would not 'do any harm'.[5] He was right to be so confident. The Colonial Secretary denied all knowledge of the Raid, although admitting that he knew of the potential Uitlander uprising. Neither Rhodes nor Chamberlain were obliged to produce the 'missing telegrams' that allegedly implicated both of them in the plot.

The Committee of Inquiry was a whitewash, and was soon being written off as the 'Lying-in-state at Westminster'. It is, of course, easy to see why neither Rhodes nor Chamberlain was brought to book over the Jameson Raid. Each could so seriously harm the career and reputation of the other, that both were as a consequence entirely safe: Rhodes could reveal the evidence of Chamberlain's complicity; for his part, the Colonial Secretary could seriously undermine Rhodes's imperial mission by stripping his British South Africa Company of its Royal Charter, the effective authorisation for its continuing rule of the Rhodesias. The truth, for the foreseeable future, was safe from discovery in their hands.

The Raid had provoked serious doubts and criticism in South Africa, even within English-speaking circles normally sympathetic to at least the principle of Rhodes's hostile policies towards the Transvaal. Although some of this arose from frustration that the coup had failed so miserably, other doubts focussed on the moral issues involved, or regretted the void created in Cape politics by Rhodes's abrupt resignation as Prime Minister. Jan Hofmeyr, Rhodes's Afrikaner Bond ally in the Cape Parliament, was to sum this up over a year after the Raid: when asked in 'one of the smaller London salons ... about things in general in the colony' he replied, 'what our politicians and people in general feel is this – we've lost a leader'.[6]

Others were convinced that Rhodes had in the last resort acted so rashly because of his conviction that time was running out for him:

> 'So much to do' ... there lies the secret of the feverish haste with which Rhodes worked especially during the last years of his life, when he knew he was doomed to die young. It explains also his mistakes. He endeavoured to take short cuts ... He was like an airman with his eyes glued anxiously to the petrol indicator – would the fluid hold out till he reached his destination?[7]

As the aftermath of the Raid was scrutinised and more rumour and evidence unravelled, a particularly unfavourable gloss emerged. It was put succinctly in a letter between Sir Percy FitzPatrick, an Uitlander leader and loyalist politician, and Alfred Beit, the gold magnate and close friend of Rhodes. Writing to Beit in December 1896, FitzPatrick recounted a recent conversation with the future Cape Prime Minister, W.P. Schreiner, who was apparently 'very open indeed, and at the end he told me this in confidence':

> I have been told lately, on what I regard as excellent authority, that Rhodes, through and in co-operation with Beit, practically doubled his fortune by huge [speculative share] operations in all parts of the world, timed to mature with the Movement [the Jameson Raid]. Now, if Rhodes has made a couple of millions out of it, the thing has a very ugly look – gaming with men's lives and the fate of a country; and I should have to re-cast my whole estimate of the man. Mind you I did not know this at the time of the Enquiry [the British parliamentary inquiry into the Raid]; and I am glad of it, because I could not have said what I said had I heard this of him.[8]

Naturally FitzPatrick tried to put another point of view to Schreiner:

> In vain I put such questions and assurances as this: 'If they meant to gamble on it, which did they expect, success or failure? And which did they gamble on?' and 'Men of solid wealth do not gamble on a rise or fall which may only last twenty-four hours, and which may come off at any time, or not at all.'[9]

Schreiner remained unconvinced:

> His answer was this: 'The evidence given me was such that – well, if I were a judge, I *wouldn't hang* a man on it, but . . .' and then he shrugged his shoulders and raised his eyebrows in an unmistakable way.[10]

Certainly Schreiner, like so many others, had earlier done his best to be circumspect when summoned to London to give evidence before the Committee of Inquiry. In 1896 he had resigned his position as Attorney General in Rhodes's Cape government in order to disassociate himself from the Jameson Raid. He was, however, tarred by association and was required to come to Britain to answer the inquiry's questions.

Despite his warm reception in London, and his meetings with, among others, the Liberal leader Campbell-Bannerman and the influential editor of the *National Review*, Leopold Maxse, Schreiner was fully aware of the thin ice under his feet. As a result, he had written an anxious letter to Chamberlain in December 1897, explaining that he had hoped for an interview with the Colonial Secretary before giving evidence and especially whether he should 'state fully, if asked, what I know relating to the closing and opening of the Vaal River drifts in 1895'. Lamenting the fact that the campaigning journalist W.T. Stead had somehow got hold of evidence relating to the pre-Jameson Raid drifts crisis, Schreiner assured Chamberlain:

> I have not the least wish to embarrass you; and that if you should decide that I should ... maintain silence as to the communications, which passed at the time, I shall accept your decision. May I say that I do not regret my part in the matter, though I personally anticipate very heavy weather regarding it when I return to the Cape Colony.[11]

With a closing of ranks like this at the time of the inquiry, no matter what Schreiner's subsequent misgivings about Rhodes's actions were to be, the British government was able to ride out the post-Jameson Raid storms and sustain very little damage in the process. For his part, Chamberlain shrugged off the attacks on his integrity and remained unbowed by the inevitable embarrassment of the official inquiry. Soon, with the support of his ministerial colleagues, the Colonial Secretary set about restructuring British policy in South Africa.

In 1897, within a year of the inquiry, he had appointed Alfred Milner, an avowed 'race-patriot', as Governor of the Cape and High Commissioner for South Africa. Milner's task was to regain the diplomatic and political initiative against Kruger's republic and to isolate and denigrate the Transvaal government. At the same time, the place of Rhodes as Prime Minister of the Cape was taken by Schreiner, who had emerged from the investigations of the Committee of Inquiry with his reputation intact, if not enhanced.

This seemed to be a brilliant stroke for the discreet furtherance of British interests in the region, hopefully in a creative partnership with Milner. Schreiner was not merely a Cambridge graduate who had gone on to be called to the bar in Britain, but he also had Afrikaner connections. He was married to Frances Hester Reitz, the sister of

F.W. Reitz, President of the Orange Free State between 1889 and 1895.[12] The fact that Schreiner habitually called his wife 'Fanny', and always wrote to her in English when they were apart, is yet another indication of how complex and intertwined the relations between South Africa's whites often were, and how rash it is to assume that there were two clearly demarcated European sides in the crisis that was to end in the Anglo-Boer War.[13] To further complicate matters, Schreiner was also the younger brother of Olive Schreiner, soon to be world famous as a shrewd and passionate writer and feminist, and a sensitive and progressive commentator upon South African affairs.

W.P. Schreiner was thus linked to the cosmopolitan, sophisticated world represented by his sister, and was at the same time also to a considerable extent able to reassure the Cape Afrikaners that with him as premier their interests were safer than under the calculating and often head-strong leadership of the now disgraced Rhodes. With his British education and his Anglophile cultural connections, his family links with the Orange Free State and his politically driven need to consider sympathetically the susceptibilities of the Afrikaans-speaking citizens of the Cape Colony, Schreiner was uniquely placed to bridge the growing gap between the British government and the two Boer republics.

Schreiner's capacity to influence events creatively was demonstrated by his efforts to avert what seemed after 1895 to be an increasingly inevitable war. Together with the Cape's Chief Justice, Sir Henry de Villiers, Schreiner honourably and persistently pursued the goal of compromise and mediation in the months leading up to the outbreak of the war. It is possible that these constructive initiatives actually deferred the military assault on the Cape Colony by the Orange Free State, under its President M.T. Steyn, rendering Natal the more favoured target of the Free State administration.[14] In any event, it kept alive the option – also of course an important, and frequently favoured, option of the British government – of reaching a settlement short of fighting.

Schreiner's efforts to avert a conflict were not some idiosyncratic, erratic and isolated display of personal initiative. Many South African statesmen, as well as business and church leaders from both sides of the growing divide, also sought ways out of the crisis short of war. There is very little evidence of consistently uncompromising and aggressive behaviour among contemporary leaders. Even

Chamberlain, for all the cold, hard, inexorable edge of his speech-making, for all his capacity to manipulate and control, was disposed to settle for a deal which delivered the substance of what he wanted. The trouble was that the Transvaal and Orange Free State leadership too often took the combative style of the Colonial Secretary's pronouncements to be the message itself, instead of seeing that behind the rhetoric there was a pragmatic politician not averse to compromise – though with a crystal clear set of criteria for public consumption and a bottom line that was irreducible.

More threatening and opaque was Alfred Milner, the paramount orchestrator of British policy in South Africa after his appointment as Governor of the Cape and High Commissioner in 1897. Although able to show to a few intimates a warm, lively and passionate nature, Milner's reputation for machiavellian, cold-blooded calculation was what marked him out for the distrust and vituperation of his many critics and foes. It is no wonder that many contemporaries felt that it was the brooding, calculating policies of Milner, his brutal brinkmanship, that were destined to lead to the outbreak of war in October 1899.

Yet even a brief analysis of Milner's thoughts and attitudes after his appointment as High Commissioner reveals a character far more complex, and a mind far more open to persuasion, than was, or is, commonly supposed. In December 1898, for example, Milner wrote thus to W.P. Schreiner from London:

> It is just as well that the policy of letting things [in South Africa] come right of themselves should have a fair trial. It largely depends of course on the internal state of the Transvaal ... The times are very exciting. Public opinion has been stirred on Imperial questions as it never yet has been in my lifetime, & it is impossible to say what may come out of it.[15]

On the other hand, Milner, like every other responsible and prudent statesman, was not a single-minded, lumbering, diplomatic automaton. The achievement of British aims in South Africa short of war was clearly a primary aim of policy for him, Chamberlain, and even for Rhodes. Nonetheless, Milner's approach to the solution of the escalating crisis in South Africa often left local statesmen and observers unsettled and distrustful, even when they might have been expected loyally to support the imperial cause. Typical of such reactions were the misgivings voiced to Schreiner in the spring of 1899 by the liberal Cape politician John X. Merriman. Describing the impression that a recent interview with Milner had left upon his mind, Merriman wrote:

> This was one of *profound* apprehension and uneasiness. Milner seems to me to be in absolute ignorance of the South African question and to be dominated by a steady and persistent hostility to the Transvaal ... He reverted more than once to the notion that a crisis must come in the Transvaal – that Kruger had done nothing to meet them ... I did not ask him what Chamberlain had done since the Raid to inspire confidence, nor did I point out ... the many instances in which Kruger *has* tried to mend matters.
>
> I feel that there is a sinister undercurrent. What do we know about Gt. Britain's attitude towards the Transvaal? Nothing! Yet Rhodes knows everything – and I feel most acutely that this is not the right position for a responsible government [the Cape Colony government].[16]

Milner's patient reconstruction of imperial policy in South Africa could not be diverted by the qualms of Cape statesmen – indeed, it is noteworthy that Merriman in his account of the meeting described above, told Schreiner that 'we were throughout the interview on the best of terms and I avoided even the smallest approach to what might be looked on as a controversial matter'.[17] In such an atmosphere there was really very little need for Milner to take much heed of local misgivings, even though he prudently sought the support of the Cape premier Schreiner and consulted him fairly frequently as the Transvaal crisis deepened and when war finally broke out.[18]

Working closely with Chamberlain and the British government, Milner was able to prepare the ground for a final showdown with the Transvaal government. A year before hostilities began, in a brilliant and unexpected diplomatic coup, the Transvaal was cut off from its most likely form of outside assistance. During 1898 the Anglo-German agreement over the possible future disposal of Portugal's southern African colonies was signed. In the half expected event of the Portuguese government's financial crisis leading to national bankruptcy and collapse, and the subsequent surrender of her colonies, it was agreed that Britain was to have Mozambique and Germany was to have Angola.

As a result, in September 1898 Arthur Balfour was able to tell the Cabinet that Germany had resigned 'all concern in Transvaal matters'. It is worth noting that this judgement was made barely two years after the Kaiser's enthusiastic telegram in support of Kruger after the Jameson Raid. Further evidence of the dramatic shift in German policy in the region occurred in the autumn of 1899, as large British forces were transferred to South Africa to fight the Boer republics. Far from attacking British policy, Kaiser Wilhelm II went out of his way to compliment the British War Office on the efficiency of its organisation. With Germany no longer obstructive, there was no other nation that was likely, or indeed able, to assist the Transvaal in a military confrontation with Britain.

At the Colonial Office, Chamberlain, although perceived by many as being morally impoverished by the Jameson Raid, faced down his critics with his usual self-confidence and, with Milner's shrewd and skilful assistance, gradually re-established the propaganda campaign on behalf of the Uitlanders and, as a result, of Britain's legitimate interests in the internal affairs of the Transvaal.

Gradually, carefully, the Uitlanders were rehabilitated, and once more represented as a worthy English-speaking community denied their basic civil rights and ill-treated by the tyrannical Kruger regime. Although in fact the Transvaal government became increasingly pre-pared to make some retrospective concessions over the Uitlander franchise, British propaganda was always quick to present such offers as too little and too late. The tone of Chamberlain and Milner's blatant propaganda campaign even left some members of the Conservative and Unionist government feeling uneasy, and Balfour argued, with commendable honesty, in a paper put to the Cabinet that 'were I a Boer ... nothing but necessity would induce me to adopt a constitution which would turn my country into an English Republic, or a system of education that would reduce my language to the "patois" of a small and helpless minority'.[19]

During 1899, however, the crisis in South Africa was moving towards a final resolution. Milner argued that what was really going on was a 'great game between ourselves and the Transvaal for the mastery of South Africa' with the object of 'uniting South Africa as a British State'. Chamberlain asserted, with characteristic clarity and hyperbole, that 'Our supremacy in South Africa, and our existence as a great power in the world are involved.'[20]

Always able to see where its best interests lay, the British-dominated industry on the Rand increased its practical backing for

Chamberlain's and Milner's progressively aggressive policies. The deep-level mining magnates, the 'Park Lane millionaires' of British Liberal demonology, had been suspected of putting up money for the Jameson Raid. As the crisis escalated it is clear that, with Rhodes and Alfred Beit at the forefront, they offered crucial financial support and thus, in effect, indemnity to the British government in the event of a full-scale war to destroy the republic of the Transvaal. Sniffing the scent of future profits, the City of London was generally enthusiastic at the prospect of the overthrow of the Kruger regime. This was understandable, given the fact that in 1899 investment in the gold-mining industry totalled some £74,000,000 of which the British share was about seventy per cent.[21]

In May 1899 the British government, represented by Milner, adroitly played a potent diplomatic card by arranging a conference at Bloemfontein in the Orange Free State. The conference was called as a last ditch and very public attempt to resolve the differences between the Transvaal and Britain. Unsurprisingly, perhaps, the Bloemfontein summit turned into a face-to-face confrontation between Kruger and Milner. The meeting predictably failed to resolve any of their differences, and left the Transvaal President fearfully convinced that 'It is our country you want.'

Less than a month after the collapse of the Bloemfontein summit conference, Chamberlain and Milner were discussing both the form of an ultimatum to the Transvaal, and more ominously the matters of military reinforcements and troop movements. In July 1899, Kruger made the substantial concession of offering the Uitlanders a seven-year retrospective franchise that would enable substantial numbers of them to vote, as well as five new seats in the Volksraad, the Transvaal's parliament. His offer, in effect a significant climb-down, was rejected.

There were, however, other negotiations, both open and covert, to avoid war. In part this reflected the understandable desire to avoid a bruising and uncertain conflict that was likely permanently to disrupt, and probably for the worst, the existing political, economic and social relationships of South Africans of all colours, nationalities and origins. In part it was predictable: impending conflicts almost always provoke last ditch attempts to prevent them.

In the South Africa of 1899 there was perhaps an even more compelling reason to seek a peaceful solution to the confrontation. Quite simply, the prospects of an Anglo-Boer struggle to the death not merely raised the terrifying spectre of uncontrollable black insurrection in the interstices of the fighting, but also seemed, on many counts, to be an unnecessary, almost self-indulgent, diversion from the real job to hand – the development and consolidation of a white dominated southern Africa.

The overwhelming majority of Afrikaans- and English-speaking South Africans knew very well that when push came to shove in the real 'race conflict' there would be no question where their common interest lay – in the maintenance of white supremacy. This explains why, after the war, Smuts felt that Britain's arming of Africans was an even greater crime than the introduction of the concentration camps, and why the Natal cabinet overwhelmingly opposed the use of armed 'natives' in the conflict.[22]

Milner, of course, protested his willingness to be patient and negotiate. Before the Bloemfontein conference he assured Schreiner:

> I don't want even to be seen to stand in the way of anything wh[ich] is likely to be thought to promote harmony in S. Africa, however much I may feel that real harmony is impossible, while the one great (& I think *sole*) abiding cause of racial bitterness remains unremoved and unmitigated.[23]

Even after the failure of the Bloemfontein summit, Milner told Schreiner:

> My influence *has* been exercised, since my return from Bloemfontein, to keep the tone of controversy moderate. You will understand, however, that it is not possible, or even desirable, that when efforts are being made to white-wash the S[outh]. A[frican]. R[epublic]. & to represent the attitude of the British Govt. as unreasonable, those who feel as I do, that the state of things in the S.A.R. is impossible, and that the British Govt. is right in insisting on some remedy, I should not reply. This controversy is bound to go on, & bound to be heated. But I don't wish to aggravate it . . .[24]

Chamberlain also was often at pains to protest his peaceful and reasonable intent. According to Milner, the Colonial Secretary wished Schreiner and his Cape Colony ministers:

to be informed that, as you will have seen from his despatch of May 10th, H.M's. Govt. is most anxious to avoid interference with the internal affairs of the S.A. Republic.

They trust that [Cape] Ministers may use all their influence to induce the Govt. of the S.A.R. to take such steps as would render it unnecessary for H.M's Govt. to consider the question of interference.[25]

South African inspired attempts to avert a war took place both covertly and openly. In 1900, John X. Merriman, writing from his office in the Cape Treasury, revealed that before the outbreak of war, President Kruger had told President Steyn that:

'A certain W.E.T. Hargrove has come here as he says from Sauer and Merriman who are ready to declare themselves openly on our side in order to set on foot propaganda in the Cape Colony provided that an official declaration be given that the republics only wish to secure their entire independence'. The inference is obvious. Viz that [Hargrove] w[as] an emissary sent by Sauer and myself with a message to President Kruger.[26]

What was the policy or attitude that Merriman was so anxious to deny? Simply that he had wished to avoid war and to counsel the British government towards caution. He was not alone. A few months later J.S. Moffat wrote to W.P. Schreiner from Mowbray in the Cape, praising him for pursuing an equally constructive policy:

I wish to thank you very heartily for your declaration that in your opinion there is no call for the active interference of the British Government in the Transvaal under present circumstances. I hope you will have the courage given to you to maintain that position in spite of the strong feelings evoked among those who hold more warlike views.[27]

Neither Schreiner, nor Merriman, nor Moffat nor the mysterious Hargrove were isolated, eccentric seekers after a settlement. Indeed, Moffat argued in his letter to Schreiner in July 1899 that Kruger's belated concessions gave 'our British Colonial Office a chance of gracefully accepting the terms and thus avoiding ... so grave a misfortune as this war would be'.[28]

None of this was able to divert the British government from its grim determination to push the crisis to the brink of war. By August

1899, both the Colonial and War Offices and the British imperial authorities in South Africa were busy preparing for war. The Sudan campaign, with its capacity to seize the public imagination and to dominate the headlines of the British press, was conveniently over. The British people, still luxuriating in the afterglow of Kitchener's crushing defeat of the dervishes at Omdurman, could now be made to concentrate upon the infinitely more complex and risky confrontation with the Transvaal. So thorough were British preparations for the looming conflict in South Africa that several weeks before the outbreak of hostilities in October, over 10,000 British and imperial troops were stationed in South Africa , and soon after the war began another 50,000 were on their way.

The British diplomatic offensive was concluded neatly in October 1899 when the threatening and unambiguous movements of imperial troops forced both the Transvaal and the Orange Free State to present an ultimatum calling for the withdrawal of these forces from the Transvaal's frontiers, and for the recall of all reinforcements dispatched since June. The British government, having provoked the ultimatum, naturally ignored it. Those in the Cabinet, and within the English-speaking community in South Africa, who doubted the wisdom of military intervention, now mostly swallowed their qualms and admitted the necessity for a military showdown in South Africa.

Essentially, of course, British policy in the region since 1895 had been a failure. Despite its increasingly strident and menacing tone, the brinkmanship of Chamberlain's and Milner's diplomatic offensive had failed to deliver the goods – or, at least, the desired first option of a bloodless surrender by the Transvaal. The various concessions that had been demanded of the Kruger government were simply too great to be practical politics. At least Britain could now protest its good intentions, point to its diplomatic initiatives, and officially regret the fact that a military confrontation now seemed unavoidable.

For its part, the Transvaal, strongly supported by the Orange Free State, and with offers of help flooding in from thousands of Cape Afrikaners, decided that it had nothing to lose by standing firm. No doubt memories of Britain's brisk humiliations during the Anglo-Transvaal War of 1880–1 influenced this determination, with echoes of the battle of Majuba Hill both misleading and inspiring a later generation. So perhaps did the feeling that the English-speakers of

South Africa included many who had worked to avoid a military showdown, and that the liberal conscience and liberal voices in the United Kingdom would soon be mobilised on their behalf. It was, moreover, October, and the spring grass was sprouting, supplying ample fodder for the horses so central to the successful deployment of Boer commandos. With a surprising initial show of purpose and solidarity the two Afrikaner republics went to war with the largest empire in the world. The Anglo-Boer War, the South African War, that had been so long anticipated, dreaded and desired, had at last begun.

Part II

The Combatants

3

The British Army

A T FIRST SIGHT the opposing forces were ludicrously unequal. The British Empire, within whose borders dwelt almost a quarter of the human race, was at war with two sparsely populated republics in South Africa. Britain was still arguably the greatest power in the world, her navy invincible and ubiquitous, her overseas trade colossal, her global influence all-pervasive. British possessions virtually surrounded the Boer republics, while the Boer ultimatum meant, in the words of Lord Lansdowne, the Secretary of State for War, 'that Portugal will wheel into line with us', thus ensuring the closure of Delagoa Bay to the Boers and preventing any outside help.[1] Within the Transvaal the remaining Uitlanders were a fifth column, and by no means all Afrikaners were spoiling for a fight. If ever a war looked as if it would be over by Christmas it was this one.

The British army went to war supremely confident that decades of reform and experience of other 'small wars' had turned it into an efficient fighting force. Its inability to defeat the Boers except after nearly three years of gruelling endeavour, shattered the confidence of both the military hierarchy and the British public. The various committees and commissions that emerged during and after the war revealed an army deficient in quality: its officers and men lacked proper training; some of its weaponry, though modern, needed improvement; and it lacked sufficient military stores. Yet, in spite of the criticism that emerged, the army was able, eventually, to adapt to the rigours of conventional and guerrilla warfare in South Africa. Indeed, the British army was to face the impact of modern weapons to an extent unknown in Europe. As one British officer noted, 'the flat trajectory of the small-bore rifle, together with the invisibility of the man who uses it, has wrought a complete revolution in the art of fighting battles.'[2] Though the British army was to receive some painful lessons, the revolution was achieved.

In one respect the British army found itself completely ill-equipped, and that was in the provision of sufficient manpower. Far more men were needed in South Africa than was at first thought and this shortfall was met by allowing the militia to serve outside Britain and then by the enlistment of enthusiastic volunteers. These were supplemented by the use of Uitlander volunteers, by British colonists from both the Cape Colony and Natal, by a steady stream of volunteers from the self-governing colonies and, lastly, by units raised from British settlers in India and Ceylon. A variety of reasons drew these men to fight: pay, adventure, patriotism, or as one writer opined, 'The spirit of *noblesse oblige*, the pride of freedom and independence, inspired the rank and file. They were in South Africa because they were eager to fight the Queen's enemies.'[3] For the self-governing colonies, taking part in the war – in essence coming to the Empire's rescue – was to have a strong influence on the way these societies perceived themselves and their place in the Empire and also on the way the British regarded them.

Yet such was the demand for manpower that the British were obliged to turn to the local black population to provide essential cover for transport services and, later, after providing them with arms, for the blockhouse lines that criss-crossed the veld from 1901. In addition, in Natal a group of leading Asian businessmen and lawyers, the most prominent perhaps being Mohandas K. Gandhi, felt it their duty to do something for the war effort and formed an ambulance unit that provided stretcher-bearers for the army in Natal. Thus the war in South Africa was truly an imperial war if one takes into account the various manpower sources used by the British, and it revealed to the world the Empire's strength in depth.

The Boers, of course, could not match this wealth of manpower but still managed to put about 60,000 men and boys into the field throughout the war, though this effort meant that they had to commit every available man. However, the Boers would be supplemented by at least 2,000 foreign volunteers, many of whom were Irish, as well as some 13,000 Afrikaners from the Cape Colony, who became rebels in order to see their dream of a united, Boer dominated South Africa fulfilled. From late 1900, after the British had captured their urban centres and completely cut off the republics from the outside world, the Boers showed their versatility and endurance by embarking on hit-and-run guerrilla tactics. The British would be kept at bay for eighteen months, but there was a price to pay for this stubbornness as it would split Boer society. Not all Boers would be content to carry on indefinitely and, encouraged by the British, would serve them as scouts and soldiers. In the end, over 5,000 Boers were serving with the British forces and doing untold harm to those still holding out.

Thus the war played merry havoc with the military institutions and forces of both sides, and few imagined the changes that would take place during its course. For the British, they would have the luxury of time to reform their army and learn the many lessons provided by the war, and could take comfort in the Empire's response. For the Boers, all that would be left to them was time to rue their lost chances and to heal the divisions caused by the war.

Four days before the outbreak of war, Lord Selborne, Chamberlain's deputy at the Colonial Office, wrote somewhat gloomily to his friend Milner: 'You cannot realise the enormous difficulty we have had with public opinion at home. We have now got four-fifths of the nation behind us because of our hesitancy (militarily almost universal) in making adequate preparations early enough, and because they believe there is now no more opening for negotiation.'[4] But when the Boers presented their ultimatum the mood in the country seemed to change dramatically, for the war could be presented, in Chamberlain's phrase, as one 'in defence of principles', thus giving Britain the high moral ground. By so doing, public opinion seemed totally in favour of teaching the Boers a lesson and for silencing those who still opposed the war. H.W. Wilson, the patriotic author and assistant editor and leader writer on the *Daily Mail*, could loftily point to the fervent response of the British public:

Employers announced that they would pay half wages to the women and children whose bread-winners had been called away; enormous funds were raised to support the widowed and the fatherless of those who should fall, and to keep in comfort the families of the soldiers. Workmen subscribed their shillings; the well-to-do their guineas; the rich their thousands of pounds. The most intensely national of poets, Mr. Rudyard Kipling, appealed in touching verse to the nation's heart. In answer to his appeal women sent their rings, children their pence, and the poor humble gifts in kind. No names were published; the giving was simple and un-ostentatious, and therefore all the nobler. Thus our soldiers were made to feel that they went forth to battle with the nation's love and with its fervent prayers ... From the Queen on her throne to the peasant in his cottage all gave liberally. The flood gates of generosity were opened; a universal impulse of patriotism moved the nation.

Indeed, the war did move those who beforehand were regarded as the opponents of government policy in South Africa. Perhaps the most prominent was Robert Blatchford, editor of the socialist paper *Clarion*, who found that the blood of being an old soldier was thicker than the water of socialism: 'My whole heart is with the British troops', he wrote, and 'when England is at war I'm English. I have no politics and no party. I am English.'[5]

Generals and politicians also shared the public's faith in the British army. Field Marshal Lord Wolseley, Commander-in-Chief and head of the army from 1895, told his wife that the South African conflict was the most important since the Crimean War, but he added: 'In the present case however we shall send out a much larger force from these shores & it will be one under the very ablest soldiers & thoroughly equipped for war – a very different condition of things from that which existed in the Army sent out to the Crimea in 1854.' Similarly, George Wyndham, the Under-Secretary of State for War, declared: 'I believe the Army is more efficient than at any time since Waterloo.' Wolseley was proud of an army he had done much to fashion. By 1899 it had undergone nearly thirty years of reform as its officers and political masters endeavoured to keep up with the development of new technologies and the debates these developments engendered.[6]

Wolseley had joined the War Office administration in 1871 following his successful command of the Red River Expedition in Canada. There he was able to consider the reforms being undertaken by the Liberal government of William Gladstone (1868–74). The War Minister, Edward Cardwell, was attempting to re-organise the army and its administration in the light of the Crimean and Franco-Prussian wars, as well as make it more cost effective at the same time. One of the main reforms was to introduce short-service into the army, whereby the recruit could serve for six years rather than sign on for life. After the six-year period, he would go into the reserve, ready for any national emergency. This was an imitation of the Prussian conscript system and was designed to meet a shortfall in soldiers which the Crimean War had exposed. By 1899 this system had produced a reserve of 80,000 men.

Reform was also intended to entice a better class of recruit into the army, but as an inducement to recruiting it was an utter failure. The army remained forever short of men and those that did join still tended to come from the lower end of society. Attempts were constantly made to alleviate this problem, through wage increases or by the reduction of physical standards, but they made hardly any difference. Increasing army pay was never enough on its own, but even the belated improvements made to barracks, food and general living standards failed to remedy recruiting deficiencies.

Another of Cardwell's reforms that was linked to the problem of recruitment was the localisation of the regiments, whereby a regular regiment of two battalions was grouped with the local militia and volunteers in a specific district. Regiments would eventually lose their numerical designation and be known by their localities, a process brought to fruition in 1881 by another Liberal War Minister, Hugh Childers, during Gladstone's second ministry (1880–6). The aim was to provide a closer link with the locality and thus attract, in Cardwell's words, 'a better class of men and a greater number than now present themselves'. Again, this failed to live up to expectations as recruitment remained poor. It was hoped that part of the attraction would be that soldiers would not have to spend so much time abroad in colonial garrisons; while one regular battalion was posted overseas, its counterpart would send a steady supply of replacements, thus allowing some men to return home. This system, however, would only work efficiently if there was an equal number of battalions at home and abroad, but with the expansion of the Empire the system broke down as home battalions were required overseas, which left only the inefficient and infirm men back at base to act as replacements for both battalions. This was a serious problem, which Wolseley and Lansdowne attempted to tackle just before the outbreak of war when together they persuaded the government to expand the army. However, recruiting for the new battalions proved problematic: known as 'specials', many were men who fell below the accepted standard, which led Wolseley to complain that '*over* one third are below even the low physical standard laid down for recruits. In fact at this moment *over* one half of the *Home* army are unfit to carry a pack or do a week's – I might perhaps say a day's – hard work in the field.' Indeed, the government would take men from the reserve to provide a foundation for the new battalions and help train the new recruits.[7]

Thus by 1898 the army numbered about 225,000 men, the highest it had been since the 1860s, but the poor quality of the recruits rendered its efficiency somewhat suspect. Although the refinements made to army life meant that soldiers enjoyed a lower mortality rate than their civilian counterparts, the health of recruits was often so poor that despite the healthier environment and regular meals, many new soldiers never fully developed physically. Most were in their late teens when they joined and many were already stunted by poverty; one glaring feature of the war would be the height difference between the officers and their men. This is not surprising given the persistence in the late-Victorian period of urban overcrowding and mass poverty. Indeed, the Boer War was to show all too clearly that conditions in Britain's cities were in vast need of improvement.

The quality of recruits was therefore never good and as the war dragged on and more men were needed, standards dropped even lower: by the end of 1901 the minimum height requirement had decreased from a pre-war 5 feet 3 inches to 5 feet; far more men who merely looked 'robust' were allowed to enlist as 'specials'; and it was reported that during the war one-third of men accepted were below the standards. Even so, the increase in volunteers meant that far more men were being rejected because of poor physical health than in peacetime, despite the lower standards. In consequence, the British army that fought in South Africa was the smallest put into the field during the nineteenth and twentieth centuries.[8] The appearance and condition of the soldiers was to surprise even the Boers, one of whom remarked that his impressions had been based on reading thrilling stories and seeing the pictures of the war artist Caton Woodville: 'How I was disillusioned by the appearance of these men! They were small, and some had naked bully beef slapped in their pockets, so that the grease oozed through. They had neither, it seemed, the accent nor the gait of Christians.'[9]

Throughout the post-Cardwell era, army chiefs and politicians wrestled continually over funding for the army in order to make it more efficient, in terms of both manpower and technology. Reform was never undertaken for the sake of it; improvements were made as weaknesses came to light. Much was eventually done to improve the army's support services; failures led to the establishment of the Army Service Corps in 1888 as a way of ensuring that the army had sufficient transport; and in 1898 the Royal Army Medical Corps (RAMC) was established.

As far as weaponry was concerned the British were well supplied with modern equipment. The standard infantry rifle, the Lee-Metford .303, was a modern, breech-loading weapon and was in the process of being replaced by the improved Lee-Enfield, which would remain in the army for much of the twentieth century because it was a good weapon and one that could be used virtually anywhere the army was needed. A weakness was that the magazine had to be loaded round by round once it had been emptied. By 1899 cordite, a smokeless chemical compound, was the favoured propellent and was a major improvement on the standard smokeless gunpowder. Such developments would change infantry tactics forever. In addition, the troops were supported by the Maxim .303 machine gun, a weapon of proven ability, as the warriors of the Mahdi and the tribesmen on India's north-west frontier had discovered.

By 1899 the artillery, too, had undergone fundamental changes since the Franco-Prussian War had demonstrated the superiority of rifled, breech-loading steel guns. In the British army the standard pieces were the 12 and 15 pounders, and the artillery's principal task was to smother the battlefield with shrapnel. The British had developed a new high explosive, lyddite, in which they placed much faith. Lyddite shells were meant to be used in howitzers against enemy entrenchments and buildings. In early 1899, Wolseley and Lansdowne had appointed Lieutenant General Brackenbury as head of the Ordnance Department, whose task was to bring the government ordnance factories under military control and examine the effectiveness of the new recoilless, quick-firing artillery being developed in Europe. Unfortunately for the British the war broke out before Brackenbury had adequately completed his reforms and investigations. During the first months of the war there would be some controversy over whether the Boer artillery was better because of its apparently superior range. Letters were written to the press, and the Duke of Portland's brother wrote home angrily saying 'the

Boers have much longer range guns and rifles than us which is a great handicap to us and a gross mistake by the War Office.' Brackenbury reacted in fury and told Lansdowne that the criticisms were 'based on irresponsible remarks made by war correspondents who are evidently ignorant of what may and may not be reasonably expected of field artillery and of what has been decided upon after, in some cases, years of experience'.

The Boers seemed to outrange the British because they often fired at long range, but they caused few casualties and were usually overwhelmed by the weight of British firepower. Nevertheless, Brackenbury was to take advantage of the reform spirit and in January 1900 urged the need 'to rearm the whole of the Horse and Field batteries that have taken part in the campaign' because they would be worn out. This paved the way for the British to begin acquiring quick-firing artillery sooner rather than later.[10]

Much of the reform of the support services had also been in response to Brackenbury's earlier work as head of the Intelligence Branch. In 1886 his recommendation that the government make a set plan for the mobilisation of a specific number of troops was accepted by Lord Salisbury's Conservative administration, which had just succeeded Gladstone's Liberals. Edward Stanhope, the new Secretary of State for War, encapsulated these proposals in a memorandum based on Wolseley's demands to set down the army's tasks. The Stanhope Memorandum, as it became known, explained 'the objects of our military organisation' in order of priority: the first was to support the civil power; the second, to garrison India; the third, to garrison fortresses at home and overseas; the fourth, once the above had been fulfilled, to mobilise two regular army corps, one made of regulars and militia, and the auxiliary forces for home defence; and lastly, if necessity demanded and everything else had been taken into account, to be able to send two regular army corps abroad, along with a cavalry division and troops for the lines of communication. This last task was meant for a European war that was, however, considered to be an unlikely event. Reforms made to the Army Ordnance Corps and the Army Service Corps, and the establishment of the RAMC, were intended to enable them to support the two army corps.

As weapons technology improved, so the need to adapt training methods and tactics became an issue of debate within the army.

British officers were alive to the fact that smokeless powder, longer ranges and rapid fire would transform the battlefield. Without the benefit of a major European conflict, however, no European army was entirely sure what these changes would entail and so even the annual manoeuvres of both the French and German armies reflected old certainties rather than uncertain eventualities. Armies supposedly at the forefront of modern thinking manoeuvred in Napoleonic-style formations with opposing sides firing at each other in rigid lines. One weakness which the British army suffered from, and which their European counterparts did not, was the inability to conduct large-scale manoeuvres and attempt to ensure the integration of all arms on the battlefield. During the 1890s limited manoeuvres were held, particularly by Sir Evelyn Wood when he was in command at Aldershot, and eventually Wolseley managed to get a large-scale exercise undertaken in 1898 on recently acquired land on Salisbury Plain. Wolseley's reports, though marking the good progress made, still revealed poor performances by the senior officers, including General Sir Redvers Buller, one of the corps commanders. The handling of the troops and their dispositions were considered very faulty.

Infantry training, though, had been reformed over the decade before the Boer War started, with Wolseley and Wood at the forefront. Wolseley had instituted a new drill book, which stressed the need for open formations, although volley firing still remained an essential part of the musketry regulations. Nevertheless, Wolseley's drill book stated: 'The conditions of modern warfare render it imperative that all ranks shall be taught to think, and, subject to their general instructions and to accepted principles, to act for themselves.'[11] But basic training was limited by several factors: a high turnover of men; numerous other duties; and limitations on expending ammunition, which meant that volley firing was used to preserve ammunition. Yet in spite of the handicaps, the army did not go to war with what might be termed a 'Napoleonic mindset', and the officers were certainly aware of the new tactical requirements on the battlefield. Some of the army's failures during the early months of the war often resulted from officers ignoring the lessons they had been taught.

Artillery tactics were also caught in a vacuum of inexperience of modern warfare conditions. Thus the 1896 *Field Artillery Drill* reflected the notion of its authors that the guns should in all cases support the infantry, meaning in the open. Little attention was given to avoiding enemy rifle fire, except to state that the gunners' best defence was to suppress the enemy's fire. The newer German preference for indirect fire, whereby the guns found cover and shot at an unseen enemy using scientific instruments, was considered unworthy of the British service and inapplicable because the enemy was expected to be 'uncivilised' natives.

As for the cavalry, Wolseley had criticised this arm at the manoeuvres for its inability to reconnoitre properly. This was the result of the cavalry's firm belief that it was primarily a fighting force whose ultimate expression was the massed charge. Although the sword and lance remained the main armament, the cavalry was equipped with modern carbines, which were infantry rifles with shortened barrels. Dismounted action was held in low esteem and cavalry commanders in general paid little attention to it.

In many ways the spirit of the late-Victorian army was willing, but the flesh was weak. Despite the intention to try to adapt the army's training and tactics to modern conditions, army life was not conducive either to the study of war or to its application beyond the requirements of Britain's small-scale colonial warfare. In part, lack of interest in the study of war reflected the failure of the Cardwell reforms to change the social composition of the officer corps. Officers were recruited from the upper, landed class, or from professions intimately connected with it, such as the army itself (where wealth did not matter as long as an officer came from a good military family and was a gentleman), the church or the law. Social status and wealth were far more important than professional expertise and most officers had too much time on their hands, which they spent in non-military pursuits. Promotion was by seniority, discouraging the idea that advancement could be attained through study. Even the reformer Wolseley still believed that being by birth a gentleman provided all the requisite qualities to enable an officer to lead men into battle.

Because of this attitude, and because army commanders did everything themselves when campaigning on the frontiers of the Empire, there was no proper general staff in the British army. There was a staff college, which produced thirty-two graduates a year, but this was not enough to fill all the staff posts and this would present a major problem once the war broke out. Although the appeal of attending the staff college increased, it was not considered the only path to promotion and was, in any case, not equipped to provide a comprehensive military education. When the staff appointments came to be made there was no system as such. Wolseley chose most of the men, with only the minimum of consultation, and made things worse by reorganising the army into what one officer later described as 'fancy brigades', which meant that any existing staffs were broken up to serve the new units. After the war Leo Amery, a journalist for *The Times* who had covered the opening phases of the conflict, took on the task of writing that paper's comprehensive history of the conflict and also promoting army reform. He scathingly remarked that 'Englishmen who would not dream of sending a crew to Henley Regatta whose members had never rowed together before, were quite content that a general's staff should be hastily improvised at the last moment from officers scraped together from every corner.'[12]

The Intelligence Department attempted under severe financial constraints to provide regular appreciations of the Boer forces and their likely intentions. These were eventually encapsulated in a document entitled *Military Notes on the Dutch Republics*, which predicted the future hostility of the Orange Free State and the scale of the Boer armaments correctly, but believed that the Boers would mount raids against British territory, not the full-scale invasion they actually launched. Indeed, one of the last appreciations estimated that after various deductions the forces of the Transvaal would number no more than 9,000, while the OFS would field about 5,000. The officers of the Intelligence Department, like many others, underestimated the military capacity of the Boers.

During the crisis months of 1899, the army prepared itself for war as far as it could. By June 1899 preparations had already been made for the mobilisation of the army corps and were constantly under review thereafter. On 7 October the order to mobilise was given by the government although the War Office had been preparing for this eventuality for a whole week beforehand. The mobilisation plan went ahead very smoothly and ninety-nine per cent of reservists answered the call, with ninety-one per cent eventually being passed fit. H.W. Wilson was mightily impressed by the response and wrote later:

The reservists answered the call like Englishmen; like men, that is to say, who know a painful duty lies before them and will do it ... Men rose from their beds of sickness that they might serve with the old colours and not betray the confidence reposed in them. There was no exultation, no desire to fight for fighting's sake, only a calm determination to end twenty years' purgatory of misrule in the Transvaal by coming to the aid of brother Englishmen.[13]

Wilson's hyperbole aside, the mobilisation was a remarkable achievement, as was the procurement of shipping to transport the army to South Africa. It must be said, however, that the reservists did not increase the number of fighting men to any real extent because they were used primarily to ensure the battalions were up to war strength with fit men. In essence, they replaced the unfit and too young, who remained behind. Overall about 50,000 men embarked for South Africa from Britain during the first month of the war, under the command of General Sir Redvers Buller, who had fought under Wolseley in the past, had won the Victoria Cross during the Anglo-Zulu War of 1879, and had recently served as Adjutant General, which had confined him to an administrator's desk and had gained him much weight as a result, but had led to a loss of self-confidence as an army commander. The infantry was organised into three divisions, with the Ladysmith garrison being considered the fourth. When it became clear that more men were needed at the front, the government authorised the mobilisation of a fifth and a sixth on 11 November and 2 December respectively; these forces too were embarked with consummate ease. Wolseley wanted the immediate mobilisation of a seventh division but this was refused by Lansdowne until Buller had tried his luck in Natal. After Buller's defeat during Black Week at Colenso on 15 December, which followed defeats inflicted on two of his subordinate commanders at Stormberg on 10 December and at Magersfontein the next day, it was clear that even more men were required. Two more divisions, the seventh and eighth, were despatched to South Africa either side of the new year, but yet more were needed. But with the eighth division gone, there were no longer any regular troops left in Britain and as far as the army was concerned the cupboard was bare. In response, the government allowed militia battalions to volunteer for overseas service and regular troops were subsequently replaced in the Channel Islands and Malta. Eventually the militia was allowed to serve in South Africa.

Since earliest times the British army had been backed by part-time volunteers known collectively as the auxiliary forces. In 1899 these comprised the militia, whose origins dated from Anglo-Saxon times, its cavalry arm the yeomanry, and the rifle volunteers, first raised in 1859.

After the regular, professional army, the militia constituted Britain's main defence force. Between 1757 and 1831 militiamen had been selected by ballot, an early form of compulsory military service that had proved to be very unpopular. When this was abolished in 1831 the militia declined, but when the country was gripped by an invasion scare in 1852, it was revived formally as a voluntary force. The militia was closely tied to the army and joining it was often a first step towards an army career. Initially, the militia recruit would train with the army for three months and then decide whether to become a full- or part-time soldier. Those who wished to remain part-time soldiers would stay in the militia and have to train for one solid month every year. Because the militia was a state institution, recruits received pay for their time. This made the militia attractive to the unemployed or the irregularly employed. Even so, men did not join the militia solely for economic reasons: many were motivated by the comradeship it offered and by patriotism. Indeed, when the militia was asked to volunteer for service in South Africa, the battalions did so to a man, according to H.W. Wilson anyway. On 18 December 1899 the entire 3rd Durham Light Infantry militia volunteered and were soon followed by the 3rd York and Lancaster and, as Wilson explained, 'In no case did any militia battalion when invited to give its services show the smallest reluctance.' To be fair to Wilson, propagandist though he was, he was not exaggerating. According to the Inspector General of Recruiting and Auxiliary Forces, Major General Borrett:

Very strict orders were given to generals to the effect that in every district where a regiment was going abroad the general should personally see it on parade, and ask the men whether they quite understood the terms, that there was no compulsion, that everything was quite voluntary and that if any man did not wish to go no questions would be asked. It was entirely voluntary and that was all carried out right through.

One wonders though if other pressures were exerted on the men to volunteer – peer-pressure for example, which is only to be expected when volunteers are called. The main problem, however, was that the militia was so short of men that eighteen year olds were allowed to go, which was not the case in the regular army, where only men twenty and over were initially sent to South Africa. There was also such a shortage of officers that Borrett, on his own authority, gave commissions to 407 'ordinary educated young gentlemen' and said afterwards that 'the juniors were quite untrained. I got them straight from school or their families. I sent them out without even Gazetting them [publishing the appointments in official journals].'

Because of these weaknesses, the militia would be used to guard the lines of communication, well away from the front line. But by the time militia units arrived at their posts, the Boers had launched a guerrilla war and many militia battalions found themselves at isolated spots deep inside Boer territory. On 7 June 1900, for example, the 4th Derbyshire militia battalion was attacked by a force commanded by the great Boer leader Christiaan de Wet at Rhenoster railway bridge and nearby Roodewal railway station. The militia had had no time to prepare an adequate defence and were overwhelmed after a brief fight. Nearly 500 men surrendered. It would take time for the militia to develop as an efficient force and time was what they got as the war dragged on. In the end over 45,000 men served in the militia during the war.[14]

The volunteers owed their immediate origins to an invasion scare in 1859, although volunteer units had previously been raised during the French revolutionary and Napoleonic wars. Like the militia, the volunteers were part-time soldiers, but other than that they differed considerably. Although many recruits were from the middle classes, most came from the skilled, regularly employed, artisan, working class. They were not a state institution and so were unpaid, but they administered themselves and were able to select their own officers. By 1899 the government was providing grants to the volunteers on condition that they fulfilled certain training requirements, such as an annual inspection or training camp of several days' duration. The main role of the volunteers was to help defend Britain from invasion and they were not permitted to serve overseas unless specially sanctioned to do so. But like their militia counterparts, volunteers were eager to prove themselves in real combat, and during the political crisis in South Africa enthusiasm among the various volunteer regiments was high, so much so that offers of help were made as early as July 1899. These continued as the crisis deepened, but even Sir Howard Vincent, a leading member of the volunteer movement, who offered to pay for 1,000 volunteers to be sent to South Africa with the main army, thus saving the War Office any major expense, was rebuffed by a government still clinging to the hope that war might not come.

Once war had begun further requests were turned down – until Black Week itself, when Lansdowne, Wolseley and the rest of the military hierarchy agreed that auxiliary forces ought now to be used. On 14 December 1899, Wolseley wrote: 'We are now face to face with a serious national crisis and unless we meet it boldly and quickly grapple with it successfully it may – in my humble opinion it will – lead to dangerous complications with Foreign powers.'[15] Wolseley was at this moment urging the mobilisation of Britain's last regular units, but also recommended the use of the militia in South Africa and, more pointedly, the acceptance of 6,000 volunteers (picked officers and men), as well as 1,000 yeomanry to serve as mounted infantry. Now, at last, the eager volunteers were granted their wish, when the Empire seemed in real danger. In many respects the government had no choice but to accommodate the wishes of Britain's part-time soldiers, for as Lansdowne explained to the Prime Minister: 'It seems to me to be impossible to refuse altogether and, apart from purely military considerations, I see some advantage in affording an outlet to public feeling, which is beginning to run high.'[16]

The volunteers who came forward were split into two groups by the nature of the recruiting that took place. The first group, which was a self-contained unit, and one of the most famous volunteer regiments of the whole war, was the City Imperial Volunteers (CIV). The idea for the CIV was inspired by the public mood after Black Week and which seemed to be 'going through a great depression'. The CIV was apparently the brainchild of the Lord Mayor of London, Sir Alfred Newton. However, Wolseley had first been approached informally and Newton had been assisted by Colonel Charles Boxhall of the Sussex Volunteer Artillery, who had prepared the paperwork. The fact that the force was to be financed entirely by the City and assorted well-wishers obviously had its effect on ministers, as did the fact that senior officers would be provided by the army and that Wolseley had the final say in appointing other officers after receiving advice from the volunteer authorities and Newton. Similarly, senior NCOs would also be provided by the regulars, while the overall commanding officer was a Guardsman, Colonel Henry Mackinnon.

It was decided to take 1,000 men picked from London's various volunteer regiments who received, apart from a smart uniform and the best equipment money could buy and the same daily rate of pay as an ordinary soldier (one shilling and threepence), the promise that they would be granted the freedom of the City. In addition, an artillery battery of four guns of the new quick-firing type was purchased from Vickers-Maxim, and two companies of mounted infantry were also raised. In all, the City paid £25,000 towards equipping the CIV and by 12 January over £100,000 had been raised altogether, which included a donation from Wernher, Beit & Co. The Hull shipowners, Wilsons, offered fitted transports for three months free of charge, which cost them about £15,000. Such generosity meant that only the arms and ammunition were provided by the War Office.

There was no shortage of volunteers: even Lord Salisbury's private secretary, the Honourable Schomberg MacDonnell joined, and the CIV was raised very quickly between 16 December 1899 and 6 January 1900. Such were the numbers that officers could afford to be choosy but even so were not as rigorous as might have been expected. All recruits had to be aged between twenty and thirty-five, be at least 5 feet 5 inches tall, and have been passed efficient by their own regiments in 1898 and 1899. According to Major General Sir Ian Hamilton, under whom the CIV would serve, and who was later Chief of Staff to Lord Kitchener, the men were 'extraordinarily intelligent fellows'. The post-war Royal Commission noted later that 'The raising of the City Imperial Volunteers is one instance of the great military improvisation which became necessary in order to overcome the Boer resistance. It appears to have been one of the most successful instances, and does credit to the City of London.' Indeed, following their baptism of fire on 15 February at Jacobsdal, the CIV played a prominent part in several subsequent engagements, acquitting themselves well each time. At Diamond Hill, fought between 11 and 12 June 1900 and one of the last set-piece battles of the war, the CIV were particularly conspicuous. They would return to London on 29 October 1900 and be accorded a rapturous reception.[17]

The ordinary volunteers who agreed to serve in South Africa, the Volunteer Service Companies (VSC), lacked the glamour of the CIV and were their 'poor relations'. This had much to do with the fact that they were not sent out as a self-contained unit, but were allocated to the regular battalions to which they were affiliated. The VSCs were thus absorbed almost anonymously into the army. The enlistment requirements were the same as those for the CIV, except that the medical examinations seemed to be more rigorous. Nevertheless, there was an ample sufficiency of men.

But when it came to organising a second draft in 1901 there was an acute shortage of men willing to serve in South Africa and it was said that the poor rate of pay was a major factor. The VSC received the same pay as an ordinary soldier, while the yeomanry received five shillings, even though the VSCs were more qualified than their yeomanry counterparts, who were recruited straight from the streets. By 1901, however, interest in the war was diminishing and the patriotic fervour that had motivated the first draft was no longer apparent. Inducements were thus offered: there was a £12 capitation grant and married men were allowed to volunteer, especially if they hoped to remain in South Africa afterwards. Their families would then be given assistance to join them.[18]

The other glamorous unit raised at the height of public excitement in late 1899 was the Imperial Yeomanry (IY). The yeomanry provided the core of the new organisation, but the rest were made up of eager volunteers, many of whom were important social and political figures. This is not surprising given that the main qualifications were that recruits should be able to ride and shoot. The determination of these important individuals to join up and do their bit was explained by the Honourable Sydney Peel, barrister-at-law and late fellow of Trinity College, Oxford: 'The thing became intolerable, it was impossible to go on doing the ordinary things of life; something had to be done; new men and new measures must be devised.' For him, as for many others, the main impetus to do something came from the shock of Britain's early military setbacks, but the genesis of the IY began a few months earlier when Lord Chesham and some fellow officers unsuccessfully appealed to the War Office. Attitudes changed, however, when Buller urgently asked: 'Would it be possible for you to raise eight thousand irregulars [meaning volunteers] in England. They should be equipped as mounted infantry, be able to shoot as well as possible and ride decently. I would amalgamate them with colonials.'[19]

'The "Imperial Yeomanry" is my child. I invented it after lunch on Sunday and it is already a fine bantling,' George Wyndham told his father and was left very much in charge of establishing the committee that would organise it.[20] Overall supervision of this new force was given to Honorary Colonel A.G. Lucas of the Loyal Suffolk Hussars, one of those who had come forward with Chesham to offer their services in October. Like the CIV, the IY attracted the attention of wealthy patrons, with Wernher, Beit & Co. again among the contributors, this time with £50,000. Just as well, because the IY had to find its own equipment and horses because Brackenbury's Ordnance Department could not cope with the extra demand: 'I cannot provide these "Imperial Yeomanry" with anything except arms, ammunition and tents. They must provide everything else for themselves ... We cannot get these things fast enough to supply the regular troops.' In consequence, the War Office and the IY competed for the same resources. The difference, though, was that the IY was wealthy and the equipment and horses it obtained were of a better quality than those provided by the army.[21]

The recruits signed up on the same terms as those of the CIV but each had to be a 'good rider and a marksman according to Yeomanry standard'. Recruits also had to be physically and medically fit. The yeomanry itself was unable to provide sufficient recruits, so recruiting was open to all who met the above qualifications. The IY had no problem filling the first contingent but not everyone was happy about this open arrangement. Unlike the CIV, the IY was not controlled by the army and Wolseley proved less enthusiastic about it: on 28 December he wrote that he wanted '*trained men accustomed to some sort of discipline*; but to go into the highways & byways & pick up any civilians who will volunteer to go to South Africa quite regardless of whether they have ever learnt even the rudiments of discipline ... is according to my knowledge of war, a dangerous experiment'. Lansdowne's response, two days later, was unequivocally against this view, a recognition that any attempt to restrain public enthusiasm was perhaps dangerous. He replied that as the demand was pressing there was no other way of meeting it and thought that the qualifications would ensure the best men, adding pointedly: 'The Boers are not, I suppose, very highly drilled or disciplined.' Even so, he believed that units raised ought to be thoroughly inspected before they went off to South Africa.[22]

The IY was famous because many of its men did not come from the highways and byways, but from stately homes and gentlemen's clubs. Indeed, thirty-four recruits were members of both houses of parliament. One was Winston Churchill's cousin, the Duke of Marlborough. Some units comprised only men of wealth and authority and these were independently raised but attached to the IY; one such was Paget's Horse, made up of a 'pretty average collection of young men of good social position and public-school education – a gentlemen corps'. The Duke of Cambridge's Own sportingly paid for their own equipment and gave their pay to the Soldiers' Widows and Orphans Fund. These were all part of the 13th Battalion, which also incorporated members of Ireland's Protestant ascendancy, including nobles and whiskey millionaires.[23] Most battalions, though, were more socially mixed: Peel recorded that his battalion was 'a miscellaneous multitude of all ages from twenty to forty, with coats of every cut and every degree of newness or shabbiness'. He listed 'barristers, solicitors, blacksmiths, cooks, bakers, farmers, land-agents, schoolmasters, architects, clerks, horse-dealers, publicans, auctioneers, grooms, ex-soldiers, butchers, drapers, ranchers and cowboys, civil servants and many more'. Belying the general perception regarding motives for enlistment, Peel affirmed that there was only one patriot amongst them 'and he was generally regarded as peculiar'. Most of the men of his battalion seem to have been attracted by the promise of a new start in South Africa, the possibility of escape from domestic problems, a change of career, or simply the prospect of glory.[24]

Before the IY embarked they were given two or three months' basic training at their district centres as mounted infantry, even though some upper-class recruits preferred to regard themselves as cavalry. As many of the men came from very good social backgrounds or had been in regular employment, their physical quality was impressive, especially compared to the usual army recruit. Major General J.P. Brabazon, the IY's overall commander between March and November 1900, was very complimentary about the quality of the men and recorded that 'In the ranks you found, in addition to the

blood, bone and sinews, the intelligence of the English nation represented.' Insubordination was virtually unknown and all this showed
the army was in need of being '"aristocratised" – if there is such a
word'. Brabazon's judgement might be called into question,
however, following his recommendations regarding suitable weaponry for 'shock tactics':

> For the Latin races the sword or the lance, for it's natural to them to
> always give the point. The Anglo-Saxon race invariably chop or strike, and
> I believe the lightest, most handy, effective, and demoralising (to your
> enemy) weapon would be a light battle-axe or tomahawk. It would be
> light, easily carried, and a desperate arm in a mêlée.

Brabazon's recommendation was not taken up.[25]

Such glowing pronouncements were not given to the second or
third contingents. In the first instance some 15,000 men were sent to
South Africa, but the War Office refused Colonel Lucas's request
that recruiting be continued to provide replacements, especially as
many professional men had been allowed to leave early and thirty per
cent were lost overall, either through unfitness or as casualties. But as
the war continued far longer than anticipated, new recruits had to be
found – and fast. Consequently, the second and third contingents
were recruited at a time when the initial enthusiasm had worn off and
so potential recruits had to be offered five shillings a day, which
induced many in the VSC to transfer. However, most of those
recruited were not of the same high standards as the first contingent
and officers had to be commissioned from whatever sources were at
hand. Speaking after the war, the Adjutant General, Sir Thomas
Kelly-Kenny, said there was a palpable difference between the first
and subsequent drafts. 'With the first lot it was not a question of
buying, and they came with a rush through patriotism, but after that
it was a question of buying.' So desperate was the need that men
were taken with no experience of shooting or riding, and as Lord
Methuen understood it the new lot 'were men from the East End,
and they were men of an inferior stamp', although he acknowledged
that many improved as time went on. This was the result of the training they received in South Africa because they received none in
Britain as they were required immediately at the front. At least the
Australians were amused: 'It is good fun to see the Imperial

Yeomanry ride, as they fall off at the rate of one a minute.' Lucas realised that the pay on offer was better than most employments in
Britain and that joining the IY meant a free passage to South Africa
for those minded to emigrate. The same mistakes were not repeated
with the third contingent, raised between September 1901 and
January 1902. Before they left for South Africa they were given three
months' training, so that useless men were weeded out, and many
officers came from the regulars. However, by the time they arrived
the war was over.[26]

4

Rallying the Empire

Britain's need for more and more troops led the government to accept volunteer forces from the self-governing colonies (later known collectively as the Dominions) of Canada, Australia – which was then a collection of colonies and would not be united in a federation until 1901– and New Zealand. In all, over 30,000 men from these disparate territories chose to serve the imperial cause in South Africa and revealed to the world the strength of imperial sentiment at the time.

To many in Britain, the Empire was where degenerate British upper- and middle-class youths could learn something of the healthy, outdoor life from rough-hewn men, made tough, honest and decent by the rigours of their colonial upbringing. This image – that colonials were somehow superior to the urban-bred British – was one that the colonies were eager to promote.

The ball started rolling following Joseph Chamberlain's telegram to the Governors of Canada, and the Australian colonies of New South Wales and Victoria on 3 July 1899, which asked whether the local governments might make a spontaneous gesture of solidarity by offering Britain colonial troops, the idea being that public offers would make the Transvaal think twice as the crisis deepened.

In Canada, Chamberlain's telegram was not acted upon by the government of Sir Wilfred Laurier, which felt more concerned about current problems with America and the reaction of French-Canadians to involvement in an imperial, rather than a Canadian, dispute. Laurier's reluctance, however, was not shared by many English-speakers and a vociferous press campaign, backed by an influential and articulate imperialist lobby, called for participation in the event of war. As relations between Britain and the Transvaal worsened in late September and early October 1899, Laurier came under severe pressure to offer Canadian soldiers. It seems that his reluctance to commit Canada to an imperial conflict was also borne of a sincere belief that Kruger would eventually back down, but when the Boers issued their ultimatum Laurier and his ministers were obliged to confront a difficult political decision. In the end Laurier gave in and authorised an official Canadian force for South Africa. By then he could no longer refuse: Chamberlain had offered to pay for the troops once in South Africa, and Laurier's supporters in his party and in the press had turned pro-war. For a long time afterwards many in Canada felt that Laurier had been bullied into sending men by the British, but it is now accepted that it was the Canadians themselves who made Laurier change his mind.

The Militia Department (the Canadian war office) had already made plans for a contingent to be sent as early as July under the enthusiastic direction of Canada's militia commander, the British soldier Major General E.T.H. Hutton. Consequently, when war broke out recruitment of volunteers from Canada's various militia districts was already well in hand. The first contingent comprised 1,000 volunteers 'thoroughly representative [of Canada] in character' and was ready to sail by 30 October. As the Minister of Militia and Defence, F.W. Borden, told Lansdowne on 10 November, there was no shortage of volunteers: 'A much larger force could have been recruited & my chief difficulty was to restrain those who seemed determined to force their services upon one & would scarcely take no for an answer.' Borden was later to lose his son in the war.[1]

The men of this and the second contingent, recruited in December 1899 following Britain's early defeats, were depicted by the Canadian and British press as the epitome of Canadian manhood. But overall, the bulk of Canada's volunteers were low-paid urban dwellers who, more often than not, volunteered in order to escape their situation and seek adventure. Few of the men conformed to the image as promoted by the press and British patriots such as H.W. Wilson, who wrote of the second contingent:

The men who were picked were active and intelligent, accustomed to an outdoor life, sitting their horses like centaurs. They speedily showed in

war that they were a full match for the Boers, man for man, in marksman-
ship, the art of taking cover, and stubborn courage, while they had that
high spirit which preaches attack rather than defence, and which the
Boers, among their many fine qualities, altogether lacked.[2]

Wilson's exaggeration aside, the men of Canada's third contingent,
raised and sent in the early months of 1900, did correspond more to
the favoured stereotype of outdoor, rugged, rough-rider types. This
unit was paid for by Lord Strathcona, the Canadian High
Commissioner in London, and was to bear his name as Lord
Strathcona's Horse. They, like the other contingents, were to see
much active service and prove themselves to be very good soldiers
indeed and better than British troops. Image and experience combined to give Canadian soldiers a sense of being superior to the class-
ridden, degenerate British army, an opinion often encouraged by
senior British officers anxious not to offend Canadian susceptibilities. In the end, the Canadians did not regard their role as a fraction
of the imperial war effort but as a distinct contribution, which compared more than favourably with that of the British. For many
Canadians, participation in the war led to the forging of a Canadian
military identity, which carried over into Canadian society in general
and enhanced Canada's own sense of nationhood.

In some respects the Canadian experience was repeated in
Australia. For many years after the war, opinion in Australia believed
that the colonial governments had been bullied into supplying contingents by the imperial authorities and the offers made were labelled
'manufactured spontaneity'. But, as in Canada, it is now thought that
the Australian governments were not forced into sending troops but,
like Laurier, reacted to internal demands.

In 1899 Australia was not a unified country and its modern states
were then self-governing colonies with more often than not separate
and localised interests. Queensland emerged as the first colonial
government to offer military support to Britain in the event of war.
This was done on 10 July 1899 after the governments of New South
Wales and Victoria, the two major colonies, had, like Canada,
declined to send contingents. Fear of spending money unnecessarily;
a belief that the situation in South Africa was not that dangerous; and
internal political difficulties all contributed to this reluctance. But as
the crisis worsened, so the demands for action became louder. From

September the various Australian governments came under severe pressure from their own defence forces to make spontaneous offers of military support. Victoria was the first to buckle and began recruiting volunteers for service in South Africa, the first colonial government to do so openly. By this time, as war appeared likely, the colonial governments were also being pushed into a response by the growing patriotic clamour in Australia. Just before the outbreak of war, vague offers of support that had been mentioned since July were turned into reality when the Colonial Office sent a note listing the military requirements to all colonial governments. In Australia this meant that each colony would send a unit and, unlike Canada, there would be no federal force. As in Canada, the Australian forces did not quite match the stereotype of the country-bred tough as described by numerous British boys' journals or the press, or even by the Australians themselves in contemporary novels such as *Tommy Cornstalk*, written by J.H.M. Abbott, a veteran of the war, and first published in June 1902. Abbott's work certainly helped perpetuate the view that Australian soldiers were bushmen, similar to the Boers. The social composition of each contingent varied: in the New South Wales force, for example, the mounted infantry were mainly country born, while the infantry detachment came from Sydney and Newcastle. The story was more or less the same in Victoria.

When Britain suffered a series of military defeats in December 1899, a definite spontaneous outburst of patriotism and volunteering pervaded Australia and led to the formation of a second contingent of mounted infantry. Although it was again recruited mainly from Australia's militia forces, this time there was a substantial leavening of civilians to make up the numbers as not enough militiamen had come forward. The men left Australia through rapturous crowds and as one observer remarked: 'An epidemic of war fever set in. It prostrated the whole continent, and even affected ... the little island of Tasmania.'[3]

Perhaps more than the other colonial contingents, the Australians were seen as quite distinctive because of their lack of discipline and their contempt for the rituals of army authority. But although this distinctiveness was played for all it was worth during and after the war – just as Canada's forces imagined their own contribution – the reality was always somewhat different. Most Australian volunteers were townsmen and of British birth and upbringing. Nevertheless, the fact that they had come from the colonies, and were citizen volunteers, did lend itself to the development of an identity separate from that of their 'cousins' in the British forces, particularly those in the regular army, a difference often indulged by British officers aware of the political advantages of doing so as well as the desire for a quiet life. For Australians, as for all the other colonial volunteers, this difference became an integral part of their own national identity.

The Australian troops did make a name for themselves, both good and bad. They did sterling service as scouts: the third, fourth and fifth contingents sent from Australia were labelled 'Bushmen' and were used in the pursuit of elusive Boer guerrillas. The sixth and last contingent, which arrived in South Africa too late to participate, was the first federal unit to be raised and was known as the Australian Commonwealth Horse. For the Boers and their sympathisers the Australians also had another reputation. John X. Merriman, an opponent of the war in the Cape Colony and one of its leading politicians, wrote of Australian depredations in areas of the Cape that had strong Boer sympathies. Near Prieska, 'These swashbucklers arrested inhabitants, drove off stock, and shot a few people without greatly caring who they were.'[4] Whatever the performance of the Australian forces, the war did contribute to the formation of an Australian military identity, which developed further during the wars of the twentieth century.

Long before the war, the novelist Anthony Trollope wrote that every colony considered itself 'to be the cream of the British Empire ... But in New Zealand the assurance is altogether different. The New Zealander among John Bulls is the most John Bullish.' In September 1899 the New Zealand parliament tried to live up to this image by being the first colonial parliament (as opposed to a colonial executive) to make a concrete offer of troops for service in South Africa. The Prime Minister, Richard 'King Dick' Seddon, was not only concerned that New Zealand should be the first colonial government to show its support for the imperial cause, but also that by doing so it should have a subsequent voice in Britain's future imperial policy.[5] Backed by a vocal and belligerent pro-war campaign, recruiting was swift and by 21 October New Zealand's first contingent – the first of ten – had set sail for South Africa. As elsewhere, Britain's defeats in December gave an extra impetus to the already strong patriotic mood in the country and Seddon took the opportunity to enhance New Zealand's imperial stature. In a major speech Seddon fervently endorsed the imperial cause: 'The people of New Zealand are determined that the prestige of the British Empire, to which they belong, shall be maintained at all hazards. Though New Zealand is Radical and Democratic, even termed by some Socialistic, there is in the present emergency an amount of imperial patriotism in the country not to be surpassed elsewhere in Her Majesty's dominions.'[6]

The New Zealanders did not seem to attract the same sort of attention that was given to the Australians, although they too had definite ideas about their place in the military scheme of things. In general, they were good and effective troops and 'by general consent [were] regarded as on average the best mounted troops in South Africa', but could, like their Australian counterparts, show an aversion to British military discipline. In December 1901, for example, following an altercation with a British officer, New Zealanders released two soldiers from undertaking field punishment.[7] For New Zealand, then, participation revived the colony's martial spirit and gave it, or Seddon at least, a platform upon which it could try to take a more prominent role in imperial affairs.

Britain's self-governing colonies were not the only English-speaking areas to offer troops to the imperial cause. As war approached, many Uitlanders in Johannesburg decided that discretion was the better part of valour and hurriedly left the city. Very soon, in fact days before the Boer ultimatum, Cape Town and Durban were already overrun with Uitlander refugees.[8] Such an influx into the British colonies soon overwhelmed the local authorities, but for the military the exiled Uitlanders were a source of vital help since many could ride and shoot and knew the country well. Kruger's regime already understood the value of the Uitlanders, having commandeered them and their goods during the Transvaal's war with a local African tribe, the Bagananwa, in 1894, which led Charles Leonard of the pro-British Transvaal National Union to remark: 'it is difficult to perform military service as a duty to the state when we are denied the rights of citizenship.'[9] Many, however, had no hesitation in joining the various Uitlander irregular units that appeared as war began.

One of the prominent Uitlander units was the Imperial Light Horse (ILH), a force whose men had been recruited secretly in

September 1899 until the Natal government gave the unit its official blessing. The man behind the ILH was Aubrey Woolls-Sampson, a Cape colonial who had seen service as a volunteer in the Anglo-Zulu and Anglo-Transvaal wars (1879 and 1880–1). Alongside his Australian friend, Walter Karri Davies, Woolls-Sampson had taken a prominent part in the Jameson Raid and the pair had been imprisoned afterwards until pardoned in 1897. They were still hostile to Kruger and the crisis of 1899 gave them a chance to get their own back. However, Woolls-Sampson's earlier attempt to persuade Lieutenant General Sir William Butler, the military commander in the Cape Colony, to sanction the raising of an Uitlander volunteer force, was rebuffed because Butler did not share his view that Kruger wanted war with Britain, and felt that any military preparations in the Cape Colony and Natal would inflame the situation. Consequently, Woolls-Sampson went to Natal and began his secret preparations. When war broke out the pre-arranged mobilisation of the ILH went very smoothly, unlike the Uitlander efforts at the time of the Jameson Raid. The men, 500 at first, were all Uitlanders or South African born, and included men from other colonies as well as Americans, many of whom lived and worked in Johannesburg and believed that Kruger's regime, which had denied them political rights, needed crushing. The men of this group were of a high standard although as the war dragged on the unit's quality declined and it earned the nickname of 'Imperial Light Looters'.[10] Their first commanding officer was a British regular, Lieutenant Colonel J.J. Scott Chisholme, who was not to last long in command. He died at the battle of Elandslaagte on 21 October 1899, leading his men on foot waving a stick upon which was tied a red handkerchief. Woolls-Sampson, who had been badly wounded during the Jameson Raid, was wounded again at Elandslaagte. The unit served throughout the war and was later joined by the Imperial Light Infantry, also made up of refugee Uitlanders. These too were commanded by a regular British officer and were to do sterling work at the battle of Spion Kop.

A force similar to the ILH and equally prominent was Rimington's Guides, who wore leopard-skin around their hats and were mistakenly dubbed Rimington's Tigers. The founder of this unit was a serving British officer, Major M.F. Rimington, who recruited mostly Uitlander refugees who spoke Afrikaans and various African languages. One of the men, Lieutenant March

Phillipps, was very complimentary about his fellow guides: 'I don't think you could wish for better material, or that a body of keener, more loyal, and more efficient men could easily be brought together ... They are darkly sunburnt; lean and wiry in figure; tall often, but never fat ... and they have the loose, careless seat on horseback, as if they were perfectly at home there.'[11] The horsemanship and scouting skills of these Uitlander forces was to prove indispensable to the British high command, particularly when the Boers resorted to guerrilla warfare.

Apart from these irregular units raised by private individuals or British officers, the volunteer units of the Cape Colony and Natal were also mobilised and used during the conflict. Both colonies had their own official volunteer forces and both acquitted themselves well throughout. In the Cape Colony there was actually a unit of regulars called the Cape Mounted Rifles (CMR) made up of men who enlisted for five years. Their immediate task was to police disaffected districts where Boer sympathisers verged on outright rebellion; this they did well enough and earned the praise of a Major Pollock, who wrote later that the CMR were: 'Smart, active fellows, in the prime of life and evidently in a most satisfactory military condition. The discipline seemed to be excellent, and the men the most willing workers that it is possible to imagine ... The Cape Mounted Rifleman is a first-rate fighting man and a downright good soldier all round.'

The CMR were joined by the Cape Police and several volunteer units collectively known as the Cape Colony Volunteers and drawn from the colony's 6,000 volunteer riflemen. In addition, there were the British South Africa Police, described as 'a most useful body of trained horsemen, good shots, and wily to the last degree', and the Rhodesian Regiment, which was led by Colonel Plumer, later famous in the First World War as Plumer of Messines and who was to keep the Boers busy on the Transvaal's northern frontier.[12]

Natal did not have any regular force but called on the Natal Volunteers, which by the outbreak of war were well prepared and organised. They were joined by new units such as the Colonial Scouts, who were sent to patrol the borders of Zululand and the Transvaal. Lieutenant Colonel Hubert Gough, who would serve under Buller in Natal and would later command his own force during the guerrilla war, called these units 'the English equivalent of a Boer commando' and found them 'a friendly, practical body, prepared to fight when required, but not at all inclined to gallop thoughtlessly into danger', a trait which Gough himself did not share as he was to reveal at Blood River Poort in September 1901, when he was ambushed by Louis Botha.[13] Unlike the forces of the Cape Colony, these units saw little action but managed to ensure that Natal had an enhanced military presence especially before the arrival of Buller's forces.

A more exotic Natal unit was that raised from among Natal's Asian community and which saw service as an ambulance corps. Indians had come to Natal in 1860 as indentured labourers for the sugar plantations, eventually settling there and from the early 1880s even moving into the Transvaal. By 1894 Indians outnumbered whites in Natal but were a substantial minority in the Transvaal, where they found themselves severely mistreated. Indian complaints were valuable ammunition to use against Kruger's government. In fact, Indians were worse off than the Uitlanders because, despite being British subjects, they had to adhere to pass laws and all the irksome restrictions imposed on those whom the Boers classed as 'coloured'. Not surprisingly, the Transvaal Indians fled as war approached but found the Natal government very unsympathetic; only pressure applied by the imperial authorities ensured that Indian refugees joined their relatives in Natal.

Natal's Indians were treated little better and as the Indian lawyer M.K. Gandhi observed, 'Every Indian, without exception is a coolie in the estimation of the general body of Europeans.' Gandhi, of course, emerged in South Africa at this time as one of the leading voices against the harsh treatment meted out to the Indian community, whether in Natal or the Transvaal. His experiences, especially in formulating a protest policy, were to be used on a much wider scale in India after 1918 and make Gandhi a revered national and international figure. The Boer invasion of Natal, however, gave Gandhi and other like-minded Indians the opportunity to reap some political benefits and to show that Indians had not gone to South Africa 'only for money-grabbing and were merely a deadweight upon the British'.

Indian opinion was not completely united in wanting to do something for the British Empire, but following a meeting of the Natal Indian Congress it was agreed that an offer should be made to the colonial and imperial authorities. Not until December, however, when Buller requested an Indian ambulance corps, was Gandhi's scheme realised, when, with the backing of an Anglican missionary, Dr Booth, as well as the Bishop of Natal, such a corps was formed and sent immediately to the front. The men had been released by the sugar estates and were paid twenty-five shillings a week by the Natal government, although Gandhi and the other leaders served without pay. The corps was to play a substantial part in the forthcoming battles and Buller would mention them in his despatches. Gandhi wrote afterwards that 'The relations formed with the whites during the war were of the sweetest' and that the ordinary British soldiers were 'friendly and thankful'.[14]

At the start of the war the African majorities in the Cape Colony and Natal were not asked by the British or local governments to show their support for the Empire. Indeed, there was concern that the war should be a 'white man's war' and that black participation would turn a civilised war into a barbaric struggle. This intention was never realised because by the end of the war in 1902, at least 30,000 Africans and mixed-race 'coloureds' were serving as armed auxiliaries (or support troops) with the British army, while another 100,000 worked for the army's transport force. In the Boer republics, thousands of Africans would die in the concentration camps alongside the Boers, having been sent to these places by the British after the destruction of their settlements and of the Boer farms upon which many lived. By so doing, the British attempted to deny the Boers supplies and intelligence. Moreover, major tribes in the Transvaal, the Pedi and Venda, would rise in revolt against their Boer overlords. In no respect, therefore, was this a war confined simply to Boer and Briton.

In the British colonies it is fair to say that those Africans and coloureds who gave any thought to the outbreak of war were solidly behind the British. In the Cape Colony, although most Africans lived on the land and provided labour for white-owned farms and the mines, especially at Kimberley, a black elite had emerged from peasant producers who benefited from a general rural prosperity, a 'colour-blind' franchise based on property ownership or a sizeable annual income, literacy and often conversion to Christianity. They provided about 8,000 voters to the electoral rolls, and many in this elite were interested in politics and in advancing the political and social rights of their community. They had formed political associations, which were the forerunners of the African National Congress, and had established their own newspapers, usually with white financial backing. *Izwi Labantu*, for example, which began circulating in 1897, was founded with money given by Cecil Rhodes. With one notable exception, this community backed Britain in the hope of gaining further civil rights after the war. The exception was John Tengo Jabavu who, through the editorship of his newspaper *Imvo Zabantsundu*, proclaimed his loyalty but also his belief that the war was being fought for reasons other than the official line. The universal execration Jabavu endured from his fellow Africans ensured that his was a lone voice.

Following the outbreak of war, Colonel R.S.S. Baden-Powell enlisted Africans and coloureds to help defend his besieged garrison at Mafeking near the border with the Bechuanaland Protectorate, much to the annoyance of the Boers. General Cronje wrote an impassioned letter to Baden-Powell complaining of his methods: 'I would ask you to pause and even at this eleventh hour, reconsider the matter, and even if it cost you the loss of Mafeking, to disarm your blacks and thereby act the part of a white man in a white man's war.' Cronje's plea cut no ice with Baden-Powell as it was a question of needs must. Indeed, Boer consternation was heightened by the hostility of the local Ngwato tribe under their king, Khama III. The Ngwato's military presence ensured that British communications between Rhodesia and southern Bechuanaland remained secure.[15]

Unlike Baden-Powell, the authorities in the Cape Colony were rather more squeamish and were reluctant to call upon Africans and coloureds to supplement their own meagre defence forces. But under pressure from the British authorities and by the desire of the colony's African and coloured communities, they were compelled to enlist non-whites because of the colony's military weakness and the subsequent Boer invasion. Generally, the recruitment of Africans took place in the east, while in the west it was the coloured community that supplied the auxiliaries. In the east, towards the end of 1899, the Transkei, an area largely devoid of white settlers and separately administered, raised 4,000 levies for local defence in case of a Boer invasion, which never came. Elsewhere, the Boers did arrive and local magistrates, military and police officials hastily raised African and coloured men to defend towns or localities. During the first months of the war these forces clashed repeatedly with the invading Boers, for example at Klipdam and Kuruman. Armed resistance by African and coloured men infuriated the Boers and as the war in the Cape continued, with the occasional lapse, until 1902, repeated defiance brought horrific reprisals: the destruction of Leliefontein in January 1902 was one such episode. There, the local coloured inhabitants defied the Boer Commandant Maritz with antiquated weapons and paid for their defiance when between twenty and thirty of their number were killed and the town was left burnt and wrecked. For those Africans and coloureds who served as scouts and were armed, capture by Boer forces could mean instant death and this was to be the fate of many. As a result of his execution in early 1901, Abraham Esau, a coloured auxiliary, was regarded as a martyr by the local population and came to occupy a central place in their identity and mythology.

Later on, the use of African and coloured auxiliaries enabled the British to police areas of the Cape Colony where the loyalty of the Afrikaner inhabitants was suspect. The British military authorities proved reluctant to take account of local susceptibilities and African police auxiliaries were given licence to treat the Afrikaners with the utmost disrespect. Most Afrikaner farmers were considered disloyal and so the British authorities turned a blind eye when they were robbed of their cattle, dispossessed of their rifles, had their property searched and were generally persecuted under military regulations.

The behaviour of these armed auxiliaries was just one horn of a dilemma for Afrikaner farmers; the other, shared with English-speaking farmers, was the loss of labour to the British army and the competition provided by African and coloured producers. Together these seemed to herald the destruction of traditional colonial society. For most Africans and coloureds, participation in the war meant serving the British army as transport workers and as general labour, but others supplied the army with cattle and grazing lands. It seems all were able to make much more money working for the army than for their usual masters, the Cape farmers, and eventually the lure of the army resulted in serious labour shortages for white farmers. The army proved very deaf to the entreaties made by the Cape farming community, because as the war progressed the demand for labour and supplies grew considerably and as long as the army's needs were fulfilled it cared little for the problems of others.

In Natal, both the Boers and the colonial authorities feared the participation of the warlike and numerous Zulus, although they, like their counterparts in the Transkei, were given permission to defend their frontiers. British weakness at the start of the war, which left Zululand without military help, was a major concern for the British and Natal authorities. Nevertheless, the Zulus stayed loyal to the British connection and eventually made gains when the guerrilla war took shape. The British army, to the dismay of the Natal government, actively connived at Zulu raiding of Boer areas for cattle and other supplies. This brought retaliation from the Boers, but on 6 May 1902 at Holkrantz, the Zulus surprised a Boer force, inflicting heavy losses and a humiliating defeat. This episode was to have profound effects on Boer attitudes during the peace negotiations.

Thus the desire that the war should be a white man's war collapsed at the very beginning, and African and coloured participation was to be ubiquitous throughout the conflict. The British and colonial authorities were thwarted in preventing non-white participation by two important factors: first, the weakness of the imperial and colonial forces over so large a battlefield, and second, the promotion in the Cape Colony at least of a liberal ideal which though weakened still endured. This ideal was that 'civilised' men should play a complete and active role in society and that the Empire was a motor by which non-white men could become full citizens. When war came, many African and coloured men wanted to demonstrate their 'civilisation' or their loyalty to this ideal by serving the imperial cause and it was a clamour that could not be resisted.

5

The Boers

WHEREAS THE BRITISH could count on the forces of a worldwide empire, as well as the bulk of the non-white population in southern Africa, the Boers could rely only on themselves. Many were prepared for the moment when the Transvaal would have to fight again to preserve its independence and they waited for events to unfold with a fatalistic expectation of war. For one Johannesburger, Roland Schikkerling, 'War was bound to come, for the Boer and Briton despised each other, and would never have been satisfied until the dispute had been settled by arms'; while the Transvaal Attorney General, J.C. Smuts, wrote in September 1899 that 'humanly speaking a war between the republics and England is certain'.[1] This anticipation of war was remarked upon by the American journalist Howard C. Hillegas in rather poetic terms, as if the Boers were about to embark on a lion hunt, the lions of course being the British and like lions a nuisance to the Boer way of life.[2] The impression given is one of unity, which did seem apparent at the outbreak of war, but this unity of purpose, of fatalistic acceptance, must not be taken too far. Before the war there were divisions in Transvaal politics and society which meant that the Boer response to the war and its subsequent prosecution was not straightforward but complicated.

First of all, Boer society was not particularly egalitarian, nor was it the rural idyll portrayed by commentators at the time. For many years before the war Transvaal society had being undergoing considerable change, which saw the emergence of the landless *bywoner* (poor white sub-farmer or sharecropper). This group, which belies the image of the Boers as all individual farmers, was of growing concern before 1899. Rural life was being transformed through increased buying and selling of land, and its accumulation and exploitation by fewer landholders. Many *bywoners* moved to towns, especially Johannesburg, but even there attempts to set up their own businesses were generally unsuccessful for a variety of reasons. In the Transvaal, therefore, there were many Boers whose loyalty to the state was not as wholehearted as was later supposed.

Kruger's economic policies were also instrumental in creating divisions within Boer society. Much of the Transvaal's economy was based on companies which had been granted monopoly rights over key services and many of those involved in these monopolies, or concessions, were Kruger's friends and associates, who regarded their companies more as money-making schemes than as providers of public services. Corruption was rife, therefore, and this led to the development of an opposition political grouping known as the Progressive party, some of whose members had lost out when the concessions were granted. The term party, however, gives the grouping a coherence it never really achieved. Kruger's main opponent was Piet Joubert, the Commandant General during the war of 1880–1, who had held the office ever since. But military command was no match for Kruger's political skills and Joubert had failed four times to beat Kruger in the presidential elections. Nevertheless, Joubert's opposition attracted many important men who would feature prominently in the war: Schalk Burgers, Louis Botha, J.H. (Koos) de la Rey and Lukas Meyer. Ludwig Krause, a lawyer originally from the Orange Free State, wrote bitterly against Kruger's 'blind obstinacy' and did not believe that war was inevitable. He felt Kruger had blundered, eyes open, into a British trap and resented the way Kruger's party criticised opposition as 'fanatical Anglophiles' or as traitors. Krause believed 'that by the exercise of patience and tact, war could be avoided and the political differences could be amicably settled', sentiments also shared by Joubert, not a good position for one expected to lead the Transvaal forces.[3]

If Kruger's enemies felt that war was not a certainty then Kruger and others did. After the Jameson Raid the Transvaal began to import arms on a lavish scale and by October 1899 had acquired a substantial arsenal. Within the Transvaal there were about 75,000 rifles, the best of which was the German Mauser of which there were some 37,000 by 1899. The Mauser rifle was an inspirational weapon, the Boers instantly taking to its light weight and the ease with which they could load a clip of five bullets. This gave the Mauser an advantage over the British Lee-Metford, whose magazine had to be reloaded bullet by bullet. For men who were connoisseurs of the rifle, the Mauser was indeed a piece of fine art.

Not only modern rifles were imported: the Transvaal's artillery, though small in number compared to Britain's, was nevertheless very modern, though none of the guns were of the ultra-modern quick-firing type. The British would be impressed by the Maxim-Nordenfeldt rapid-firing guns, which delivered one-pound shells and were christened 'pom-poms' because of the noise they made when firing. Also impressive were the four 155mm Creusot fortress guns, which were hauled from Pretoria's forts to be used as siege artillery and were given the name of 'Long Toms'. Although they were formidable weapons they were so few in number that their impact was to be marginal. Imposing though this armament was it was not nearly enough to match the British arsenal and for this Joubert was largely to blame because of his dilatoriness as Commandant General.

The Orange Free State had also begun an armaments programme following the Jameson Raid and by October 1899 had acquired some 12,000 Mausers to add to the 12,000 or so older and virtually obsolete Martini-Henry rifles. For the Mauser and other rifles, the Transvaal and Orange Free State had stockpiled some 40–50 million rounds of ammunition. The Free State artillery consisted of some fourteen modern Krupp 75mm guns, about ten other assorted pieces, as well as three 'pom-poms'. The republics, while unable to meet Britain on equal terms, were nevertheless formidably prepared and would be an altogether different foe than the ones the British usually encountered.

On 27 September 1900 Joubert was ordered to begin mobilisation and the Orange Free State followed on 2 October as part of its treaty obligations. In both republics the system was the same: every male between sixteen and sixty was liable for military service and had to undertake it. Both armies were citizen forces whose members ordinarily provided their own rifles, except that before the war each republic had given its men the imported Mausers and had taken in their obsolete Martini-Henrys. The men also had to provide ammunition and rations for the first eight days, after which the government provided the necessary supplies.

Each citizen, or burgher, was part of a ward commanded by a veldkornet ('field-cornet'), which was a sub-division of a district under a commandant. Every district despatched a commando, the main Boer military unit, to the front, the size of which varied depending on the size of the local population. It is estimated that at the start of the war the republics had about 55,000 men liable for military service. The veldkornets, commandants and even the Commandant General were all elected officers and in the first two cases had been elected before war broke out and so were voted into office for other than military reasons. Family ties, party allegiance and age, among other things, were usually the reasons for election. Thus, unlike the British army, there was no military hierarchy, as Howard Hillegas explained:

> The burgher who had assisted in electing his field-cornet felt that that official owed him a certain amount of gratitude for having voted for him, and obeyed his orders or disobeyed them whenever he chose to do so. The field-cornet represented authority over his men, but of real authority there was none. The commandants were presumed to have authority over the field-cornets and the generals over the commandants, but whether the authority was of any value could not be ascertained until the will of those in lower rank was discovered. By this extraordinary process it happened that every burgher was a general and that no general was greater than a burgher.[4]

Thus, while the burgher was obliged to go on commando, he had to be persuaded to fight. Decisions were made by the officers of the commando in what was known as a *krijgsraad* or war council, often by a vote. This meant that all officers were equal whatever their rank and decisions could be influenced by the least experienced. This did not mean that once a decision had been made everyone stuck to it; a Boer officer would often interpret decisions in his own way, sometimes to the point of contrariness. Once a decision had been made the officers would have to explain it to their commando members and then ask the men to carry it out. It was a process that did little to enhance Boer prospects during the coming conflict.

There was no great *krijgsraad* where the officers of both states met and consequently there was no planning for war. Smuts did prepare a strategy for the Transvaal government in which he outlined the coming struggle as a 'long and exhausting one' which required an early success against the British to stave off subsequent Boer defeatism. His recipe for success was an immediate offensive *'and doing it before the British force now in South Africa is markedly strengthened'*. Smuts's Napoleonic belief in the offensive was based on the need to undermine the confidence of the British Empire, which he argued 'rests more upon prestige and moral intimidation than true military strength'; if the Boers overran Natal it would 'cause an immediate shaking of the British Empire in very important parts of it'. This initial defeat would complicate Britain's relations with France, America, Germany and Russia and 'All these countries will try to take advantage of a defeat inflicted on England, but will quite possibly remain sitting still if the Boers suffer a defeat.' He also contended that the Boers should attack immediately once war was imminent and so encourage an uprising in the Cape Colony. Smuts recognised that the British would attempt to retake Natal and so the republics needed to prepare for a long struggle. To survive a protracted conflict Smuts made several recommendations: he advised the continuation of agriculture by women and 'kaffirs'; a twenty per cent war tax on the mines and the need to keep the mines working; the manufacture of arms and ammunition in the Transvaal and thus the need to establish a Mauser factory; the need to obtain advice from German military experts; and the need to encourage rebellion in India. All this was necessary 'because in my opinion South Africa stands on the eve of a frightful blood-bath out of which our people will come, either as an exhausted remnant, hewers of wood and drawers of water for a hated race, or as victors, founders of a United South Africa, of one of the great empires of the world'.[5]

Unfortunately for Smuts, and possibly the Boer cause, the Transvaal government did not take his advice and nor did Joubert. For Joubert, the coming of war was a crushing blow that bore down on his already pessimistic nature, although his wife, who accompanied him on campaign, seemed invigorated by the call to arms. Deneys Reitz, the son of the Transvaal's State Secretary, saw Joubert at this time and described him as 'a kindly, well-meaning old man who had done useful service in the smaller campaigns of the past, but he gave me the impression of being bewildered at the heavy responsibility now resting upon him and I felt that he was unequal to the burden'. Nevertheless, as Conan Doyle remarked, Joubert might not have been a live-wire any more, 'but he was experienced, crafty, and war wise, never dashing and never brilliant, but steady, solid, and inexorable'.[6]

It was Conan Doyle who described the ordinary burgher in terms that helped create the image of the mounted Boer rifleman as brave, resourceful, full bearded, a superb horseman and better marksman, 'fired with a strange religious enthusiasm. They were all of the seventeenth century, except their rifles.'[7] The truth was somewhat different, as many accounts left by Boer fighters reveal. We have, for example, accounts of Boer indiscipline. General F.A. Grobler, who commanded at Pietersburg, was described by Ludwig Krause in very unflattering terms: 'His chief qualification seemed to be the power to utter silly jokes and to laugh at them himself with a roar that was almost a yell.' Krause's opinion, though, might have been coloured by the fact that Grobler was a supporter of Kruger. Yet Grobler's subsequent actions said a great deal about Boer discipline. On receiving an order from Joubert to take Rhodes Drift and Fort Tuli, Grobler despatched just one commando, while he and the rest went in search of a local chief to settle some feud. The Zoutpansberg commando did not obey their orders to seize the drift (ford), having been abandoned by their officers who had fled a dust cloud caused by a swarm of locusts. Krause eventually took his leave and went off to Natal.[8]

Barend Daniel (Ben) Bouwer joined the Ermelo commando from his office as public prosecutor and later stated that life in a laager (wagon encampment or headquarters) was not all about singing hymns; he alleged that he became the commando's heavyweight boxing champion. Yet he acknowledged that Boer discipline left something to be desired, describing it as 'seventeenth-century' and remarking: 'It cannot be claimed that the discipline in the Boer forces was satisfactory, at least not until the weaker element had been weeded out, but its latitude was eminently suited to the national character.'[9]

Not all Boers were the typically rural folk so often described. Many men came from Pretoria and Johannesburg and did not have the skills with a horse or rifle as portrayed by Conan Doyle. Dietlof van Warmelo joined the Pretoria commando as did Deneys Reitz, but whereas Reitz had grown up in the country, Van Warmelo corresponded more to the typical Pretoria burgher, 'mostly young fellows from the Civil Service and legal offices and shops in the town', who were more like a Great War 'pals battalion' than a Boer commando. Reitz also remarked on the fact that few had any military training. Van Warmelo noted that they were all well dressed but found that the government had prepared nothing for their arrival at Zandspruit and so they had to spend several nights out in the open. Moreover, he hardly knew how to handle a horse and could not distinguish his unit's horses when they wandered because they 'all looked exactly alike in the eyes of an inexperienced townsman'. The invasion of Natal was no picnic: 'They were wet, cold days, and we were still unaccustomed to preparing our own food and looking after ourselves.'[10]

Ben Viljoen had little to say in favour of the Johannesburg commando. He recounts how he was surrounded by men wanting exemptions, complaining of new-found illnesses, and women begging him to release their men. Without irony it seems, Viljoen recorded that 'It is necessary that the reader should know, that the main part of the population was composed of all nationalities and lacked every element of Boer discipline.' He complained that only one of his original three veldkornets went on commando, the other two being substitutes for the original office holders.[11]

The reluctance of some burghers to fight helps explain why many would become *hensoppers* ('hand-uppers') in 1900, men who preferred to surrender once the British army had overrun the republics rather than become *bittereinders*, those wishing to fight until the bitter end. Others would pack up everything and take their families and livestock into neighbouring territories. A substantial number of Boers, however, would join the British in varying capacities. Initially, armed units were formed to guard towns and farms from marauding commandos and to help establish the rudiments of civil government. Then some Boers assisted the British as scouts, often lured by the prospect of loot as they helped clear the countryside. But another group of Boers emerged from the shattered remains of the republican cause and preferred to be absorbed into the British army and accept British pay. The most prominent group of *joiners*, known as the National Scouts, achieved notoriety in South Africa by helping the British to carry the war to the commandos. From October 1901 the British began to raise men from inside the concentration camps. The reasons for joining the British cause were varied: the bulk were landless *bywoners* hoping for British rewards; others enlisted because life in the camps had become unbearable;

and some joined to obtain preferential treatment from the British for their families. As already mentioned, some 5,000 men overall joined the British forces, generally to act as scouts, but sometimes to take part in the fighting.[12]

Thus the war was to tear a large hole in the fabric of Boer society and take on elements of a civil war. This is best illustrated by the fact that two prominent *joiners* were Andries Cronje, who helped form the National Scouts and Piet de Wet, who eventually changed sides and fought with the Orange River Colony Volunteers, for the British. These two were the brothers of prominent Boer generals, Piet Cronje who was to command in the west and defy British attempts to relieve Kimberley, and Christiaan de Wet, who was to become one of the greatest of the Boer guerrilla leaders. Christiaan de Wet later threatened to shoot his brother like a dog.

Petrus Jacobus du Toit was a National Scout but did not conform to the *bywoner* stereotype of most of his colleagues. At the start of the war he worked for the Commissioner of Mines at Klerksdorp in the Transvaal and was called up three times, finally serving as secretary to General P.J. Liebenberg. Du Toit was someone who was never enthusiastic about the war and noted in his diary on the first anniversary of the war's start: 'I feel sad at the thought of so many good and useful lives having been sacrificed for – now to me seeming – a fruitless cause.' By the end of May 1901, Du Toit was heartily sick of the war and deliberately surrendered to a British column, his reasons he informed his diary were 'because I consider further resistance useless, my health is failing and out of consideration for the poor families in the camps and our prisoners in Ceylon and elsewhere'. This last remark referred to the fact the Boer prisoners of war were being sent out of South Africa for security reasons, in case they were freed by Boer guerrillas or sympathetic Afrikaners in the Cape Colony. The British were keen for him to join as a scout and eventually he accepted their offer. In his diary he wrote:

> I am convinced in my mind that nothing in the world can save us, then why should I wait to do my share towards bringing this horrible and miserable state of affairs to a speedy termination, for the sake of the country at large, for the sake of humanity, and lastly for the sake of the women and children in refugee camps, and the prisoners of war on Ceylon, St. Helena and [in] India. This I consider the duty of every true patriot.[13]

Not everyone would agree with Du Toit's belief that he was patriotic. National Scouts and other *joiners* would be vilified by their own people, who saw them as nothing but traitors who could be summarily shot if captured. Writing in 1903, Ben Viljoen could not bring himself to understand or forgive these 'wretched' men: 'Oh, day of judgment! The Afrikander [sic] nation will yet avenge your treachery.' Roland Schikkerling could not forgive either and realised that the National Scouts had helped turn the war against the *bitter-einders* because without them 'the enemy would never have penetrated our fastness. Time will no more erase the black from their souls than it will the blue from the heavens.' Far from being the great unifying force against British imperialism, the war was to have serious divisive effects on Boer society that were to continue long after.[14]

Unfortunately for the Boers the war was not to have the same divisive impact on their opponents, although in one instance there was a split in the English-speaking community. In the Transvaal town of Heidelberg, as we have already seen, at least sixteen English-speakers actually went off to fight in the local Boer commando unit. Of these men half a dozen were killed in action: among them Frederick Flanagan at Spion Kop, Charles Cothill at Platrand, David Anderson at Lake Chrissie and Benjamin Russell at the siege of Ladysmith. Those English-speakers in Heidelberg who did not join the conflict 'were generally left alone to their own devices, as long as they did not interfere in the war. To the credit of the Boers, no victimisation took place, but rather they were shunned by not being approached for any help with the war effort. This probably avoided unnecessary friction.'[15] As it turned out, only the Afrikaans-speakers of the Cape Colony would provide the Transvaal and the OFS with the same sort of help given by the National Scouts to the British.

In the Cape Colony, the Afrikaners (that is, the Boers who had remained under British rule rather than join the trek northwards) were still the dominant white group in terms of numbers. For many imperial officials, soldiers and commentators, the Cape Afrikaners were considered a 'fifth column'. This perception was intensified by political developments since the Jameson Raid, notably the election of the Afrikaner Bond and their liberal allies in May 1898 under William Schreiner. Indeed, it was felt that in August 1899 Kruger's agents were already at work in the Cape Colony distributing arms. Although this perception of all Cape Afrikaners as potential rebels was far from correct, a substantial number were sympathetic towards and supportive of their republican brethren rather than the British Empire. Consequently, through the course of the war some 13,000 Cape Afrikaners – all British subjects – would fight for the republican cause.

There was good reason for the British to be wary, for certain districts were well known to be disloyal. The war correspondent G.W. Steevens travelled through some of them on his way to Ladysmith. He passed through Burgersdorp, described as 'famous throughout South Africa as a stronghold of bitter Dutch partisanship ... and Capetown turns anxious ears towards it for the first muttering of insurrection'. Around Aliwal North he found that Afrikaners had sent their sons to serve in the forces of the Free State and 'promise that loyal inhabitants will be "sjambokked" [flogged with a rhinoceros-hide whip] ... when the Boer force passes through'. To Steevens, every local Afrikaner man, woman and child was 'a potential Boer secret service agent'.[16] For Sir Alfred Milner the position was straightforward – all Cape Afrikaners were disloyal at heart. Thus when the Boers invaded the colony to besiege Mafeking and Kimberley, his worst nightmare was apparently about to become reality. On 18 October 1899 his response, in agreement with Schreiner, was to issue a treason proclamation which warned the population 'to abstain from all treasonable and seditious acts or words' and 'not to enlist or engage themselves in the military service' of the republics, nor 'aid, abet and assist' them, nor trade with the enemy. Anyone caught contravening the above would be liable to the full penalty of the law.[17] From then on, the government and Milner lived in fear of someone or something provoking an uprising, although some political opponents believed that Milner was doing that already. 'Milner has goaded and stung our folk to an almost incredible degree,' wrote John X. Merriman, 'and though their self-control is wonderful there is a store of bitterness laid up.' Merriman was in contact with leading Afrikaner figures in the frontier districts and was assured by several that they were doing their utmost to keep their people quiet. However, Merriman's appeals had been in vain and some of his correspondents, such as C.J. van Pletzen and J.F. de Wet, were already conspiring with the enemy and would later join them.[18]

Milner's worst fears became reality first on 1 November 1899, when Boer units from the Orange Free State invaded bordering districts, and then on 13 November when the Boers under Commandants Olivier, Grobler (different from the one mentioned above) and Schoeman crossed the Orange River and launched a more substantial invasion, taking Aliwal North and Colesberg early on. Until then President Steyn had been reluctant to attack the heartlands of the Cape Colony, owing to the pleas of Schreiner, who initially opposed the deployment of British troops near the frontier and the use of Cape forces by the imperial authorities. Moreover, although many of Steyn's commanders had wanted war they had proved reluctant to carry that war to the enemy and preferred to sit on their side of the Orange River in a more familiar defensive posture. This failure to act promptly cost the Boers a major strategic opportunity because, until November, the north-central heartlands of the Cape Colony were virtually defenceless. But in those Cape districts bordering the Orange River there were few defenders to oppose Steyn's forces when they arrived, and for the first few days the Boer invasion was a promenade, the commandos being joined by thousands of rebels. Many prominent Afrikaners welcomed the invaders, including members of the Cape Colony's legislative council. The imposition of martial law did nothing in many ways to dampen the spirit of rebellion, but merely inflamed it because many Afrikaners thought it meant they would be conscripted to fight their Boer brethren. Moreover, because of the shortage of regular troops, the British authorities had to rely on colonial volunteers to administer martial law, and some, like Colonel Crewe of Brabant's Horse, had pre-war scores to settle. The arming of Africans and coloureds and their use in law courts to denounce their former Afrikaner masters, all added to the sense of grievance and inspired many to rebel.

During this first invasion of the Cape Colony it is believed that some 10,000 Afrikaners joined the Boer commandos and were, for the most part, amply supplied with arms and ammunition, either their own or that provided by the Free State forces. It would be a different story when the Boers invaded a second time. Then, in December 1900, provoking a rebellion in the Cape Colony had become the main strategic priority of the Boers, but it proved a futile exercise even though the British would be hard pressed to deal with the various commandos that appeared and which proved to be extremely elusive. Most Afrikaners had had their rifles removed, many of the better men were prisoners and those that joined needed virtually every item of equipment, including rifles. The failure of the first invasion made its mark and only about 3,000 Afrikaners would join the second attack. Many were now too fearful or had reconciled themselves to the fact of a Boer defeat. Cape Afrikaners were in the end to disappoint republican expectations.

A last word must be said about the numbers of Africans who served in various capacities with the Boer forces. Although it is true that the vast majority of Africans and coloureds supported the British, it is estimated that during the first, conventional phase of the war some 9,000 were with the Boers, this number steadily dropping off as Boer fortunes dwindled. In the first instance, many Africans were forced labour, needed to help construct the field fortifications along the various fronts and so were a vital part of the early war effort. Most Africans, and a few coloureds, were more commonly servants, known as *agterryers*, a term that is not readily translatable and can mean 'after-rider', 'retainer' or even 'lackey'. Many of these were often personal servants of the burghers who accompanied their masters to the front. They were often tenants on their master's farm, their families having worked there for many years. Some Boer farmers had to provide *agterryers* for others and quite often they sent their worst servants. It is calculated that at the start there was one *agterryer* to every four, possibly five Boers. Their tasks were essentially menial, to look after the horses and keep the riding equipment clean and serviceable, to cook and generally look after the basic needs of the Boers. The relationship between the *agterryers* and their masters varied: some Boers exercised a dutiful, paternalistic attitude towards their men, which might engender devotion in return. There were many instances of loyalty shown by the *agterryers*, some of whom remained to the bitter end or accompanied their masters to prisoner-of-war camps overseas. Some were armed, deliberately by the Boers, to be used as guards and scouts, some even took part in the early battles. Many, however, deserted, particularly when it seemed the Boer cause was lost in 1900. Bad treatment – and most Boers would have applied the *sjambok* at one time or other – lack of food, and the prospect of pay led many to go over to the British. Criticisms by the Boers of the British use of non-whites rang rather hollow given that they too had recourse to the services of Africans and coloureds. Thus even on the Boer side, the war was not exclusively a 'white man's war'.[19]

Part III
The Campaigns, 1899–1902

6

The Opening Battles

OCTOBER 1899

WHILE BULLER AND his retinue steamed towards the Cape, bearing a heavy and in the event unrealistic load of patriotic expectation on their braided shoulders, British fortunes in South Africa were suffering sharp and unexpected reverses. The Boers, far from waiting like bemused rabbits to be devoured by their ponderous enemies, immediately struck against the Cape Colony and Natal. Three Afrikaner columns invaded Natal, the soft underbelly of British power: Utrecht, Dundee and Newcastle were occupied, and soon Ladysmith, on the junction of the railway lines between Natal, the Orange Free State and the Transvaal, was under siege.

Further west, Afrikaner troops advanced upon two more towns that lay on the strategically significant railway line that ran from the important junction at De Aar, in the Cape, roughly parallel with the western borders of the Free State and the Transvaal until it finally entered the British protectorate of Bechuanaland. The name of Kimberley was already world famous owing to its diamond mines; that of Mafeking was about to become so. Crossing the Free State's southern border into the Cape Colony, Boer columns also pushed towards the railway junction of Stormberg and towards the rail link between Noupoort and De Aar.

A young girl of Russian parentage, Freda Schlosberg, recorded the excitement of these early days of the war in a journal she kept at her select boarding school in Pretoria. On 20 October she wrote:

Newcastle has been occupied by the Boers. The news brings great rejoicing. Mafeking and Kimberley are besieged, and Ladysmith is threatened.

'Victory follows victory.' 'The English are being driven into the sea.' 'Boer arms are successful everywhere.' The Transvaal is very gay. The Hollanders, Irish and Germans are celebrating. 'The Boers will soon be masters of South Africa.'[1]

At this early stage of the war, Boer strategy was based on the belief (a belief to be amply justified by events) that time was not on their side. They hoped, therefore, to achieve such striking early military successes that the British would become disheartened and negotiate a settlement, just as had happened after General Colley's defeat at Majuba Hill in 1881 during the Anglo-Transvaal War. The Boers also hoped that a string of early victories would encourage the Cape Afrikaners to flock to the republics' standards, and would rally international opinion against the oppressions of John Bull.

The first engagements of the war came in northern Natal. Here British forces consisted of a brigade of 4,000 men under Major General Sir William Penn Symons at Dundee, and 8,000 men at Ladysmith under the veteran Sir George White VC. Boer columns were pressing towards Ladysmith from the north (Transvaal commandos crossing the Drakensberg range at Botha's Pass and Laing's Nek) and from the west (where Free Staters began to move through Van Reenen's Pass and Tintura Pass). Newcastle, to the north of Dundee and Ladysmith, was occupied without a fight. General White almost immediately gave a demonstration of the wavering indecisiveness that was to lead to such embarrassment for British arms in Natal. At first he ordered Symons to retire and join him in Ladysmith; this Symons declined to do, and White finally let him have his way.

At 2.30 a.m. on 20 October the first battle of the war, Talana, began when Lukas Meyer's scouts clashed with a British picket of the Royal Dublin Fusiliers at Smith's Nek, the pass running between Talana Hill and Lennox Hill, to the east of Dundee. General Symons, on hearing this news, concluded that it was merely a raid, and of no great significance. When the mist cleared at 5.30 a.m., however, the British troops positioned on the partly dried up bed of Sand Spruit saw to their dismay that the crests of both Talana Hill and Lennox Hill were thick with Afrikaners. Within seconds Boer gunners fired the first shell of the war over the heads of the British troops.

Symons immediately ordered his infantry to join the Royal Dublin Fusiliers, the mounted infantry of the 60th, the 18th Hussars and some field batteries at Sand Spruit. The 13th, 67th and 69th Field Batteries eventually opened fire upon the Boers on Talana. So effective was their bombardment that the Boer guns were silenced, and over 1,000 burghers panicked, leapt onto their horses, and made off. The bulk of the Afrikaner forces, however, stayed, concealed among the boulders upon the summit.

General Symons now prepared to drive the enemy off Talana by a frontal attack backed by artillery fire. By about 7.30 a.m. units of the Royal Dublin Fusiliers, the Royal Irish Fusiliers, and the 60th Foot Regiment had taken cover in a plantation of eucalyptus trees between Sand Spruit and Talana Hill. The Dublin Fusiliers soon moved northwards out of the wood, but they were raked with such crippling fire that they were virtually knocked out of the battle.

The frontal attack on Talana was mounted by the 60th Foot and the Irish Fusiliers, supported by the 69th and 13th Field Batteries. For some time, however, nothing happened, and General Symons rode into the eucalyptus wood to see what was holding up the advance. He dismounted and walked among the men shouting 'Push on', and other words of encouragement. Several walls ran along the edge of the wood and on the slopes of Talana, and Symons stepped through a gap in one of them and was almost immediately shot in the stomach. Though his wound proved to be fatal, he coolly instructed General Yule, the artillery commander, to press the attack, and then rode back to the field dressing station, where he subsequently died.

While General Symons lay dying, the men of the 60th and the Irish Fusiliers were fighting their way doggedly up the slopes of Talana, using the various walls for cover where possible. Despite a hail of accurate fire from the Boers' Mausers, the men made a final assault on the summit, driving off many of their foes with the bayonet. As the British troops made for the summit, however, their own artillery, hampered by the now poor light, brought down a heavy fire on both attackers and defenders alike. Once this terrible error was rectified, the British line was able to surge forward again, and found that the Boers had deserted the summit of Talana. The Afrikaners on Lennox Hill also withdrew.

Amid the noisy confusion of the Boer retreat, the British artillery, shocked at having fired on their own men, failed to punish the enemy as they withdrew to the east. Nor did the cavalry cut them off, for Colonel Möller with the men of the 18th Hussars and some mounted infantry of the 60th got himself trapped by a Boer commando at Adelaide Farm some four miles to the north of Talana Hill. By 4 p.m. Möller was forced to surrender, together with nine officers and 205 men; eight of his troopers had been killed and twenty-three wounded.

As a result of the fighting, the British lost some 500 men, including killed, wounded and prisoners. The Boers lost 150. It was a pyrrhic British victory – indeed, in a sense a defeat, for General Yule soon decided to move his forces back to Ladysmith, leaving Dundee open for enemy occupation.

Some twenty-five miles to the south-west, meanwhile, Boer forces, led by old General Kock wearing his top hat, were advancing on Elandslaagte, halfway between Dundee and Ladysmith. As a result, on 19 October, advance units of Kock's men took Elandslaagte station and its environs, completely cutting rail, road and telegraphic communications between Dundee and Ladysmith. By 20 October Kock's main force reached Elandslaagte. That evening the Boers held a smoking concert in the hotel near the railway station; some British prisoners from a captured supply train were invited, and both *God Save the Queen* and the Transvaal's *Volkslied* were sung vociferously at the concert.

The battle of Elandslaagte took place the next day, when General Sir John French moved north from Ladysmith to clear the path for General Yule's forces retreating after the battle of Talana. French's patrols made contact with the Afrikaners holding the station, and the Natal Volunteer Field Battery cleared both friend and foe out of the station buildings with fire from their 7-pounder guns. But the Boers on the kopjes (small hills) to the south-east in turn shelled the 7 pounders, causing French to fall back to where the Modder Spruit crossed both the railway to Elandslaagte and the road north to Newcastle.

French had telegraphed Ladysmith for reinforcements, and as they began to arrive the main battle got under way. Sir John had squadrons of the Imperial Light Horse, the 5th Dragoon Guards and the 5th Lancers; besides the 7 pounders, he had some 15 pounders of the 21st and 42nd Field Batteries. Half a battalion of the 1st Manchesters arrived, followed by seven companies of the 1st

Battalion of the Devonshires and five companies of the 2nd Battalion of the Gordon Highlanders.

Advancing up the Newcastle road, French delayed his main attack until three o'clock in the afternoon, by which time all the reinforcements had arrived. The battle area was south of Elandslaagte station, and consisted of a plain ringed by a horseshoe of hills, with the opening of the horseshoe in the north; the Boer laager (headquarters) was near the top of the eastern side of the hill formation. The commander of the infantry, Colonel Ian Hamilton, a survivor of Majuba Hill, and much favoured by General White, addressed his men in stirring words, telling them that they would throw the Boers off the hills before sunset and that London newsboys would be shouting the news of their victory the next day. The infantrymen cheered lustily, shouting out 'We'll do it, sir! We'll do it!'.

At first the attack went well. Sir George White arrived from Ladysmith with an escort of Natal Mounted Rifles to watch the progress of the battle. A huge thunderstorm closed in upon the battle area, however, thus reducing visibility. Since the daylight was also beginning to fade, French ordered Hamilton's infantry to advance after the Boer positions had been shelled for a mere half hour. The Afrikaners were easily dislodged from the western side of the horseshoe of hills, but the eastern side – including a formidable hogback – was to prove a more difficult objective.

The Devonshires advanced across the plain towards the hogback, and made good progress owing to their open formation – a lesson Hamilton had learnt the hard way during the Majuba campaign. But 1,200 yards from the Boer positions, they were halted by heavy and accurate rifle fire.

The Manchesters and the Gordons had meanwhile cut round the inside bend of the horseshoe, accompanied on foot by Uitlanders of the Imperial Light Horse, who moved along the bend of the horseshoe, to their right.

To mount an attack on the southern flank of the hogback was a difficult task, and one rendered doubly hazardous by the breaking thunderstorm. However, as the rain eased off the infantry began to climb the rock-strewn slope towards the barbed wire fences protecting the Afrikaners. Many British troops were shot down, especially when they bunched together to cut paths through the wire. The men of the Imperial Light Horse, who had virtually annihilated a force of

Germans under Colonel Schiel, were in turn decimated; half of the Gordons' officers were out of action, and the Manchesters were cut to pieces.

Colonel Hamilton then decided to order the Devonshires to resume their advance. The bugles of the approaching Devonshires put new heart into the other battered infantry units and, fixing bayonets, they swept the Boers from the hogback, capturing two guns in the process.

As it turned out, the infantry's triumph was short-lived. Noticing some Boers in the laager waving white flags, Hamilton ordered a ceasefire, but this was rudely interrupted when about forty men under General Kock, in his frockcoat and top hat, suddenly appeared below the crest of the hogback and blazed away at the British troops. Driven from the summit, the infantry were rallied by Hamilton and by French himself; joined by the Devonshires, they once more hurled the enemy off the heights, the Gordons, with considerable presence of mind, shouting 'Remember Majuba!'.

The defeated Boers mounted their horses and streamed away from the hills, hoping to fight another day. As they retreated, the 5th Dragoon Guards and the 5th Lancers charged upon them in the dusk. The Afrikaners were sabred down, and speared by the British lances (two Boers clinging to one pony were impaled by the same lance). The cavalrymen wrought havoc among the Boers until darkness called a halt to their activities.

Elandslaagte was a clear-cut British victory. The Boers had been driven from their chosen positions through a good cooperative effort by artillery, cavalry and infantry, and three VCs were awarded to British soldiers. Though infantry losses had been heavy in the final stages of the assault, the news of the victory was encouraging for the British, and on 21 October Freda Schlosberg recorded the following in her journal:

The English language paper, *Standard and Digger News*, which arrives by post from Johannesburg, reports that 'General French shelled strongly entrenched Boer forces at Elandslaagte, fifteen miles north of Ladysmith and after a bayonet attack put them to flight. General Kock was wounded and he and 300 of his men, and General Schiel, commander of the German Corps, was taken prisoner. Boer officials in Pretoria are reported to be uneasy and hospitals are preparing to receive the wounded.'[2]

In fact, General Kock was mortally wounded and died in Ladysmith. The triumphant General French's reputation was boosted by the encounter and proved to be durable enough to survive the later tribulations of the war.

Despite this victory at Elandslaagte, the prospects for the British forces in northern Natal remained bleak. Columns of Transvaalers and Free Staters continued to close in upon the forces around Ladysmith. General Yule, retreating south from Dundee towards Ladysmith, made a bold detour over rain-drenched hills and through dangerously high rivers, away from the main road; eventually, exhausted, they reached Ladysmith, to the cheers of the garrison.

Yule's retreating column had passed close to Rietfontein, between Elandslaagte and Ladysmith. Here on 24 October, 5,000 British troops had held off the Free State commandos, led by General Erasmus, who had just occupied and looted Dundee. Once this British force learnt that Yule's men had reached Ladysmith, they too pulled back.

On 25 October Dr Alec Kay, having arrived in Ladysmith as a civil surgeon at the Stationary Hospital, wrote:

> Ladysmith is full of spies. I met one today, a man who had fought against us in the Boer War of 1880 and I knew him to be very bitter towards us. I sent a friend with a message to the Intelligence Department that he had better be arrested; but the reply was, 'Ladysmith is so full of spies that one more or less makes no difference.'[3]

Three days later, on 28 October, Dr Kay wrote gloomily, 'The Boers are all around us; the water supply of Ladysmith is cut off. Our war balloons went up and charted the Boer positions.' The siege of Ladysmith had begun.

General White's position was an unenviable one. Cavalry reconnaissance and balloon observations showed that thousands of the enemy were closing in. To the west, Free State commandos, though not apparently making for Ladysmith, were moving down towards Colenso, thus cutting off communications to the south. In the northwest Piet Cronje, in command of units of Free Staters, was situated near Nicholson's Nek and Tchrengula Mountain. To the north, General Erasmus and his men lay between Pepworth Hill and the

Modder Spruit. To the east Lukas Meyer's commandos were spread out from the east bank of the Modder Spruit. Further round to the north-east there were Afrikaners around Long Hill, but these forces were soon withdrawn to a laager east of the Modder Spruit.

In an attempt to break this menacing semicircle of Boer forces, General White planned to strike to the north with what he called a 'reconnaissance in force'. The object was to turn the enemy's east flank on Long Hill, and to close the pass of Nicholson's Nek to reinforcements from the north. White originally planned this countermanoeuvre for Sunday 29 October, but reconsidered the timing when reminded of the Boers' reluctance to fight on a Sunday. The fateful battle of Majuba Hill had been forced on the Transvaalers on the sabbath, and afterwards Piet Joubert had remarked scornfully, 'What can you expect from fighting on a Sunday?' Superstitiously, the British commanders feared that a Sunday counter-attack could stiffen Boer resistance even further.

So Monday 30 October was chosen instead. It was no more propitious, and was soon to become known throughout the Empire as 'Mournful Monday'.

At 10.30 a.m. on Monday, Colonel Carleton led a force of 1,000 men out of Ladysmith towards Nicholson's Nek. He had the 1st Battalion of the Gloucesters, the 1st Battalion of the Royal Irish Fusiliers, and the 10th Mountain Battery. They got off to a poor start: the artillery mules were difficult and subsequently stampeded on the slopes of Tchrengula Mountain – obstinately carrying the mountain guns and a good deal of the spare ammunition back to camp. The clatter, and some nervy firing by some of the troops, alerted the Boers who began to move against Carleton.

Colonel Grimwood, meanwhile, led out a brigade to bombard and capture Long Hill. He had under his command the 1st and 2nd Battalions of the 60th, the 1st Liverpools, the 1st Leicesters, the 2nd Dublin Fusiliers, the 21st, 42nd and 53rd Field Batteries and the Natal Field Battery.

Colonel Hamilton, basking in his success at Elandslaagte, also left Ladysmith to help in the shelling of Long Hill and then to storm Pepworth Hill with Grimwood's brigade. Hamilton's force consisted of the 1st Devonshires, the 1st Manchesters, the 2nd Gordon Highlanders and the 13th, 67th and 69th Field Batteries. The cavalry was divided between these two infantry brigades, though

Hamilton's troopers were allotted the task of galloping up Bell Spruit and harassing the Boers after they had been swept off the hills.

The advance of Colonel Grimwood's troops towards Long Hill was little short of disastrous. As they marched under cover of darkness, his artillery units unaccountably left the advancing column and stationed themselves at Flag Hill. The Liverpools, the Dublin Fusiliers, and mounted infantry units of the Leicesters and the 60th, also turned aside at Flag Hill – to the south of Long Hill. Grimwood, knowing nothing of this, plodded on to within a mile of Long Hill and proceeded to launch a dawn attack in accordance with General White's orders. Ian Hamilton's brigade had meanwhile moved to its agreed position south of Pepworth Hill, ready to cooperate with Grimwood's attack.

Shortly after dawn Grimwood discovered that Long Hill was unoccupied, but his men soon came under enfilading fire from across the Modder Spruit. The brigade commander then sensibly spread his men out, facing east. But where was the cavalry? General French, who had oversight of cavalry manoeuvres, promptly sent in some of his own horsemen and summoned Hamilton's cavalry as reinforcements. This extended British line, though lacking the units that had dropped by the wayside at Flag Hill, was thus well placed to hold off the Boers from the Modder Spruit area.

In the region of Pepworth Hill, things had been going better. Colonel Hamilton's artillery silenced the Boer guns on Pepworth and drove most of the enemy off the summit. The Afrikaner positions were submitted to a positive hail of shrapnel shells – which were thudding down in batches of twenty and more. Boer dead and wounded were scattered over the hillside. Despite this success, Hamilton denied the active and pre-arranged cooperation of Grimwood's brigade, felt disinclined to advance, and little more occurred in this sector of the battle area.

Further east, Grimwood's men came under determined Boer pressure. The Afrikaner commander Lukas Meyer, who had in earlier times established the petty republic of Vryheid, collapsed from nervous strain and left the field. His place was taken by his subordinate and fellow-founder of Vryheid, Louis Botha. Botha was intelligent and authoritative, a man of wide vision and considerable military competence – and destined to become one of the great Boer generals and the first Prime Minister of the Union of South Africa. Profiting from the arrival of reinforcements, Botha began to press hard against Grimwood's brigade – which was left virtually leaderless by its increasingly anxious commander.

Back in Ladysmith, General White grew despondent at the situation. He was threatened by a new Boer attack from the north-east, and morale had hardly been raised by the unexpected reappearance of Colonel Carleton's runaway artillery mules. The Boers' 'Long Tom' on Pepworth Hill, moreover, had been steadily firing its massive 94-pound shells into Ladysmith, though it inflicted little damage. Later a naval brigade landed from HMS *Powerful* and brought 12-pounder guns with them. Arriving at Ladysmith they promptly went out and silenced 'Long Tom', but by 2 November the big 6-inch Creusot gun was again pounding away.

At any rate, White decided to recall his forces, and sent out a heliograph message to that effect. Hamilton's brigade made an orderly withdrawal, but Grimwood's men pulled back with a storm of Mauser bullets and shells whistling about their ears. Colonel Carleton's men at Tchrengula Mountain, however, received no order to withdraw, and were soon to be disgraced.

On Tchrengula Carleton's position quickly became untenable – through both indifferent British leadership and expert Boer assaults. The Afrikaner commandos, led by the able Christiaan de Wet, wriggled stealthily towards the British defences, shooting any soldiers who showed themselves or tried to withdraw. Soon the forward infantry units had been driven back. At this point, one company of the Gloucesters, left stranded by their fellows and believing that the main body of troops was marching back to Ladysmith, raised the white flag by tying a towel onto a sword.

This apparent surrender was soon reported to Colonel Carleton, who eventually ordered his bugler to sound the ceasefire. The wretched man struggled to produce the appropriate call and at last gave out such a strangled blast that it was later rumoured that the Boers were responsible for it. More white flags were raised and the Boers waved their hats to acknowledge the ceasefire. A unit of the Irish Fusiliers saw things differently, however, and their enraged officers snapped their sword-blades across their knees in a dramatic gesture of protest. But it was of no avail, and more than 800 prisoners were taken by the Boers, who, according to Dr Kay:

told the dejected prisoners that they had heard them during the night and by the time the day dawned they had 2,000 men around the hill.

They behaved very well to the wounded, riding some distance for water and giving them blankets. One or two, however, were objectionable, trying to loot medical stores and medical comforts, but on complaint being made to the Boer in command, he abused the looters and sent them away calling them 'low Hollanders'. The prisoners had their water-bottles, haversacks, glasses and anything of value taken from them, and some were shoved about and treated roughly, but not the wounded.[4]

While some of the captured officers were talking to the triumphant Boers, they caught sight of the British force of some 10,000 men in full retreat for Ladysmith, great clouds of dust rising above them. General Joubert deliberately held back from unleashing his horsemen upon them, subsequently explaining that 'When God holds out a finger, don't take the whole hand.'

For those besieged in Ladysmith there had been humiliation enough, and Dr Kay wrote on 31 October:

Yesterday, Mournful Monday, was the first day of the bombardment of the town after our defeat at Nicholson's Nek and a mournful day for all of us. The Boers opened fire from Pepworth Hill at about 5.30 a.m. with their Long Tom, the first shot pitching near the station but doing no damage. The gun is a 6 in. Creusot, one of the Pretoria Fort guns, a matchless advertisement for its French factory, for despite firing steadily all day it did little or no damage. We have christened it 'Puffing Billy'.

Nicholson's Nek turned out a disaster for us. Our men were so scattered because they had to cover such an enormous area of ground, the country so broken, and the mobility of the Boers turned to such good account, that we were forced to retreat. Some of our men being isolated and without support, retired at the double amid a great deal of confusion. The Boers followed and poured in very heavy fire with their mausers, their artillery using shrapnel and making excellent shooting, but luckily most of the shells burst too high. Had the Boers pressed home their advantage, there is little doubt that Ladysmith would have been taken that day.

Fortunately the Naval Brigade arrived at 10 a.m. They had managed to get through the Boer lines before they finally closed around us. I went to the railway station to meet them but they had no reception as all the troops and staff were busy engaged with the enemy.

Within half an hour the Brigade was on its way to the fight with their guns and maxims, and real good service they did, for their fourth shot either struck Puffing Billy or killed some of the men serving it, for the gun was silent for the rest of the day.

There was a dinner that night at the Royal Hotel for the officers of the Naval Brigade who were loudly cheered as their advent was both welcome and reassuring. There were many regular soldiers present, volunteers, war correspondents, civilians, and the usual hangers-on one meets in colonial towns. The situation was freely discussed and the general opinion was that the British had been outmanoeuvred and beaten, and that the Boers were very strong.

The General [White] and his staff were freely criticised; and there was almost a panic when later in the evening an officer came in and declared that the British losses were 30 killed, 97 wounded and 830 taken prisoner, and a mountain battery lost. Dismay was on every face, and all felt that bad times were in store.[5]

With Ladysmith under siege, and British forces dramatically rebuffed in northern Natal, the war was clearly going badly for the Empire. In Britain, Arthur Balfour, First Lord of the Treasury and nephew of the Prime Minister Lord Salisbury, told his sister Alice that he was surprised that at Ladysmith 'so large a garrison ... amply supplied as I believe they are with ammunition and food can be in any danger ... On the whole ... I am dissatisfied'.

Further afield than Ladysmith there were other causes of dissatisfaction. Mafeking and Kimberley would have to be relieved – yet there was no immediate prospect of this. Though the Boers had not been able to sweep into the potentially supportive, though for the British 'disloyal', area of the northern Cape, they had shown resourcefulness and guile in their encounters with the British.

In Pretoria, Freda Schlosberg chronicled these events in her journal, and also mentioned the capture of the young Winston Churchill, the war correspondent for the *Morning Post*:

2 November
A great multitude went to Pretoria station to witness the arrival of more British prisoners. The captured officers are said to be comfortably accommodated at the State Model School.

16 November
An armoured train is wrecked near Estcourt [in Natal] and an important man by the name of Winston Churchill is taken prisoner.

19 November

Sixty prisoners taken when the armoured train was wrecked near Estcourt, including this Mr. Churchill, arrived at Pretoria at noon yesterday. Two officers and Mr. Churchill were taken to the State Model School, and the rest of the prisoners to the Racecourse Prisoners Camp. Nobody was at the station to notice their arrival. The general situation is splendid and hopeful for the Boers. Besieged Mafeking, Kimberley and Ladysmith are expected to surrender soon.[6]

In Mafeking, meanwhile, Solomon Plaatje, an ironic and erudite African interpreter at the local court, was writing elegantly in his diary:

Friday, 17th [November]

What a lovely morning after yesterday's rains. It is really evil to disturb a beautiful morning like this with the rattling of Mausers and whizzes and explosions of shells. 'Au Sanna' [the 94-pound Creusot siege gun] appears to have sharpened up, for her fire was very vigorous and quick since 3 o'clock. Mausers were also very brisk today. Goodness knows what these Boers are shooting: they kill on the average only one goat, sheep or fowl after spending 5,000 rounds of Mauser ammunition – but very rarely a man.[7]

The following day Plaatje wrote 'We have just got definite information that the Troops [the Army Corps of 50,000 men] landed at Cape Town on the 4th Instant and that they are given 6 days rest prior to proceeding north.'[8] With Buller now safely disembarked, it seemed certain that a series of crushing blows would be delivered against the Boers. In the event, however, the British forces were on the brink of disaster.

7

The Disasters of Black Week

December 1899: the battles of Stormberg, Magersfontein and Colenso, and their less disastrous prelude

As November 1899 drew to its close, substantial British forces under Generals Gatacre and French moved to counter the threatened Boer invasion of the potentially rebellious northern region of the Cape Colony. Meanwhile in Natal, Buller established a huge base camp at Frere, twenty-five miles south of Ladysmith, where he mustered nearly 20,000 amply equipped men; at the pain-fully-gained Modder River station, some twenty-seven miles to the south of Kimberley, Lord Methuen was preparing to lead 13,000 men to the relief of the besieged diamond mining town.

During a single week in December, however, these three British offensives were each to suffer such serious rebuffs that the nation was finally shocked out of its lazy assumption that the war could be won quite easily.

In many ways, the prelude to what came to be known as Black Week had not gone badly from the British point of view. At first, Lord Methuen's drive towards Kimberley – where the diamond millionaire Cecil Rhodes fretted like a caged lion – went pretty well. On 20 November Methuen moved north from the Orange River station with a force of 8,000 men, which included the 9th Infantry Brigade and the Guards Brigade. He was in an aggressive mood and not inclined to skirt the main obstacles that lay in his path – some groups of hills at Belmont and Graspan, the river at the Modder River station, and a triangle of hills at Magersfontein. 'My good fellow,' the self-confident Methuen said to a fellow-officer who suggested a prudent detour round Belmont, 'I intend to put the fear of God into these people; and the only way is to fight them.'

What accounted for this excessive optimism? It seems that Methuen had convinced himself, by carefully considering the course of the recent battles of Talana and Elandslaagte, that direct, forceful attacks on Boer positions would be more fruitful than canny manoeuvres. Furthermore, he was anxious to get to grips with the enemy as soon as possible and to go on to relieve Kimberley. He therefore planned to push on along the railway line, repairing the sabotaged sections as he went.

Seventeen miles north of the Orange River the railway ran through Belmont station, where a group of hills, or kopjes, occupied by Boer forces blocked the way. Methuen planned a night march and a dawn attack on the enemy positions on Table Mountain, Gun Hill and Mont Blanc. The 9th Infantry Brigade was to clear Table Mountain while the Guards drove the Boers from Gun Hill. Once this was achieved, both brigades would sweep the enemy off Mont Blanc.

This perfectly coherent plan of action went badly wrong. The Guards were late in taking up their positions, having been held up while cutting their way through wire fences. By the time they were ready it was nearly light, and the element of surprise had vanished. The Boers on the hills began firing rapidly at their foes. The 1st Scots Guards and the 3rd Grenadiers nevertheless fixed bayonets and drove the Boers from Gun Hill. The Coldstreams meanwhile began attacking the wrong hills, to the south of Mont Blanc. Although the 2nd Battalion was recalled, the 1st Battalion pressed on. At the same time, the 9th Infantry Brigade was successfully storming Table Mountain.

Once the fighting got underway, Methuen let the shifting, disorganised conflict follow its own path, and was fortunate enough to see his infantry put the Boers to flight everywhere. After the battle he spoke to his men, praising them, and claiming that 'With troops like you no general can fear the result of his plans.'

In the aftermath of this encouraging encounter, the British troops rested at Belmont. On 24 November, however, they were on the move again, marching northwards towards Graspan sidings on the railway line. Methuen's scouts told him that a mere 500 Boers were on the Rooilaagte Hills near Graspan, but in fact by the time the British drew near there were 2,300 of the enemy, composed of General Prinsloo's defeated men from Belmont and a commando led by the austere, formidable and inspiring General Koos de la Rey. The Boers had three Krupp 75mm guns and two pom-poms.

The guns under Methuen's command began to bombard the enemy positions on the hills, but it was soon evident that this alone would not be enough to shift them. The general therefore sent the 9th Brigade and a naval detachment to capture the occupied eastern kopje, a hogback running from north to south and dominating the surrounding hills.

The sailors, marines, Northamptonshires, North Lancashires and the King's Own Yorkshire Light Infantry got to within 1,000 yards of the enemy before the Boers opened fire. Enemy bullets did terrible damage among the closely-packed ranks, and the officers, with their swords and glossy Sam Browne belts, were easily picked off.

The advance continued to within 200 yards of the kopje, when the survivors – by now about half of the original force – lay down to fix bayonets and quench their thirst. Refreshed and determined, they made their final charge, aided by men from the Northumberland Fusiliers from the north-east. The Boers broke and ran to their horses to escape. The British cavalry, exhausted by its reconnaissance work, was in no state to pursue them, and the Afrikaners were able to escape to the Modder River.

Regrouping at Modder River, the Boers held a council of war. Orange Free State forces, led by General Jacobus Prinsloo, were dispirited by their recent defeats and some made off home. But De la Rey argued that the Boers would do better if they took up defensive positions as low down as possible, from which they could fire upon their enemies with a flat trajectory. Thus, lying close to the plain, they could sweep their front for over a mile in range. De la Rey managed to convince his fellow-commanders, who now included Piet Cronje, that such a change in tactics would pay dividends. He argued that the Boers' smokeless powder would not give away their positions, and that they could expect to stop the British advance before the bayonet charge they so much feared. The Afrikaners prepared their ground admirably, making use of the south banks of the Riet and

Modder rivers for shelter, and even placing whitewashed posts and stones in front of them to act as markers and thus ensure even more accurate fire.

At 4 a.m. on 28 November, Lord Methuen's forces began the march to the Modder River station. The men were full of confidence and a beautiful day was breaking over the veld. As they drew near to the banks of the Riet and Modder they little suspected the ambush that awaited them. Methuen himself was firmly of the conviction that a mere 500 Boers blocked his path. He had, however, an inaccurate map that showed the Riet River running east to west, not south to north.

Having surveyed the river banks, Methuen then said decisively to General Colvile, 'They are not here.' Colvile replied, 'They are sitting uncommonly tight if they are, sir.' As if in response, the Boers suddenly opened fire. Men fell on all sides, and if they had been allowed to approach any closer the British would have been slaughtered wholesale. As it was, the Guards, on the right flank of the attack, were pinned down for hours under the scorching sun, unable to stir without inviting a hail of bullets.

On the left flank the 9th Brigade had better luck, and some of them drove Prinsloo's Free Staters over the Modder towards Rosmead village. Lord Methuen, however, was wounded at 4.15 p.m. while observing this sector of the battle area and took no further part in the engagement. Prior to this he had moved too freely along his front line, thus depriving his men of effective central control.

The 9th Brigade's success in crossing the Modder River also included the eventual capture of Rosmead village, but elsewhere there was little progress. The British artillery poured over 2,000 rounds into the Boers' positions, but little real damage was inflicted. General Colvile, who took over command from the wounded Methuen, toyed with the idea of a night attack on the Afrikaners, but eventually dropped the plan in view of the Guards' exhaustion after their gruelling day under the blazing sun.

Although the British hoped to exploit the uncertain situation the next day, they were doomed to disappointment for the Boers slipped away under cover of darkness. Methuen had won the crossing of the Modder, but at the cost of 70 dead and 413 wounded, or seven per cent of his force. He made the best of it by describing the battle as 'one of the hardest fights in the annals of the British Army'. Not all would have agreed with this description, and it was evident that more hard fighting would take place over the horizon where the Boers were digging trenches in front of the Magersfontein hills.

Before attempting to drive the Boers off the hills at Magersfontein, however, Lord Methuen gave his men, and himself, two weeks to recover from the battles of 23, 25 and 28 November. This period of rest, though perfectly sensible, gave the Afrikaners an invaluable period in which to prepare their defences – which consisted mainly of a line of trenches, camouflaged by thornbush branches and tufts of scrub, at the foot of Magersfontein Kop.

Even as the Boers were digging in at Magersfontein, the first British disaster of Black Week occurred at the battle of Stormberg on 10 December. The battle at Stormberg was fought to prevent Boer columns from striking into the potentially disloyal area of the northern Cape Colony and encouraging disaffection and rebellion. Crucially, Stormberg was also on the junction of the railway lines between Port Elizabeth, East London and the Orange Free State.

On 9 December 1899, the gaunt, energetic General Gatacre (known ruefully to his troops as 'General Backacher') ordered 3,000 men on to the train for Molteno, the nearest friendly station before Stormberg junction. There were about 2,300 Boers, led by General Olivier, defending the pass that led to Stormberg. Gatacre was a gung-ho, over-enthusiastic exponent of the night march and the dawn attack, perhaps cherishing the illusion that he could thus bring off a coup as spectacular as Garnet Wolseley's brilliant victory at Tel-el-Kabir during the 1882 invasion of Egypt. But on this occasion things went badly wrong.

Gatacre's men were up at 4 a.m. on 9 December, ready to take on the enemy. Due to bungled transport arrangements, however, the entire force did not reach Molteno until 8.30 in the evening. It was not until 9.15 p.m. that men of the Irish Rifles and the Northumberland Fusiliers moved out of Molteno towards Stormberg junction. Gatacre had decided that it was foolhardy to push on down the main pass, and instead planned to take the western end of a range of kopjes called the Kissieberg, from where he could dominate the route into Stormberg.

By some inexplicable oversight, however, the one guide who knew the terrain well had been left behind, and Gatacre had to rely on less skilful guides who were soon lost and, worse still, refused to admit it.

With bayonets fixed, the men stumbled on through the darkness. They had by now been without sleep for twenty-four hours and would soon have to fight a well-rested enemy. To make matters even worse, as dawn broke on 10 December the British forces were actually behind the Kissieberg and moving in the wrong direction, whereas Gatacre believed that they were in front of it and about to advance into the railway pass.

Afrikaner pickets watching from the eastern end of the Kissieberg suddenly saw the British forces beneath them. They gave the alarm and their comrades opened fire. Lacking clear orders, the British infantry hurled themselves heroically at the steep slopes of the hills and a few of them scrambled to the top of the range, where they were dispersed by misdirected fire from their own artillery.

In half an hour it was all over, and most of the battered and disorganised troops, fired on from two sides, were making an undignified retreat to Molteno. But 600 men of the Northumberland Fusiliers had received no orders to withdraw and were left behind on the Kissieberg. Most of these were forced to surrender to the Boers, which meant that, together with the ninety-odd battle casualties, the British lost nearly 700 troops at Stormberg and despite this the railway junction remained in enemy hands. So inexplicable did this reverse seem to the authorities in London, that when the news of the disaster was published on 11 December it was asserted that Gatacre had been led into an ambush by treacherous guides.

On the same day that Gatacre's drive on Stormberg disintegrated, Lord Methuen was preparing to march on Kimberley, where an irate and jumpy Cecil Rhodes was at odds with the garrison commander, Colonel Kekewich, and inveighing against military men in general. Between Methuen and Kimberley lay the Magersfontein hills, dominated on the right by Magersfontein Kop itself, upon whose slopes the Boers were entrenched. Methuen decided that the best way to carry Magersfontein Kop, and thus to open the way to Kimberley, was by an artillery bombardment followed by a dawn assault headed by the redoubtable Highland Brigade.

Methuen's guns opened fire on Magersfontein on Sunday 10 December. The hill rocked under its one and a half hour's pounding, and it seemed certain to British observers that the Boer entrenchments must be shattered and the enemy dispersed. But ironically the vast bulk of General Piet Cronje's force of 8,500 men were not on

Magersfontein Kop at all. They were concealed in a long line of narrow trenches running along the foot of Magersfontein and almost to the Modder River twelve miles away. The decision to forsake the traditional protection of the hills had been taken against Cronje's advice when the Orange Free State's President Marthinus Steyn had backed General Koos de la Rey's plan to entrench an extended position on the plain at the base of Magersfontein.

As a result of this tactical innovation the British forces walked straight into a devastating ambush. In the early hours of 11 December the Highland Brigade, composed of the Seaforths, the Gordons, the Argylls, the Black Watch and the Highland Light Infantry, moved off towards Magersfontein. Despite a violent storm overhead, and tacky going underfoot, the Highlanders had got to within half a mile of Magersfontein by 4 a.m. Their commander, Major General Andy Wauchope ordered them to extend their line prior to the assault. But as the 4,000 men began to spread out, a murderous fusillade from the Boer trenches cut them to pieces. Within seconds hundreds were killed or wounded, and General Wauchope lay dead. Amazingly about a hundred Highlanders pressed on, broke through the trenches, and began climbing Magersfontein. But by an extraordinary coincidence Piet Cronje and six of his adjutants, who were lost, wandered into their path and blazed away at them until reinforcements sealed the gap in the Boer entrenchments.

As the sun rose, the Afrikaners saw hundreds of the Highland Brigade lying face downwards on the sandy plain not daring to move. Despite a suicidal attempt by some men to rush the enemy's trenches, and a defiant, fitful skirl or two of the bagpipes, the majority of the survivors sweated it out in the scorching heat until at about 1.30 p.m. their morale understandably crumbled and they rose and escaped as best they could. Night fell with hundreds of wounded still lying unattended before the trenches.

General Methuen decided on the next day, 12 December, to order a general withdrawal, after an armistice had allowed both sides to deal with their wounded and dead. The Boers, as so often in this war, were disinclined or unable mercilessly to harry the retreating British troops. By 4 p.m. the shattered force was back at its camp on the Modder River. Their losses were 210 killed and 738 wounded. Among the dead were Major General Wauchope, and Britain's premier Marquess, Major Lord Winchester. The leading companies of the Highland Brigade lost sixty per cent of their officers. In painful and humiliating contrast, the Afrikaners suffered comparatively trifling losses with 87 killed and 188 wounded. Methuen's devastating bombardment of Magersfontein Kop had merely wounded three of the enemy.

Heavy criticism can be directed at Methuen for his generalship at Magersfontein. He set too much store on night marches and dawn attacks that were risky and apt to exhaust the troops. He had no knowledge of the real Boer positions and too few cavalry to reconnoitre properly. It is also arguable that he withdrew too soon, since his other brigades, including the Guards, were hardly thrown into the battle and might even have turned the Afrikaner flank.

Even as the defeated Methuen fell back towards the Modder River, the British Commander-in-Chief in South Africa, General Sir Redvers Buller, with an army of 18,000 was setting out to dislodge 8,000 men under General Louis Botha from Colenso, where the railway and road to Ladysmith crossed the Tugela River. The Boers were understandably apprehensive about the coming battle, not merely because they were heavily outnumbered but also because of Buller's martial reputation. They need not have worried. Botha was a commander of supreme gifts, and Buller was about to reveal his inadequacies for all to see.

At the besieged town of Ladysmith, Sir George White, the garrison's commander, was expecting to coordinate with Buller's attack on Colenso by dispatching a sizeable field force against his Afrikaner besiegers. Unfortunately Buller failed to inform him of the date of his own attack and the first that White knew of it was the rumble of guns across the Tugela. For two days Buller's artillery pounded Botha's positions. But the Boers gave nothing away; indeed, they did not budge, and their exact whereabouts remained a mystery to the British.

Buller's men moved towards the Tugela at dawn on 15 December. At the front Colonel Long forged ahead with twelve field pieces and six naval guns under his command. But within 200 yards of the river the concealed Boers poured a withering fire into the field-piece batteries. In under an hour hundreds of them had fallen, including the foolhardy Long, who shouted, though seriously wounded, 'Abandon be damned! We never abandon guns!' But the twelve field pieces could be defended no longer, and they were left useless and marooned on the banks of the Tugela.

On the left flank, meanwhile, Major General Hart muffed an attack with his Irish Brigade. A firm believer in strict discipline and close, parade-ground order, Hart rashly led his unfortunate troops into the northern loop of the river where Botha's men were presented with a glorious target. The Irish Brigade was soon pinned down. British fortunes were no better on the right flank where detachments of the Mounted Brigade made an unsuccessful attack on Hlangwane, a hill that dominated Colenso to the east.

Buller, who had sat impassively watching these abortive assaults, munching some sandwiches, at last decided to withdraw. Dismayed that he had lost so many of his guns, he ordered a desperate rescue attempt which in fact succeeded in dragging two of the field-pieces clear, though at the cost of several lives. Among those mortally wounded was Captain the Honourable F.H.S. Roberts, only son of Field Marshal Lord Roberts of Kandahar. By a painful irony, Buller's indecisive tactics at Colenso not only contributed indirectly to Captain Robert's death but also to the home government's decision to replace him as Commander-in-Chief in South Africa with the bereaved Lord Roberts.

Captain Roberts was not the only casualty at Colenso. The British lost 143 killed and 1,002 wounded. Botha's men lost a mere seven killed and twenty-two wounded, a result of their well-entrenched positions and also of the smokeless powder used to fire their Mauser rifles which made their location difficult to assess.

Black Week stunned the British public. There was a confused, partly troubled partly defiant response. On the one hand, patriots thumped the imperial drum with renewed, even hysterical vigour; on the other, a mounting volume of criticism was directed against the conduct of the war, and even against the justice of the British cause.

In January 1900 Arthur Balfour, the First Lord of the Treasury and in effect deputy Prime Minister, expressed his private opinions in a letter to his brother-in-law, the philosopher Henry Sidgwick: 'I not only think blunders have been committed, but I think they have been of the most serious kind, imperilling the whole progress of the war ... The chief blunders have been made ... by our Generals in the field.' *Punch* magazine tried to extract some wry humour from the enforced immobility of the British forces when it announced, 'Nigger News from Transvaal: De British hab got alongside o' Modder. But they habn't got no Farder.'

Back at the front, Private Thomas Atkins, who was supposed to be 'wiping something off a slate', had little to laugh at. Earl de la Warr, on active service in South Africa, thought that the common soldier's lot in the campaign was a far from happy one:

> Modder River, South Africa, December 25th. The battles in this campaign do not consist of a few hours' fighting, then a grand charge, resulting in the rout of the enemy, when men can see the effect of their work. No; this is very different. Think of it, a two-mile march under the fire of an invisible foe, then perhaps eight or ten hours' crouching behind any available cover – an ant hill or a scrubby bush – when the slightest movement on a man's part at once enables the hidden enemy to put him out of action, whereas he never has a chance of retaliating. Certainly this is fighting in circumstances which require extraordinarily good nerve and courage. And when the day is over 'Tommy' has not even the satisfaction of knowing what he has accomplished. When the day comes which will give him an opportunity of getting at close quarters with the Boer, he will remember the long and weary hours he has spent facing the enemy's trenches.[1]

Robust British patriots were mostly either unaware of this sober, chastened mood, or disinclined to take serious note of it. Instead they preferred to revel in the mawkish sentiment surrounding the story of the fourteen-year-old bugler, John Dunne, who had lost his bugle in the Tugela at the battle of Colenso. Queen Victoria gave the youngster a new bugle at Osborne, and the incident was preserved for a more cynical posterity in a popular verse:

> What shall we give, my little Bugelar,
> What for the bugle you lost at Tugelar?
> Give me another! that I may go
> To the front and return them blow for blow.

In Ladysmith, Dr Kay wrote on 12 December:

> There was heavy firing Colenso way; it turns out Buller was repulsed and lost ten guns. Very serious for us, as no one knows when we shall be relieved. No one believes in our generals. If what the Russians said about our army in the Crimea was true, we are an army of lions led by asses.[2]

Aboard the SS *Induna* sailing from Lourenço Marques in Mozambique for Durban, Winston Churchill, having recently and controversially escaped from his Boer captors, pondered over the implications of Black Week. The defeats of Stormberg and Magersfontein had stiffened his resolve to escape, for he did not fancy the lengthy imprisonment implied by these Boer victories. So, aboard the *Induna*, Churchill composed a stirring cable for his paper the *Morning Post*, in which he argued that Britain could only negotiate with the Boers after achieving victory. He concluded:

> The individual Boer, mounted, in a suitable country, is worth four or five regular soldiers. The power of modern rifles is so tremendous that frontal attacks must often be repulsed. The extraordinary mobility of the enemy protects his flanks. The only way of treating them is either to get men equal in character and intelligence as riflemen, or, failing the individual, huge masses of troops ... We should show no hurry, but we should collect huge masses of troops. It would be much cheaper in the end to send more than is necessary. There is plenty of work here for a quarter of a million men, and South Africa is well worth the cost in blood and money. Are the gentlemen of England all fox-hunting? Why not an English Light Horse? For the sake of our manhood, our devoted Colonists, and our dead soldiers, we must persevere with the war.[3]

Back in Britain, Arthur Balfour was one senior member of the government who had already formed a low opinion of Buller, telling his relation Violet Cecil on 19 December 1899 that

> ... the case against him [Buller] could be made so strong that it is hard to justify retaining him in command even of a portion of our Army. He seems quite capable of forming a good plan, but quite incapable of sticking to it ... I think this is a most melancholy story and I can only account for it by the theory that for the last ten years Buller has allowed himself to go downhill, and, for the moment at least, is not the man he once was.[4]

Queen Victoria, very old and almost blind, struggled to read the newspapers by candlelight during Black Week, and one morning misread defeat for victory. Her high spirits at breakfast were promptly dampened by her youngest child, Princess Beatrice, who told her the unpalatable truth. After a pause, the old Queen said, 'Now perhaps they will take my advice, and send out Lord Roberts and Lord Kitchener, as I urged them to do from the first.' When Balfour visited Windsor Castle at this time, Victoria was determined to uphold national morale, and told him plainly, 'Please understand that there is no one depressed in this house; we are not interested in the possibilities of defeat; they do not exist.'

It is clear that the old Queen was determined to be of use to her people during these dark days. Though eighty years old, she undertook a strenuous round of military reviews and hospital visiting. She also sent off parcels of knitting to her 'dear brave soldiers'; when these gifts were appropriated instead by her dear brave officers, she had 100,000 tins of chocolates sent to the men. She was doubtless gratified to hear subsequently that one of these tins had stopped a Boer bullet!

The government now moved swiftly to address the rapidly deteriorating situation. Acting in concert with, though not in response to, the Queen's breakfast-time advice, it was decided in December 1899 to remove Buller from his command and to replace him with Field Marshal Roberts, supported by General Kitchener.

Lord Roberts, the new Commander-in-Chief in South Africa, was widely popular, indeed something of a national hero. He had won the VC during the 1857–8 Indian Mutiny, and further distinction during the Afghan War of 1879–80. A teetotaller, a firm believer in the need for a form of national service, of diminutive stature but charismatic, Lord Roberts of Kandahar was affectionately known to the Victorian public as the 'Bobs' of Rudyard Kipling's poem:

> There's a little red-faced man,
> > Which is Bobs,
> Rides the tallest 'orse 'e can –
> > *Our* Bobs.
> If it bucks or kicks or rears,
> 'E can sit for twenty years
> With a smile round both 'is ears –
> > Can't yer, Bobs?[5]

Lord Kitchener of Khartoum, the victor of the 1898 battle of Omdurman, reserved, complicated and ruthless, went as Roberts's second in command. Roberts was enthusiastic about having Kitchener serving under him. They were certainly an impressive team, and Roberts dismissed doubts as to his own physical vigour and age (he was sixty-seven) with the words 'for years I have led a most active and abstemious life, waiting for this day'.

Roberts's appointment was rendered almost agonisingly poignant by the heroic death of his only son at the lost battle of Colenso. But the man whose blunders had been chiefly responsible for the Colenso defeat, Sir Redvers Buller, was still in command in South Africa, waiting for Roberts's arrival. Before he could be superseded, Buller (now cruelly nicknamed 'Sir Reverse' and the 'Ferryman of the Tugela') led his men in another drive to relieve Ladysmith.

8

Humiliation

GENERAL BULLER WAS of course aware that he would soon be released of the burden of the overall command of British forces in South Africa, or, more bluntly, that he had been sacked. However, he was still commander in northern Natal and anxious to do something to make amends. In what seems like an act of propitiation, he undertook three further attempts to relieve Ladysmith. The fates, or rather his own shortcomings, denied him the victories he so desperately desired. Two of these offensives, unfortunately for him and Britain, led to the battles of Spion Kop and Vaal Krantz; in the event, just two more disasters to be added to the list of the wretched man's blunders.

The most dramatic and humiliating of these encounters, the battle of Spion Kop, was fought on 24 January 1900. It was far from being the New Year's gift that the Empire wanted at the opening of the twentieth century – the century that was to witness its eventual decline and disintegration. Indeed, Spion Kop ranks as possibly the sharpest defeat of the war, and made such an impact on opinion at home that football grounds from Liverpool to Northampton named their high terraced ends 'the Kop' or 'Spion Kop'.

Buller's preparations for the battle were characteristically thorough. He was not the man to fight on an empty stomach, and he ensured that his troops should likewise not do so. Nor did he believe in the heroic exertions of 'thin red lines' of ill-equipped men. As a consequence, he built up substantial forces with which to campaign, and guaranteed them ample supplies and creature comforts.

From early January Buller had 30,000 men under his command in northern Natal, with the addition of a new division under General Sir Charles Warren. On 16 January 1900 he set off with 24,000 infantry, 2,500 mounted troops, eight field batteries and ten naval guns, planning to cross the Tugela at Trichardt's Drift and 'gain the open plain north of Spion Kop'. To do this he proposed to send Warren's division on a sweeping left flanking movement round the Rangeworthy Hills then on eastwards to the town of Dewdrop where it would link up with General Lyttelton's brigade forging up from the south over Potgieter's Drift. The Boer's hill entrenchments would thus have been turned, and the combined columns could press on to Ladysmith fifteen miles away.

The advance began well. The Tugela was efficiently bridged and the troops and their bountiful supplies taken across in excellent order. Lord Dundonald's cavalry moved in a great leftwards arc towards Acton Homes on the road to Ladysmith. To their rear, General Warren found the route too difficult for his wagons. He therefore halted at Fairview at the foot of the Rangeworthy Hills. Calling back Dundonald's cavalry, he now proposed to dislodge the Boers by a direct attack on the hills. Surveying the terrain he decided to occupy the highest peak on the ridge – Spion Kop. From this vantage point he could then enfilade the Afrikaner trenches and dominate the Fairview-Rosalie road to Ladysmith.

After obtaining grudging approval from Buller for his assault on Spion Kop, General Warren divided his force into a 'left attack' and a 'right attack'. The latter group, under Major General Coke, was chosen to seize Spion Kop, though Lieutenant Colonel Thorneycroft, who had sketched out the landmarks on the route up the mountain, acted as guide. The assault column set off before midnight and grappled in the mist with the steep, rock-strewn slope of Spion Kop, fearing detection at any moment. But in fact the men managed to attain the summit before a Boer picket challenged them. Even so the troops were able to dislodge the seventy or so Afrikaners with a brisk bayonet charge, and at 4 a.m. on 24 January Spion Kop was in British hands.

The troops dug themselves in for three hours, while the mist hung over the summit. But the rock strewn, hard ground prevented the construction of anything more than a dangerously shallow entrenchment with a parapet. Then, at about 7 a.m., the mist began to lift, revealing the true situation. The British had won only part of the summit. Worse still, their entrenchments were pitifully exposed to enemy fire from all directions; field guns, pom-poms and rifles could be directed at the British positions.

Within an hour the Lancashire Fusiliers, the Scottish Rifles and General Thorneycroft's mounted infantry were being systematically shot to pieces. The Lancashire Fusiliers were caught in a terrible enfilading fire from the Twin Peaks to the east, and soon their shallow trench was piled high with bodies. Before long the surviving Lancashires were waving white handkerchiefs or trying to slip off down the hill. The redoubtable Thorneycroft, reinforced by men of the Middlesex Regiment and the Imperial Light Infantry, managed, however, to retrieve the situation on the summit and, with further assistance from the Scottish Rifles, held the hilltop for the rest of the day.

Potentially bad as the British position on Spion Kop seemed to be, it was made worse by Buller's generalship. There was great confusion as to who was in command at the summit: General Woodgate, the brigade commander, was severely wounded, and Buller at last told General Warren to put Thorneycroft in charge; but Major General Coke, the officer commanding the 'right attack', and Lieutenant Colonel Hill of the Middlesex Regiment, were mysteriously not informed of this crucial decision. More serious still was Buller's reaction to the success of General Lyttelton's brigade, which had crossed the Tugela at Potgieter's Drift and then stormed the Twin Peaks, east of Spion Kop and the source of some of the most destructive enfilading fire. Lyttelton's triumph on the Twin Peaks was not in accordance with Buller's overall plan and at sunset the troops were recalled. A real chance of averting defeat was thus, almost perversely, cast away.

As night fell Thorneycroft was still holding on to the summit. But when the young war correspondent Winston Churchill managed to reach him in the darkness with messages from Warren, he found that the summit commander had decided to withdraw. Churchill was shocked at the sight of the exhausted, wounded and dead troops on Spion Kop, and appreciated Thorneycroft's conviction that he had been sacrificed to the incompetence of his superiors who had allowed thousands of fresh troops to stand idly by while he and his men had struggled for survival.

Even as Thorneycroft's men were staggering down from the summit, the Boers were similarly drifting away from Spion Kop. An earlier assault on the British position by nearly 900 of the enemy had been beaten back; and Lyttelton's temporary occupation of the Twin Peaks was an ominous challenge. At about 2 a.m., however, the tireless efforts of Louis Botha halted the Boer dispersal. As the Afrikaners reluctantly returned to the foot of Spion Kop some of them saw in the breaking dawn two men on the summit waving their hats in triumph. They had scaled the hill and found it deserted.

At Spion Kop the British had withdrawn first, thus handing victory to their opponents. Buller had insisted on a complete retreat across the Tugela, which he supervised with his characteristic care. But he had lost 1,750 men killed, wounded and captured on Spion Kop, while the Boers had lost a mere 300. Moreover, Ladysmith was not relieved.

The British were defeated at Spion Kop partly because both Buller and Warren stuck to plans which Dundonald's cavalry dash towards Acton Homes and Lyttelton's occupation of the Twin Peaks ought to have been allowed to amend. There was also appalling lack of communication between the senior officers involved, and the British, once Thorneycroft had accepted defeat, did not have anyone of the calibre of Botha to rally their men for one last effort.

The news of the 'sickening fiasco', as Joseph Chamberlain called the defeat at Spion Kop, struck Britain like a thunderbolt. Accusations of muddle and incompetence multiplied. The radical, rising star of the Liberal Opposition, the eloquent Welsh member of parliament David Lloyd George and countless other 'pro-Boers' redoubled their criticisms of the war, and the great powers of Europe, now regularly indulging in understandable bouts of *schadenfreude*, took further delight in British discomfiture.

Even before the disaster of Spion Kop, the embarrassingly poor showing of the British armed forces had provoked recrimination and fostered discontent. Arthur Bigge, Queen Victoria's Principal Private Secretary, had written to the influential First Lord of the Treasury, Arthur Balfour, on 2 January 1900:

No-one has ever laid down what is expected of our army – until this is done we shall never have a satisfactory organised force. If only someone in authority could have realised that we might be called upon to conduct a campaign against 45,000 Boers fully armed and equipped, and we had organised accordingly – not forgetting India, our other colonies and Home Defence – we might have been better prepared. However I see that you think everything has now been supplied to Generals but brains! In these I imagine the Primate is arranging a special day of intercession![1]

In Ladysmith Dr Kay wrote on 27 January:

Headquarters received very bad news from Buller yesterday but wouldn't let it out. Today's *Orders* state that last Wednesday [24 January], after shelling the Boers for a whole week, General Warren took the Boer position at Spion Kop, fourteen miles from here, but the Boers made a night attack and re-took it, and of course there's the usual remark, 'The Boer losses were very heavy'. We all expected bad news and now we have it with a vengeance. Everyone is very down and depressed.[2]

In the aftermath of the battle of Spion Kop there was a two-week lull in the campaign in northern Natal. Many Boers retired to their laagers around Ladysmith, or went home to rest and to see their families. Among their high command there was a good deal of skirmishing as to who should take charge of the forces besieging Ladysmith: President Kruger did not want Prinsloo, the nominee of the Orange Free State's President Steyn; the Transvaaler General Piet Joubert did not want the position, which was eventually given to Louis Botha.

Now even more anxious to secure a success of some sort, Buller made plans for a third offensive to clear the path to Ladysmith. The plans were complicated, though well considered, but unfortunately, and predictably, their execution was marred by Buller's vacillation and lack of confidence.

His troops moved off on 5 February, committed to driving the enemy from a group of hills some six miles to the east of Spion Kop. The Tugela would have to be crossed and then an assault mounted on Vaal Krantz, Green Hill and Doorn Kop, which guarded the eastern route to Ladysmith. Buller proposed to bluff the Boers by a diversionary attack to the west of Vaal Krantz via a specially constructed pontoon bridge. The real attack was to go in further east, again over a pontoon bridge.

The opening stages of the operation were reasonably successful. The diversionary advance westwards began well, but unfortunately more field batteries than planned went over the western pontoon. Some of these batteries were needed for the genuine eastern push, so three vital hours were lost while the missing batteries were retrieved. The Royal Engineers worked heroically at the pontoon bridges, completing the eastern one in fifty minutes though under persistent rifle and maxim gunfire. The artillery had meanwhile subjected the Boer positions to a heavy bombardment.

The scene was now set for a successful climax to the operation. The Durham Light Infantry and the Rifle Brigade crossed the eastern pontoon bridge and, though coming under heavy fire, made straight for their objectives. The Durhams moved rapidly through mealie fields towards the foot of Vaal Krantz, while the Rifle Brigade cleared the enemy from their position at Munger's Farm.

With sickening inevitability, Buller's nerve gave way at this point. Fire from Green Hill and Doorn Kop to the east was disconcertingly heavy, and he decided to break off the attack and forbade the 60th Foot and the Scottish Rifles to go to the support of General Lyttelton and the troops approaching Vaal Krantz. The enraged and astounded Lyttelton pointed out that his men were already committed to the attack, and reluctantly Buller allowed the 60th and the Scottish Rifles to cross the pontoon bridge. He still kept back the forces that were meant to take Green Hill, however, as well as the cavalry.

Lyttelton's infantry pressed on, and eventually took the southernmost hill of the Vaal Krantz ridge – which was all that Buller authorised them to do. Despite inconvenient enfilading fire, the men managed to shelter behind loose rocks and thus avoided heavy casualties. Night fell with the main attack aborted by Buller's indecision.

The despairing Buller sent a telegram to his newly-arrived Commander-in-Chief Lord Roberts, who was about to strike across the Modder River and relieve Kimberley. Roberts had not wanted Buller to launch his third attack across the Tugela, since he believed that his own advance through the Free State would ease the pressure in northern Natal. But now that Buller had committed himself to a fresh offensive, he saw no convincing reason why the operation should be called off. Thus, in reply to Buller's query as to whether he should persevere, Roberts stated that in his opinion the attack should go forward, and that the troops' morale should be boosted by the message that if they relieved Ladysmith they would also strike a great blow for the honour of the Empire.

Despite Roberts's advice, Buller dithered in a crisis of self-confidence. But on 8 February he made up his mind to withdraw – something, at least, that he always did with considerable finesse and good sense. He fell back, through Springfield, to Chievely, the base from which he had started out a month before. There he began to plan yet another offensive, but was unable to achieve his long-awaited breakthrough until 27 February.

Although he had as usual managed to keep his troops' morale reasonably high through good feeding and care, Buller prompted the war correspondent J.B. Atkins to write after the battle of Vaal Krantz, 'The fault of this and all other battles, was the cumbrous nature of our transport. How should it be otherwise than that jam and pickles should be at a disadvantage against biltong?' But in Ladysmith there was little enough jam and pickles; indeed food supplies were almost exhausted, and 'waiting for Buller' had become a hungry, macabre and frustrating game. The privations of Ladysmith were, however, soon to be ended, as were those of Kimberley. The relief of Mafeking would take a little longer.

9

'I thank God we have kept the flag flying'

THE BESIEGED TOWNS OF LADYSMITH,
KIMBERLEY AND MAFEKING

THE SIEGES OF these three towns became symbolic of the dilemma of British arms in South Africa. While they remained under threat, the prospect of beating the Boers and rapidly realising the aims of the war seemed remote. Worse still, the sieges were humiliating and painful spectacles, military failures relished by what seemed to be the legions of foreign and domestic critics of Britain's aggression in South Africa. The sieges also provided excellent daily copy for the rapidly expanding popular press back in the United Kingdom. This meant that even if the British government had wished to divert the nation's attention from the sieges they were powerless to do so, short of muzzling the press.

The siege of Ladysmith lasted from October 1899 to the end of February 1900 – 118 days in all. The Boers encircled the town within a six mile radius, mostly from hill positions like Pepworth, Gun Hill, Long Hill, Lombard's Kop, Middle Hill, Umbulwana, Rifleman's Ridge, Lancer's Hill, Telegraph Ridge and Tchrengula. The British manned a smaller defensive ring within the Boer circle, taking up positions on Observation Hill, Tunnel Hill, Rifleman's Post and Bester's Ridge. General White placed his headquarters upon Convent Hill, from which central site he could oversee the town's defences.

The Boer tactics were self-evident and quite straightforward. They planned to starve and bombard Ladysmith into surrender, while keeping the inept Buller at bay along the Tugela. The Afrikaner forces made only one major attempt actually to break through the British defensive circle by an assault on Bester's Ridge on 6 January 1900.

For the British defenders – the soldiers, some 10,000 of them – and the white civilians of Ladysmith, the siege required greater reserves of patience than deeds of heroic self-sacrifice. Eyewitness accounts of it are particularly revealing and interesting. For example, Colonel R.W. Mapleton was the Principal Medical Officer in charge of the Ladysmith hospital, and was later allowed by the Boers to set up a neutral camp at Intombi (some four miles south-east of the town) where the wounded and non-combatants could take refuge. He wrote, in a number of letters:

> We are besieged by a large force of Boers, and although we have 10,000 men here we can't get out and so are waiting until we are relieved. We had about three very hot days in Ladysmith as the Boers shelled the town and the shells were screaming and bursting all over the place and considering the number of shells very few people were hit though there were many narrow escapes. I had no particular near-shave myself but one lump of shell about six by four inches fell pretty close to me and nearer to where I had passed ... We are close to the enemy position and can see them with the naked eye. I think we are all glad to get out of here for the shell-fire was too hot to be pleasant and someone must have been hit if we had stayed where we were.
>
> I have seen some of the Boers for as I am in charge of the hospital out here, I have several times met the Boers under a flag of truce to discuss sundry matters. Those I have seen have all been very pleasant fellows indeed and very friendly. They have behaved extremely well to our wounded prisoners, attending to them and giving them everything they had themselves. All our wounded speak highly of the kindness they have received at their hands ...
>
> The bullet the Boers use is an extraordinary missile: it is about one and a quarter inches long and as thin as a lead pencil. It incapacitates a man but it does not kill him like the old Martini and other bullets. I have seen men shot through the brain, matter oozing out of the hole in the skull and yet the man recovered very shortly too. Men shot through the lungs have very little trouble from the wounds. If it catches a hard bone it at times smashes it, but generally drills a hole right through it. The shell wounds are of course ghastly to a degree ...

The shops are all shut in Ladysmith, and some of the civil population have been cleared out into this camp which is a very big one ... We get lots to eat though I dare say you would turn up your snout at it, for the quality though all right for camp is not what one would select for choice, still besieged people have to be thankful for what they can get. The water is like pea soup but we boil it and filter it.

A good deal of big gun firing goes on all day, and now and again the Boers let off all their guns into the town at midnight – no one knows why. They have knocked down a lot of houses in Ladysmith but have done comparatively little damage. Two of our officers were sitting side by side having lunch at the hotel; a shell burst just outside the house, and a big lump of it came through the window and actually went between them as they sat, and hurt no one. Pretty close shave that! One shell came into our camp, but did not burst, but rolled through the camp and through a tent and hurt no one. Many shells have burst close to people and not hurt them. One burst in a room in which were thirteen people, and no one was hurt. Of course there is a reverse side of the picture.

I get about fifty-five sick a day into this hospital, and I am now in charge of no less than 1,270 sick and wounded, including sixty-five officers. I have a very insufficient staff of both officers and men to do the enormous amount of work: about 500 cases of enteric fever, 180 of dysentery and 150 wounded.[1]

Another excellent insight into the conditions in Ladysmith can be derived from the letters of Dr Alec Kay. Becoming increasingly disillusioned with the game of 'Waiting for Buller', Dr Kay wrote savagely of Britain's 'phantom army'. His morale was doubtless boosted by being allowed a brief leave on Christmas Day 1899, when he left Intombi Camp for Ladysmith. He saw a room at the back of the Standard Bank at Ladysmith, which had been decorated 'very nicely and there were four Christmas trees labelled, "Canada", "Australia", "Britain" and "South Africa". At 7 p.m. all the children in Ladysmith were to be there – plenty of cakes, lemonade and other things for them. I trust they enjoyed themselves.'

On Boxing Day Dr Kay walked with some friends to the naval camp, an outing which he recorded in a letter to his wife, Alice:

From there we walked slowly up to the naval camp. The Boers had not fired a shot all day. Just as we got there their guns began plugging away and put in shell after shell as hard as they could, which riled everyone, thinking Christmas Day should be 'Peace on earth and goodwill towards all men'. I am very glad that they did so, as it shows what swine they are. And yet that very morning the gun on Bulwana fired two shots, the shells pitching in the town without exploding. When dug up, they were found to be stuffed with rough plum pudding and outside on the shell was painted 'A Merry Christmas'. Which forced many to say or think, 'There is some humour and some good in the Boers after all'. One of these shells was bought by a curio hunter for £15. The subsequent shelling dispelled these favourable thoughts about them and made some of us very savage.

When we got to the mess tent I had a long whisky and soda – the first one for ages; I shall never forget that drink, it was over too soon.

At about seven o'clock Captain Lampton came in and we prepared for dinner. Am glad sailors are superstitious, as thirteen were going to sit down, so they sent for a petty officer who came in to make it fourteen.

We had excellent soup, turkey, sucking pig and plum pudding – a real good one both for quality and size. Sherry, champagne-and-stout (black velvet) and whisky and soda ad lib. A toast to Her Most Gracious Majesty the Queen, which we most enthusiastically drank. Then someone, riled by the Boer shelling that day, proposed, 'To Hell with the Boers!' which we drank with enthusiasm and laughter, considering the surroundings. It was the most enjoyable and successful dinner it was possible to have.

After dinner a lot of the 19th Hussars came in, and officers of other regiments, and a lively time it was.

I thoroughly enjoyed myself, and was very sorry to return at 5.15 a.m. to Intombi Camp.[2]

But after the Christmas festivities, which were evidently reasonably lavish, the grim realities of the siege reasserted. The 'music of the guns' accompanied the worsening of conditions within Ladysmith and its environs:

27 December
There was a false alarm that the Boers were attacking the town, but our men did not fire. We could see the flashes of the rifles and a line of fire to the right.

Every now and then we are cheered up with the news 'Buller is certain to be here on such and such a day', but it is one disappointment after another.

They say 'Everything comes to he who waits' but oh, it is a very weary waiting, especially on an empty stomach.

I have just been told that there's a reliable runner leaving at any minute. So in haste and with lots of love to you all,

Your ever loving,

Alec[3]

On 21 February Dr Kay gave an account of the soaring prices of food and luxuries in the besieged town (in order to compare these prices with today's it is necessary to multiply them approximately tenfold!):

21 February

The prices of luxuries are astounding. I myself paid £5 for four tins of milk, £3 for a bottle of port, £7 for a bottle of whisky, and I am sure that if £20 had been offered no one who had it would have parted with it. I was ill at the time, and I believe that it meant life to me. A tin of condensed milk was always cheap at £1 and when I bought four tins I could easily have made a substantial profit had I waited to sell. Here is a list of prices published by Joe Dyson, an auctioneer in Ladysmith:

	£	s.	d.
14 lbs. Oatmeal	2	19	6
1 lb. beef fat		11	0
1 tin coffee		17	0
2 lb. tin of tongue	1	6	0
1 sucking pig	1	17	0
Eggs, per dozen	2	8	0
Fowls, each		18	6
4 small cucumbers		15	6
Green mealies, each		3	8
1 small plate of grapes	1	5	0
1 small plate of apples		12	6
1 plate of tomatoes		18	0
1 vegetable marrow		18	0
1 plate of potatoes		19	0
3 small bunches of carrots		9	0
1 glass jar jelly		18	0
1 lb. bottle of jam	1	11	0
1 lb. tin of marmalade	1	10	0
1 doz. boxes matches		13	6

	£	s.	d.
1 packet of cigarettes	1	5	0
50 cigars	9	5	0
¼ lb. cake 'Fair Maid' tobacco	2	5	0
½ lb. " " " "	3	5	0
1 lb. Sailors tobacco	2	3	0
¾ lb. tin 'Capstan' Navy tobacco	3	0	0

The Boer guns have been pounding us incessantly. Their shooting is remarkably good, superior to ours. Their Long Toms are six-inch Creusots and are heavier than our 4.7 naval guns which however have greater range and greater penetration. The ordinary Boer field guns are far superior to ours – greater range and higher velocity; but our gunners say they are much heavier, which naturally means they are less mobile and require more horses, but I am not sure they are right for I have myself seen the Boer pieces going across country with only six horses and at a good gallop – as fast as our artillery go with their guns and they are only twelve-pounders. Many of their gunners are French or German.

We frequently hold open-air concerts at Intombi. If the music is not first-class and the songs are not drawing-room, we none the less appreciate them.[4]

The defenders of Ladysmith had other discomforts. The heat, during the South African summer, was often intense, and on 17 February 1900 Dr Kay wrote, 'Heat lately has been awful, temperature in my tent 116 degrees [Fahrenheit] with an accurate thermometer.' There were scorpions and tarantulas; the bread was 'as hard as stones and with no more nutrition. It often produces violent pains and diarrhoea ... Matches are scarce and candles are unobtainable ... The amount of theft in Ladysmith and at Intombi is astounding.'

Sir George White was not completely supine during these long weeks. There were some ill-fated attempts to cooperate with Buller's sporadic relief operations, and an ineffective cavalry sortie took place. Two attacks were made on Boer gun positions during December 1899: the first attack destroyed a 4.7 howitzer and the 'Long Tom' on Gun Hill; the second succeeded in knocking out another 4.7 howitzer on Surprise Hill. These forays were, however, expensive: seventy-five British soldiers were killed or wounded, and the 'Long Tom' was repaired at Pretoria in three weeks and was dispatched to the siege of Kimberley.

On 6 January 1900 the Boers made their one full-scale attempt to break through the British defences when they attacked Bester's Ridge (or the Platrand); there were three hills comprising this ridge – Wagon Point to the west, Wagon Hill in the centre, and Caesar's Camp to the east. The Afrikaners planned to assault the ridge with 2,000 men, while 3,000 more would give support if necessary or make a diversionary attack against Observation Hill to the north of Ladysmith. The Transvaal commandos were to be led by the republic's Vice-President, Schalk Burgers, and the Free Staters by General de Villiers; the overall command was given to Piet Joubert, accompanied by his sharp-eyed wife who had proved herself an able tactician twenty years earlier at Majuba Hill.

For the British, the inspiring and courageous Colonel Ian Hamilton was in command of the 1,000 men defending Bester's Ridge. Though Caesar's Camp was well fortified, Wagon Hill had only two fortified posts. The Manchester Regiment was stationed at Caesar's Camp; the Imperial Light Horse, dismounted, together with the 60th, held Wagon Hill and Wagon Point; the Gordon Highlanders provided reinforcements, as did other units of dismounted cavalry.

The men defending Wagon Hill and Wagon Point were the first to be aware of the Boer approach. This was partly fortuitous, since units of infantry were guarding sappers who were preparing gun pits for two naval guns.

The advancing columns of Afrikaners were challenged at 2.45 a.m. by British troops, and the two sides began to blaze away in the darkness. In the confusion, the Gordons mistook the slouch-hatted Imperial Light Horse for the enemy and were on the point of shooting them down when they realised their mistake. Fierce hand-to-hand fighting took place, while the British officers tried to organise their lines of defence. Caesar's Camp was apparently secure, so Hamilton, awoken by the firing, sent a message calling for reinforcements to Sir George White, and then went off to Wagon Hill.

At Wagon Hill, the British were being hard pressed by units of Free Staters. As day broke, neither side could dislodge the other from their positions. Not long after midday, however, the Boers made a determined attempt to oust the British from the 4.7-inch gun emplacement on Wagon Point; happily, from their point of view, they caught a considerable number of troops literally napping. Many of the British troops stumbled, panic-stricken, down the hill, while

Hamilton and some of his officers and NCOs tried desperately to check the disorderly rout. Hamilton was ably supported by Lieutenant Digby Jones of the Royal Engineers and Trooper Albrecht of the cavalry; together they led a counter-charge which scattered the Boers and sent them scurrying from the summit. Both Digby Jones and Albrecht were killed in this action and were posthumously awarded the Victoria Cross.

The British commanders sent up more reinforcements, which were mostly composed of dismounted cavalrymen. But the hills were still occupied by the Boers. At 5.30 p.m. the Manchesters managed to drive the enemy from the edge of Caesar's Camp. Sir George White, however, also wanted Wagon Hill cleared by nightfall. Hamilton passed on this order to the Devonshires, confident that they would carry out their mission. The Devons promptly made a heroic bayonet charge at the enemy, cheering as they went and falling like nine pins; other units joined them. Half an hour later darkness fell, and the Boers slipped away – a good many of them drowning in the flooded Fouries Spruit.

The attack on Caesar's Camp and Wagon Hill had failed. There were 400 British casualties and some 200 Afrikaner losses. Both sides had displayed remarkable bravery as well as cowardice. White, preoccupied with the defence of Ladysmith, made haste to tell Buller that he could no longer cooperate in any further attempts to relieve the town. In Britain, the sixteen-hour struggle had raised fears that Ladysmith would fall, and the situation was viewed gloomily. Even by 7 January, when it was evident that the Boers had been repulsed, British opinion remained jittery, and there were some who now reconciled themselves to the inevitable surrender of the besieged town.

At Kimberley, 4,000 Boers hemmed in the 500 British troops and some 50,000 civilians. There were about 13,000 Europeans, 7,000 coloureds and 30,000 Africans. In one sense, Kimberley belonged to Cecil Rhodes and De Beers – his great diamond-mining company. Appropriately enough, Rhodes himself was in Kimberley and De Beers supplied 450 rifles to the defenders, as well as being able to manufacture ammunition in its workshops. The commanding officer was Colonel Kekewich; apart from his 500 regulars, 3,500 civilians were eventually enrolled in the Town Guard.

Kimberley's ordeal, compared with the sieges of Ladysmith and Mafeking, lacked some of the military melodrama of Buller's campaign in northern Natal, or the lengthy time-span of Mafeking's encirclement. The garrison was not idle, however, and made a number of sorties against the enemy. One of the most important of these expeditions took place the day before Lord Methuen fought the battle of Modder River on 28 November. Three columns left Kimberley, planning to attack the Boers on Carter's Ridge five miles west of the town. Though the British force did tolerably well, they failed to take the ridge and withdrew at nightfall, having sustained fifty-six casualties; nor were they able to break through and give first-hand assistance to Lord Methuen. The foray did, however, succeed in engaging part of the besieging force, just as the defence of Kimberley itself effectively pinned down 4,000 of the enemy who might otherwise have raised rebellion in the northern Cape Colony.

As it turned out, Kimberley was in no real danger of being taken by the Boers. There were no dominating, surrounding kopjes from which the Boers could bombard the town, though they did manage to situate some siege guns on the few low ridges nearby. Kimberley's mining economy also aided the defenders in a variety of ways: heaps of mining debris, sixty to seventy feet high, were used as perimeter strong points; an observation tower was built on top of a mine shaft's hauling gear, and, connected by telephone to the perimeter strong points, ensured that any enemy movements in the surrounding countryside would be quickly spotted; and De Beers lent powerful searchlights with which to survey the surroundings at night.

Nor did Kimberley suffer the acute food shortages of Ladysmith and Mafeking, though towards the end of the siege many civilians seem to have endured considerable hardship. Predictably, the Africans in the population were unlucky in the treatment they received; a large number of their babies and infants died from lack of milk, and scurvy also affected many African adults. For the defenders as a whole, especially the Europeans, it was fortunate that De Beers had a large stock of food and fuel. Colonel Kekewich also took the sensible step of issuing a proclamation fixing the price of basic commodities at the pre-siege figure. In addition, from time to time bands of Africans raided Boer herds, and thus supplemented the town's food supply.

At Kimberley the chief drama centred upon the increasingly histrionic clash between Cecil Rhodes and Colonel Kekewich.

Rhodes – ailing, restless, preoccupied and barely two years away from death – was not content to wait passively for Methuen, or even for Roberts and French; he was, moreover, bitterly critical of Kekewich's handling of the town's defences. As early as 16 October he sent a message to Milner in Cape Town, using the heliograph link from Kimberley to the next telegraph station, in which he said, 'Strain everything. Send immediate relief to Kimberley. I cannot understand the delay.' The next day Rhodes set the mirrors flashing again, while local wags speculated that he must be selling or buying shares; this time he sent a message via Lord Rothschild in London to the British Cabinet: 'Relief is perfectly possible, but the military authorities in Cape Town will do nothing.'

Lord Methuen's sharp rebuff at Magersfontein during Black Week had the effect of pulling Rhodes up short. Clearly the relief of Kimberley would be a longer business than he had imagined. Christmas came, and with it a message, carried by a runner, from Queen Victoria: 'I wish you and all my brave soldiers a happy Christmas. God protect and bless you all.'

The Boers began to bombard the town heavily – though inconsistently. In reply, the De Beers workshops built a big gun, with a 4.1 inch bore and able to fire a 28-pound shell. Affectionately and inevitably nicknamed 'Long Cecil', its shell cases stamped with the message 'With C.J.R.'s Comps.', the gun began to roar out its daily defiance at the besiegers. 'Long Cecil' was in action from the middle of January, when Colonel Kekewich reckoned that his ammunition, food supply and forage would last until 28 February.

On 7 February, however, with morale in Kimberley already low, provisions running out, and relief still some way off, the Boers began to shell the town with the 'Long Tom' that had been damaged at the siege of Ladysmith and subsequently repaired in Pretoria. The huge shells screeched into Kimberley's residential quarters, killing and maiming a good many civilians, including women and children. 'Long Tom' began to terrorise the town's defenders and desperate efforts were made to dig appropriate shelters. In an attempt to cut down casualties, Kekewich devised an early-warning system: a signaller on the observation tower waved a flag whenever he saw 'Long Tom's' puff of smoke four miles away, then buglers situated throughout the town sounded the alarm, and the townspeople had approximately fifteen seconds to take cover. Though this system lacked the efficiency of modern radar and early-warning techniques, it undoubtedly saved some lives.

This most recent hazard, however, was too much for Cecil Rhodes, especially with Lord Roberts's relief column inactive a few miles away on the Modder River. He let the mayor of Kimberley and Kekewich know that he would call a public meeting unless he was informed, within forty-eight hours, of the precise and definite plans to relieve the town. Kekewich was appalled at this ultimatum, believing that Rhodes would persuade the public meeting to surrender Kimberley to the Boers. Rhodes, indeed, spelled out his intentions to Kekewich by shouting: 'Before Kimberley surrenders I will take good care that the English people know what I think of all this.'

Kekewich at once informed Lords Roberts and Methuen of the situation by heliograph. Roberts replied, urging patience, and Kekewich, encouraged at having the new Commander-in-Chief so near at hand, heliographed back on 9 February 1900:

> Will do my best but fear will have great difficulty restraining Rhodes and others from precipitating matters. Rhodes informed me today he would call meeting in two days' time unless definite information column movements given him. Can forbid meeting but difficulty in preventing same his influence here so great. He is quite unreasonable. Shelling here severe and causing great alarm.[5]

In character, the impatient Rhodes kept up the pressure for a speedy relief. On 10 February the scanty Kimberley newspaper the *Diamond Fields Advertiser* carried a vehement article entitled 'Why Kimberley Cannot Wait', which was more or less unadulterated Rhodes:

> After the disturbing events of the last three days, we think it must have been brought home to Lord Roberts and to the whole world that, in the interests of humanity, the relief of this beleaguered city can no longer be delayed. How utterly the public and the authorities have failed to grasp the claim which Kimberley, by the heroic exertions of her citizens, has established upon the British Empire is only too apparent ... [from] the utter indifference with which our fate appears to be regarded by the military hierarchy. Yet what are the facts? We have stood a siege which is rapidly approaching the duration of the Siege of Paris; we have practically defended ourselves with citizen soldiers ... and through the genius of Mr Labram we have been able not merely to supply ammunition for the pop-

guns sent to Kimberley, but also to produce in our own workshops the only weapon capable of minimizing the terrible havoc and destruction caused by the enemy's six-inch gun ... Although the difficulties of getting news have been almost insuperable, we are fully aware there are at the present moment 120,000 British troops in South Africa ... Arrayed against this vast Army – the largest by far that England has ever got together since the Napoleonic wars – are the burghers of two small republics ... and why in the name of common sense should Kimberley wait? ... Military men may make maps at the War Office, and may chatter in Cape Town; they may continue to evolve the most wonderful schemes and plans to take the place of those which one by one they have had to abandon, but they cannot, save at the risk of jeopardizing the whole campaign, evade the task of relieving Kimberley. [Magersfontein] is said to be an impregnable position, but what of that? There is a way into Kimberley over perfectly flat country ... We have held our tongues for long, believing that relief was merely a question of days, or at most a week. We have now reached a situation when either a newspaper must speak out or it has no *raison d'être*, and should cease to exist. They shout to us 'Have patience'. Will they remember that we have fought alone and unaided for four long months? Will they remember that we are situated practically in the centre of a desert 600 miles from the coast? ... Is it unreasonable, when our women and children are being slaughtered, and our buildings fired, to expect something better than that a large British Army should remain inactive in the presence of eight or ten thousand peasant soldiers?[6]

Enraged at the way in which the article broke censorship and revealed military information, Kekewich ordered the editor's arrest. But Cecil Rhodes had prudently hidden the editor down a mine and Kekewich had to be content with closing down the newspaper. Kekewich was also determined that Rhodes should not call his threatened public meeting. Instead the latter held a smaller meeting with twelve of Kimberley's leading citizens, and then went to Kekewich and demanded that the statement drawn up by the meeting should immediately be sent to Roberts over the heliograph. Kekewich told Rhodes that the signallers were working under great pressure and could not send the message for some time. At this Rhodes flew into a violent rage and flung himself at Kekewich shouting 'You low, damned mean cur'. Not content with upbraiding the colonel in the tones of a G.A. Henty hero, Rhodes also tried to punch him in the face. Fortunately the mayor of Kimberley, who was present, intervened and prevented the two men from coming to blows. Rhodes then stormed off, with the mayor at his heels.

Rhodes's message was as follows:

> On behalf of the inhabitants of these towns, we respectfully desire to be informed whether there is any intention on your part to make an immediate effort for our relief. Your troops have been for more than two months within a distance of little over twenty miles from Kimberley ... Scurvy is rampant among the natives; children, owing to a lack of proper food, are dying in great numbers, and dysentery and typhoid are very prevalent. The chief food of the whites have been bread and horsemeat for a long time past ... a six-inch gun is daily causing death among the population ... It is absolutely essential that immediate relief should be afforded to this place.[7]

Kekewich duly flashed an abbreviated version of this message to Lord Roberts on the Modder River. Within an hour Roberts had sent his reply, telling Kekewich to arrest anyone, no matter how illustrious, if they were a danger to security. Roberts at the same time sent encouraging words to Rhodes and his fellow leading citizens:

> I beg you to represent to the Mayor and Rhodes as strongly as you possibly can disastrous and humiliating effect of surrendering after so prolonged and glorious defence. Many days cannot possibly pass before Kimberley will be relieved, as we commence active operations tomorrow. Our further military operations depend in a large degree on your maintaining your position a very short time longer.[8]

All of Kimberley soon knew that the relief force would start operations the next day, 11 February 1900. Rhodes was partly placated, though he drafted a strongly worded reply to Roberts, which ended, 'It is high time you did something.' Colonel Kekewich refused to relay this message, which he considered to be offensive, and Rhodes subsequently sent a milder though still forceful one.

Determined to defend his reputation, Kekewich wrote to Roberts trying to explain why Rhodes and he had clashed so dramatically: 'Rhodes during the siege has done excellent work. And also, when his views on military questions have coincided with mine, he has readily assisted me, but he desires to control the military situation. I have refused to be dictated to by him. On such occasions he has been grossly insulting ... I have put up with insults so as not to risk the safety of the defence.'

On 11 February, with most of the women, children and civilian males crammed into the galleries of the De Beers mines, the defenders of Kimberley knew that the nearby British forces were moving to their relief. Looking south towards Jacobsdal and the Magersfontein hills, observers could see a huge column of dust or smoke in the sky. Perhaps it was rising from the tumult of a great battle, or from the movement of thousands of troops. At any rate, it was coming northwards towards them.

Mafeking was a small border town situated at the junction of three territories – the Cape Colony, the Bechuanaland Protectorate and the South African Republic. The Western Railway line, which started in Cape Town and reached Bulawayo in Rhodesia, passed through Mafeking, thus giving it some strategic significance. Arguably, however, the Boers were mistaken in committing a large force to its encirclement, but for them, as for the British, it became a symbolic prize, squeezed between conflicting interests. It was a neat, new little town of some 1,500 white inhabitants, built round a spacious market square; it had the Victoria Hospital, a convent, the railway station, a racecourse, a recreation ground, a bank, a library, a courthouse, a gaol, hotels, schools, churches, shops, and a Masonic hall. It was not unlike scores of small towns in southern Africa, yet it was destined to endure a siege of 217 days.

In July 1899 Colonel R.S.S. Baden-Powell arrived in South Africa and was sent to the north-west Cape to raise and train two regiments of mounted infantry, and to take charge of the defence of that area and of Bechuanaland and Rhodesia. He had successfully raised his troops, and garnered some units from the Bechuanaland Police and from Rhodesia's British South Africa Police force, by the time war broke out on 11 October. In all, Baden-Powell had 745 soldiers under his command – too few to take on the Boers in the field. He therefore withdrew to Mafeking and prepared to defend it against the enemy forces invading the north-west Cape.

Inside Mafeking, Baden-Powell mustered 450 citizens as volunteers, some of whom grumbled at the personal inconvenience of it all and at the disruption that the war was causing to their business lives. Even these volunteers meant that in all he had only some 1,200 men to defend the town against Piet Cronje's 9,000 Transvaalers.

Baden-Powell was also short of guns: he had four muzzle-loading 7 pounders, two small quick firers, a three-quarter-pounder Nordenfeldt, a one-pounder Hotchkiss, and seven Maxim guns. The Boers had at least ten modern pieces of artillery, and towards the end of October 1899 a 94-pounder Creusot. The great Creusot siege gun could hurl its heavy shell right into the centre of Mafeking; the Afrikaners nicknamed it 'Grietje', which the British adapted to 'Creechy' and then 'Old Creaky'.

The defences of Mafeking stretched in a five-mile perimeter encompassing the European township, a small village occupied by Fingos, and a large settlement of the Barolong people at Mafikeng (the 'place of rocks'). The fortifications, which had to be constructed hastily when hostilities broke out, connected a series of small forts of which the two most formidable were Cannon Kopje in the south and Fort Ayr in the north-west. In addition to these fortifications and his antiquated guns, Baden-Powell had plenty of dynamite. He ordered that mines should be made by filling wooden boxes with dynamite; the boxes were then placed at various points on the defensive perimeter and connected by wires to his headquarters next to Dixon's Hotel in the centre of the town. In fact, most of the boxes were filled with sand, but several genuine mines were detonated to impress the Boers, and their spies within the defences. This largely fictitious mine network apparently did have a deterrent effect on the besieging Boers. Underground shelters were also dug for the women and children, and Baden-Powell tried to ensure that the citizens were given early warning by carefully placed lookouts whenever 'Old Creaky' fired.

Baden-Powell's defence of Mafeking became a legend cherished throughout the Empire and even beyond. Autocratic, imaginative, firm-minded, humorous and, on occasion, ruthless, B-P came to symbolise 'British pluck' at a time when British power looked fallible if not ludicrously inadequate. He was also a tireless self-publicist, conceited, cranky and opinionated. A controversy still rages as to whether he precipitated the deaths of many of the Africans besieged in Mafeking by denying them adequate rations and forcing them outside the town's perimeters to fend for themselves. Certainly he played down the part that Africans had played in Mafeking's defence, even claiming that 'at the first shots they ran away'.

Under Baden-Powell's direction, the improvisations of Mafeking's defenders were undeniably impressive. The railway staff constructed an armoured train out of freight trucks by fixing spare rails horizontally down the sides of the trucks, leaving gaps as loopholes. An old cannon was dug up; it turned out to be a 1770 bronze ship's gun, bearing the propitious letters B.P. on its breech. It was transformed in the railway workshops into a workable piece of artillery, named 'Lord Nelson', and was able to fire some 3,000 yards. Another gun was actually manufactured in the workshops, and proved able to throw its home-made 18-pound shell a distance of 4,000 yards, making it the most powerful gun inside Mafeking.

His activities in Mafeking also helped to advance Baden-Powell's ideas on scouting. Before the siege he had written a book, *Aids to Scouting*, which described scouting techniques for soldiers. Once the siege was underway, he got Major Lord Edward Cecil (son of Lord Salisbury, the British Prime Minister) to set up the Mafeking Cadet Corps. This organisation was made up of boys aged between nine and fifteen, dressed in khaki, with forage caps. They acted as postmen and messengers. Baden-Powell later wrote: 'The possibility of putting responsibility onto boys and treating them seriously was brought to proof in Mafeking with the corps of boys raised by Lord Edward Cecil there in 1899 and led me to go into it further.' So, in a very real sense, the world scouting movement grew out of a battle for supremacy in southern Africa.

The siege was, on the whole, conducted along honourable lines, at least as far as the white combatants were concerned. Baden-Powell agreed with Cronje that there should be no belligerent activity on Sundays; nor should there be any firing on the convent, the Victoria Hospital, the mule-drawn ambulances flying the red cross, or the camp that was eventually established outside the town for women and children. When these understandings were violated, the two sides tended to engage in a lengthy correspondence. Within Mafeking, Baden-Powell quickly replaced civil law with martial law, under which some stern (perhaps too stern) sentences were meted out in the interests of security.

On one issue regarding the conduct of the siege, however, Baden-Powell and Cronje had a sharp and significant disagreement. Like so many of the Boer commanders, Cronje objected profoundly to the British use of armed Africans in the fighting. Despite his subsequent disclaimers, Baden-Powell relied far more than he cared to admit upon the services of black combatants and non-combatants. Eventually, as mentioned earlier, an exasperated Cronje was obliged to make a request that was also partly a demand: 'I would ask you to pause and ... even if it cost you the loss of Mafeking, to disarm your blacks and ... act the part of a white man in a white man's war.'

Away from this apparently ideological clash, apart from the artillery duel and the occasional skirmish, there were few serious clashes between the two sides. In many ways the siege was a dreary and inconsequential military encounter. On 31 October 1899, however, the Boers did launch a determined attack on Cannon Kopje, but were successfully rebuffed. Solomon Plaatje, the African interpreter to the Mafeking court, wrote a wry account of this attack and its prelude:

Monday, 30th

During this day we received another ultimatum that if we did not surrender we would be bombarded early next day. We knew that the big gun had been with us for more than a week and as she failed to shake us in eight days I am afraid that the Boers are merely fooling themselves to imagine that we entertain any fear in being bombarded – for so far from being alarmed, we are getting used to it. I look back to reflect on the slight damage caused by these shells, nearly 200 of which have already been wasted on the town. Considering the expense of one of them (opinion on this point differs, some saying £35 and some £47), she is really not worth the fuss. Meanwhile the position of the big commando at Lothlakane is being moved down the river to a spot about three miles west of here, and one from the eastern to another spot three miles to the north. We are anxiously waiting to see what tomorrow's day will bring forth.

Tuesday, 31st

Long before 5 o'clock we were aroused by reports of Ben [the Creusot 94 pounder] going as rapidly as she did last week. She was accompanied by the enemy's 7-pounder and all other pounders. We woke, dressed in a hurry, and went to the rocks to find things really very serious at Makane. They were shelling Makane and the dust was simply like a cloud around our little fort. The Boers were advancing towards the koppie like a swarm of voetgangers [wingless locusts]: they came creeping under cover of their shells, which were flying over their heads and preceding them like a lot of lifeless but terrific vanguards, until they opened fire with their muskets at long range. Their fire was very heavy, for the whole of the Dutch army had come over from all round Mafeking and turned their attention towards our little fort at Makane. They have evidently discovered that to capture the whole place at once was a hopeless task and they had therefore decided on capturing one by one of our forts until they have nipped every one of them in the bud . . .

To return to the subject. I think I have already stated that the Boers attributed their failure to the fact that we never leave our trenches to give them a chance of tackling us in the open: this morning they must have thought that they would easily compel us to do so by weakening Makane and naturally getting us to run to her assistance, thereby affording them an opportunity of going for us in the plain between this and there. If this was their expectation they were sorely disappointed, for nobody cared. They went for the little fort from east, south and west with muskets and artillery, the former being volleys from about 800 hands. But nobody in town, or anywhere else, troubled his soul about it. The volunteers round the place, seeing that all of the guns were turned towards Makane, stood up and admired the operation as though it was a performance on a theatre stage. It must have given them a headache to find such a multitude of them advancing towards a fort occupied by 70 officers and men of the B.S.A. Police – and nobody caring to go to their assistance. But this was not all: the enemy came quite close and still not a shot came from within the mysterious little fort. I believe the Boers (who always let off a number of rounds unnecessarily) must have thought that everyone was dead, for nearly 20 tons of bombs had already been plugged into the fort. The fortifications looked quite old and ragged in consequence. All of a sudden there came volley after volley from the dumb fort and we could see them fall when the Maxim began to play; some dead, some wounded, and some presumably to wait until dark . . . Our losses were 2 officers and 5 men killed, and 6 wounded.[9]

Shortly after Christmas, the British also made an attack on Game Tree Fort. The armoured train opened fire, two 7 pounders blazed away, and two squadrons of troops attacked the fort in extended line. The Boers, however, had been forewarned of the attack by their spies, and they shot down their attackers, killing twenty-four. This was the heaviest loss the defenders suffered during the siege.

Relentlessly the siege continued. Baden-Powell's main problems were those of food supplies and keeping up morale. There were sufficient provisions to last the Europeans until the end of April 1900, but the local tribe, the Barolong, were less fortunate, caught as they were in this 'white man's war', and many faced starvation at worst, deprivation at best. There was, in addition, insufficient pasture for the Barolong cattle, and no mealies to crop. At least Baden-Powell set up soup kitchens, and later explained how horses were shot and utilised:

> When a horse was killed, his mane and tail were cut off and sent to the hospital for stuffing mattresses and pillows. His shoes went to the foundry for making shells. His skin after having the hair scalded off, was boiled with his head and feet for many hours, chopped up small, and ... served out as 'brawn'.
>
> His flesh was taken from the bones and minced in a great mincing machine and from his inside were made skins into which the meat was crammed and each man received a sausage as his ration.
>
> The bones were then boiled into rich soup, which was dealt out at the different soup kitchens; and they were afterwards pounded into powder with which to adulterate the flour.[10]

There were, however, not many horses available to be eaten by the besieged Africans. They subsisted on a barely palatable porridge made out of the husks of forage oats; locusts were raked up and devoured; stray dogs were also shot and eaten. The markedly different rations available to Europeans and Africans emphasised commonplace racial assumptions in southern Africa. That Africans' lives were worth less was taken for granted by most of the British and Afrikaners.

Throughout the siege, Baden-Powell proved adept at keeping morale high. For example he posted a casualty list outside his headquarters which read:

Killed:	one hen
Wounded:	one yellow dog
Smashed:	one hotel window[11]

But when Kimberley and Ladysmith had been relieved, when the British under Roberts and Kitchener were pressing triumphantly into the Orange Free State and towards Pretoria, the citizens of Mafeking began to feel aggrieved. On 30 March 1900 Baden-Powell published a warm rejoinder in the *Mafeking Mail* to the Jeremiahs and rumour-mongers:

THE COLONEL ON 'GROUSING'

I hear that again wiseacres are busy in town, informing people as to what I am doing and what I am leaving undone. As their deductions are somewhat inaccurate I wish to state that the condition of affairs is in no way altered by my last general notice, which stated we must be prepared to remain besieged [for some] time. Indeed I hope that we may be free within the next fortnight or three weeks, but it would be folly on our part not to be prepared against possible unforeseen delays. Had we not been thus prepared in the first instance we should all have been prisoners in Pretoria by the beginning of January, and the Boers would have now been enjoying the use of our property in Mafeking.

I am, I suppose, the most anxious of anybody in Mafeking to see a Relief Column here and the siege at an end; all that can be done for our relief, from both North and South, is being done, but the moves of troops in the face of the enemy must necessarily be slow, and we have to sit in patience until they develop.

As regards the smallness of our rations, we could, of course, live well on full rations for a week or two and then give in to the 'women slaughterers' and let them take their vengeance on the town, whereas by limiting our amount of daily food we can make certain of outlasting all their efforts against us. The present ration, properly utilised, is a fairly full one as compared with those issued in other sieges – in fact I and my staff have, during the past few days, been living on a far smaller ration without any kind of extras to improve it – and we still live. There are, by the way, two hints I should like to give for making small rations go further – hints derived from personal experience of previous hungry times – and these are:-

1. To lump your rations together as much as possible for cooking, and not every man to have his little amount cooked separately.
2. To make the whole into a big thick stew, from which, even three quarter lbs. of ingredients per man, three good meals can be got per day.

It is just possible that we may have to take 2 ozs. off the bread stuffs, but otherwise our supplies will last well over the period indicated. It has been objected that we are feeding horses on oats, but the oats so used are a lot (of Colonial oats) that have been found quite useless for making flour from for human consumption.

I am told that I keep back news from the public. This is not in accordance with facts, for I make a point of publishing all news of general interest as soon as possible after receipt, first by telephone, then by notices posted about, and lastly through Mr Whales, in the Mafeking Mail Slips; I have no object whatever in keeping news back. Occasionally, of course, items of military information have to be kept quiet because, as we all know, their publication in Mafeking means their transmission within a few hours, to the enemy's camp . . .

I am always, not only willing, but anxious to personally hear any reasonable complaints or suggestions, and those who have them to make, need only bring their grievances to me to get what redress is in my power, but veiled hints and growls cannot be permitted; at such times as these they are apt to put people 'on edge' and to alarm the ladies, and for these reasons they must be suppressed. 'Grousing' is generally the outcome of funk on the part of the individual who grouses, and I hope that every right-minded man who hears any of it will shut it up with an appropriate remark, or the toe of his boot. Cavillers should keep quiet until the siege is over and then they are welcome to write or talk until they are blue in the face.[12]

Meanwhile, Britain, and indeed much of the Empire, waited anxiously for news of Mafeking's relief. Amid his tribulations Baden-Powell may have taken some comfort from a message from Queen Victoria sent in April 1900, which said: 'I continue watching with confidence and admiration in the patient and resolute defence which is so gallantly maintained under your ever resourceful command. V.R.I.'

10

The Turn of the Tide

FEBRUARY 1900: THE RELIEF OF KIMBERLEY, THE
BATTLE OF PAARDEBERG, THE RELIEF OF LADYSMITH

D ETERMINED TO TURN the tide of the war as soon as possible, the
newly installed Commander-in-Chief, Lord Roberts, summoned his senior officers to his camp on the Modder River, and on
10 February addressed them:

> I have asked General French to call you together as I want to tell you that
> I am going to give you some very hard work to do, but at the same time
> you are to get the greatest chance cavalry has ever had. I am certain you
> will do well ... You will remember what you are going to do all your lives,
> and when you have grown to be old men you will tell the story of the relief
> of Kimberley. My intention is for you to make a detour and get on the
> railway north of the town. The enemy are afraid of the British cavalry, and
> I hope that when you get them into the open you will make an example of
> them.[1]

Roberts was determined to strike quickly and boldly against the
enemy. He was acutely aware of Rhodes and Kekewich's quarrel at
Kimberley; further east, in the northern Cape Colony, Generals
Schoeman and De la Rey were poised to harry his communications;
and he knew, moreover, that in northern Natal Buller had once more
failed to relieve Ladysmith.

Although short of fit horses, and with his organisation incom-
plete, Roberts put his faith in speed and surprise. Basically, he

planned to move south from the Modder River camp to Ramdam, east of Graspan station, where Lord Methuen had earlier fought a successful minor battle. His forces would then sweep eastwards to cross the Riet River, and would next press northwards, on Cronje's east flank, and ford the Modder River. Once across the Modder, General French would surge forward to the relief of Kimberley; Roberts would then decide whether to support French in the west or make for Bloemfontein, capital of the Orange Free State.

It is clear that Cronje did not suspect that he was about to be outflanked. Shortly after midnight, in the early hours of 11 February, the British forces began to move off: there were 25,000 infantry, nearly 8,000 cavalry and mounted infantry, more than 100 guns and thousands of supply wagons. In order to deceive the Boers, French's cavalry, which was the first to move, left all their tents standing. By daybreak the whole column was uncoiling, making for Ramdam, which provided the only water before the Riet River.

As French's troops approached the fords of the Riet, Cronje and De Wet struggled to interpret Lord Roberts's intentions. At first De Wet thought the cavalry were going to raid Fauresmith thirty miles to the south-east; then Jacobsdal, just north of the Riet, seemed a likely objective. By 13 February Cronje was none the wiser as to his enemy's strategy. At this time the main force had reached the Riet, where a confused pile-up of supply wagons ensued until Lord Kitchener diverted some of the columns to another ford.

Finally French was able to lead off his 6,000 horsemen with all their supplies, ammunition, forty-two guns, and a cart that unwound telegraph wire as it went. De Wet, grossly outnumbered, made no attempt to intercept this force, though he reported its progress to Cronje who said to the messenger, Gideon Scheepers, 'Are you afraid of things like that? Just you go and shoot them down, and catch them when they run.'

There was, however, no chance of shooting down French and his men. By the early afternoon on 13 February he was nearing the Modder River, and though harassed by a small enemy force on his right, he went through the textbook manoeuvre of turning his horse-men half-right and edging his way towards the river. When the green banks of the Modder came in sight, the whole cavalry force wheeled towards the river and galloped for the crossing. A few Boers were scattered, and the British troops forded the river.

The operation had now reached a crucial stage, although at the cost of 500 dead or unfit horses. The British cavalry held Klip Drift and Rondavel Drift, French's men making full use of abandoned Boer food wagons and feeding their exhausted horses on forage left behind in the enemy's laagers. The Modder River quenched the thirst of man and beast alike. It was now a question of waiting for the rest of the force to arrive so that the infantry could guard the drifts across the Modder and allow the cavalry to make for Kimberley.

The infantry and the wagons reached the banks of the Modder two days later. General Kitchener, the Chief of Staff, arrived to supervise the rear, while French prepared for the final ride to Kimberley, setting out at 8.30 a.m. on 15 February. General Cronje, now realising with dismay that he had been outflanked, was determined with De Wet to put up some sort of opposition to French's forces. The Boers had thus taken up strong positions on two adjoining ridges to the north of Klip Drift. There were about 800 men, and two guns. As French's men rode towards the ridges they came under shell fire, but the British artillery was turned on the Boer guns and they were silenced.

French now decided to force his way between the two ridges and out into the open country beyond. If he succeeded Kimberley would certainly be relieved within hours. The stage was now set for one of the last great cavalry charges of history. With the 9th and 16th Lancers leading, wave after wave of horsemen galloped into the valley between the two ridges, pennants flying, lances and sabres at the ready. A great cloud of dust billowed up from the horses' hooves, making it difficult for the Boers to aim properly, and the British artillery kept firing until the last possible moment. The Boers fled, leaving a score captured or speared. French had broken through with spectacular ease and at the cost of only seven dead and little more than thirty wounded.

After taking a vital hour's rest, French led his cavalry straight for Kimberley. The dispirited and panic-stricken Boers were reeling from the cavalry's success and, to the west, staggering from the ferocious bombardment Lord Methuen had unleashed upon the Magersfontein hills. Their opposition faded away.

A little after 4 p.m. a patrol of Australian horsemen rode into Kimberley, and the townspeople emerged from the mine shafts to cheer and gape. Towards evening General French arrived with the main body of the force. For the first time in months British arms had achieved a striking success, and the telegraph lines bore the proud and perhaps unexpected message, 'Kimberley has been relieved'.

The *Daily Mail* was overjoyed, announcing on 17 February: 'Kimberley is won, Mr Cecil Rhodes is free, the De Beers' shareholders are all full of themselves, and the beginning of the war is at an end. It is a great feat to have accomplished, and the happiest omen for the future. There is no one like Bobs!'[2]

The *New York Tribune* commented more soberly on 18 February:

The relief of Kimberley and the retreat of Cronje have completely transformed the whole aspect of the war. The fighting is now transferred from British to Boer soil. The advance on Bloemfontein and Pretoria has actually begun and the investment of Ladysmith is likely to be abandoned. The Boers must relinquish their schemes of conquest and fall back in defence of their own territory.[3]

A talented cavalry officer, Major Edmund Allenby (later to achieve fame as Field Marshal Allenby, the conqueror of Jerusalem in the Great War), wrote of the entry into Kimberley:

We got in here after a very hard week. We are in a beastly bivouac, tentless, blanketless, unwashed and dusty. We lost about 10 officers killed and wounded, and I think about 30 men. My property now consists of the dirty clothes I live and sleep in day and night, a cloak, a saddle blanket, a toothbrush, a box of cigarettes and a tube of lanoline. On the march I lived chiefly on biscuits and beef tongues. The horses are half-starved. Rhodes is behaving very well. He sent over some soup, firewood, etc. I dined with him last night. He's much the same as I remember him 15 years ago ... Last week was the longest week I ever have spent. It feels like six months.[4]

Describing the conditions which the relieving forces had found at Kimberley, a war correspondent wrote:

What one noticed first was the number of holes and shelters and warrens into which people had crept for safety. Hundreds of them, like human ant-hills ... The menu at the principal hotel, where I dined, would (if it had been printed) have consisted of one item – horseflesh. I noticed that the residents ate it eagerly, and even talked about it; but most of us strangers arose hungry and went quickly into the fresh air ... One found man after man thin, listless and (in spite of the joy of salvation) dispirited; talking with a tired voice and hopeless air, and with a queer, shifty, nervous, scared look in the eye ... The thing was scarcely human, scarcely of this world. These men were not like oneself ... All this fear and horror to be borne upon an empty stomach, for the horrors of partial starvation were added to the constant fear of a violent death. Mothers had to see their babies die because there was no milk or other suitable nourishment; a baby cannot live on horse and mule flesh. There was hardly a coloured baby left alive.[5]

Now that Kimberley had been relieved and Boer hopes dashed, General Cronje's will to resist temporarily crumbled. He sat in his laager as if paralysed, with Methuen's guns roaring in the distance. His wife, more indomitable than he, sought to comfort him by patting his head. At last he shook off his lethargy and despair and considered what to do. He could not go north since French held Kimberley. To the south were the forces led by Methuen. To the west was barren wasteland. Although the main British force was marching up from the south-east, there was still a gap through which he could slip eastwards towards Bloemfontein.

On 15 February Cronje's army abandoned the Magersfontein hills before midnight and made off to the east. There were about 5,000 men, many wives and children, 400 wagons and several thousand horses. By the time dawn broke on 16 February Cronje had got away, though an infantry division and a brigade of mounted infantry, urged on by the relentless Kitchener, snapped at his heels as he crossed the Modder.

Although buoyed up by their success in relieving Kimberley, the British forces also faced some frustrations. Roberts failed to get a message to French ordering him to cut off Cronje's retreat, because the Boers had cut the telegraph wires. French himself pursued the main Afrikaner force, under J.S. Ferreira, that had been besieging Kimberley and was now making off northwards, dragging the Creusot siege gun. He failed to run them down, however, as his horses were desperate for water and the Boers fought a brisk rear-guard action. Worse still, De Wet with about 1,000 men swooped onto the great British supply park at Waterval on the north bank of the Riet and swept aside all resistance. Roberts decided to abandon the supply park so as not to slow down his advance by turning back to fight for it, but four days' supplies were lost and the men were on short rations for some time.

Roberts now ordered all available forces to pursue Cronje's convoy. On 17 February French, who could muster only 1,200 sound horses, set off to intercept Cronje and bar his retreat until the main British force caught up with him. The Boer column pressed on, not knowing that Kitchener was pushing the infantry along behind them with forced marches and that Sir John French was bearing down on them from the north-west.

Cronje's army prepared to cross to the south bank of the Modder shortly before noon in order to get onto the Bloemfontein road. They had just passed a hill called Paardeberg on the north bank of the river and halted their wagons while the midday meal was prepared. It must have seemed to the Boers that they had virtually made their escape and that the British infantry were struggling along in their rear.

Without any warning, a salvo of shells crashed among them. Panic followed, as men, women and children desperately sought shelter. It was French's guns that had opened fire. He had slogged to his present position on a line of hills called the Koedoesrand, north-east of Cronje, in seven hours. The Boers were, for the moment, a sitting target.

Despite this, French was not wholly confident or comfortable. Cronje's force outnumbered his by nearly five to one; moreover, Ferreira's men, retreating from Kimberley, might come up upon his rear at any moment. He anxiously scanned the western skyline. At last he could see large forces approaching to within two and a half miles of the Boer positions. It was Kitchener, who had driven the infantry along for a thirty-mile march, mostly under a burning sun, and who had accomplished the feat within twenty-four hours. Roberts, meanwhile, had fallen ill at Jacobsdal, but had confirmed Kitchener in command (a decision which reduced the more senior General Kelly-Kenny, the commander of the 6th Division, to a mood of sulky, limited cooperation).

Cronje was trapped. As night fell he decided to stand and fight instead of trying to escape. He had 5,000 men and had sent for further reinforcements from Bloemfontein; General Ferreira was nearby with 1,500 troops, and De Wet, with a similar force, was closing in from the south.

*

The battle of Paardeberg began early in the morning on 18 February. Kitchener was determined to smash Cronje's army and inflict heavy losses upon it; in contrast, General Kelly-Kenny suggested a leisurely bombardment while waiting for the enemy to surrender. This was not Kitchener's way at all. He had not force-marched his sweat-soaked regiments of foot to Paardeberg in order to engage in a gentlemanly joust of 'the white man's war'. As he saw it, here was a notoriously elusive foe in a trap, and he was determined to move in for the kill. He surveyed the Boer positions through his field glasses and decided to order an immediate attack.

Cronje's defensive laager was north of the Modder, surrounded by trenches and set among trees; on the dry river bed below were sheltered the ox wagons, and the women and children. Two miles to the west of the main laager there was a formidable defensive position in a donga (gully). On the other side of the laager there were more posts, stretching for three miles eastwards and capable of pouring out deadly low-trajectory fire. Kitchener's headquarters were two miles due south of Cronje's laager. He was confident of success and, as the main action began, said to his staff officers, 'It is now seven o'clock. We shall be in the laager at half past ten, then I'll load up French and send him on to Bloemfontein.'

Kitchener's divisional commanders were not so optimistic. Kelly-Kenny was still resentful, and General Colvile and Colonel Smith-Dorrien were by no means enthusiastic supporters of Kitchener's plan of attack. These, and other senior officers, were fearful that heavy casualties would result from a full-blooded assault on the Boer positions. It is likely that their views permeated their divisions and led to a certain half-heartedness in the approach of some units. For Kitchener there was no cause for hesitation. He planned to attack Cronje's laager from both the east and the west on both banks of the river; he also wanted a frontal attack to take place from the south.

Unfortunately the frontal attack from the south got off to a bad start and the troops were soon pinned down by accurate enemy rifle fire. British casualties mounted steadily, and in the end the assault ground to a halt some 300 yards from the river bank. In the east, and south of the river, the British forces were unexpectedly attacked from the rear by several hundred Boers with two guns, who had come hotfoot from Bloemfontein and were led by Commandant Steyn. Although the British turned on Steyn, silenced his guns, and eventually drove him off the hills near Stinkfontein, large numbers of men were diverted from the pincer movement that Kitchener had planned. In the west, meanwhile, British troops attacked on both sides of the river but made little progress, though two spirited attacks were made on the defensive position in the donga, first by Canadian forces and the Duke of Cornwall's Light Infantry together, and then by the Canadians alone.

Amid the battle's noise and turmoil General Cronje sat, once more holding his wife's hand, while shells landed among his wagons and rifle fire crackled around him. He seemed calm and gloomily fatalistic. Kitchener, on the other hand, positively exulted in the battle; but he lacked the staff to carry orders efficiently to the different units engaged in the struggle, and, as at Omdurman, he spent a good deal of time galloping hither and thither issuing instructions to the officers nearest at hand.

Very little had been achieved, however, by 10.30 a.m., and British casualties were high. Kitchener now decided to throw in the mounted infantry, under Colonel Hannay, who had just driven off Steyn's Free Staters. The mounted infantry moved up and joined the Essex and Welsh Regiments who had got to within 800 yards of the main laager. Kitchener sent a curt message to Hannay, when the latter reported the progress he had made, saying, 'The time has now come for a final effort. All troops have been warned that the laager must be rushed at all costs. Try and carry the Essex and the Welsh on with you. But if they cannot go, the M.I. should do it. Gallop up if necessary and fire into the laager.'

The risks of carrying out this implacable order were tremendous, but Hannay in a fit of boy's adventure-story bravado decided to do so. He gathered up a handful of men and rode straight towards the enemy. The Boers hesitated to shoot him down, so forlorn and mis-guided did he seem at the head of his men, but he came on relent-lessly and at last they had no alternative but to kill him. After Hannay's self-sacrifice, the Essex and Welsh Regiments made an attempt to storm the laager, but were decisively checked by enemy fire. Almost simultaneously, the Cornwalls, the Canadians, and the Highland Brigade launched another attack on the donga in the west. The assault was ill-coordinated, however, and Smith-Dorrien held back his reserves.

It seemed that everywhere British commanding officers were

holding back. The light was fading fast and they saw no point in amassing further casualties. De Wet, moreover, now created an awkward diversion by occupying Stinkfontein Farm and the freshly named Kitchener's Kopje, just to the east of Kitchener's headquarters. Although De Wet had only 600 men, it took three days and a foray by General French's cavalry to drive him off.

The crucial battle of Paardeberg ended as night closed in. Both sides had fought themselves to a standstill. Although the British had suffered 1,262 casualties (more than for any other day throughout the war) they had had the best of it: Cronje was still penned within his laager, surrounded by over 300 casualties and the corpses of many of his trek-oxen; he had no doctors to tend his wounded; and unless substantial reinforcements arrived promptly he was doomed. Kitchener's abrupt assault on the laager had at least left no time for the Boers to wriggle out of the trap, and if his divisional commanders had shown more enthusiasm for his ruthless tactics the day might have ended in a spectacular triumph for British arms.

Lord Roberts arrived at Paardeberg the next day, 19 February, having shaken off his illness. Disinclined himself to risk heavy casualties, he tactfully sent Kitchener to the rear to supervise the vital supply links. To the relief of most of his subordinates, Roberts decided upon an investment of the Boer positions. It is arguable that a further full-blooded assault would have settled matters within twenty-four hours, and would also have dealt the Boers such a crippling blow in terms of casualties and morale that they would never have recovered. This did not happen. Even the British artillery bombardment was a desultory affair, though aided by an observation balloon overhead. The enemy, however, were unable to break out and escape.

On 26 and 27 February the British made two attempts to storm the laager. The assault troops came within 250 yards of their objective in the east, and within 550 yards in the west. Shortly after 6 a.m. on 27 February the Boers raised white flags. Cronje had accepted defeat.

Field Marshal Roberts immediately ordered a ceasefire. At 7 a.m. Cronje rode up to the British headquarters, where men of the Highland Brigade formed a hollow square. Lord Roberts greeted him cordially, shaking his hand and saying, 'I am glad to see you. You have made a gallant defence, sir.' Cronje, face to face with the realities of his failure, made no reply. The contrast between the appearance of the two commanders reflected their respective fortunes: Roberts was clad in a well-tailored khaki uniform, unadorned save for the jewelled Kandahar sword at his side; Cronje wore an old, bulky, green over-coat, a slouch hat, and rough *veldskoen* boots.

The defeated Boers stacked their arms upon the river bank and were then led away into captivity. In all, 2,500 Transvaalers and 1,500 Free Staters surrendered. Cronje and his wife were taken to Cape Town, though the vanquished commander was later shipped, like Napoleon before him, to St Helena for safe keeping.

The victory at Paardeberg had great significance, much of it sym-bolic. In Britain there was relieved celebration, and brokers danced for joy in the London stock exchange. For the Boer republics the news came as a great blow, particularly since the surrender fell on the anniversary of their crushing victory at Majuba nineteen years before. 'The English', Paul Kruger complained, 'have taken our Majuba Day away from us.' But this was not all, for the British had also decisively taken the initiative in the war. With Kimberley relieved, and the Boers falling back on Bloemfontein, the British were poised for a final breakthrough in northern Natal.

The indefatigable General Buller had formulated yet one more plan for the relief of Ladysmith. It consisted of a right-flanking move-ment that would drive the Boers off the group of hills dominated by Hlangwane and within a great loop in the Tugela on what was then the British side of the river. Buller had 25,000 men with, as usual, ample food and supplies, and on 17 and 18 February a substantial part of this force drove about 2,000 Boers off Hlangwane and two nearby hills. As cautious as ever, Buller spent the next two days bringing up the rest of his army, while, to the west, Cronje was being brought to the point of surrender at Paardeberg.

Despite Buller's slow-footed advance, Boer morale sagged and many began to make for home. General Botha tried in vain to stop the rot, and in despair telegraphed to President Kruger that he feared the Tugela and even Ladysmith would have to be abandoned. Kruger replied in defiant vein, his exhortation owing much to the lessons of the Old Testament and also containing references to his people's historical sense of mission and their earlier experiences of persecution. The reply is worth quoting in full to give the flavour of Boer fundamentalist thinking:

The moment you cease to hold firm and fight in the name of the Lord, then you have unbelief in you; and the moment unbelief is present cowardice follows, and the moment that you turn your backs on the enemy then there remains no place for us to seek refuge, for in that case we have ceased to trust in the Lord. No, no, my brethren; let it not be so; let it not be so. Has not the Lord hitherto given us double proof that He stands on our side? Wherever our burghers have stood fast, however hard the task, the Lord has beaten back the enemy with a small number of our burghers. My brethren, is it not the same Lord that cleft the Red Sea and routed Pharaoh and all his host, when Moses stood firm in his faith? Is it not, again, the same Lord that caused the stream of water to spring from the rocks whence thousands could drink? Is it not still the same Lord who walked on the sea and rebuked the waves of the sea and the winds, and they obeyed Him? ... It seems to me from a study of God's word that we live at a point of time spoken of in the Revelation, in which the Beast has received power to persecute the Church of Christ in order to purify her, as gold is purified through fire ... This, indeed, is the struggle for the crown, both in a material and a spiritual sense. Read Psalm XXVII, verse 7, where the Lord says, 'Be of good courage, little band of god-fearing ones'. The Lord is faithful, and in your weakness shall He make perfect His strength. Read Psalm XXXIII, verse 7, to the end, where it says that victory is in the hand of the Lord alone, and not with the multitude of horses and chariots ... No brethren, let us not bring all our posterity to destruction. Stand fast in faith to fight, and you shall be convinced that the Lord shall arise and shall scatter His enemies (Psalm LXVIII). Our faith is now at its utmost test, but the Lord will now shortly prove that He alone lives and reigns. The young men preferred death in the fiery furnace to forsaking their faith. Our ancestors preferred the stake to abandoning their faith, and the Church has been preserved, and all those who have preferred death to forsaking their faith have been as a sacrifice on the altar. Read this out to all officers and burghers, and my faith and prayer lie in my firm confidence that the Lord shall strengthen His people in their faith. Even if they have no earthly rock behind which to seek cover, they shall win on the open plain.[6]

Perhaps Kruger's stern rallying call had the power of a miraculous transformation; or, far more likely, perhaps Buller's characteristically ponderous manoeuvres improved Boer morale. At any rate, the dis-integration of Botha's forces was halted. By 21 February about 5,000 Afrikaners were prepared to face the greatly superior numbers of their enemy. The British forces crossed the Tugela and foot slogged northwards against a group of hills that included Horseshoe Hill, Hedge Hill and Terrace Hill. By 25 February the British were draped painfully across these hills and subjected to enfilading fire that was uncomfortably reminiscent of Spion Kop. But the 25th was also a Sunday and the Afrikaners were anxious for an armistice and a chance to tend the wounded and bury the dead. Buller was only too pleased to agree to this, and on the Sunday British troops and Boers fraternised and exchanged gossip. One Afrikaner said to General Lyttelton 'We've all been having a rough time', to which Lyttelton replied stoically, 'Yes, I suppose so. But for us of course it's nothing. This is what we are paid for. This is the life we always lead – you understand?' 'Great God!' said the Boer, shocked.

Buller, during this pause in the operations, consulted with General Warren and decided to alter his plans. He now proposed to bring back most of his force to the eastern bank of the Tugela and then to launch a three-pronged attack over a pontoon bridge on the northern hills guarding the route, and the railway line, to Ladysmith. The attacking troops would be supported by artillery fire from seventy-six guns. The battle went better than Buller expected: his forces attacked along a three-mile front, concentrating on Pieter's Hill, Railway Hill and the still partially occupied Terrace Hill. The Boers were overwhelmed by the textbook assault of British troops, both infantry and artillery working in close coordination.

Deneys Reitz, who was near Pieter's Hill, later described the attack in his book *Commando*:

[the crest of Pieter's Hill was] almost invisible under the clouds of flying earth and fumes, while the volume of sound was beyond anything that I have ever heard. At intervals the curtain lifted, letting us catch a glimpse of trenches above, but we could see no sign of movement, nor could we hear whether the men up there were still firing, for the din of the guns drowned all lesser sounds ... then, suddenly, the gun-fire ceased, and for a space we caught the fierce rattle of Mauser rifles followed by British infantry swarming over the skyline, their bayonets flashing in the sun. Shouts and cries reached us, and we could see men desperately thrusting

and clubbing. Then a rout of burghers broke back from the hill, stream-
ing towards us in disorderly flight. The soldiers fired into them, bringing
many down as they made blindly past us, not looking to right or left.[7]

Fatefully, it was 27 February, the anniversary of the battle of Majuba
Hill. Buller, elated by the unusual taste of success, spent a good deal
of the next day on Railway Hill watching the Boers retreating to the
north-east. He made no attempt to harry the enemy further, and
indeed an exceptionally violent storm on the night of the 27th had
achieved as much as a massed cavalry charge might have done:

> The thunder was terrific, the rain was like an incessant water-spout, and
> the fearful lightning in its vivid play along the rocks and down the hill-
> sides revealed thousands of men bedraggled and drenched, rushing as fast
> as they could, no one seemed to know where. Some were on horseback,
> some in mule and bullock wagons, and many afoot, all hurrying on, along
> mountain-sides, over rushing rivers and slits now turned into raging tor-
> rents; cattle and men, in some instances, being caught by the wild waters
> and hurled down by their fury to destruction; but on and on went the
> main body pell-mell, nobody apparently pursuing, only the frightful
> storm fiend and awful panic speeding them; and no human power could
> stay that rush on that memorable night.[8]

Botha's force was broken. As they struggled to escape, the Boers
heard the news of Cronje's surrender at Paardeberg. They knew then
that the siege of Ladysmith would have to be abandoned.

Within the Ladysmith defences Dr Kay chronicled these events:

27 February
News has arrived of the surrender of General Cronje after he lost 1,700
killed and wounded. Everyone very pleased. But the Boers in camp look
miserable.

   In the afternoon, after very heavy gunfire, we could hear Buller hard at
it with rifle-firing; then as it began to get dusk it gradually slacked off.

28 February
Cloudy up to ten o'clock and not a shot to be heard, except one from
Bulwana. About ten the sun came out and the helio was going gaily. A few
shots fired in the morning. At about three o'clock our 4.7 naval gun
started blazing away at Bulwana. The opinion was that the guns were

keeping the Boers from moving, and as we have not got much ammunition for the guns, we are sure we are near relief. But this morning we were put on half rations again.

Heavy rifle-fire was heard behind Bulwana about 4 p.m. At about 6 p.m. some mounted men were seen on the horizon going towards Caesar's Camp. Some said they were Boers, but as our guns did not open on them and as they were making towards Caesar's Camp, I felt sure they were part of Buller's forces.

Colonel Fawcett, 5th Lancers, who had a pair of field glasses, took a good look at them and said, 'Most decidedly they are British cavalry; the horses' tails are all cut short and it is relief at last.'

I don't know how others felt, speech was beyond me; and when we saw them turn towards Caesar's Camp, all knew his words were true. At last Ladysmith is relieved. Our 119 days of suffering are over, and with feelings impossible to describe I go to my tent and sit down alone. Thoughts of the past give way to hope for the future.[9]

Back in Britain, patriots exulted in the news that Ladysmith had been relieved. Enormous crowds rejoiced in the London streets, stopping the hansom cabs and delivery carts. Pall Mall blazed with torches, and art students from South Kensington marched to cheer Joseph Chamberlain.

In Ladysmith the citizens, though gratified, did not greet the relieving forces of Buller's army with wild enthusiasm. Hollow-eyed, and in their best clothes, they lined the streets and gave the soldiers a dutiful welcome. The war correspondent, J.B. Atkins, wrote ruefully, 'I have been greeted with as much ardour in an afternoon in London by a man with whom I had lunched two hours before.' Perhaps the garrison was too exhausted and listless to indulge in more dramatic displays. They had suffered considerable hardship, and few had enjoyed the lengthy game of 'waiting for Buller'. Sir George White, however, put a much-needed gloss on the whole affair in the brief speech he made as the 118-day siege ended. 'I thank God', he said, 'we have kept the flag flying.' It was just what the Empire wanted to hear.

11

Marching to Pretoria (and Johannesburg)

THE BRITISH ADVANCE THROUGH THE BOER
REPUBLICS, THE RELIEF OF MAFEKING, THE
START OF THE GUERRILLA WAR

A T THE BEGINNING of March 1900 it was clear that the tide of war
had well and truly turned. As things seemed to fall apart, the
Boer generals struggled desperately to restore morale and halt
the break-up of their forces. It was no easy task. In northern Natal
the Boers flooded through Elandslaagte on their way home. Louis
Botha and Lukas Meyer sought in vain for General Joubert, and
threatened to shoot the horses of those who wanted to leave. But
Elandslaagte, crammed with Boer supplies, had to be abandoned;
rather than let its stores fall into British hands it was set on fire and
the great column of smoke could be seen for fifty miles around.

No wonder that so many Boers shouted to their commanders
'*Huis toe!*' ('Off home!'), for their cause seemed lost beyond hope.
Kimberley and Ladysmith had been relieved; in the west almost an
entire army had surrendered with Cronje; the Boer offensive in
northern Natal had been broken, and their invading columns
ejected from the Cape Midlands; and Lord Roberts stood at the
head of a well-equipped and confident army ready to advance on
Bloemfontein. Nor was there any sign of foreign intervention on
their behalf – not that this possibility had ever been anything more

than a comforting fantasy. The British had now had a taste of victory and would undoubtedly drive home their advantages to the full.

President Kruger actively intervened to try to stop demoralised Boers forces from fleeing into the most northerly reaches of Natal, to Glencoe and even Newcastle. By his entreaties and exhortations he managed to patch up the situation in northern Natal, then departed for Bloemfontein on 5 March leaving Joubert to cope with Boer strategy in that area.

In Bloemfontein Kruger and President Steyn conferred. They made a peace proposal to the British government but, since it stipulated the full independence of the two republics, it was hardly likely to be accepted. More significant was their determination to stand firm against Roberts's threatened advance from the west. They reckoned that, with reinforcements drawn from Natal, Colesberg and Stormberg, they could put 12,000 men into the field against the invaders. Poplar Grove, fifty miles from Bloemfontein and set among a line of hills extending for twenty-five miles, was chosen as the first line of defence; Christiaan de Wet was entrenched there with 6,000 men.

Confronting this puny and over-extended force, Roberts could count upon 30,000 troops, and on 7 March he resumed his march westwards. The line at Poplar Grove did not hold, the Boers not waiting to be enveloped by the infantry columns or encircled by French's cavalry. They hitched up their wagons and made off, President Kruger travelling with them in his Cape cart. French was particularly lethargic that day, nursing some petty grievances against Roberts, and making slow progress. If he had shown the dash that had relieved Kimberley and stopped Cronje in his tracks at Paardeberg, then another substantial Boer army might have been captured and President Kruger with it. Given such a catastrophe for the Afrikaners it is difficult to see how they could have persevered with the war.

In effect, Kruger was being carried along amid a panic-stricken mob. At Abraham's Kraal, thirty-five miles from Bloemfontein, Kruger, aided by De Wet and De la Rey, managed partially to stop the rout, though units of the Zarps (the South African Republic's police force) disobeyed his orders to shoot the fugitives. While Kruger and De Wet hastened back to Bloemfontein to organise its defences, De la Rey, with a mere 1,500 men (including 1,000 Zarps), stayed at Abraham's Kraal to resist Roberts.

On 10 March the British army, refurbished with fresh supplies, approached in three columns from the east. On the 11th, as Roberts rode out to join General French's cavalrymen at the front of the advance, he was troubled by rumours of heavy Boer reinforcements closing in from the north. Knowing how crucial it was to seize Bloemfontein, with its vital railway rolling-stock, he decided to send French off to take Brand Kop, four miles south-east of the city. Once this dominating hill was taken, Bloemfontein would be at the mercy of the British army.

As daylight faded, French's weary horsemen, having earlier cut the railway line that left Bloemfontein, approached Brand Kop and hustled about 400 Boers off the ridge.

The capture of Brand Kop sealed the fate of Bloemfontein. The Afrikaners accepted the inevitability of its fall, and thousands of them trekked away to the north. President Steyn and his government left at night by train; the state archives had already been sent to Kroonstad, 100 miles away to the north.

Lord Roberts was able to make his formal entry into Bloemfontein at the head of his cavalrymen on 13 March. As he rode along the decorated streets, past pretty gardens and respectable buildings, the citizens gave him a warm reception. There were several reasons for this unexpected welcome: the hard-core resistance had left, to fight another day: there were a considerable number of British citizens in the city; the Orange Free State had traditionally enjoyed close economic links with the Cape, and hence with British power; and the rock-solid basis of militant Afrikaner nationalism was not to be found in Bloemfontein.

Britain erupted with scenes of rejoicing. Both Houses of Parliament assembled in the courtyard of Buckingham Palace and serenaded Queen Victoria with a rendering of the national anthem. The crowds in the streets were almost hysterical with joy, exulting in the turn of events that seemed to bring the war close to its end. There was also a solid feeling of satisfaction that the continental critics of Britain would now have little to crow about. Yet the war was by no means universally popular; there were pro-Boers on the left wing of the Liberal Party and among socialist groups, and both David Lloyd George and Keir Hardie got rough receptions at public meetings; and in addition, the Peace Society and the League of Liberals Against Aggression and Militarism made their voices heard.

But the national mood was perhaps more accurately captured by *Punch*, which showed a baby saying 'Bang!' as his first word.

In South Africa, while Roberts nursed his tired troops in preparation for the next big push, Kitchener busied himself with crushing rebellion in the western Cape, and other British columns brought much of the southern Orange Free State under imperial control. More than 8,000 Free Staters and Cape rebels laid down their arms, though the ultimate fate of the latter (pardon or punishment) was left to the British authorities to decide. At Bloemfontein, Roberts's main task was to restore the railway system necessary for the supplies that were so vital to his future progress, and to make proper use of the 200,000 men now in South Africa.

The Boers tried to cope with the gloom that had seized so many of them. In Pretoria President Kruger was confronted by a legal deputation led by Chief Justice Gregorowski, which urged him, unsuccessfully, to call a halt to the war. President Steyn, ousted from his capital, physically imposing, cultured and intelligent, did his utmost to restore morale. On 27 March Commandant General Piet Joubert died, and Louis Botha took his place. This promotion led to a greater drive for efficiency among the remaining Boer forces, of which there were about 12,500 near Bloemfontein and 15,500 on other fronts. It was agreed, for example, that military courts should impose sterner discipline, and that the regulations for leave should be tightened up.

It also was resolved that generals should have the power to limit the amount of transport wagons under their command. This was meant to reduce the numbers of wives and children attached to the Afrikaner columns, an encumbrance which had, arguably, brought Cronje to disaster at Paardeberg. Not all Boers accepted these new regulations, and De Wet, for instance, had to force Commandant Vilonel of Winberg to resign because he refused to abide by the decision of the Council of War regarding excess wagons.

As it turned out, it was De Wet and his brother Piet who gave the British at Bloemfontein the most trouble. He decided to move down from the north and to attack the waterworks on the Modder River upon which Bloemfontein largely depended. This resulted in the battle of Sannah's Post, named after the railway station on the unfinished line to the east.

De Wet's tactics were simple: his brother Piet was to lead the larger part of his force of 2,000 men in an attack upon the water-

1. 'Make us masters of the situation in South Africa!' Joseph Chamberlain, Secretary of State for the Colonies, 1895–1903

2. 'I precipitated the crisis': Sir Alfred (later Lord) Milner, British High Commissioner

3. Rhodes's men: Dr L. S. Jameson and friends rest in Rhodesia before the Raid

4. The Colossus at home: Cecil Rhodes enjoying the opulence of Groote Schuur

5. President J.P. (Paul) Kruger, at his somewhat more modest retreat

6. Man of peace turned man of war: President Marthinus Steyn of the Orange Free State

7. The great Boer triumvirate of generals: (*left to right*) Christiaan De Wet, 'Koos' de la Rey and Louis Botha

8. 'Slim Jannie': Jan Christiaan Smuts, Cambridge graduate and lawyer turned commando leader

9. 'A kindly, well-meaning old man': the Transvaal's Commandant General, Piet Joubert

10. 'The pocket Wellington': Field Marshal Lord Roberts

11. 'A grim, iron-conqueror': Lord Kitchener of Khartoum

13. The hero of Mafeking and the original Boy Scout: Colonel Robert Baden-Powell

12. 'The ferry-man of the Tugela': General Sir Redvers Buller

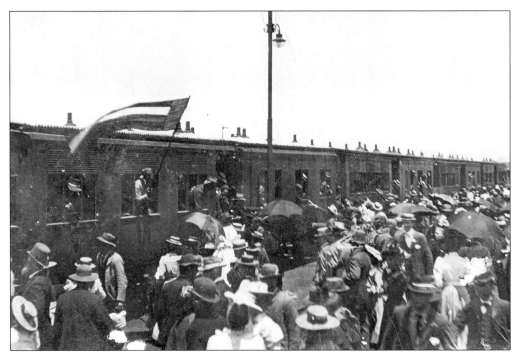

14. Off to the front: Boers entraining at Pretoria

15. 'Marching as to war': Milner inspects the Rand Rifles, 1901

16. The Boer 'Long Tom' sends a greeting to the besieged British garrison at Ladysmith

17. 'The caged lion': Cecil Rhodes (*third from left*), trapped in Kimberley, oversees a soup-kitchen

18. 'Neither the accent nor the gait of Christians': British prisoners–of–war enter Pretoria

19. 'They were all of the seventeenth century except their rifles': Boer commandos with their deadly Mausers

20. 'Imperial warriors': Canadians at the front

21. 'We're thinking of you, Mother': British soldiers at rest

22. British soldiers at war: Royal Munster Fusiliers repel a Boer attack

23. Casualties of war: wounded British officers recover, in some comfort

24. British power on parade: the occupation of Bloemfontein, 13 March 1900

25. 'In the bag': Boer prisoners-of-war ponder their fate after the battle of Paardeberg

26. The guerrilla war: a train wrecked by Boer commandos

27. Britain's allies: black armed auxiliaries man the blockhouse lines

28. Off to the concentration camps: Boer refugees entrain at Dundee

29. At the camps: new arrivals unload the remains of their possessions

30. The camps – one aspect: Kate Meintjes (*second left*), later wife of Dr J.J. Ross, enjoys a peaceful moment

31. The camps – 'methods of barbarism': a busy camp mortuary

32. 'That bloody woman':
Emily Hobhouse

33. The nation rejoices: peace is announced in London

34. The road to Union: the Transvaal receives self-government in 1907

works from the east bank of the Modder; meanwhile he would wait on the west side of the river and destroy the small British force guarding the waterworks (200 men) as they were driven towards him. De Wet did not envisage interference from other British troops. There were some British twelve miles away at Springfield, a few at Boesman's Kop (about eight miles from the waterworks), and also a convoy of wagons, escorted by cavalry under Colonel Broadwood, somewhere to the east of the Modder, but De Wet fancied that they might run up against Commandant Olivier with several thousand Boers who were in that area.

An hour before dawn on the day De Wet had picked for his attack, some of his men discovered that a column of carts carrying English-speaking refugees were starting to cross the river from the east. He described the scene in his book *Three Years' War*:

> As soon as it became light enough to see anything we discovered that just above the Spruit stood a waggon with some Kaffirs and a number of sheep and cattle beside it. The Kaffirs told us that the waggon belonged to one of the 'hands-uppers' from Thaba 'Nchu, and that they had been ordered to get it down to Bloemfontein as quickly as possible and sell it to the English. The owner of the sheep and of the cattle, they said, was with General Broadwood whose troops had just arrived at the waterworks. The light grew brighter and there, three thousand paces from us, was Broadwood's huge force.[1]

De Wet quickly saw that he had almost stumbled into a trap himself. A large force of cavalry, about 2,000 men in all, were bivouacked around the waterworks. De Wet decided, however, that he could deal with this force using the same tactics he had prepared for the small one. Anxiously he waited for the sound of his brother's guns opening fire. He did not have long to wait:

> Then our guns began to fire; and the result was a scene of confusion. Towards us over the brow of the hill came the waggons pell-mell, with a few carts moving rapidly to the front. When the first of these reached the Spruit its occupants – a man and a woman beside him – became aware that something was wrong. I was standing at the top of the drift with Commandants Fourie and Nel. I immediately ordered two of my adjutants to mount the cart and sit at the driver's side. The other carts came one after another into the drift, and I ordered them to follow close behind

the first cart, at the same time warning the occupants that if they gave any signal to the enemy they would be shot. The carts were filled with English from Thaba 'Nchu. I was very glad that the women and children should reach a place of safety before the fighting began. So speedily did the carts follow each other that the English had no suspicion of what was occurring, and very shortly the soldiers began to pour into the drift in the greatest disorder. As soon as they reached the stream, they were met by the cry of 'Hands up!' Directly they heard the words a forest of hands rose in the air. More troops quickly followed, and we had disarmed two hundred before they had time to know what was happening.[2]

Very probably De Wet might have captured more of the British troops, but for a couple of artillery officers who came down to the drift across the river imagining that there was some sort of transport tangle to sort out. Both officers were surprised to encounter De Wet, who said quietly, 'Dismount. You are prisoners. Go to the wagons.' The leading battery came on, and was also captured. Suddenly one of the captured officers decided to run for it; he broke away, yelling a warning to the second battery, that was now approaching the drift. The battery (Q Battery) immediately wheeled round, and galloped off.

At this point, De Wet and his men opened fire on them. Q Battery in fact halted a little further off and, joined by an escaped gun team from the drift, began to bombard De Wet's positions, but to little effect. Colonel Broadwood's men were now uncomfortably caught between the fire of the two De Wets' forces, and a small British force that had arrived at Boesman's Kop was split in two and thus of little real help.

At 10 a.m. Broadwood decided to rescue the guns of Q Battery and to try to escape to the south-west. There now followed an episode that was much cherished by patriots at home; volunteers ran out to drag off the threatened guns and limbers, though subjected to merciless rifle fire. Four VCs were won, and when the attempt was at last called off the watching British troops rose to cheer the gallant rescuers.

Broadwood eventually made his escape, but De Wet had won the day. The British lost 600 men, eighty out of ninety wagons, and seven of the twelve guns; Bloemfontein's water supply was cut off, and within a month 2,000 inhabitants had died of enteric fever. De Wet crowned his triumph at Sannah's Post by next day swooping down on 400 of General Gatacre's troops at Mostert's Hoek. By the time Gatacre himself arrived on the scene he found that his men had tamely surrendered and had been taken off.

Neither this episode nor the disaster at Sannah's Post boded well for Britain's hope to finish off Boer resistance quickly. De Wet's mobility and incisiveness showed what even small numbers of determined men could achieve; moreover, he had been aided in his coup at Mostert's Hoek by burghers who had been prepared to break their recently taken oath of non-participation in the fighting.

However, by now (the beginning of April 1900), Lord Roberts was ready to lead his army out of Bloemfontein. He was determined to march straight for the Transvaal's capital of Pretoria, believing that its capture would effectively end the war, not merely because of the influence of its fall upon Boer morale, but also because it was the railway centre for all the main lines except the Western Railway. En route he would enter Johannesburg, the golden city, citadel of the Uitlanders, and the source of so much of the wealth of Kruger's republic.

There seemed very little chance of the Boers stopping the British march on Pretoria. Roberts had over 170,000 men in the field and proposed to use 100,000 of them in his great northwards advance; the rest were to be left behind in garrisons, or to guard the vitally important supply and communications lines for the main army. The Afrikaners had about 30,000 fighting men – mostly in small forces scattered over a large area.

Roberts proposed to head the main advance himself: three columns, totalling 38,000 troops, and with over 100 guns. Meanwhile, to the west of the railway line north, Lord Methuen would also march towards the Transvaal. The eastern flank of the British advance was, however, vulnerable. At first Roberts tried to persuade Buller, in northern Natal, to swing his army across in support. But, as usual, Buller prevaricated, piling excuse upon excuse: he had, he said, insufficient cavalry, infantry, engineers, equipment, boots, clothes (but not insufficient food!). Roberts finally gave up trying to pin him down to a definite plan of campaign and left him to make his own way, at his own speed, into the Transvaal.

Mafeking was still under siege while Roberts was laying his plans. Baden-Powell, ever one for the dramatic proclamation, had let his

Commander-in-Chief know that his supplies would be finished by 22 May. Roberts therefore ordered a flying column to be detached from the forces stationed at Kimberley and to go to the relief of Mafeking.

Roberts took the train from Bloemfontein at 5 a.m. on 3 May. Alighting at Karee Siding he placed himself at the head of the column that he was confident he would soon be leading into Pretoria. This column included units representing all those countries of the Empire that had sent troops to support the British cause in South Africa. As the infantry stepped it out, spirits were high, and on all sides men were singing 'We are marching to Pretoria!' The refrain had an ominous ring for the waiting Afrikaners.

The Boer forces waiting to meet the tide of the British advance had an almost impossible task. De la Rey's men were appalled at the sight of tens of thousands of enemy troops spilling towards them over open ground; they retreated smartly from Brandfort, which was fifteen miles from Bloemfontein, and made a brief stand at the Vet River on 5 May.

The Free State President, Marthinus Steyn, was at Kroonstad, his temporary capital, with Louis Botha and about 8,000 men to support him. As he awaited the onslaught, he struggled to inspire his people's will to resist:

> Look, burghers! There are your brothers [men on a train drawing out of Kroonstad for the front] going forward to take part in the struggle which you and I have to carry on to its end; and are you going to stand here while they are fighting for their country? ... We have fought against the hordes of Great Britain for more than seven months; we can fight seven times as long if necessary. Go, then, burghers, in God's name, for the cause of your dear country, for your wives and children. It is better to die on the battlefield than to become slaves of your ancient enemy.[3]

But at Sand River the British columns threatened to envelop the Boers, and their only alternative to encirclement was flight. Steyn saw the realities too, and on 11 May he declared Heilbron, sixty miles to the north-east, to be his new capital. On 12 May Roberts marched into Kroonstad. There was no resistance.

While Roberts's men swarmed northwards, the Transvaal's parliament, the Volksraad, met. With the news that more British reinforcements, and heavy siege guns, had recently arrived in South Africa, the

Volksraad decided that Pretoria could not be properly defended. It was agreed, therefore, to fight the British before they reached the Transvaal's capital. As they dispersed, many delegates must have been privately convinced that they would never again assemble under an independent republican constitution.

Even as the British were occupying Kroonstad, the flying column under Colonel Mahon was approaching Mafeking. As the British drew near, a determined group of Boers led by Veldkornet Sarel Eloff, a grandson of Paul Kruger, broke through Mafeking's outer defences on 12 May 1900. Baden-Powell drummed up all available troops and soon forced Eloff to surrender, at the same time personally inviting him to dinner.

The following day, 13 May, Mahon's column joined up with Colonel Plumer who had marched to the Malopo twenty miles from Mafeking. On 16 May the combined British forces drove several thousand Boers off the Malopo River at a place called Israel's Farm. This was the effective end of the siege of Mafeking. At 7 p.m. on 17 May ten troopers of the Imperial Light Horse, led by Major Karri Davies, rode into the town.

At about 9.30 p.m. on 18 May a Reuters message reached London saying that Mafeking had been relieved. Soon the Mansion House dangled a placard from the window announcing the good tidings. As the news spread like a forest fire throughout the capital, theatre performances were interrupted and huge crowds whirled into the streets, cheering, dancing and singing patriotic songs. But it was not merely London that was caught up in the tumultuous celebrations:

> Liverpool was alive with parading crowds; Newcastle was startled by the explosion and flare of rockets; Birmingham spread the news like wildfire from its theatres; the brass band of the volunteers roused the streets of York; Glasgow illuminated its Municipal Buildings; Leicester and Brighton swarmed with madly cheering people; the Yorkshire dales reverberated with the sound of strangely blown mill and factory sirens.[4]

The following day, Saturday, was a half-holiday for many people anyway. The pandemonium continued unabated; red, white and blue bunting was everywhere; London's main streets were clogged with revellers, and street-hawkers (and pickpockets) did a roaring trade. As evening fell, bonfires were lit and there was singing and dancing in the street. There was also a good deal of drunkenness and hooliganism, and one policeman who had been deluged with kisses at Aldgate said plainly, 'I wouldn't go through that kissing again for something. Right in the public street it was.'

The celebrations marking the relief of Mafeking added a verb, to 'maffick', to the language; they disgusted opponents of the war and even gave pause to serious-minded supporters of imperial expansion; they were both vulgar and fun, distressing and exhilarating. Essentially the pandemonium was pathetic, the relieved reaction of a nation fed on grandiose notions of imperial might, but, underneath all the glitter, pomp and circumstance, insecure, resentful of international hostility, and embarrassed at the war's early fiascos. Posterity may be forgiven, indeed, for asking what all the fuss was about.

Lord Roberts's army rested at Kroonstad for ten days. Then, on 22 May, it struck off again northwards, for Johannesburg and Pretoria. British forces were pressing on the Transvaal from all sides and there was little active opposition to their advance.

On 24 May French's cavalry reached the Vaal River, and on the same day Roberts announced the annexation of the Orange Free State. Inexorably the march on Johannesburg continued. Louis Botha fell back before it, his numbers dwindling as the British came on. At last he and 3,000 men stood barring Roberts's way at Klip River a few miles south of Johannesburg. Here Botha, supported by Koos de la Rey, newly arrived from Mafeking, managed to hold up the British advance for the best part of two days. But the enemy's numbers, and French's swooping raids, proved too much; the Boers found themselves outflanked and retreated.

The triumphant Roberts marched into Johannesburg on 31 May 1900 and a silken Union Jack, made by his wife, was hoisted at the courthouse. Most of the Uitlanders – for whom, in theory, the war was being fought – had left, and as a result Johannesburg was something of a ghost town. In nearby Pretoria, Paul Kruger prepared to move sixty miles down the Delagoa Bay railway towards Mozambique. In Britain, the fall of Johannesburg aroused little enthusiasm – certainly nothing like the reaction to the news of Paardeberg or the relief of the besieged towns. On the Stock Exchange, however, there was gratification that, contrary to the earlier threats that they had made, the Boers had not blown up the gold mines and valuable industrial equipment. Perhaps an instinctive prudence and a glimmer of hope that they might sometime in the future still benefit from the Rand's prosperity played its part in the decision.

By 3 June Roberts was poised for the climax of his 300 mile march to Pretoria. With General French riding ahead with orders to sweep round Pretoria from the west and cut the central railway line north of the city, the British columns moved off over the rolling grasslands of the Transvaal highveld. They had forty miles to go.

In Pretoria panic had gripped much of the populace. Government stores were looted and there was a mass exodus in whatever trains were still running (to the east), in carts and wagons, or on foot, pushing wheelbarrows and handcarts laden with private possessions. Kruger left his capital and entrained for Machadodorp, which was destined to be his seat of government until he was forced to flee the country in September. Schalk Burgers, the Vice-President, stayed on in Pretoria, as, for a while, did the State Attorney Jan Smuts, who would soon to go into the field as a commando leader. The courageous and unfortunate Louis Botha was entrusted with the defence of Pretoria – a thankless task, since he had barely 2,000 men and the city's modern forts had been stripped of guns in the earlier part of the war.

Botha, ever a realist, and perhaps looking to the future, proposed that the Transvaal should now surrender. Koos de la Rey, however, swore that he would never accept this and would continue to fight on in the east. But Botha decided that Pretoria was indefensible and he abandoned the city and withdrew whatever loyal troops he had eastwards.

Field Marshal Roberts, with Lord Kitchener at his side, arrived at Pretoria's central square at 2.15 p.m. on 5 June, and the Union Jack – in fact the same one that had been hauled down after the 1881 defeat at Majuba – was re-instated amid thunderous cheers. A victory march past followed, 'Bobs' savouring the triumphant climax to his epic advance from Bloemfontein. He had made the 300 mile march in thirty-four days, the vast bulk of his army slogging away on foot, carrying all his food and supplies with him. His foes had been scattered like chaff before him. The war seemed well and truly won.

There was still some mopping-up to be done. On 7 June, moreover, De Wet overran some garrisons along the railway line north of Kroonstad, causing the British over 700 losses. While Kitchener was sent south to restore the severed communication links, Roberts turned against Botha's remaining forces astride the railway line to Mozambique at Diamond Hill, twenty-five miles east of Pretoria. With considerable difficulty the British troops managed to occupy part of Diamond Hill by nightfall on 11 June. But the next morning when the offensive was renewed, it was discovered that the Boers had slipped away under cover of darkness, and had made off down the railway line towards Kruger at Machadodorp. The battle of Diamond Hill was one of the last formal, face-to-face encounters of the war.

In July 1900 there was one more significant operation, when the British tried to break continuing Boer resistance in the north-east of the Orange Free State. South of Bethlehem, in the mountainous basin of the Brandwater River, about 9,000 Afrikaners were hemmed in by 16,000 British troops. Among the Boers were President Steyn, who had been harried from one makeshift capital after another, and Commandants de Wet and Prinsloo. In desperation the trapped Boers decided to try to break out through the few as yet unguarded passes. Four columns were formed, but only that under De Wet and President Steyn managed to escape. The others were less fortunate and over 4,000 men under Prinsloo, with 4,000 sheep and 6,000 horses were eventually forced to surrender. De Wet, whose escape was to cause the British untold tribulation later in the war, afterwards wrote scathingly of these events:

> On 17 and 18 July the enemy had broken through at Slabbert's Nek and Retief's Nek, causing the greatest confusion among our forces. Many of the officers and burghers were for an immediate surrender, as appears from the fact that the same assembly which, in defiance of law, elected Mr Prinsloo as Commander-in-Chief, also decided by seventeen votes to thirteen, to give up their forces to the enemy. But this decision was at once rescinded, and it was agreed to ask for an armistice of six days to enable them to take counsel with the Government. A more senseless course of action could hardly be imagined. The Boer Army, as anyone could see, was in a very tight place. Did its officers think that the English would be so foolish as to grant an armistice at such a time as this when all the burghers wanted was a few days in which to effect their escape? Either the officers were remarkably short-sighted or . . . something worse. It was still possible for the commanders to retire in the direction of Witzieshoek (through Golden Gate). But instead of getting this done with all speed, Mr Prinsloo began a correspondence with General Hunter about this

ridiculous armistice, which the English of course refused to grant. On 29 July 1900 Prinsloo, with all the burghers on the mountains, surrendered unconditionally to the enemy. What then is to be our judgment on this act of Prinsloo and the other chief officers there? That it was nothing short of an act of murder, committed on the Government, the country and the Nation, to surrender three thousand men [sic] in such a way. Even the burghers themselves cannot be held to have been altogether without guilt, though they can justly plead that they were obeying orders. The sequel of Prinsloo's surrender was on a par with it. A large number of burghers from Harrismith and a small part of the Vrede commando, although they had already made good their escape, rode quietly from their farms into Harrismith and there surrendered to General Sir Hector Macdonald – one could gnash one's teeth to think that a nation should so readily rush to its own ruin![5]

In August, while Roberts was concentrating on linking up with Buller (at last) and scouring the north-east Transvaal for the enemy, De Wet, De la Rey and others were making a nuisance of themselves south and west of Pretoria. Though the British managed to scatter Botha's forces once more, near Belfast, after an heroic resistance by the Zarps, it was the commando operations in the west that had greater portent. Unless the British could promptly round up the widely separated groups of Boers that were still fighting, there seemed no end to the havoc they could create by attacking lines of communications, garrisons, store depots and the like.

For President Kruger, though, the war had ended. On 11 September he entrained for Delagoa Bay, and thence sailed for Holland. Few imagined that he would return. He had, as a boy, taken part in the Great Trek; he now saw, as an old man, his republic smashed to pieces by the British army. In fact, with the annexation of the Transvaal, both Afrikaner states had ceased to exist, and in Cape Town Sir Alfred Milner would soon be chafing to 'suspend' the Cape constitution and forcibly federate all of South Africa.

In Britain, the Unionist government sought to cash in on the apparent victory in South Africa by appealing to the electorate for a renewed mandate. The 'Khaki Election' of October 1900 was bitterly contested, particularly by those who hated 'Chamberlain's War'. The results confirmed the Unionists in office with a slightly enlarged majority; though this could be interpreted as a mandate for pushing the war through to the bitter end, it did not escape notice that for every eight votes cast for the government seven were cast against it – though for several parties and thus split.

In the same month General Buller departed for home, leaving the care of his soldiers' stomachs to others. At the end of November, Lord Roberts laid down his command and returned to a triumphant and rapturous reception in Britain. Queen Victoria bestowed an earldom upon him and also made him a Knight of the Garter; Parliament voted him £100,000, and everywhere he was fêted and admired. In fact, the celebrations were sadly premature. The commandos in the field did not lay down their arms. The fall of Bloemfontein and Pretoria, even the flight of Kruger, did not bring about the pacification of South Africa. The war still had one and a half years to run.

12

Methods of Barbarism?

ON HIS RETURN to Britain, Lord Roberts was greeted, under-standably enough, as a conquering hero. In South Africa, however, his successor, Kitchener of Khartoum, was grappling with the less glamorous, pressing realities of the military situation. Having annexed the Boer republics the British government was now demanding unconditional surrender from the Afrikaner forces that were still at large. But unconditional surrender could only come if the commandos were decisively beaten in the field, or trapped, by the overwhelmingly large British army in South Africa.

The fall of Bloemfontein and Pretoria, the defeat and capture of Cronje's army at Paardeberg, the flight of President Kruger, the discomfiture of President Steyn, though serious blows to the Afrikaner cause did not in themselves force capitulation upon those Boers who were still prepared to fight. Just as Napoleon had fought his way to Moscow in 1812 and had then found no government with which to negotiate a peace settlement, the British discovered that their recent triumphs did not lead directly to the conference table.

The Boers had a huge area within which to continue their resist-ance. There were railway lines to cut, garrisons to surprise, supply columns to ambush. Given skilful leadership, the Boer forces would be extraordinarily difficult to run to earth. They would, moreover, be sustained and aided by the Afrikaner civilian population. It should not be supposed that the Boers hoped to defeat their enemies – the odds against them were too heavy for that. On the other hand, if they could protract the war they might well force Britain to negotiate a reasonable peace settlement; or a Liberal government might succeed the Unionist administration and be more inclined to treat the defeated republics gently.

Perhaps it was Christiaan de Wet who best represented the spirit of Boer resistance. Elusive, wily, brave and imaginative, De Wet's exploits thrilled not only his own people but also a substantial section of the British public; indeed, they accorded him a hero's welcome when eventually he came to London, with Botha and De la Rey, to negotiate with the British government in August 1902.

In December 1900 it looked as if De Wet would be caught in a trap sprung by Kitchener as he tried to cross the Orange River to raid the Cape Colony:

That evening we reached the Orange River; but alas! what a sight met our eyes! The river was quite impassable owing to the floods, and, in addition, the ford was held by English troops stationed on the south bank. Our position was beginning to be critical, for there were English garrisons guarding the bridges and fords of the Orange on our south, and those of the Caledon on our north. There was still Basutoland [north-east between the rivers] but we did not wish to cross its borders – we were on good terms with the Basutos and we could not afford to make enemies of them. Surely we had enough enemies already! The reader will now perceive how it was my projected inroad into the Cape Colony did not become a fact. My dear old friend, General Charles Knox [in charge of the British columns] was against it, and he had the best of the argument for the river was unfordable. What then was I to do? Retreat I could not, for the Caledon was also now full. Again, as I have already explained, it would not do for me to take refuge in Basutoland ... I knew that the Orange and Caledon Rivers sometimes remained unfordable for weeks together. How could I escape then? Oh, the English had caught me at last! They hemmed me in on every side; I could not get away from them. In fact they had 'cornered me', to use one of their own favourite expressions. That they also thought so appears from what I read afterwards in the *South African News* where I saw that Lord Kitchener had given orders to General Charles Knox 'not to take prisoners there'! For the truth of this I cannot positively vouch; but it was a very suspicious circumstance that the editor of the newspaper was afterwards thrown into prison for having published this very anecdote about Lord Kitchener ...

Without delay I proceeded to the Commissiedrift bridge over the Caledon. As I feared it was occupied by the enemy (Highland Light Infantry). Entrenchments had been dug, and schanzes thrown up at both ends. Foiled here, I at once sent a man to see if the river was still rising. It might be the case that there had not been so much rain higher up. The man reported that the river was falling, and would be fordable (upstream) by the evening. This was good news indeed ... Accordingly we made for Sevenfontein, a ford ten or twelve miles further up the river. If it were not already in the enemy's hands, we would surely be able to get across there. Shortly before sunset we arrived at Sevenfontein. To our immense joy, it was unoccupied and fordable.[1]

Thus encouraged, De Wet made his way north towards Dewetsdorp (named after an ancestor) and Thaba Nchu. Once more British forces closed in on him – General Knox's men stood before him and other columns pressed in. But General Piet Fourie, who was with De Wet, saw a gap in the British line and, despite fierce fire from either side, the Boers burst through. De Wet later described this narrow escape:

On either side of the way we passed, there were two strong forts at a distance of from 1,000 to 1,200 paces from each other. In the space between them was absolutely no cover; and the distance from the point where the burghers were first visible to the men in these forts, to the point where they again disappeared from view was at least 3,000 paces. Over these terrible 3,000 paces our burghers raced, while a storm of bullets was poured in upon them from both sides. And of all that force – 8,000 strong – no single man was killed, and only one was wounded! Our marvellous escape can only be described to the providence and irresistible protection of Almighty God, who kept His hand graciously over us. What the enemy's loss was I never heard. In addition to the burghers, a few carts and wagons, and one gun got safely through the English lines.[2]

This meant that De Wet had escaped again. Whether or not this was due to the intervention of the Almighty, Kitchener had come to the conclusion by the beginning of 1901 that a massive series of barbed-wire fences must be built across the veld; at intervals there should be blockhouses, encased with two layers of corrugated iron packed with stones. At first the wire barriers and blockhouses were widely separated from each other, but gradually the British closed the distances by building more fences. Some commandos were indeed trapped by this system. De Wet, however, was more elusive, and later wrote, in somewhat dismissive tones:

> I learnt that the enemy were occupied in building a line of blockhouses from Heilbron to Frankfort [N.E. Orange Free State]. It had always seemed to me a most unaccountable circumstance that England – the all-powerful – could not catch the Boers without the aid of these block-houses … Still, narrower and narrower did the circle become, hemming us in more closely at every moment. The result was that they 'bagged' an enormous number of men and cattle, without a solitary burgher or, for the matter of that, a solitary ox, having been captured by means of their famous blockhouse system. The English have been constantly boasting in the newspapers about the advantages of their blockhouses; but they have never been able to give an instance of a capture effected by them. On the contrary, when during the later stages of the war, it happened, as it often did, that they drove some of our men against one or other of the great blockhouse lines which then intersected the country, and it became neces-sary for us to fight our way through, we generally succeeded in doing so … There were thousands of miles of blockhouse lines which made a sort of spider's web of the South African Republics. The blockhouses themselves were sometimes round, sometimes angled erections. The roofs were always of iron. The walls were pierced with loop-holes four feet from the ground, and from four to six feet from each other. Between the block-houses were fences, made with five strands of barbed-wire. Parallel with these was a trench, three feet deep and four to five feet across the top, but narrower at the bottom. Where the material could be procured, there was also a stone wall to serve as an additional obstacle. Sometimes there were two lines of fences, the upper one – erected on top of the earth thrown up from the trench – consisting of three or four strands only. There was thus a regular network of wires in the vicinity of the blockhouses – the English seemed to think that a Boer might be netted like a fish.[3]

Still, the blockhouse system undeniably put great pressure upon De Wet and others. So did the attempt by the British to keep a watch on the drifts over the rivers. De Wet described yet another narrow escape as he approached the Vaal River near the appropriately named Bothaville in the north-west of the Orange Free State:

> On the night of 12 March we broke through the blockhouse line, some five miles to the west of Bothaville. When we were about fifty paces from the line, somebody to our left challenged us:

'Halt! Who goes there?'

He challenged us a second time, and then fired. At once seven or eight sentries fired upon us. Shots also were directed at us from the right. Nevertheless we cut through the barbed-wire and crossed in safety, the firing still continuing until we were about fifteen hundred paces on the far side of the line. Fortunately no one was hit. Having thus escaped the last 'White Elephant' that we should have to reckon with, the next obstacle to be encountered was the Vaal River. For President Steyn [who was in the field with De Wet] ... had decided to visit De la Rey in order to place himself under medical advice. His eyes had become very weak during the last fortnight or so, and he thought that Dr van Rennenkampf might be able to do something for them. Thus we had to cross the Vaal River.

But we heard that there was a military post at Commando Drift where we wanted to cross, and further, that all the other fords were occupied by the English. We should have been in a great difficulty had not one of our burghers, Pieterson, who knew the district thoroughly, brought us across the river by a footpath ford. We crossed on 15 March. The current was so strong that in places the river-bed was strewn with huge boulders, over which our steeds had to climb. However we all managed to get safely over ... [and] on the following day we joined General de la Rey.[4]

De Wet's exploits made him a household name throughout the world. In Britain, where his elusiveness was the despair of patriots and a consolation to pro-Boers, he became a legend. King Edward VII once said jocularly of a hostess bent on finding a suitor for her daughter 'they ought to set her to catch De Wet'.[5] Rudyard Kipling, bard of Empire and a journalist in South Africa during the war, wrote wryly in his poem dedicated to the Royal Artillery and entitled *Ubique*:

> Ubique means 'They've caught De Wet, an' now we shan't be long.'
> Ubique means 'I much regret, the beggar's goin' strong!'[6]

To enable the British forces to track down commando leaders like De Wet, and also to punish those who aided them, Lord Roberts had begun a policy of farm burning in the Orange Free State in June 1900. Technically those Free Staters who aided Boer forces were rebels, since the republic had been annexed by the British crown in May, and between June and November 1900 more than 600 farms were burnt. Farm burning was also practised in the Transvaal and actively prosecuted by Kitchener in his attempts to smash Afrikaner resistance. It was a policy that aroused bitter resentment among the Afrikaners and mixed feeling among the British troops that actually set fire to the homesteads.

Captain R.F. Talbot of the Royal Horse Artillery wrote in his diary for 1901:

> I went out this morning with some of my men ostensibly to get vegetables, but joined the provost marshal and the sappers in a farm burning party, and we burnt and blew up two farms with gun-cotton, turning out the inhabitants first. It is a bit sickening at first turning out the women and children, but they are such brutes and the former all spies; we don't mind it now. Only those are done which belong to men who are sniping or otherwise behaving badly.[7]

Captain Phillipps, of Rimington's Guides, gave another, more poignant account of farm burning in his book *With Rimington* published in 1902:

> I had to go myself the other day, at the General's bidding, to burn a farm near the line of march. We got to the place and I gave the inmates, three women and some children, ten minutes to clear their clothes and things out of the house, and my men then fetched bundles of straw and we proceeded to burn it down. The old grandmother was very angry. She told me that, though I was making a fine blaze now, it was nothing compared to the flames that I myself should be consumed in hereafter. Most of them however, were too miserable to curse. The women cried and the children stood by holding on to them and looking with large frightened eyes at the burning house. They won't forget that sight, I'll bet a sovereign, not even when they grow up. We rode away and left them, a forlorn little group, standing among their household goods – beds, furniture, and gimcracks strewn about the veld; the crackling of the fire in their ears, and smoke and flame streaming overhead. The worst moment is when you first come to the house. The people thought we had called for refreshments, and one of the women went to get milk. Then we had to tell them that we had come to burn the place down. I simply didn't know which way to look. One of the women's husbands had been killed at Magersfontein. There were others, men and boys, away fighting; whether dead or alive they did not know ...
>
> We can't exterminate the Dutch or seriously reduce their numbers. We can do enough to make hatred of England and thirst for revenge the first

duty of every Dutchman, and we can't effectively reduce the numbers of the men who will carry that duty out. Of course it is not a question of the war only. It is a question of governing the country afterwards.

So far we only really hold the ground on which our armies stand. If I were to walk out from this tent a mile or two over the hills yonder, I should probably be shot. Kroonstad has been ours for four months. It is on the main railway. The country all round is being repeatedly crossed by our troops. Yet an Englishman would not be safe for a minute out of range of those guns on the hill ...

At another farm a small girl interrupted her preparation for departure to play indignantly their national anthem at us on an old piano. We were carting the people off. It was raining hard and blowing – a miserable, hurried home-leaving; ransacked house, muddy soldiers, a distracted mother saving one or two trifles and pushing along her children to the ox-waggon outside, and this poor little wretch in the midst of it all pulling herself together to strum a final defiance. One smiled, but it was rather dramatic all the same, and exactly like a picture.[8]

Farm burning was, in the short term, of some benefit to the British army. De Wet admitted as much when he wrote:

I had to wait there [near Heilbron] till the evening of 31 December until the necessary waggons and oxen had been got together for carrying the ammunition with us. Waggons were now no longer easily to be got, because the British had not only taken them away from the farms but had also burnt many of them ... even where there were waggons the women had always to keep them in readiness to fly in them before the columns of the enemy, who had now already a command to carry the women away from their dwellings to the concentration camps – which the British called Refugee Camps. Proclamations had been issued by Lord Roberts, prescribing that any building within ten miles of the railways, where the Boers had blown up the railway line should be burnt down.[9]

In the long term, however, farm burning antagonised many South African moderates, and made the policy of post-war reconstruction more difficult and, incidentally, much more expensive. Three Cape Colony editors were put on trial for criticising farm burning among other aspects of British military policy, and in the fallen Afrikaner republics enraged villagers often refused to allow British dead to be buried in their cemeteries.

But the outraged reaction to farm burning was overshadowed by the concentration camp controversy. The camps were first established in the summer of 1900, chiefly to protect the *hensoppers* from the vengeance of their fellow Boers. As the war progressed, however, the families of prisoners of war (who were themselves mostly sent to relatively comfortable confinement in Ceylon, Bermuda and St Helena), of the men still fighting, or simply those whose farms had been burnt, were placed in the camps.

It may be assumed, though many contemporaries thought otherwise, that the British authorities had no malevolent motive in the establishment of the concentration camps, despite the latter-day emotive connotations of the term. The camps were set up mostly in the Free State and the Transvaal, though there was also a number in the Cape and Natal. At one time they contained as many as 160,000 inmates. A direct result of the British occupation of the Boer republics and of the scorched-earth aftermath of that success, the camps were simply a pragmatic response to certain problems.

By October 1901, however, the concentration camps had acquired a terrible notoriety. Overcrowding, insanitary conditions, an insufficiently balanced diet, and inadequate planning caused a tragic loss of life. Women and children, swept into the camps from isolated farms, were easy prey to a variety of diseases, and measles, typhoid, jaundice, malaria, bronchitis and pneumonia all took their toll. In October 1901 there were as many as 3,156 deaths, and the annual average was running at 344 per thousand.

Not only did the death rate in the concentration camps convince many Afrikaners that the British were bent on destroying their race, but it led to a persistent and noisy outcry in the United Kingdom. The Liberal leader of the opposition, Sir Henry Campbell-Bannerman, felt moved to ask 'When is a war not a war?' and to provide the answer: 'When it is carried on by methods of barbarism in South Africa.' 'Methods of barbarism' was a phrase that highlighted a memorable controversy. But the actual improvement in conditions in the camps owed much to the persistent agitation of Emily Hobhouse, women's Secretary of the South Africa Conciliation Committee, and the impatient Kitchener's *bête noire*. As a result, conditions were drastically improved and by the end of the war the death rate was down to sixty-nine per thousand.

Despite the liberal and humanitarian outcry, there were plenty willing to defend the camps. Dr Alec Kay, safely out of Ladysmith, wrote scathingly of the 'agitation ... raised by a few unsexed and hysterical women who are prepared to sacrifice everything for notoriety'. He went on, writing in 1901:

> The whole question of the camps is bound up with that of guerrilla warfare. If it is lawful and necessary to destroy such Boer houses and farms that are used as bases for warfare is it not more humane to establish camps where women and children can be housed? And even at those Boer farms which have not been destroyed, the exigencies of war have brought a desperate shortage of food and medical attention and a constant danger from marauding natives against unarmed women and children. Is it not better for them to be taken to camps than be left where they are? All the misery, the burning and the camps are the result of war; it has always happened, and will happen again. After all it was the Boer Government which declared war.
>
> It is true that there has been sickness in the camps and that conditions have been primitive. But they were set up hurriedly by the military authorities, and there is always disorganisation and lack of careful planning where large numbers of people are moved. Improvements are taking place rapidly, and they would have taken place whether or not there was this agitation by sexless busybodies with nothing better to do than decry everything and everybody ...
>
> I have myself worked at one of these camps when measles and influenza were raging. To children and adults, already debilitated by the results of war, anxiety, bad food and other hardships, any illness would be likely to become serious in the severe winter weather, especially when people are living under canvas; even those in comfortable homes in Johannesburg, Pretoria and other towns suffer.
>
> The Boers in the camps often depend on home remedies, with deplorable results. Inflammation of the lungs and enteric fever are frequently treated by the stomach of a sheep or goat which has been killed at the bedside of a patient being placed hot and bloody over the chest or abdomen; cow-dung poultices are a favourite remedy for many skin diseases; lice are given for jaundice; and crushed bugs for convulsions in children. These are common remedies in everyday use on the farms.
>
> As far as the authorities are concerned, everything is done in the camps that can be done: good food, good clothing and blankets are provided and British soldiers are employed to keep the camps clean, carrying water, serving rations and assisting in every way. It is my firm belief that if the

camps had not been established, sickness and mortality would have been far greater on the farms and villages, and even in the towns.[10]

Despite Dr Kay's apologia, at least 25,000 Afrikaner concentration camp inmates had died by the end of the war – a bitter legacy for the ensuing era of reconstruction and conciliation. Incidentally, it went barely noticed at the time that at least as many blacks also died in their own segregated and even more poorly equipped and managed concentration camps.

13

Seeking Peace

MARCH 1900 TO JUNE 1901

Lthough more and more civilians were caught up by the British
army's attempts to bring the Boer commandos to heel, the prospect of peace was never far from the minds of the soldiers and politicians. In late 1900, Ludwig Krause, a critic of Kruger whom we
last saw leaving the incompetent Boer commanders in northern
Transvaal for the Natal front, was now a prisoner of war of the British
and in the process of concluding his journal with a heartfelt plea for
justice for his people. He urged Englishmen to treat the Boers as
Gladstone had done in 1881, when he had agreed to let them keep
their independence. Not only would Englishmen gain the gratitude
of the Boers and the world, he declared they would also gain the
approbation of 'all future generations of Mankind, by giving back my
country, my liberty, my independence of which you have no right to
rob me, in spite of all the gold therein, and in spite of all the vanity of
"extending your Empire"'.[1] For most Boers, however, as Krause's
somewhat melodramatic appeal makes clear, their independence
remained non-negotiable. Separation from British rule had been a
constant desire since the British had arrived in South Africa and now,
after numerous sacrifices, they were not prepared to give up their precious freedom, whatever the military situation might suggest. By
launching a guerrilla war and by attempting to provoke a massive
rebellion in the Cape Colony, the Boers hoped to exhaust the British
will to fight. Even if they had to make certain concessions, most
Boers believed their independence was still an achievable goal.

Krause's appeal was one of many made during the war for a negotiated and equitable settlement between Boer and Briton. But by the time of his plea the military situation was now so unfavourable to the Boers no one on the other side was prepared to listen. By then, the British had determined that after the shock of Black Week the Boers should never again threaten British interests with their military might. Annexation, not toleration, of the Boer republics was now the unequivocal goal of British statesmen.

Even so, between 1900 and 1901, as the war raged across the veld, attempts were made to reach a *modus vivendi*, as each side hoped the other might alter its rigid stance.

In March 1900, when the Boer armies faced the massive onslaught of the British forces under Lord Roberts and Sir Redvers Buller, some in the Boer camp felt the time had come to cut their losses and save what little remained. Under the circumstances and given his reluctance to go to war in the first place, it probably came as no surprise to his comrades that Joubert should urge Kruger to make overtures to the British. Surprisingly perhaps, Kruger agreed and persuaded Steyn that the time had come to seek some sort of accommodation based on the retention of independence, and a telegram was sent directly to Lord Salisbury on 5 March. Kruger's intention, however, was not to forestall a British invasion of the Transvaal, but to get the British to reveal their desire to annex the Boer republics. Kruger wanted something specific with which to revitalise the energies of his commandos and British obduracy seemed to work.

For the British the past five months had been a revelation. A war entered into with such confidence, and a degree of levity, had proved to be one humiliation after another. With the realisation that the Boers meant business, so too came the realisation that the fate of the Boer republics would have to be given serious consideration. At first, the government had not given the war's aims much thought beyond the view that the Boers, once quickly chastised, would settle down under British tutelage and behave themselves for ever more. No thought was given to annexation because territorial aggrandisement was not what the war was about. For the government it was about securing British interests and ensuring that the Boers acknowledged these in a satisfactory manner. After all, Lord Salisbury had publicly stated that the British were not after the goldfields and territory but the 'equal rights for men of all races and security for our fellow-subjects and for the

Empire'. But the failure of the army at Magersfontein, Stormberg and Colenso awoke British ministers to the fact that moderation would not do in the face of Mausers and Creusot artillery. And so it was that Kruger's parleying was rebuffed, just as he had anticipated, and in May 1900 both Salisbury and Chamberlain made it clear that the republics were to be terminated. The safety of the Empire was paramount and the republics had forfeited their right to exist. In any case, after a council of war at Kroonstad on 17 March, the Boer governments had already decided that the war would continue, but this time fought not in entrenchments but with hit-and-run tactics more suited to South Africa's wide open spaces. For the Boers the war was about saving their independence – nothing else mattered – and it would carry on regardless.[2]

For the time being the positions of the belligerents had set hard. But as the year ended, the British began to try to chip away at the edifice of Boer intransigence. In spite of the occupation of both republics the guerrilla war continued unabated and with Lord Roberts about to go home to become Commander-in-Chief in Britain, it was Chamberlain who resuscitated the peace process with a reminder to Milner that the effort to find a peaceful end to the war was an equal partner to the military effort. For Chamberlain and his ministerial colleagues it was imperative that the fighting Boers should realise that, while the annexations stood, it was in their interests to give up as they would still retain most of their former liberties, laws, property and municipalities. In urging Milner to make these terms known to the Boers on 13 December, Chamberlain hoped that the British people would realise that the government was doing its best to secure peace and that it was the Boers who were the main obstacle to that goal.[3] Despite the money being spent on the war and the many troops being sent to South Africa, the public was losing interest. British casualties, mostly from disease, were high by the standards of the time and set-piece battles, which everyone could follow, were no longer being fought because of the guerrilla war. The British authorities, therefore, were keen to put the onus of responsibility on the Boers. The response, however, was not encouraging: on 11 January Kitchener told his confidant Lady Cranborne, the daughter-in-law of Lord Salisbury, that the Boers 'mean to stick to it for some time yet. I have let them know what Chamberlain said about the future, but it does not seem to have much effect.'

Kitchener himself had his own ideas about the best way to make peace. Two weeks later he told the new Secretary of State for War, St John Brodrick, that he was trying his luck through 'burgher peace committees'. By this he meant using prominent, malleable but earnest Boers, like ex-President Pretorius of the Transvaal, to persuade their irreconcilable brethren that the cause was hopeless. This initiative proved a dismal failure and extremely dangerous for the Boers who actually went out to the commandos. Two, Morgendaal and Meyer de Kock, were executed by their outraged countrymen. With an eye to the future, Kitchener offered his own view of the terms he expected the Boers to seek. First, with regard to the question of the treatment of Africans, Kitchener felt the answer was to use the laws of the former Orange Free State because they were supposed to be more liberal than the Transvaal's laws. Second, in dealing with the problem of compensation for the destruction of private property Kitchener believed the mines could pay for this, naively arguing that 'a million would go a long way to putting matters right, and when the Rand is working they turn out 2 millions a week'. Third, he asked if an amnesty for Cape rebels (there were no Natal rebels to speak of) was permissible. Finally, he wanted a guarantee that the Boers would not be ruled by capitalists, meaning the mine owners of Johannesburg. 'They are I believe absurdly afraid of getting into the hands of certain Jews, who *no doubt wield great influence in this country.*' Kitchener's knowledge of the Boer leadership was extremely accurate, and he was thus aware that Louis Botha was more accommodating than either Steyn or De Wet. In a remark he was to repeat in the future, he put his finger on one of the major dilemmas facing the Boers: 'a great difficulty with them is who will be the first man to give in, as he will be held up as a disgrace to his country ever afterwards.' With some understatement he concluded that 'On the whole the chances of peace in this way are not very promising.'[4]

Indeed, Kitchener's assessment of the Boer leaders was spot-on. In August 1900 Botha had evidently tried to persuade Kruger to make another overture to the British, but had been stopped by Steyn's intransigence. From then on, relations between the two remained strained and this clash was to ensure that the Boers were far from united when the final talks came. Several attempts had already been made by leading Boers and others, such as Samuel

Marks, to convince Botha that the war was lost, but nothing came of these attempts. It was not long, however, before another chance to work on Botha arrived. At the beginning of February, Botha had asked that his wife, who was living in Pretoria, be allowed to visit him at his base in the eastern Transvaal, and for Kitchener the opportunity was too good to miss. He would be available any time to meet and discuss matters with her husband, he told her as she left, but would not discuss the question of independence, which he was well aware was the main sticking point. When Mrs Botha returned she came with good news; her husband would talk to Kitchener. A conciliatory attitude would be best, Kitchener informed Brodrick on 22 February, and after requesting to know the extent of his bargaining powers, he continued: 'I [hope I] may be allowed to do away with anything humiliating to them in the surrender if it comes off.' If he could detach Botha, he felt that De Wet and the equally intransigent De la Rey would also give in.[5]

Kitchener's verbal message via his wife had intrigued Botha enough to agree to talks, having already been invited to meet Kitchener by the Transvaal's ex-President Pretorius. Botha's intentions did not go down well with De Wet, when appraised of his plans, and he was now added to the list of those who questioned Botha's loyalty to the cause.

Kitchener and Botha met on 28 February 1901 at 10 a.m. in Middelburg, a town situated almost halfway between Pretoria and Komatipoort on the Delagoa Bay railway. Two days earlier Kitchener had been instructed not to make promises without consulting the government beforehand, which waited for Botha's conditions to become known.[6] The talks that followed were apparently very amicable, and Botha was taught how to play bridge by Kitchener during the evenings! It emerged that a major sticking point was Milner's recent appointment to the governorship of the Transvaal, and, although Kitchener thought this a point not worth pursuing, he mentioned it to the British government because Botha wanted him to. More specifically, Botha wanted answers to those questions foreseen earlier by Kitchener. If the British reply was acceptable, Botha would then try to convince his government, De la Rey and the Orange Free State to make peace. Kitchener confidently remarked that Botha seemed 'fully assured that he could, in a very short time, bring about peace and good feeling between Boer and Briton'.[7]

Kitchener met Milner in order to discuss his proposed answers to Botha's questions, and the proposal was then sent to their superiors, Brodrick and Chamberlain, who also had the benefit of Milner's opinions.

Kitchener's terms were that on the complete surrender of the Boers and all their equipment, the British government would give an amnesty for all lawful acts of war, although rebels would be disenfranchised; all prisoners of war would be returned; a crown colony government would replace military government in the former republics, followed by representative government once circumstances permitted; both English and Dutch would be used in ordinary, state schools and the law courts; a sum of £1,000,000 would be given to pay debts owed by the Boers to their people for supplies during the course of the war; the British government would give financial assistance to farmers to rebuild their farms and they would not pay any special tax towards war costs; burghers would be allowed to keep rifles under licence; and finally, no franchise would be given to Africans before the establishment of self-government.[8]

Milner, however, remained unconvinced by the whole business of peace talks. While only disagreeing with Kitchener on the issue of the amnesty for rebels because, he said, 'I think it would have a deplorable effect in the Cape Colony and Natal to obtain peace with such a concession,' underneath he was appalled by the very idea of negotiating. As he told his friends and acquaintances, only total victory was acceptable; to one friend he wrote more bluntly that he wanted 'to knock the bottom out of the "great Afrikander [sic] nation"'.[9] Milner had by this time formulated a specific set of war aims, which fitted into his vision of South Africa's place in the Empire. He had once described the area as the 'weak link in the imperial chain' and by 1901 he had worked out how this weakness could be strengthened. Total victory, whereby the irreconcilable Boers and their leaders would be defeated both physically and psychologically, thus ensuring they would have no part to play in post-war South Africa, would guarantee the new colony's loyalty to the Empire. He expected that British immigrants, preferably made up of men from a 'superior' class with capital to spare, would be brought in to Anglicise the Transvaal, especially the rural areas on land bought by the government. Milner realised, however, that such a scheme would never succeed in outnumbering the rural Boers, but it would dilute them significantly. A continual influx of British immigrants into the towns would cement overall British numerical superiority. He hoped many ex-soldiers would remain in South Africa – in the police, in the railway service, in the Post Office and in civil employment. Basically, his aim was make South Africa at least sixty per cent British.[10] Thus, when Milner learned that Kitchener had met Botha, he feared that a compromise peace might be all too real. In his scheme, there was no place for irreconcilable Boers no matter what their immediate, peaceful intentions. For Milner, they would remain forever irreconcilable and a permanent stumbling block to the future peace of British South Africa.

On 6 March 1901, Chamberlain telegraphed to Milner the government's reply, which contained several amendments to Kitchener's earlier proposal. First, the total cessation of hostilities should mean just that, and did not imply only the surrender of Botha, who would have to ensure that all the other Boers agreed. Second, complete amnesty was rejected as it could not be granted to rebels. Third, the 'privilege' of self-government would only be granted after a period of representative, or crown colony, government – in other words, self-government was to be attained by degrees, with the Boers having to earn the trust of the British over a length of time, which was not fixed. Fourth, regarding the debts of state, Kitchener's promise seemed to ministers to be 'dangerous'. Instead, they proposed to provide £1,000,000 to be paid out *pro rata* to claims, satisfactorily confirmed, by those who were obliged to pay requisitions before and after the annexation of the republics 'in the face of superior force'. This sum would also cover the claims of Uitlanders. Fifth, the government could not promise assistance to Boer farmers following the destruction of their farms because the loyalists might feel that they were being left out. Farmers would, alternatively, be provided with loans. Lastly, Chamberlain insisted on an extra paragraph regarding the question of the African franchise: 'And if then given [the franchise] will be so limited as to secure the just predominance of the white races, but the legal position of Kaffirs will be similar to that which they hold in the Cape Colony.' And for good measure Chamberlain asserted that peace would not be purchased by leaving the 'coloured population' of the former republics as servile as they were before the war.

Kitchener was plainly irked by the government's amendments and while he realised that the question of independence was still the key issue, he felt that the matter of loans and the 'native' question would make peace doubtful. As he explained to Lady Cranborne, 'I was amazed that the Govt. were not more anxious for peace.'[11]

Kitchener forwarded the peace plan to Botha and received his reply just over a week later. Botha stated that he could not recommend the terms contained therein to his government, and that his government and generals all agreed with him. A disappointed Kitchener, on further reflection, was sure that the main stumbling block now appeared to be the lack of an amnesty for rebels: 'As I thought,' he wrote, 'he [Botha] feels bound in honour not to give in and leave in prison those who came out to help his cause.' Chamberlain, on the other hand, was relieved by Botha's reply and was glad the talks had not dragged on. Milner was far more emphatic in expressing his relief; to his confidante Lady Violet Cecil, another daughter-in-law of Lord Salisbury, he summed up his feelings: 'I hope we shall take warning and avoid such rotten ground in the future.'[12]

At Middelburg, Botha had certainly tested the water and although he now realised that Kitchener was a man with whom he could do business, the terms offered by the British government were plainly not acceptable at that time. In a proclamation to the burghers on 15 March 1901, Botha starkly concluded that the British government 'desires nothing else but the destruction of our Afrikander [sic] people'. There would be no more independence and this remained at the heart of the matter: 'The blood and tears that this war has cost has been hard, but giving up our country will be doubly hard.' It was a sentiment shared by others: one burgher noted the fury of his comrades when appraised of the terms because 'However great their longing for peace, nobody wanted to hear about it if it was going to cost their independence.' This view was echoed by Dietlof van Warmelo who wrote: 'Had we indeed fought so long and so fiercely only to become an English colony, and not to be allowed to carry arms unless we had a licence? And for the Kaffirs to be eventually allowed to vote?' Many were strengthened by their religious faith and the conviction that God would ultimately lead them to victory. The desire to fight for their independence was in itself an article of that faith and one that could not be compromised. For the moment then, the Boers would fight on.[13]

In spite of the apparent finality of Botha's answer, the question of peace talks continued to rumble on through most of the South African winter of 1901. In part this was a result of Kitchener's anger at the failure of the talks themselves and his refusal to believe that they had irrevocably failed. In his letter and telegrams to Brodrick he lashed out apportioning blame to all and sundry for what he felt was a wasted opportunity. On 22 March, while describing Milner's view as vindictive, Kitchener was too ready to accept that the Boers were prepared to give up their independence and consequently he put too much emphasis on the question of amnesty for rebels as the main sticking point. He complained about it to Brodrick:

> We are now carrying the war on to be able to put 2 or 300 Dutchmen in prison at the end of it. It seems to me absurd and wrong and I wonder the Chancellor of the Exchequer did not have a fit. Mrs Botha has written to ask her husband if the amnesty question is the only one they are now fighting for. If he replies in the affirmative, could anything be done if Botha was induced to ask for better terms for the rebels & for a recommendation of their case?

Botha, sadly for Kitchener, chose not to pursue the issue, but evidently Ben Viljoen let it be known 'that [the] amnesty question was [the] principal difficulty' and wondered whether Kitchener would meet him, Botha and De la Rey, to which Kitchener replied that he was always ready to talk.[14]

The government, however, chose to look at it differently, as Brodrick indicated to Kitchener. An amnesty would be a 'surviving reproach on us. The loyalists at the least have surely a right to see the very moderate Cape punishments inflicted on the rebels.' Furthermore, the government stated that the terms offered at Middelburg had been withdrawn and that further negotiations should not be reopened. The government would only consider suggestions offered by the Boers themselves, but would not contemplate conceding terms more favourable than those already declined.[15]

The prospect of further talks was now remote but reverberations from the Middelburg discussions continued still. Although Kitchener finally conceded in June that the amnesty question was not the main reason for the Boers refusing to compromise, Brodrick's earlier mention of the loyalists sent him off on another tack. To Kitchener, pandering to the whims of the loyalists, or as he referred to them ,'the South African white', would not be in the best interests of peace. They were inferior to the Boers in virtually every respect, which the Boers knew, and if not for the presence of British troops the Boers 'would still make short work of the local whites, and carry out their original scheme of a united South Africa under the Dutch'. The Boers would never be subordinated to the colonists and Uitlanders. According to Kitchener's thinking if the British authorities wanted peace then they would have recourse to two options: either the government would have to deport the irreconcilable Boer population, whom he described as 'uncivilized Afrikander [sic] savages with a thin white veneer', to places such as Fiji or Madagascar; or, alternatively, the British government would have to offer terms such as those proposed at Middelburg, even if the Boers surrendered unconditionally, 'if you really want to live in peace and security with them and be able to give them self-government'. Once the Boers had agreed to give up their independence they could be left to quarrel amongst themselves. He concluded with a warning: 'The howls with which the terms were received in England and by the Cape loyalists have to my mind put off the termination of the war for a very long time, and made it almost impossible for Boer and Briton to settle down peaceably, so this course having failed we are, as far as I can see, forced into the more objectionable ... course proposed.'

Kitchener had thus told the government to pay its money and take its choice. This was not the thinking of an officer desperate to end the war and get away to pastures new. It was the considered opinion, albeit eccentrically put, of a hard-headed general with an eye for political realities. It would take another year before the British government fell in with Kitchener's mode of thinking and until then he pursued the Boers with added vigour, resulting in the devastation of the former republics.[16]

Questions of peace, in spite of the renewed British offensive, continued to bubble under the surface. In the Middelburg discussions one factor had been overlooked and only in May 1901 did Botha broach the subject with Kitchener. He wrote that while he was anxious to end the war, it would be necessary for him to inform Kruger of the current situation and of recent events. Kitchener's reaction, as told to Brodrick, was to refuse because, since the annexation of the Transvaal, Kruger was no longer President and his authority was no longer recognised; Kitchener would negotiate only with Botha and his generals. Surprisingly, perhaps, the British government thought otherwise and suggested that Kitchener allow Botha to send messages to Kruger in Europe. This was done via the Netherlands Consul, and on 20 June 1901 Botha published Kruger's reply as well as the recommendations of a recent council of war between the two Boer governments and their generals. The document stated that having put the facts in the worst possible light so that Kruger and the other Boer deputies gave them their utmost consideration, the exiles replied that they 'have still great hopes of a satisfactory end'. With this in mind, the council of war decided that the conflict in the Cape Colony was proceeding satisfactorily; that it would be wrong to abandon their rebel 'brothers'; and that the women and children had already made too many sacrifices. It was thus resolved 'That no peace will be made and no peace conditions accepted by which our independence and national existence, or the interests of our colonial brothers shall be the price paid, and that the war will be vigorously prosecuted by taking all measures necessary for [the] maintenance of independence and interests'.

After such an uncompromising statement Kitchener asked Brodrick, 'Can you give me any hint whether stronger measures will be taken now that the Boers have resolved on no peace?'[17]

14

The Final Battles

MAY 1901 TO MAY 1902

WITH THE APPARENT failure to reach a compromise peace with the Boer leaders, the British government, Milner and Kitchener began to consider how the next phase of the war should be carried out. The British government, stuck far away in London and receiving little tangible information from Kitchener, was at a loss how to proceed next. Beyond the desire for the Boers to surrender unconditionally, the government had no policy to speak of and was becoming acutely aware of the spiralling costs of the war and the continual need for manpower in South Africa.

Milner, on the other hand, did have a policy in mind and because he believed he could not personally deflect Kitchener from his strategy of drives, farm burning and concentration camps, he set sail for Britain under the pretext of taking a holiday on 8 May 1901. When he arrived sixteen days later, he was welcomed back as a great imperial hero, and as a reward for his hard work in South Africa he was ennobled as Baron Milner of St James's and Cape Town.

For Milner, all this was fluff; the real business at hand was to do something about Kitchener and to get South Africa working again. As far as he was concerned, restarting both farming and industry in the Orange River Colony and the Transvaal would, perhaps more than anything, induce the Boers to surrender. Milner wanted to see the establishment of protected zones, one of which had already been set up around Bloemfontein, and in which normal life, or as normal as could be expected, would carry on. The irreconcilable Boers, languishing outside, would be stopped from interfering by British troops, who would chase and harry them until they surrendered. Milner wanted to establish a feeling of permanence and encourage those Boers who had had enough of fighting to settle down in well-protected areas and get back to normality. For this scheme to work, and be given a chance to work, Milner knew that he had to have control of the army in South Africa. Moreover, he was thoroughly displeased that nothing substantial had been done to restart Johannesburg's industries, particularly the gold mines. Although by May a few mines were working and a steady trickle of mining personnel was returning, events had not moved quickly enough for Milner. As a result, his plans for rural recovery and mining production had barely come to fruition, and the main stumbling block was Kitchener. Thus on 29 March, just before he left South Africa, he told Chamberlain: 'If I could get four or five fundamental points settled, it would immensely facilitate my, and I venture to think, *your* task.'[1]

Milner found ministers receptive to his arguments because he was now giving them a policy upon which they could focus. When in Britain, Milner outlined his ideas to Chamberlain between 31 May and 2 June and these were then presented to the Cabinet for discussion. By this time, ministers had become exasperated by Kitchener's constant demands for men and his gloomy prognostications about the course of the war and its eventual end. But they lacked the wherewithal to present an alternative scheme, especially as Kitchener pleaded quite rightly that as the Boers had carried the war into the Cape Colony, he could not reduce troop numbers because they were needed there. Thus, for the Cabinet to override the great warlord in South Africa was not an easy business and there was apprehension that Kitchener might resign and so cause a public outcry. Milner, however, found the Cabinet's deliberations took too long and became quite exasperated by ministerial pusillanimity. After addressing the Cabinet himself on 21 June, he drove home his views with another memorandum criticising Kitchener's 'aggressive and destructive policy'. Although he did not offer a quick and easy solution to the war, Milner nevertheless forwarded a hopeful prognosis in contrast to Kitchener's gloom and, by so doing, won the government over to his way of thinking. On 29 June Kitchener was ordered to comply with the government's demands that large-scale gold mining was to be resumed and that after the South African winter he was to scale down military operations in favour of hunting down selected commandos.[2]

Furthermore, in his hour of triumph, Milner felt that Kitchener's military operations should be aided by complementary measures against the Boer commandos. He was in fact endorsing some earlier pronouncements of Kitchener, who in April had suggested that the government confiscate the property of the Boer *bittereinders* as a way of inducing them to surrender. Kitchener had also advocated the banishment from South Africa of the *bittereinders* and their families, but the government rejected this particular idea as far too severe and were unwilling to keep the banished Boers locked up somewhere in the British Empire, or to offload them on foreign territory. Nevertheless, Milner felt that a limited form of banishment confined to the Boer leadership would work. Not only would fewer Boers be involved, but it would mean the removal of those men Milner feared would be the main obstacles to his reconstruction plans after the war. With both Milner and Kitchener endorsing such a scheme, the government agreed to threaten the Boer leaders with banishment and on 7 August 1901 a proclamation was issued which demanded the surrender of Boer commandants, veldkornets, and 'leaders of armed bands' by 15 September, otherwise they would face banishment from South Africa if they were subsequently captured. Kitchener had therefore got his severe measures with which to complement his military operations.

He had, meanwhile, become more obstructive to the government's wishes and used an argument that Milner found very difficult to refute. He argued that until the situation in the Cape Colony had been resolved, he could not implement the measures asked for by the government on 29 June. This indeed was Milner's weak spot: if the Boer commandos were left to run free in the Cape Colony then they might very well inspire the Afrikaner uprising which he so dreaded. On 29 July 1901 Kitchener had already launched his second great drive in the Cape Colony, the first having commenced eleven days earlier. Boer commandos under Commandants Gideon Scheepers and P.H. Kritzinger were already causing the British army some anxiety, and the situation worsened on 3 September 1901 when Jan Christiaan Smuts, the Transvaal's State Attorney and now an Assistant Commandant General, entered the Cape Colony with his commando, which included Deneys Reitz, in order to assess the prospects for a major incursion to divert British attention from De Wet, Steyn and Botha. Indeed, Kitchener had been pressing the Boers hard during the last few months: on 11 July, for example, President Steyn, his staff and accompanying men, had been ambushed by the forces of Brigadier General R.G. Broadwood at the town of Reitz, where they had stopped for the night. Steyn barely managed to escape and only did so thanks to the loyalty of his black servant, Jan Ruiter.

For a moment the situation did seem to change in favour of the British in the Cape Colony. On 5 and 10 September respectively, the commandos of Commandants Lötter and Scheepers were defeated by British forces under Lieutenant Colonels Scobell and Crabbe, and Lötter himself was captured. But this good news did not last long. For on 7 September Louis Botha invaded Natal and ten days later defeated Lieutenant Colonel Hubert Gough at Blood River Poort. Gough attacked what he thought was a small Boer force, his patrols having failed to detect that Botha's larger contingent was in the vicinity. Gough's troops were quickly defeated and Gough himself was taken prisoner, along with over 240 of his men. The Boers did not realise they had actually captured the British commander and Gough was able to escape that night.

On the very same day in the Cape Colony, Smuts's commando attacked a position held by C Squadron of the 17th Lancers at Modderfontein, near Cradock, taking them completely by surprise. Their camp was completely overrun and looted by the Boers, who by this time were in rags or wearing captured British uniforms (which entitled the British to shoot them under the rules of war if they were captured), and were short of food and ammunition. In the camp they found enough supplies of all kinds to replenish their stocks completely; Deneys Reitz later wrote that he began the day dressed in a grain bag, with an old rifle and a couple of bullets, but ended it 'in a handsome cavalry tunic, riding breeches, etc., with a sporting Lee-Metford, full bandoliers and a superb mount, a little grey Arab'.[3]

In spite of this success Botha was soon chased out of Natal and his forces made hardly any impact, but the Boer commandos in the Cape Colony remained elusive and extremely active. Yet Smuts's victory over the 17th Lancers was not decisive in the long term, and superior numbers of British troops continued to harass his commando. But

Smuts's success proved that it was still too early for the British government to think about sending troops home. Indeed, Lord Roberts, now alarmed by Milner's schemes, which he believed would undermine Kitchener's authority, told the government on 20 September:

> As regards any reduction of the force now in South Africa, we need not trouble ourselves. I consider that an impossibility until peace has been established throughout the Cape Colony, and a reliable Police Force has been raised ... *The Times* of to-day takes the view, which I feel pretty sure is generally held throughout the country, and it is for us at the War Office to see that everything is done to keep the Army in South Africa in a thoroughly efficient state.[4]

Roberts's view could not be ignored and it was one that Brodrick found difficult to refute. Brodrick, though, was already coming round to the idea that the Cape Colony had to be cleared first and that Kitchener should be backed with more men and money. At the time he was in dispute with Sir Michael Hicks Beach, the Chancellor of the Exchequer, over the costs of his plans to reform the army, and Hicks Beach was also demanding cuts right across the board, including the forces in South Africa. In defending his own corner Brodrick now put his support firmly behind Kitchener. Even Chamberlain, no great admirer of Kitchener, now felt that the demand for troop reductions in South Africa was unrealistic and that public opinion favoured a more hard-hitting approach towards the elusive Boers. He told Hicks Beach that reductions would not be supported by the party or public 'against the advice of all the experts and merely to save taxation and pay off debt'.[5] Thus the mood in the government was changing. Disputes between ministers over other issues, such as army and naval reform and taxation, were sapping ministerial energies and confidence. They no longer presented a united front in favour of Milner's ideas and preferred to rely on their political instincts, which decreed that public opinion, the electorate, and the party be mollified by meeting Kitchener's demands. The war was to be prosecuted as before; the objective to defeat the Boers before reconstruction could take place.

Moreover, further Boer successes, particularly one at Bakenlaagte in the Transvaal on 30 October, where Colonel G.E. Benson, one of Kitchener's best operatives, was killed, seemed to confirm

Kitchener's views. He explained to Brodrick that 'if a column like Benson's, operating 20 miles outside our lines is not fairly safe it is a very serious matter and will require a large addition to our forces to carry on the war ... As we drive them out of areas it takes more troops to keep them out, and I consider that more troops will hasten the end which we all so much long for.'[6]

For Milner, the government's backtracking proved too much and on 1 November he openly campaigned for Kitchener to be removed, claiming he was stale and that 'It is impossible to *guide* a military dictator of very strong views & strong character', and he also wrote again of the need for civil reconstruction to start in earnest. Milner's views, expressed to Chamberlain in a memorandum, were shown to the Cabinet between 15 and 16 November 1901. There was a ministerial split over whether Kitchener should be removed, but ten days later Lord Salisbury provided the casting vote – decisively in favour of Kitchener, an officer he had always admired. Salisbury pointed out that Milner offered no guaranteed alternative policy and that there was no reason to suppose that the officer he suggested as Kitchener's replacement, Major General N.G. Lyttelton, who had done well recently in Natal, would have greater success. 'We must know much more fully in detail what it is that Milner has asked *in vain* of K. before we make it ground for superseding K. by a commander chosen by Milner.'[7]

From that moment Milner realised he could no longer influence the direction of military strategy and that his earlier schemes lay dead in the water. The government lacked the resolution to confront its military expert in South Africa and all he could do was wait, with growing frustration and annoyance, for the military situation to improve. In the meantime, he could look forward to the better administration of the concentration camps, which were now well in the hands of his civil administration, and had passed their worst month, October, when 3,205 deaths had been recorded. Moreover, the gold-mining industry was gradually improving its production, and slowly, but surely, civil life was being restored.

Kitchener could now get down to the job of hunting down the Boer commandos without having to look over his shoulder at Milner. Nevertheless he knew, and ministers constantly informed him, that he did not have carte blanche to do as he pleased. He had to keep to the task in hand and to that end the government, following the advice of Lord Roberts, sent Lieutenant General Sir Ian Hamilton to be Kitchener's Chief of Staff, in order to relieve him of some of the burdens he faced and to keep ministers informed. Kitchener was notoriously loth to delegate and by the end of 1901 had taken on too much responsibility by overseeing virtually every aspect of the drives and sweeps he had initiated. He was always at his desk by 6 a.m., worked into the night on his correspondence, and was often up during the early hours as important news came in. Sometimes the strain became too much and he asked the government if there was another officer who could take over. He did at times let his anxieties and disappointments get the better of him, such as Benson's defeat and death. The appointment of Hamilton thus relieved Kitchener of some of his arduous duties, but he was not someone who could let go entirely. The column commanders had to send in constant reports to him personally, and he responded by sending out streams of instructions. He could never divest himself of responsibility for any military operations, and for his own emotional well-being he had to keep a grip on everything. He was lucky that his constitution, in general, was able to withstand the pressure.

Meanwhile, the building of the blockhouse lines continued apace and by the end of 1901 great areas of the former republics were criss-crossed by barbed wire and the more recently designed blockhouses of Major Spring R. Rice, which consisted of two layers of circular, corrugated iron, the gap between the two filled with earth and later with hard shingle. These were easy to construct and were quickly turned into mini-fortresses with sandbags and barbed wire surrounding the blockhouse itself. In all, about 8,000 were built. The wire was then joined to another blockhouse about 1,000 yards away, and they were also linked by telegraph and telephone lines. Tin cans filled with stones were often placed along the wire and acted as alarm bells. The blockhouses spread over 3,700 miles and enclosed over 31,000 square miles of territory in the former republics. Eventually the blockhouse lines were garrisoned by 50,000 British troops and 16,000 African auxiliaries, hence Kitchener's continual need for troops to operate within the enclosed zones.

The Boers found that space was gradually being denied them and they had little room to manoeuvre. The blockhouse lines could be breached, but by 1902 it was becoming extremely difficult to do so without being detected. Moreover, within the enclosed spaces the

British continued to destroy farms, livestock and foodstuffs, and in December 1901 Kitchener refused to take any more Boer civilians into the concentration camps, thus leaving them on the veld for the Boer commandos to succour. With their own supplies now even more limited, the Boer fighters found it very difficult to help these civilian refugees. The one benefit for the Boers of this change of policy was that the concentration camps would no longer be unexpectedly inundated by civilians, and Milner's civil administration could now make set plans for the care of the inmates.

On their own the blockhouse lines could not have worked, but Kitchener used these now as an adjunct to his military strategy. Between 5 and 8 February 1902 he set in motion four parallel columns of troops designed to shepherd De Wet against the barrier of the blockhouse lines. The columns were to present a solid mass and were to channel the Boers into an ever narrowing strip of territory at the junction of two lines, in this case a blockhouse line and a railway. De Wet had recently made a nuisance of himself by defeating a force of British yeomanry at Tweefontein on Christmas Day 1901, and was considered the main prize. Unfortunately for the British, on the night of 7 February De Wet escaped, as he did again, along with President Steyn, during Kitchener's second great drive (13–27 February). But the haul of those who did not escape was impressive, as was the number of wagons and cattle taken. Nearly 800 Boers were captured, including De Wet's son. Consequently, Kitchener gave the Boers no respite. A third great drive began on 4 March, but yet again De Wet and Steyn escaped, fleeing to De la Rey's lair in the western Transvaal, and this time few Boers were captured.

For some British officers the campaign had all the qualities of a pheasant shoot or a tiger hunt, with good 'bags' and big 'drives'. Captain Talbot of the Royal Horse Artillery wrote cheerily in his diary early in 1902:

> The capture of Ben Viljoen is a good bag. The general opinion here is that the war ends the day De Wet is collared. Botha wants to chuck but daren't until the Free Staters chuck. An enormous concentration is going on all round De Wet – 25,000 troops at least in about 40 columns not to speak of blockhouses, etc. You can get some idea of the blockhouse lines by taking a map as follows: all railways of course in O.R.C.; a line from Heilbron to Frankfort and Standerton; Kroonstad to Lindley, Bethlehem,

Harrismith, Winberg, Senekal and Bethlehem; Bloemfontein, Ladybrand, Basuto border; Orange River and Caledon.[8]

A little later he described another determined British effort to end the war:

> The big drive is over with a total of 850 Boers and all their stock. The bag last week was 1,100, splendid, and two or three more big drives will knock them out. Arthur Scott seems to have done very well in the mountains. Vilonel, the Boer, is here now, and takes the field as soon as he gets his men together. He and K. of K. calculate there are 8,000 to 9,000 left. This was before the drive I believe. There is also a rumour that Botha has sent to De Wet and Steyn to say that if they don't chuck it soon, he is going to do so in any case. On the whole things are brightening every day.[9]

But even as Viljoen was in the process of surrendering, Jan Smuts was boldly striking deep into the Cape Colony at the head of his commando. By the end of February 1902 he was less than 150 miles from Cape Town, and an official report contained some uneasy observations:

> As the forces of the enemy under General Smuts now south of Calvinia appear to be moving in a westerly direction towards Clanwilliam, I am sending a further 100 of the Cape Police to strengthen Major Hennessy. I can spare these for the present as Major Corbett reports the Sutherland district is clear of the enemy ... he states that every farm has furnished its quota to the rebels and that there is hardly a loyal farmer in the district. He further informs me that there are not many supplies left, and the enemy will find it difficult to live for any length of time near there ... the blockhouse line is now completed on the east to beyond Carnarvon ... The general scheme is now to drive the enemy north of the line Clanwilliam, Williston and Victoria West.[10]

De la Rey too managed to retrieve some of the Boer confidence lost by Kitchener's drives and the constant harrying. On 24 February he had ambushed a British force at Yzer Spruit. Lord Methuen, who was operating in the area, decided to deal with De la Rey and risked everything by launching his offensive with only 1,300 men, who had been drawn from fourteen different units and were mostly raw troops. Unsurprisingly, Methuen's force met with disaster at Tweebosch on 7 March 1902. Methuen himself was seriously wounded in the leg, which was then broken when his horse fell and crushed it. Along with Methuen, over 300 of his men were wounded or captured. Methuen was treated with care and respect by De la Rey and his wife and was soon released, as were his men. The Boers had trouble feeding themselves and could not cope with so many prisoners.

On hearing the news of Tweebosch, Kitchener's emotional barrier collapsed and he locked himself away for two days, not speaking to anyone or eating. Eventually he composed himself and on 9 March wrote despairingly to Roberts: 'We had got De la Rey's men well down, short of ammunition, and very anxious for the end of the war. Now they are all up again, and we have to begin afresh.' Kitchener was determined to make sure that the Boers did not enjoy their success for too long. De la Rey's forces were to be the next target of his great drives, as he told the government on 30 March: 'I am doing all in my power to hit De la Rey hard as soon as possible and hope soon to succeed.'[11]

From late March four columns scoured the western Transvaal but were unsuccessful in their quest – De la Rey still managed to evade capture. Recognising that such a large-scale operation could not be directed from Pretoria, Kitchener sent Hamilton to co-ordinate the campaign and added another column to the British effort. On 11 April 1902 the column of Lieutenant Colonel Kekewich, the saviour of Kimberley, was attacked at Rooiwal by Commandant F.J. Potgieter. In this extraordinary battle, 1,500 Boers charged head on against Kekewich's dismounted force of 3,000. Although the Boer charge was stopped in its tracks, only about fifty men were killed, including Potgieter.

De la Rey was not involved in these operations because he, Steyn, De Wet, Botha and others were talking peace with Kitchener and Milner in Pretoria. And throughout the next few months, when peace talks began in earnest, the war continued unabated. Between 6 and 11 May, Hamilton led one last drive across the western Transvaal, his forces devastating the countryside. During these operations he managed to capture both De la Rey's wife and brother. This constant, unrelenting pressure upon the Boers finally took its toll. The combination of blockhouses, barbed wire, scorched earth and great offensive sweeps and drives had paid off. By May 1902, the Boers were exhausted and at the end of their tether. For many the peace could not come soon enough.

Part IV

The Ambivalences of War

15

Big Business, Capitalism and the War

IT WAS EASY at the time, and has ever since remained a strong temptation, simply to attribute the outbreak of the war to the inexorable demands of capitalism and big business. There is, of course, no doubt that the owners of the deep-level gold mining companies had become exasperated in varying degrees with the Kruger government for some considerable time before the final descent into confrontation and war. In Britain and elsewhere Liberals, radicals and various critics of the increasingly bellicose British approach to the Transvaal crisis were quick to accuse the 'Park Lane millionaires' – those magnates with financial interests in the South African economy and particularly in the gold-mining industry – of complicity in the policies and tactics that eventually precipitated the war in October 1899.

These suspicions were confirmed by the range of indemnities and assistance offered by big business to the British authorities as they prepared for the showdown with the Transvaal government. In the event, it was the post-war British demand for indemnities from the Transvaal to pay for part of the cost of the war that yielded the most concrete results.[1] Certainly it was one of the central issues to be discussed when Chamberlain made his 'conquering hero' – or possibly his 'conquering villain' – visit to South Africa to assess the situation early in 1903.[2]

In many ways it is compelling, certainly easier on the intellectual faculties, simply to accept the 'capitalist conspiracy' theory of the war, rather than to tease out all the ambivalence, confusion and paradox. This is partly because the original case, put so eloquently and persuasively by the British radical writer J.A. Hobson in 1900, is

neat and sufficiently comprehensive.[3] It may also be that it is sometimes hard to abandon conspiracy theories, chiefly because of their
inherent attractiveness – which owes much to the promise that they
will unravel mysteries hitherto deliberately obscured by powerful,
perhaps sinister, forces. At any rate, historians as distinguished as
Eric Hobsbawm have stuck to the view that 'whatever the ideology,
the motive for the Boer War was gold'.[4]

There are, however, many other ways of interpreting the role of big
business and capitalism in the prelude, course and aftermath of the
South African War. To start with the influence of the gold-mining
companies: we have already seen that there was a fundamental diver-
gence of interests, perhaps something as dramatic as a split, between
the deep-level mining companies in the Transvaal and the shallow-
level or outcrop mining companies over how far to seek the overthrow
of the Kruger government. Nor is it possible to view the management
of the deep-level companies as some sort of monolith; many of the
gold magnates were men of strong individualism and unbounded self-
belief, unlikely to follow a lead unless it served their interests.

Within this context, however, it is plain that there had been a
widely held view – not a consensus exactly, but certainly a meeting of
minds – among leading magnates in 1895 that the Jameson Raid was
worth backing. Rhodes, Alfred Beit, Lionel Phillips and Rhodes's key
adviser, the American mining engineer John Hays Hammond, all
supported the Raid.[5] On the other hand, there were as many if not
more Rand mine owners who kept clear of entanglement in Rhodes's
and Chamberlain's plotting. These sceptics were not, it should be
noted, merely drawn from the outcrop mining magnates, but
included men like Sammy Marks, who was closely associated at a personal and business level with Paul Kruger, and Joseph Robinson.

It is naive either to see the Rand business owners as a coherent,
well organised group of conspirators, or as a uniform, united lobby.
After all, nobody would seriously view, say, contemporary British
generals or bishops, even trade union leaders, in such a fashion. As
has been clearly stated elsewhere:

> In reality, Rand capitalists were not a united pro-war front; if anything,
> war looked costly and frightening for mine operations, and the most that
> can be said is that the anti-Kruger antagonisms of the mining interests
> and its local press allies helped to feed an atmosphere of crisis.[6]

Lest anyone should doubt that many Rand capitalists, and particularly mine owners, were right to fear the disruptive consequences of war, they should note what happened once hostilities were over. After 1902 the large quantity of cheap black labour on which the gold industry depended, had been so dispersed and run down that the desperate measure was taken of importing some 50,000 Chinese indentured labourers into the Transvaal. That the British government and the local business and political leadership needed to take so controversial a step, with its virtually inevitable backlash of liberal protest at 'disguised slavery', is further confirmation of the uncertainties and risks that war brought to one of the fastest expanding economies in the world.

Indeed, in many ways Transvaal capitalism as it had become established in the wake of the great Rand gold strike of 1886, was perfectly willing to do business and come to an accommodation with the Kruger regime – a regime which, incidentally, had few of the qualms that a British administration would have expressed over the treatment and terms of employment of black workers. This is partly because, at least until the Jameson Raid, this seemed the most fruitful way of proceeding, but it also arose from the essential willingness of capitalism, especially international capitalism, to seek smoother rather than rougher paths to profits and success. No doubt the financial experts of the contemporary City of London, whose advice investors relied on and who generally knew a good thing when they saw it, viewed the situation very similarly.

It could even be argued that British intervention in the internal affairs of the Transvaal, even if there had existed a fervently united lobby in its favour, was unnecessary. Why did British forces need to invade a state that had already been so comprehensively penetrated by largely British capital, business expertise and technological know-how? Even if the British government needed secure access to gold bullion in order to maintain sterling as a great international currency, the Transvaal had to sell its gold on the open market – and hence why not to the United Kingdom? – and there were, moreover, other suppliers of bullion worldwide.

In most ways it is unhelpful to see the outbreak of hostilities as primarily the result of either a capitalist conspiracy or the machinations of Chamberlain, Milner or Rhodes and their assorted allies and spin doctors. Almost until the first shots were fired, the British and imperial side seems to have been ready to accept a reasonable deal, a compromise.

What in the end made the war a cruel necessity from the capitalist and business point of view was the failure of the government of the South African Republic to deal with them as sympathetically and constructively as they wanted. In comparison with other quasi-imperial and client states, and certainly with other British colonies, the Transvaal, quite understandably, wished to maximise its profits from the rapid post-1886 process of industrialisation. One way of doing this was by the raising of taxes, both direct and indirect.

On the issue of direct taxes there was little cause for quarrel. Indirect taxation, however, was another matter. The Kruger government's desire to enrich itself through the imposition of state monopolies – such as the provision of the dynamite so essential to the gold-mining industry – was understandable, but also enhanced the Rand industrialist's perception of a regime that cared little for the need to keep production costs to a minimum. The government's creation of the national bank and the state control of the increasingly profitable railway system all served to confirm the impression that industry would have to pay through the nose for its profits.

It is not difficult to see why the Transvaal government wanted to gather in as much revenue as possible from the industrialisation of the country. Hitherto the pastoral, rural economy of the Afrikaner people had provided central government with only a meagre income. The discovery of gold, and the burgeoning of related industrial and commercial developments, was like manna from heaven. It enabled the regime not only to build up its supply of armaments, but also to feel that its chances of successful survival in a potentially hostile economic and political environment were greatly improved. In short, gold and industry were the equivalent of valuable insurance policies.

The price to be paid for this apparent security was, in the last resort, to prove too high. While the Transvaal was perceived as a backward, passive host body over which the modernisers and capitalist entrepreneurs of British and western capitalism could swarm and eat their fill, all was relatively well. The more assertive, protectionist policies of the Kruger administration, however, disrupted this process and raised the question of who was really in control in the South African Republic, big business or the government.

This in turn raised the even more awkward, and in the end, deadly question from the Afrikaner point of view: who was truly in control throughout the whole of South Africa – Britain or the Boers? The fact that this issue had been at the root of so much of the conflict between the imperial power and the Afrikaner people over the previous century did not make the problem any less urgent in 1899. Rather it gave it an edge, promoting on both sides – certainly in the aftermath of the Jameson Raid – a feeling that the whole tangled business needed sorting out once and for all. The growing British anxiety that the newly prosperous and increasingly powerful Transvaal, rather than Britain and its imperial client states, would come to dominate the region was crucial in the brinkmanship of major players like Rhodes, Chamberlain, and finally Milner.

Amid all of this, the role of big business and capitalism was never as clear cut as both their critics and supporters claimed. The Uitlander elite, the men who dominated the expanding Transvaal economy, were indeed overwhelmingly 'outsiders' rather than firmly-rooted old stock. It seemed often as if they were living on borrowed time on the Rand, seeking maximum profits before their varied business interests demanded that they apply their minds and energies elsewhere. They were pragmatists rather than ideologues; men with an eye for the main business chance rather than solid founding fathers of a reconstituted, reinvented state. The wonder is not that the Kruger government dragged its feet over the enfranchising of the Uitlander population, but that it was so willing to extend citizenship to so many of them between the Jameson Raid and the outbreak of war.

In these circumstances, there was an ambivalence, a variety of interests, even a sharp clash of interests, among the Transvaal's mostly expatriate business community that made it difficult to marshal them one way or another over so large an issue as peace or war.

In the end it was the British government that decided to go to war, allegedly on behalf of the civil rights of the Uitlanders. Even so, the cabinet was hardly packed with hawkish ministers. The Prime Minister, Lord Salisbury, and his increasingly influential nephew, Arthur James Balfour – in effect the deputy premier – were plainly reluctant to commit themselves to hostilities. Repeatedly there is the impression, backed up in official documentation, of the Colonial Secretary leading his colleagues by the nose towards a violent resolution of a crisis, the outcome of which was uncertain.[7]

The decision to enter into war with the South African Republic and the Orange Free State owed much to the British government's desire finally to assert British imperial supremacy over the whole region. Once brought under control South Africa, including perhaps the Rhodesias, would provide an environment within which big business, loyalist English-speaking South Africans, and those Afrikaners who wished to do so, could thrive and prosper within the British Empire.

Such an environment would also eliminate the danger that the Transvaal government's increasingly protectionist policies would seriously disadvantage commercial expansion within the region of the free-trading economies of Britain, the Cape and Natal. It is no coincidence that during the war Chamberlain was becoming increasingly preoccupied with the issue of protectionism versus free trade, and that within a year of its conclusion was to launch his highly controversial tariff reform campaign designed to restructure the whole imperial fiscal system.[8] The conquest of the Transvaal therefore carried this extra economic bonus for the Colonial Secretary.

There were several other reasons why the British government wished to assert its supremacy. Although some of these appear to be strategic or military in nature, on closer examination they nearly all reveal an economic or commercial perspective. For example, the 1890s railway link between the Transvaal and Delagoa Bay in the Portuguese colony of Mozambique carried the additional threat that it might prove a conduit through which German, French and other European influence might spread into the region, further destabilising an already shaky British presence. Although the 1898 Anglo-German agreement over the future of Mozambique and Angola generally calmed British anxieties over potential foreign incursions, the business development of Delagoa Bay was at the same time conceded to a German-backed company – thus keeping the door open to future, foreign penetration of the southern African commercial sphere. Worse still, it was possible, with the rapid expansion of the German navy after 1898, that imperial Germany could use its continuing influence in the region to establish at least some minimal maritime facilities in Mozambique.[9]

In the last resort, the British government needed to show that it could not be scorned and out-manoeuvred throughout the southern African region – whether by the Transvaal, Germany, or even Cecil

Rhodes. The end of the nineteenth century seemed almost a make or break time for Britain, its economy, its navy, its Empire, and by implication its world standing. Prestige is an odd commodity; it is not possible to eat, wear or trade in it. Nonetheless, nations cherish it, and at the century's climax, beset by powerful rivals and troubled by competition, Britain needed to assert its global power as never before. In these circumstances it was felt that it could not afford to have its standing in South Africa undermined to any significant degree. That the Boer War stood to benefit the interests of big business and capitalism in the Transvaal and elsewhere in the region was almost incidental to the grander design and purpose.

16

The Last of the Gentlemen's Wars?

'A GENTLEMEN'S WAR' was the almost nostalgic view of Major General J.F.C. Fuller, whose retrospection was influenced by having witnessed the horrors of the First World War. Yet all wars are rarely gentlemanly affairs and more often than not it is the unscrupulous who profit by regarding war as opportunity. During the Boer War, corruption was soon evident and even touched Joseph Chamberlain, who was hounded in 1900 by the Welsh radical David Lloyd George for his apparent profiteering from the war. Chamberlain's brother Arthur was prominent in the armaments firm Kynoch Ltd, which supplied cordite to the army, and Lloyd George insinuated that Joseph had helped his brother's business. Nothing was ever proved, but the accusations stung Chamberlain and mud stuck.

After the war, it was apparent to the Auditor General's office that unscrupulous officers in the Stores Department had made large sums of money by defrauding the army and the War Office, and eventually, in 1905, Lieutenant General Sir William Butler headed a committee to investigate. His report clearly showed that one officer in particular, Colonel Morgan, had conspired with his brother Frank Morgan, to make themselves rich. The latter had been allowed to make deals with a select group of companies to buy surplus food and forage from the army at a cheap rate; the army then bought the stuff back at hugely inflated prices. It would seem, although nothing concrete was ever proved, that the Morgans must have shared in the profits made by the favoured companies, one of which was the well-known Weil & Co., which had supplied Mafeking just before the outbreak of war and the army during it. On one transaction alone the company made a profit of more than £20,000. Butler's committee 'considered that in allowing his brother to enter into agencies or connections with contractors or army purchasers in South Africa, he contravened not only the letter of the regulations defining the conduct of officers, but that he acted entirely in opposition to the spirit and traditions of the army'.[1] A subsequent Royal Commission refused to follow up the accusations of the Butler report and preferred to sweep the whole affair under the carpet. The army in South Africa had been well supplied even if some officers and men had behaved incompetently or corruptly, and by 1905 no one was particularly interested. Nevertheless, for those who were, the war had ended on a sour note.

Corruption and dodgy dealing aside, Fuller's description of the war as a 'gentlemen's war' reflected his belief that the war had been fought chivalrously by the two sides, a sentiment echoed by Lieutenant Colonel H. de Watteville, who believed the British soldier thought too highly of the Boers and sometimes lacked resolution. 'Such being the case, it was easy for the war to degenerate, in the eyes of very many men at least, into a species of glorified football league in which they might win one day and lose another.'[2] On the other side, there were many acts that gave an impression that the Boers also bore little animosity towards the British. De la Rey's treatment of the wounded Lord Methuen after the latter's defeat at Tweebosch on 7 March 1902 apparently bears this out. But war and chivalry rarely go hand in hand and the Boer War was no exception.

The case of 'Breaker' Morant and his comrades, who were shot or imprisoned for executing captured Boers, is perhaps well known, although a reiteration of this story is needed in the light of more recent evidence. This episode was not, however, the only case of acts committed against the rules of war and there were numerous allegations that Boers shot Britons out of hand, and there developed tit-for-tat actions whereby Boers wantonly killed blacks and the British authorities executed those Boers they considered guilty of such crimes. With South Africa placed under martial law the British army had far greater scope to deal harshly and summarily with captured Boers and rebels than under an ordinary civil jurisdiction.

The trial and execution of the Australian Lieutenants H.H. Morant and P.J. Handcock, and the sentencing to life imprisonment of their countryman Lieutenant Witton (a British officer, Lieutenant H. Picton, was cashiered), revealed that in the northern extremes of the Transvaal, in the Zoutpansberg and Spelonken areas, a dirty war had been in progress throughout much of 1901. Although other officers were brought to trial, both Australian and British, and escaped severe punishment, the three Australians mentioned above have gone down in history as 'scapegoats of Empire'.

This was certainly the view of Witton, whose book of the same name supposedly recounted 'the true story of Breaker Morant's Bushveldt Carbineers'. The Bushveldt Carbineers (BVC) was an irregular force raised in early 1901 for operations in the northern Transvaal. It was not an entirely Australian force as later suggested, but there were more Australians than other nationalities. The case against the officers was that they had murdered eight Boer prisoners, in front of numerous witnesses, in revenge for the supposed murder of Morant's friend, Captain P.F. Hunt. These events occurred between July and September 1901 and also included the suspicious death of a Carbineer trooper, who was a Boer, and the death of one C.A.D. Heese, who worked for German missionaries. Witton and others later argued that the two Australian officers had been executed at the behest of the German government and that he and his companions had, in fact, obeyed Kitchener's orders not to take prisoners.

The view that orders had been given to shoot Boer prisoners was certainly doing the rounds in South Africa. On 18 January 1901 Lord Roberts, now Commander-in-Chief in Britain, asked Kitchener if newspaper reports 'that all captured are ordered to be shot' were true. Evidently a letter had appeared from a soldier in the 'Royal Welsh Regiment' alleging that Boer wounded were killed and five prisoners were shot after being forced to dig their own graves. Kitchener's reply was uncompromising: 'Absolutely untrue', he telegraphed back. Not only had the regiment in question not taken any prisoners, they had 'only been slightly engaging the enemy' and therefore it was unlikely that allegations had come from that regiment.[3] These, and other claims, were hungrily seized upon by a press which, because it toiled under heavy censorship, had few newsworthy items and so gave attention seekers the publicity they craved. As early as December 1899 Buller had to demand why Reuters had published a spurious telegram from one of their correspondents accusing the Boers of indulging in 'uncivilised warfare' because horses had been shot at the battle of Modder River. It was, as Buller remarked, 'contrary to honourable conduct to abuse a brave enemy'.[4]

There were, however, major flaws in the view that the executed officers were scapegoats of Empire. First, they were acquitted of the murder of Heese and so the concern of the German authorities would have had no bearing on their trial. If anything, it was the murder of Heese that brought events in the north to Kitchener's attention and initiated the proceedings against the officers. Already, in early October, fifteen men of the BVC had petitioned Lieutenant Colonel F.H. Hall, the commanding officer at the main base in Pietersburg, about the killings. Hall knew something was afoot but had done little about it. In any case, men of the Intelligence Department, an Australian Captain F.R. de Bertodano and Lieutenant N. McWilliam, were already on the case and in the process of obtaining vital information from their sources. Second, the prosecution was aided by one R.M. Cochrane, a trooper of the BVC, who happened to be a Western Australian Justice of the Peace. He had witnessed the earlier petition of his comrades and would be instrumental in procuring witnesses against the officers involved. Finally, and more generally, Boer prisoners continued to be brought in from areas patrolled by other units of the BVC.

In this instance military justice was not as swift as Kitchener would have liked because many of the witnesses had served their time in the BVC and had left the area. This was why the men were not tried until mid-January 1902, after being arrested the previous October. Morant's defence was based on the assertion that the Boers were 'train wreckers and marauders' and that Captain Hunt had ordered them not to take prisoners. These claims were dismissed and he was found guilty of three murders, while Handcock was found guilty of two murders and one manslaughter. Witton was condemned for one murder and one manslaughter, but was regarded to be under the influence of the others. Kitchener told Brodrick, Secretary of State for War since November 1900: 'I propose to confirm death sentences on Morant, who originated [the] crimes, on Hancock [sic], who carried out several cold-blooded murders, and in the case of Whitton [sic], who was present but under influence, commutation to penal servitude for life.' Later he added, 'I do not think any regulations other than those existing can restrain from such acts, but punishment may deter. It is the only case of this sort that has occurred.'[5]

Morant and Handcock were executed on 27 February 1902, and on 4 April an official statement was issued by the War Office. Unfortunately the court martial proceedings, as well as all those between 1851 and 1914 (except for that dealing with the death of the Prince Imperial, the son of the former French Emperor Napoleon III, who was with the British army in Zululand in 1879), were destroyed during the London blitz. We will therefore never know the whole story, although the idea of a cover-up by the authorities cannot be taken seriously, even if Morant and Handcock were the only officers executed by the British during the war. Their responsibility for the murders is beyond doubt.[6]

In contrast, many more Boers were executed by the British: some thirty-three were killed while Kitchener was Commander-in-Chief, and although 500 overall were sentenced to death they had their sentences commuted to terms of imprisonment. Most were rebels, the vast majority citizens of the Cape Colony, and some were executed under suspicious circumstances. Indeed, on 2 March 1901 the first execution of a Cape citizen took place under the auspices of martial law. A certain Van Heerden, who allowed his property to be used to ambush British forces, was wounded and captured. He was tried before a drumhead court martial comprising four officers, three of whom were members of the Cape defence forces, was condemned to death and was shot immediately. Kitchener heard of this and relieved Colonel Gorringe, the main British officer concerned, of his command, believing that Van Heerden had not been tried, though not long after he told Brodrick that 'the case was legally tried and correct'. However, it was not until October 1902 that Gorringe was officially exonerated by the War Office after it transpired that Van Heerden had not been brought before the court martial, but his answers to questions the day before had been entered into the proceedings of the court. Brodrick considered that 'substantial justice had been done'. The Colonial Office, however, felt it would have been better to have shot Van Heerden out of hand, rather than hold a trial 'which was no trial'.[7] That same month, three rebels were executed at De Aar for high treason, robbery and murder. There were no more executions until June.

The British authorities agreed that rebels deserved the death sentence, but the practice of executing convicted prisoners publicly caused outrage. In July 1901, the Cape government complained to the Governor, Sir Walter Hely-Hutchinson, that the men of Cradock, including all rebel prisoners, were obliged to witness an execution. A rebel had already been publicly hanged at Middelburg. Although Kitchener agreed to abide by the Cape government's wishes and stopped further public executions, he explained to Brodrick that 'When two prisoners were quietly executed here [in Pretoria] in gaol, the Dutch people refused absolutely to believe that they had been executed and insisted that they had been quietly removed.' Nevertheless, there were no more public executions.[8]

Although the British did deal harshly with captured rebels, they were condemned on specific charges and given the rudiments of a fair trial under martial law regulations. And this was in spite of continual provocation. In one instance there was strong evidence that the Boers had killed British wounded. At the battle of Vlakfontein on 29 May 1901, it was alleged by Reuters that British soldiers had been shot after capture for not showing the Boers how the artillery worked, and by the *Daily Mail* that British wounded were shot on the ground. The Reuters report proved false, the journalist having believed rumours abounding in Johannesburg, but with regard to the second allegation Kitchener reported that seven men had testified that they saw British wounded killed.

Kitchener sent letters of complaint to the Boer leaders but by the end of August had received no reply. Brodrick then suggested that Kitchener issue a proclamation notifying the Boers that if anything of the sort happened again, any Boer captured who had been present at the time would be found guilty and might face the death penalty depending on the scale of complicity. The leader of such a commando would be sentenced to death. This time it was Kitchener who took a more lenient approach, having by then received assurances from Steyn and the Transvaal commander Ben Viljoen, who both condemned the killings. Kitchener felt that such a proclamation would increase the likelihood of further outrages. 'We are getting down to men the bulk of whom are desperate and not under the control of leaders. Result of my letter has been a number of counter charges against our men which I am enquiring.' He was also assured as follows by Louis Botha, the Transvaal's Commandant General: 'I shall most severely punish such when proved, as it has always been my endeavour to continue this war in accordance with all the rules of civilized warfare.' Nevertheless, following the British defeat at Tweefontein on 25 December 1901, a British soldier informed his family that drunken Boers had killed British wounded with bayonets and rifle butts.[9] Nothing, it seems, was done to follow up these allegations.

One area where the British thought the Boers transgressed the 'rules of civilized warfare' was with regard to their treatment of Africans. Throughout 1901, the Boers were executing increasing numbers of Africans for helping the British either as despatch riders or armed scouts. This took a nasty turn when the commando leader Commandant P.H. Kritzinger, who was operating in the Cape Colony, sanctioned the killing of armed or unarmed Africans who were helping the British or were suspected of giving aid in any form. The Boers usually dealt harshly with Africans serving the British as armed scouts, and by the end of 1901 the British authorities were becoming concerned about Boer outrages against Africans. Kitchener told Brodrick that 'Cold-blooded murder of natives by Boers are frequent. On 10 November, 2 dead bodies of natives, with hands tied behind them, were found in mine shaft near Graylingstadt. They had not been shot. Sworn evidence is being collected.'

In response to a request for further information from Brodrick, Kitchener told him of another incident: 'on or about 17 July, 8 kaffir boys, between ages 12 and 14, went out from Uitkijk, near Edenburg, to get oranges. None were armed. Boers opening fire, shot 1, captured 6, 1 escaped ... Corporal Willet of Damant's Horse, afterwards saw boys' bodies near farm, but so disfigured as to be unrecognizable ... Lieutenant Kentish, Royal Irish Fusiliers, saw bodies, and substantially confirms murder.'[10] Consequently, Kitchener was determined that captured Boer leaders be brought to trial.

The court martial and subsequent execution of Commandant Johannes Lötter was fairly straightforward in that Lötter was a citizen of the Cape Colony and therefore a rebel. Lötter had raised a rebel commando that was noted for its indiscipline and brutality. In 1901 he and his men were hunted down and captured at Paardefontein. At Graaff-Reinet Lötter was put on trial for his life and among the charges against him were treason, the murder of unarmed scouts, the flogging of two Afrikaners for bringing his commando surrender terms, the destruction of a railway line and marauding. Lötter's defence was thin and was based on his assertion that he was actually a citizen of the OFS. This, however, was easily disproved. Consequently, he was taken to Middelburg and hanged there on 12 October 1901.

The execution of Commandant Gideon Scheepers was on the surface as straightforward as that of Lötter. A diehard *bittereinder*, he was charged with at least thirty crimes and convicted on twenty-nine, including, as Kitchener informed Brodrick, 'the shooting of 7 natives, the wrecking of and firing on passenger train carrying unarmed men, women and children ... flogging a white man and 2 natives ... Lieutenant Jones, 5th Lancers, saw him personally shoot a wounded native with a revolver'. Both Kitchener and Brodrick confirmed the sentence of death. On 18 January 1902, while seriously ill, Scheepers was tied to a chair and shot. For the British, Scheepers's guilt was not in doubt, but he was a burgher of the OFS and a leading officer. De Wet sent a plea to Kitchener to spare Scheepers and stated that he had been acting under his orders. De Wet argued against the murder charges, declaring that 'the ungovernable barbarity of the natives realised itself in practice in such a manner that we felt ourselves obliged to give quarter to no native and for these reasons we gave general instructions to our Officers to have all armed natives and native spies shot'. If anyone was responsible for shooting natives then it was himself and his government. Scheepers was acting under orders, 'orders that agree in every sense with the precepts of International Law as that law holds good for civilized nations, and I and my Government are in no way obliged to attribute the privileges thereby allowed to barbarians who violate the same every hour of the day'. De Wet then threatened retaliatory measures should Scheepers be shot (he already had been) and said his argument also applied to Commandant Kritzinger who was then in British custody.

Kitchener's reply was as unequivocal. Boer officers were personally responsible for their actions: '[I am] astonished at the barbarous instructions you have given as regards the murder of natives who ... have behaved, in my opinion, in an exemplary manner during the war.' De Wet was then informed that Scheepers was already dead. For good measure, Kitchener also informed Botha of his views.[11]

The execution of Scheepers, however, elicited sympathy and attracted attention in Britain. Two Irish nationalist MPs, Tim Healy and Swift MacNeil, repeatedly questioned Brodrick on the nature of

Scheepers's trial and, as Brodrick told Kitchener, gave a 'heartrending account' of Scheepers's death. Kitchener sent back the version of events by the officer who conducted the execution, Colonel Henniker: Scheepers was composed, he did not need help to walk to the chair and everything was done quickly. Brodrick acknowledged that Britain had a right to try leading Boer officers by court martial, but was concerned that they should be properly constituted. Kitchener felt that the only problem was constituting the court with officers of an equal rank to the accused because 'Boer ranks are very doubtful'. It transpired that Scheepers's court comprised a lieutenant colonel, a captain and a subaltern. Scheepers had his own defence counsel and he was condemned by white witnesses. The inclusion of a subaltern in Scheepers's court worried the British authorities and Kitchener was asked to drop one who was lined up for Kritzinger's trial and ensure that there were five officers on the court martial. 'The feeling here', Brodrick informed Kitchener, 'is very strong that unless personal guilt of murder is brought home to Kritzinger he should not be executed.' Already a campaign of sorts had been mounting to preserve Kritzinger from a death sentence. From Ceylon, where many Boer prisoners were kept, the Governor, Sir J. West Ridgeway, said that Kritzinger was well thought of and that his execution would be resented. While Kitchener felt that Kritzinger was as guilty as Scheepers, he ordered his legal advisers to review the charges against him: subsequently, those of train-wrecking were dropped, while only one murder charge was deemed of any value but that was based on African witnesses, something which the British authorities were against. The British government was now very cool towards the idea of inflicting the death penalty and Kitchener was informed that 'if an acquittal results, no harm will be done'. Unsurprisingly, perhaps, Kritzinger was subsequently acquitted.[12]

In many respects, therefore, the Boer War was a dirty war, which at times raged beyond the control of the higher military authorities, and often it was the Africans and the coloureds who were caught in the middle. No war, of course, is ever a 'gentlemen's war', yet in the interests of imperial solidarity this was how the Boer War came to be perceived. At the end, the British granted a general amnesty in the peace terms and so the culpability of the likes of De Wet were ignored because of his status, despite the fact that he had ordered the deaths of Africans and renegade Boers. The killing of a British officer, however, could not go unpunished, and Salmon van As was not included in the general amnesty. In June 1902, Van As was found guilty of killing one Captain Miers and executed. Only later did the British authorities acknowledge that Van As had not been tried fairly and that he had been the victim of perjury.[13] He joined the pantheon of martyrs that was already being established by nationalists to keep alive the hopes of Boer republicanism.

17

The Pro-Boers

FOR MANY PEOPLE in Britain the existence of the Empire was a fact they could not ignore but of which they did not necessarily approve. Many others were able to reconcile themselves to the Empire by believing that as empires went, the British Empire was somehow moral and upright and existed for the ultimate benefit of its native peoples. This imperial ideal was shared right across the political and social spectrum and engendered a sense of pride in Britain's imperial mission. But as the crisis between Britain and the Transvaal deepened many would question those assumptions and feel unable to support the government as it apparently moved relentlessly towards war. The prospect of war with the Transvaal appalled those who felt keenly about what Britain stood for in the wider world. Even before war was declared opponents of the government's stance were organising and once war erupted they attempted to make their opinions known.

The pro-Boers, as their enemies described them, would over the course of time develop a nuanced critique of the war, at first adopting an attitude of outraged high morality, then attacking the economic reasons for going to war (which combined with a scurrilous anti-Semitism), then expressing admiration for the fighting prowess of the Boers, and finally calling for a negotiated peace. Yet to see the pro-Boers as a homogeneous group united in their distaste for British policy in South Africa is too strong. The pro-Boers were a mixed bag who did not agree on everything and some would never have considered themselves to be pro-Boer anyway. The label 'pro-Boer', at the time a term of abuse, does however have its uses to describe those who were never supportive of the British government and who questioned the motives for going to war, as well as those who believed the Boers should be chastised but treated leniently thereafter and be absorbed into the Empire for the Empire's greater good. Thus pro-Boerism of whatever sort brought together differing groups and individuals: middle-class intellectuals; politicians from both major parties; most of the labour movement; and even, surprisingly perhaps, army officers. All, however, were united by their distaste for a war they considered dirty and by the feeling that Britain should make amends.

The classical pro-Boers were those who spoke out during the crisis months preceding the war and who were organised through the Transvaal Committee. Most of the committee's adherents were Liberals, but a few had broken rank from the Unionists. One such was Leonard Courtney, who spoke at a meeting organised by the Manchester branch at the behest of John Morley, the radical Liberal and biographer of Gladstone, and another was C.P. Scott, the editor of the *Manchester Guardian*. To Courtney, Milner was 'a lost mind', while the Boers were intransigent simply because they desired to keep their independence, but were not conspiring to overrun South Africa and remove the British presence. Such publicly stated views did not endear Courtney to his electors in Liskeard, Cornwall, and in one hate letter sent to him the writer thought it 'a pity that a soft-nosed bullet cannot be lodged in the place where your brains are supposed to be'.[1]

Such an angry response was something pro-Boers in Britain would get used to over the next two years. Their cause was not helped by the Boers having given the British an ultimatum before invading Natal and the Cape Colony. In consequence, pro-Boers who tried to speak at public meetings were often attacked, verbally and physically. Courtney's speech before his constituents was not only badly timed but let him in for howls of derision and the subsequent hate mail. Indeed, Leslie Stephen, a radical man of letters and father of Virginia Woolf, recognised the futility of speaking out during these months. When asked to sign a letter of protest he replied: 'I confess that it seems to me to be not only useless but mischievous to protest against the war now! The thing is horrible – it distracts & torments me – but it has got to be; and we must, in my opinion, keep what we have to say for a better time.'[2] Nevertheless, in spite of the flood of patriotic fervour released by the Boer ultimatum and then by the Boer victories during Black Week, those opposed to the war persevered in their quest to persuade others that the war ought to be stopped.

To this end, in January 1900, a South African Conciliation Committee was formed and campaigned, without any success, against British policy in South Africa and desired that the government withdraw its demand for unconditional surrender. Numerous meetings were organised under the SACC's auspices, several of which turned violent when they were disrupted by opponents. In two well-known cases, the radical Liberal MP David Lloyd George, who had been stalking Chamberlain in parliament and criticising his links with the armaments firm Kynochs, which was run by Chamberlain's brother Arthur, tried to address meetings in Liskeard and Birmingham in 1901. In the first instance he was unable to proceed because the meeting was disrupted, and in the second he barely escaped with his life as the meeting turned into a riot. He had to be whisked away from the hall disguised as a policeman.

By far the most vociferous of the pro-Boers was the eminent journalist W.T. Stead, who founded the Stop the War Committee, and who used the printed word to convey his message, mostly in the form of pamphlets, the most famous being *Shall I slay my brother Boer?*, but also through his journal *Review of Reviews*.

Yet in spite of their best efforts the pro-Boers never managed to gather enough support to make the government listen. There are several reasons for this. First, the pro-Boers lacked leadership: Stead was his own man and too much a pro-Boer, while Courtney did not inspire confidence. According to Beatrice Webb, the Fabian socialist, 'The Tories regard him [Courtney] as a wholly unendurable person; the vast majority of Liberals consider him to be a quixotic crank. Even the tiny group of pro-Boer Radicals think that his speeches and manifestoes are often out of season.'[3]

Second, the pro-Boers lacked powerful support in the press and only a few newspapers rallied to their cause, such as the *Manchester Guardian* and the *Morning Leader*, a London working-class daily. In general, the Labour press was solidly against the war, although the editor of *Clarion*, Robert Blatchford, broke ranks and supported the war effort. Nevertheless, he allowed every shade of opinion to be heard in his newspaper's columns.

A third factor that undermined the effectiveness of the pro-Boers was that no party or religion was solidly pro-Boer. The Liberal Party failed to present a united front against the Unionist administration and was divided between those against the war and those, the Liberal imperialists, who broadly supported its aims. The non-conformist churches, most of whom supported the Liberal Party, were riven by disagreements, especially after the outbreak of war. All the churches were split, Methodists, Congregationalists and Baptists, and without a united front they made no impact on the government. Even the labour movement, despite being the most solid of all, espoused differing interpretations about the war's origins and what it was being fought for. Beatrice Webb recalled in her diary that the Liberal imperialist Richard Haldane had told her that '"The Liberal Party is completely smashed".' She continued:

> The cleavage goes right through the Liberal Party into the Fabian society. [George Bernard] Shaw, Wallas and Whelan being almost in favour of the war, J.R[amsay] MacDonald and Sydney Olivier desperately against it, while Sidney [Webb] occupies a middle position, thinks that better management might have prevented it but that now that it has begun recrimination is useless and that we must face the fact that henceforth the Transvaal and the Orange Free State must be within the British Empire.[4]

Beatrice admitted that even her own family 'is rent asunder', her sisters dividing between 'raging imperialists' and 'pro-Boers of the most ultra character', one of the latter being the wife of Leonard Courtney. She confessed that she was 'on the "war was inevitable" side', which was close enough to her husband Sidney's views to enable them to 'still go on holding hands! our habitual attitude!'.[5]

Even the solidly socialist Social Democratic Federation had its divisions. Like other socialists they were split on whether the British Empire stood for freedom and liberty against Boer tyranny, or was merely a tool of capitalism. However, one of its leaders, the Marxist Old Etonian Henry Hyndman, infuriated other members by blaming Jewish capitalists for starting the war: already, in the aftermath of the Jameson raid, he had said that British imperialism was 'part of a great project for the constitution of an Anglo-Hebraic Empire in Africa'.[6]

Anti-Semitism pervaded all areas of British society and was not unusual at this time. In 1900 David Lindsay, later twenty-seventh Earl of Crawford and tenth Earl of Balcarres, remarked on a gathering brought together by Lords Rothschild and Rosebery in honour of the Prince of Wales:

> The number of Jews in the place was past belief. I have studied the anti-Semite question with some attention, always hoping to stem an ignoble movement: but when confronted by the herd of Ickleheimers and Pappenbergs, Raphaels, Sassoons, and the rest of the breed, my emotions gain the better of logic and justice … John Burns, by the way, says the Jew is the tapeworm of civilization.[7]

John Burns was a well-known Liberal MP, who started his political life as a socialist and whose pro-Boerism was prone to anti-Semitic outbursts, such as his assertion that the British army had 'become in Africa a janissary of the Jews'. The labour movement had a virulent strand of anti-Semitism running throughout its pronouncements on the war, much to the dismay of many Jews who supported socialism. Hyndman was not alone: the Independent Labour Party, Blatchford's *Clarion*, and even the Trades Union Congress all condemned Jewish capitalists for being behind the outbreak of war and imperialism in general.

By far the most important published work which latched on to this theme, and which added weight to the idea that the war was being fought not for Britain but for the benefit of financial capitalists 'of which the foreign Jew must be taken as the leading type', was that by the liberal journalist J.A. Hobson. In his influential book, *The War in South Africa: Its Causes and Effects*, published in 1900, Hobson argued that the gold mines 'are almost entirely in their [Jews'] hands'. Based on his earlier reports for the *Manchester Guardian*, written from Johannesburg just before the outbreak of war, Hobson modified them in order to show that:

> We are fighting in order to place a small international oligarchy of mine-owners and speculators in power at Pretoria. Englishmen will surely do well to recognise that the economic and political destinies of South Africa are, and seem likely to remain, in the hands of men most of whom are foreigners by origin, whose trade is finance, and whose trade interests are not chiefly British.

Virtually every major activity in Johannesburg, he claimed, was under their control: 'That greatest of gambling instruments, the

Stock Exchange, is needless to say, mostly Jewish.' Even the ordinary gambling industry was run by a Jew, as was the liquor trade and, of course, the money-lending business. Most important of all was the fact that the Johannesburg press was in Jewish hands and formulating propaganda which merely served capitalist interests. Hobson concluded by stating: 'it is at any rate open to serious question whether the civilisation of Johannesburg, the typical British product in South Africa, is higher, better, or more desirable than the simpler, ruder civilisation of the burgher population of the land'.[8] Such views, having been conceived after actually visiting South Africa, gave added weight to Hobson's thesis and were repeated by other pro-Boers, including the publisher A.M.S. Methuen in his *Peace or War in South Africa*, published in 1901. Hobson's empirical 'evidence', though, was not to be the only sort emanating from South Africa.

Hobson's concluding point, which suggested that the Boer way of life was worth preserving, struck a chord with many other pro-Boers, particularly within the labour movement. Keir Hardie, for example, felt that the Boers' rural way of life was idyllic and something that had been lost in Britain. Indeed, the theme of a medieval 'merrie England' before the onset of industrialisation and the capitalist economy was a powerful idea which bound many socialists. It was a perception that would be shared by others, who might at first be considered as unlikely pro-Boers, but who in many ways shared similar viewpoints to those already mentioned.

Certain army officers, most of whom were recruited from the landed classes in Britain and Ireland, found that campaigning in South Africa sharpened existing prejudices and outlooks. Like other members of the upper class they looked down on Jews whatever their wealth and social standing and joined readily in the chorus against 'Jewburg' or 'Jewhannesburg'. Lieutenant General Sir William Butler, an Irish Catholic officer and no stranger to prejudice, was particularly scathing in his attacks. He regarded Johannesburg as a cross between Monte Carlo and Sodom and Gomorrah, and during his brief tenure as Commander-in-Chief in South Africa in 1899 he wrote that 'If the Jews were out of the question, it would be easy enough to come to an agreement; but they are apparently intent upon plunging the country into civil strife.' These views would be shared by other officers of all ranks: Captain Ballard of the Norfolk Regiment agreed with his brother officer Ernest Swinton of the

Royal Engineers, who thought 'it a great pity that good English soldiers and good yeoman Boers should be killed in order that a lot of German Jews may wax more fat and oily'; while in 1902, Kitchener's Chief of Staff, Ian Hamilton wrote to Winston Churchill saying, 'I cannot tell you how strongly I feel that if we could incorporate these Boers into the Empire, we should be doing a vast deal more for the future of our race and language, than by assimilating a million Johannesburg Jews.' These expressions also reveal how many officers believed that a rural, familiar world was being lost, or had been lost, in industrial Britain and that somehow absorbing the Boers would regain some of that lost, rural vitality. According to Lieutenant Colonel E.S. May, 'Their [the Boers'] bodies developed and expanded in the generous air, and in a few generations the white settlers had become in bodily strength and vigour one of the finest races on the globe.' This, of course, was in stark contrast to the way the British race was deteriorating.[9] Other officers were dismayed by the resort to farm burning and a scorched-earth policy. Major Seely's complaints about farm burning to Joseph Chamberlain earned him the rebuke that 'all you soldiers are what we call pro-Boer'. Indeed, the pro-Boer A.M.S. Methuen used numerous military opinions in his book mentioned above to show how British soldiers admired the fighting qualities of the Boers. By the end of the war many officers favoured treating the Boers leniently and welcomed a negotiated peace.

Yet we should never lump together British army officers and the pro-Boers back home in Britain. For one thing, officers felt that pro-Boer utterances merely inspired the Boers to carry on despite the hopelessness of their cause, and Campbell-Bannerman's speech condemning 'methods of barbarism' was one of a number of public statements which appeared to attack the army and enraged officers who resented these 'armchair' critics. One must also not forget that many other officers never shared these 'pro-Boer' sentiments and remained resolutely disparaging about Boer fighting methods and their lifestyle. Even so, many officers, like the pro-Boers in Britain, found that warfare in South Africa tested their notions of what the British Empire stood for.

The pro-Boers in Britain thus managed to make a noise and get noticed, far more than any other peace movement hitherto. Yet they remained totally ineffective and more often than not put their own lives at risk. This changed, however, in mid-1901 when Emily Hobhouse publicised the appalling conditions in the concentration camps.

Hobhouse, whose uncle Lord Hobhouse was a distinguished Liberal and pro-Boer, had readily joined Leonard Courtney when he asked for her assistance on the South African Conciliation Committee. She herself hailed from Liskeard and had taken a prominent role in organising the failed meeting at which Lloyd George had tried to speak. In mid-1901 she managed to get to South Africa in order to distribute funds for those Boer women and children made homeless by the farm burning campaign. While there she was given permission, first by Milner and then by Kitchener, to travel north, though only to Bloemfontein. When she arrived there she managed to inspect some of the local camps and was horrified by what she saw. Although one or two were well run, those that were not were effectively death camps and on hearing that those in the Transvaal were as bad, if not worse, especially the camp at Irene, Emily returned to Britain determined to reveal the appalling conditions, which had so far gone unnoticed. By interviewing Brodrick, by writing a detailed pamphlet and eventually by undertaking a lecture tour, all of which encouraged radicals like Lloyd George to ask questions in parliament, Emily Hobhouse finally alerted the world to what was going on in South Africa.

The fact that she was not chosen for the subsequent Ladies Committee to investigate conditions simply made her determined to return to South Africa, which she attempted in October 1901. She was not allowed to land at Cape Town and eventually had to be manhandled off the boat on to another that was about to sail to Britain. In spite of threatening to publicise her treatment once back in England and signing herself 'in bitter shame for England', the authorities remained unmoved, particularly as Kitchener was determined she should not be allowed to roam South Africa. Although she had failed to do more for the inmates of the camps, Emily Hobhouse had scored a major success for the pro-Boers because her earlier publicity had finally galvanised the civil and military authorities to act. She herself became a political 'hot potato' and on receiving her protests at the treatment she had suffered trying to get back to South Africa, Colonial Office officials recognised that she was trouble: one official said she was a War Office matter, and it would be

'better if the Colonial Office knew as little as possible on the subject',
to which Joseph Chamberlain readily agreed.[10]

This, though, was the only success the pro-Boers achieved in actually getting the government to act and change tack. Overall, the campaign, first to prevent war and then to end it quickly, failed; the war
would take its own course and be left to the political and military
authorities. What eventually helped the pro-Boer cause, allowing
their meetings to go ahead more often than not and their publicity to
be given a wider hearing, was the length of the war, the way it
dragged on, sapping resources and public interest. But the persistent
pro-Boer campaign did gnaw away at public perceptions and perhaps
sowed seeds of doubt about Britain's moral right to govern other
peoples. The writer George Sturt had not agreed with the pro-Boers
at the start of the war but became profoundly disillusioned by the
end of 1900. He felt the pro-Boer case, the 'prostitution of our
Empire to the greed of capitalists and the dishonesty of ministers of
state' [had] 'never been fairly met'. He now wanted:

> an idea of England and of the honour of Englishmen, such as is not
> wholly wrapped up in brute strength and insolence towards all who may
> be too feeble to resist. A worthier ideal should be inculcated – where we
> have the power to inculcate ideals, when we have the will; in our schools,
> namely. By the agency of arts and games, we should be training the young
> man and woman to find in their patriotism a sanction and explanation of
> their daily and hourly behaviour.[11]

If anything, then, the activities of the pro-Boers made some people
think again about the war.

18

Foreigners and the War

W HEN THE BOER War began, the British found themselves very much alone as public opinion around the world was virtually solidly pro-Boer. At government level, Britain's European and imperial rivals, France and Russia, were openly hostile, and, to a lesser extent, so were more recent competitors like Germany. All relished Britain's military discomforts and did next to nothing to stem the vociferous anti-British tirades in their newspapers. In spite of lingering Boer hopes, however, none of Britain's rivals would intervene directly owing to the strength of the Royal Navy, but some could still make life difficult. For example, in 1900 France undertook military manoeuvres along the Channel coast, which sparked an invasion scare in Britain because the country was devoid of regular troops, virtually all of whom had been sent to South Africa. The Russian Tsar basked in his own self-importance because he felt he could threaten India and ruin the British Empire. He told his sister: 'I possess the ultimate means of deciding the course of the war in South Africa. It is very simple – just a telegraphic order to all the troops in Turkestan to mobilise and advance towards the frontier. Not even the strongest fleet in the world can keep us from striking England in this her most vulnerable point.'[1]

Although foreign governments could be annoying, individual foreigners could be altogether deadlier. During the war about 2,000 foreigners volunteered to fight for the Boers and were organised in several national units or were placed within Boer commandos.

The foreign volunteers were a diverse group that came from all over Europe and from North America. The most numerous were the Germans and Dutch, although both their initial units did not last long after suffering terrible losses at Elandslaagte. The Scandinavians also suffered a similar fate at Magersfontein, losing forty-five men out of fifty-two engaged. The Irish and the Irish-Americans formed two brigades during the war and along the Tugela River faced their countrymen in Britain's own Irish Brigade. The war provided the Irish volunteers with another opportunity to attack the hated British and at the start about 300 were organised under an Irish-American former soldier, Colonel John Blake, whose deputy was the staunch Irish nationalist John MacBride, who was later executed by the British following the Easter uprising in Dublin in 1916. He was thoroughly committed to the brigade, later taking over command, and as a result the unit was often referred to as 'MacBride's Brigade'. Perhaps almost inevitably a rival group, called the Irish-Transvaal Brigade, emerged under the Irish-Australian Arthur Lynch. This group had scant regard for Blake and MacBride's men, an attitude that was reciprocated. Roland Schikkerling came across some of the Irish and Irish/Americans and noted: 'Where the Germans and Hollanders, nearer to us in blood perhaps, felt and looked out of place, you could not pick Patrick out of a herd of the wildest Boers.'[2]

There were some foreign individuals who were more famous for their family connections than anything else: for example, a Count von Zeppelin fought in the German corps, while one of Vincent van Gogh's brothers fought among the Hollanders and eventually also killed himself, after falling into the hands of the British. But the most prominent individual to emerge among the foreigners and who commanded the European Legion was the French nobleman Colonel Georges de Villebois-Mareuil. He had joined the Boer cause in order to seek fame and fortune and regain some honour for France, whose name he felt had been tarnished by the Fashoda incident in 1898, when Britain had forced France to give up any claim to southern Sudan, by the ongoing Dreyfus affair, and by several recent political scandals. The French volunteers, the most numerous after the Germans and Dutch, were, according to the American journalist H.C. Hillegas, 'undoubtedly of more actual service to the Boers than the volunteers of any other nationality, inasmuch as they were given the opportunities of doing valuable work',[3] especially as many could handle the Boers' French-made artillery. Villebois-Mareuil was particularly useful as an adviser, first to Joubert and then to Cronje, whom he later joined. After escaping from Paardeberg he was made a Vecht-generaal (combat general), the highest ranking foreigner in the Boer forces. However, Villebois-Mareuil's love of fighting and his disdain for Boer military practice and discipline, led him to expose his troops in a rather quixotic battle at Boshof on 5 April 1900. Here some of the European Legion and a Boer commando were attacked by numerically superior British forces under Lord Methuen. While the Boers took to their heels, the Europeans remained and fought on until they were overwhelmed and Villebois-Mareuil was killed. The nature of his death finally earned him the fame he had craved. Methuen's chivalrous conduct in giving him a military funeral and a headstone paid for by himself, was appreciated by friend and foe alike. In this respect, the war was certainly one fought by gentlemen.

Villebois-Mareuil was succeeded by Colonel Yevgeny Maximov, a Russian who also was fascinated by 'civilised warfare which attracts men of certain descriptions, and to them a well-fought battle is the highest form of exciting amusement'.[4] The Boer War was for Maximov just one incident in an action-packed life that included fighting a duel afterwards back in Russia. He was a splendid marksman and could shoot a springbok from a moving train, which endeared him to the Boers who witnessed it. The European Legion had, however, by this time broken up into its constituent detachments and Maximov was left in command of the reconstituted Hollander Corps. He was badly wounded at Thaba Nchu on 30 April 1900 after a pulsating fight with a smaller British detachment, which the Hollanders tried to overwhelm but were driven off after coming under heavy artillery fire. Maximov took no further part in the war and was later killed during the Russo-Japanese War of 1904–5.

These daring, quixotic individuals added a certain glamour to the early phases of the war and fitted perfectly into contemporary notions about the chivalry of warfare. Although Villebois-Mareuil volunteered because of his love of battle, he was committed to the Boer cause which, despite his professional contempt for Boer amateurism, was appreciated by the Boers themselves. The efforts of the foreign volunteers in general, however, were not appreciated and in most instances the Boers felt them to be a burden rather than a help. Most were urban dwellers living in Johannesburg or Pretoria and in the case of the Hollanders were government employees. Although they were not paid they had to be provided with horses and equipment and even then many could not ride or shoot, which exasperated the Boers when the volunteers arrived at the front. The Hollanders, in particular, were considered too superior or haughty and were resented. Roland Schikkerling wrote disparagingly of some Hollanders who got so drunk on stolen liquor that they never even noticed the battle of Elandslaagte raging around them.[5] The Germans were considered to be thieves who stole from the Boers and were 'disorderly'. Only those foreigners who showed sensitivity towards Boer susceptibilities, learned Afrikaans, or showed prowess, as in the case of Maximov, were eventually accepted by them.

By the time Britain had overrun the Boer republics and was about to cut them off from the outside world, most foreign volunteers had left, having crossed the frontier into Mozambique. Very few stayed behind with the *bittereinders*, although Blake did. The year of war between 1899 and 1900 was a time of adventure for many, especially for those professional soldiers languishing during a time of un-broken peace in Europe. For others it was a time when they fought for what they saw as the right of a small nation to exist, most conven-iently forgetting how the Boers treated Africans; indeed, Russian volunteers received an early lesson in Boer behaviour towards Africans, especially those considered to be working for the British. A group witnessed the shooting of an African immediately after he had been condemned for spying on the Boers.[6] Nevertheless, whatever motivated these foreign volunteers, they were too few in number to make any real difference to the outcome of the war, and Boer suspi-ciousness and aloofness ensured that their professional advice was rarely accepted. The foreigners merely added an exotic footnote to the main aspects of the Boer War.

19

The Press and the War

IN KEEPING WITH the sheer scale of the Boer War, the press coverage, particularly during the first phase of the war, was itself immense and fed a huge appetite back home for information about every aspect of the conflict. As this was the first major war the British had been involved in since the Crimea, press enthusiasm for the war, and the public's desire for news is understandable. George Sturt's journal gives a flavour of people's hunger for some exciting tidings. On 24 October 1899 he wrote:

> behind the boy who brought his bundle of evening papers into Frank's shop, there followed thick, until the shop was crowded, men eager for War News. For so long they had been waiting about, with nothing to do, expectant of the stimulus, and desiring something truly stirring. They would like a bloody battle twice a day, so that breakfast and supper might have a relish, and ennui be chased away.[1]

Indeed, the demand for news had seen the growth of the press during the late-nineteenth century and especially of those newspapers that supported imperial expansion. The *Daily Mail*, founded in 1896, was by its positive coverage of Britain's imperial wars the best-selling daily at the outbreak of the Boer War. The numerous colonial campaigns undertaken by the British provided a rich source of newsworthy items and led to the rise of war correspondents, some of whom became well-known figures, such as William Howard Russell, who found fame in the Crimean War, and Archibald Forbes, famous particularly after his 'death-ride' through Zululand in 1879. When the Boer War began, well-known correspondents were sent to

South Africa, such as Bennett Burleigh of the *Daily Telegraph*, J.B. Atkins of the *Manchester Guardian* and G.W. Steevens of the *Daily Mail*. War was beneficial for newspapers as it usually saw their sales figures increase, and if one of their star reporters was at the front then this, too, could enhance sales. Other special correspondents also went and one who was especially to catch public attention was Winston Churchill, sent by the *Morning Post*, who knew that a good war could advance a career. The illustrated weeklies, such as the *Illustrated London News* and the *Graphic* were well represented, the former by two of the most famous war artists, Frederic Villiers and Melton Prior.

There were of course differences in outlook among newspapers, but only one of the main dailies, the *Manchester Guardian*, stood out against the war. This principled stand cost the paper dear and by the war's end it had lost much of its readership. The *Manchester Guardian*'s only ally at the start among the dailies, the *Daily Chronicle*, soon became pro-war following a change of editor in order to stop the loss of readers. Only when the *Daily News* was bought by a Liberal consortium in 1901 did the *Manchester Guardian* gain a friend, but even they lost readers. Thus for many radicals there was concern that the news coming from South Africa would be tainted and the British public deceived about the reasons for going to war and about what was actually occurring. John X. Merriman, for example, told Professor Goldwin Smith in Canada that in the Cape Colony under martial law 'Men are sentenced by court martial to penal servitude for terms of years: of course absolutely illegal, but approved by the press at home, which seems to take its cue from the ravings of Kipling.'[2] There was some good reason for this because the English-language press in South Africa was largely in the hands of Cecil Rhodes and his allies and so supported the British line uncritically. One of those allies was Milner, who used his own experience of journalism and his appreciation of the power of a press-formed public opinion, to ensure that the right news emanated from the region. For example, Edmund Garrett was editor of the influential *Cape Times*, a newspaper virtually owned by the Rhodes camp and which therefore supported the work of Rhodes. He became a staunch ally of Milner because of their shared outlook and gave Milner an invaluable outlet for his imperial vision. When it is remembered that most British papers obtained their information from the local press, Milner's desire to send out the right signals is understandable. For the *Manchester Guardian* the need to combat this one-sided view of events in South Africa was vital. Apart from sending its own correspondents to the front, the paper made determined efforts to secure the services of leading local journalists who were not part of Rhodes's camp.[3]

Yet, despite the fact that most newspapers supported Britain's imperial aims, their reporters' relations with the military and the government were often hostile. The early confidence of the press in a quick British victory was soon undermined by the events of Black Week, which led to growing criticism by newspapers of the military and the government. The tightening of censorship, especially during the guerrilla phase, also led to acrimonious relations between the press and the military. Thus even though the government, army and the press were supposedly imperialist bedfellows the nature of the war in South Africa would often lead to estrangement.

This happened quite quickly, in fact, when it became clear that the war was not going to be a walkover. In the beginning press and public confidence in the army was high, as the military writer H. Spenser Wilkinson remembered; his editor on the *Morning Post* 'shared the almost universal opinion that a war with the Transvaal would be a small affair, resembling the autumn manoeuvres and lasting for a few weeks'. Wilkinson himself was to be disillusioned as the war progressed but he, like many journalists of the time, refused to blame the army for the unsatisfactory situation and instead rounded on the politicians. For Wilkinson, Lord Lansdowne was the main culprit and in a series of articles in late 1899 he attacked the War Minister for among other things his 'unbusiness-like way of playing with national affairs'. Even the staunchly pro-government *The Times* attacked ministers when they made somewhat feeble attempts to defend their records. Balfour's public assertion in January 1900 that 'I don't feel the need, so far as my colleagues and I are concerned, of any apology whatever', brought upon him the wrath of the *The Times*, which stated 'There is need of apology on the part of the Cabinet for serious errors, both in policy and warlike preparations.'[4] The press, which had flourished owing to successful imperial campaigns, found failure hard to stomach and showed no compunction in lashing out against its political allies.

The correspondents at the front were themselves largely uncritical of the conduct of the war and limited themselves to describing the military events, although there were always one or two willing to stick their necks out. Bennett Burleigh, for example, was critical of the army's performance in Natal following Black Week. But correspondents had to be careful because if they proved too critical or became a nuisance in some way they could lose their accreditation. Buller was notoriously anti-press, like his mentor Wolseley, and seemed not to understand that cultivating the press might be a wise career move. He was unsympathetic to the needs and desires of correspondents and failed to strike up a good relationship with the 'gentlemen' of the press. Lord Roberts, on the other hand, was very aware of the press and the way favourable reports helped construct a successful commander's image. He instituted a policy whereby despatches, but not telegrams, remained uncensored, as long as they were sent after his own official despatch. Consequently, his relations with the press passed off smoothly. When Kitchener took over, press censorship became more stringent, particularly as he knew that the Boers could get hold of British newspapers and he did not want them to read anything that might encourage them and so prolong the war. Nevertheless, he also knew the value of good publicity, having cultivated tame journalists before; in the Sudan for example, he befriended G.W. Steevens, who wrote glowing accounts of the machine-like, never erring Kitchener. In South Africa, he utilised the services of H.A. Gwynne of Reuters news agency, who defended the conduct of the war in return for regular briefings from Kitchener.

The strident censorship imposed during Kitchener's tenure as Commander-in-Chief irked those journalists who had remained behind to cover the guerrilla war. Deprived of good stories and with little apparently happening anyway, one or two correspondents grabbed hold of anything that might prove interesting. Edgar Wallace, a former army private and now a correspondent for the *Daily Mail*, first annoyed Kitchener by writing of the Vlakfontein incident mentioned in Chapter 16, where British wounded were allegedly killed by the Boers. Then, in his published unofficial despatches, he wrote: 'But Lord Kitchener has never thoroughly understood his Boer; indeed, it is as a student of men, real live men, with hearts and bowels and souls, that Lord Kitchener has been a failure. The men who have thought: the men who have schemed: the men of guile have set their wits against his, and they have triumphed.'[5] Kitchener was exasperated by the press, and in particular the *Daily Mail*, for reporting minor Boer successes as terrible British disasters. All he could do was to complain to Lord Roberts that 'I only wish the English papers would take up a sounder line, they do all in their power to encourage the Boers and to dishearten our troops.'[6]

Wallace had one more trick up his sleeve with which to infuriate Kitchener. When the peace talks were nearing their conclusion at Vereeniging in May 1902, each journalist was desperate for a scoop, wanting to be the first to report the end of the war. Four days before peace was signed, Kitchener telegraphed Brodrick: 'I should like to know if you are going to publish anything in London, as the correspondents have behaved extremely well, and I should like to give them a chance.' Although the government wanted to give nothing away, Kitchener was evidently in a better humour with the press. But when peace was signed late on 31 May Wallace, with the help of a British soldier, managed to get the news promptly and by use of a pre-arranged code telegraphed the information to the *Daily Mail*, which knew of the peace before the government. For such an act, which was reminiscent of one that followed the conclusion of the peace talks in 1881 after the battle of Majuba, Wallace gained both fame and notoriety: fame because he broke the news and notoriety because his career as a war correspondent was finished forever. He had proved too difficult for the military to control.

From 1901, the correspondents in South Africa had lost interest in a war that offered no great battles and only the discomforts of chasing Boers. In Britain, fewer newspapers carried war news although opinions were aired about army reform and the state of the nation in general. The focus on war news, the desire to augment what little was being provided by the military, kept correspondents fixed to the great sweeps and drives because writing about fighting and skirmishes was something they did best. The civilian dimension to the war, namely the fate of the civilians after they had been taken from their farms, was something beyond their notion of what warfare was all about. In consequence, the military-minded male correspondents missed the growing disaster within the concentration camps, the revelation of which was left to Emily Hobhouse and ultimately the *Manchester Guardian*.[7]

The war, then, caused the press to question notions of British imperialism and revealed that even those newspapers most in

harmony with the government would not tolerate what they perceived as a failure to uphold British interests properly. The
deficiencies revealed by the war also meant that it was not only the
press and the government that fell out; relations between the military
and newspapers had also changed, and this ended the uneasy give
and take of the nineteenth century for a more one-sided relationship
dominated by the military authorities.

20

The Literature of the War

ESPECIALLY ITS POETRY

THERE WAS AN enormous quantity of literature written and published during, and very soon after the South African War. As
with other aspects of the conflict, it reflected widely differing views
and opinions as well the ambivalences and paradoxes that were so
strikingly evident during the conflict. The writing was designed to
describe, analyse, respond to and bring alive the tumultuous events
of 1899 to 1902. Quite apart from the *The Times History of the War in
South Africa* in seven volumes there were several other serious historical accounts and the memoirs of many of those who fought in the
war on both sides. The world's press often sent out their top journalists to cover the campaign, and early moving film crews were also
present. Then there were the poets and the novelists who covered
the war, as well as the writers of fiction for children. The common
description of the confrontation as the first 'media war' is thus quite
justifiable.

Of course, this great outpouring was partly the result of the
almost insatiable public demand for information, images, and
accounts – some of it inevitably sensationalist. More than that, the
written word was enjoying its heyday. In Britain the late-Victorian
and Edwardian eras were a golden period for English literature,
and books of all sorts were very much in demand. Writers like
Rudyard Kipling, Thomas Hardy, H.G. Wells, Arnold Bennett, John
Galsworthy, E.M. Forster and George Bernard Shaw were at the
height of their creative powers; novelists such as D.H. Lawrence and

John Buchan were about to make their marks. In children's literature, too, not only were the adventure stories of writers like G.A. Henty in great demand but there was also a flood of what we now regard as classics. The Beatrix Potter tales, *The Wind in the Willows*, *The Secret Garden*, *The Railway Children*, *Stalky and Co.*, and many more books were being eagerly devoured by an increasingly literate and affluent juvenile readership. There was, in other words, a huge and eager market for writing about the war.

Apart from the many publications that derived from the conflict, there was another source of information and comment. The late-Victorian drive for improvement through educational reform – most obviously precipitated by the great 1870 Education Act – meant that the vast majority of rank-and-file troops were literate and thus able to write home or, less commonly, to keep diaries. Photographs of soldiers reading beside their tents, or pressing with stubby pencils onto writing paper, are there in the pictorial archive. The implications of this were stated by a contemporary observer: 'Never before has Britain sent forth to the battlefield so large a force of men sufficiently educated to write home. The war, therefore, has been described from day to day, not like all other wars, by professional journalists or by literary officers, but by the rank and file.'[1]

So, one way or another, there was a colossal literary response to the Boer War. Nor was the output simply derived from Britain and the Empire. Afrikaner writers, especially poets, put their perception of their people's experience, painful and doom-ridden as it eventually became, into often vivid, moving literary forms. French, American, German and other foreign writers were also anxious to have their say. The high profile and increasingly controversial nature of the conflict in South Africa, its capacity to grab the headlines, demanded a literary response; it was most certainly forthcoming.

Since poetry was among the most popular and evocative literary forms that engaged with the events of the Boer War, it seems appropriate to gauge the content and quality of this medium in particular. British patriots could take comfort from some of the robust verse produced during the war. There was single-minded, sub-Kiplingesque doggerel:

> When Tommy joins the 'unt
> With the stabbin' of the baynit

> The baynit, the bloody baynit
> Gawd 'elp the man in front![2]

Unashamedly inspired by, and sometimes replicating, the rhythms and structures of such considerable British poets as Tennyson and Kipling, a crop of patriotic versifiers rushed into publication, from Percy Ingrams in *Songs of the Transvaal War* to Frederick Langbridge in *Ballads and Legends*. More considerable talents, such as Swinburne or the Poet Laureate Alfred Austin, were quick to bang the patriotic drum. Even before the war had begun, Swinburne was longing in the pages of *The Times*:

> To scourge these dogs, agape with jaws afoam,
> Down out of life. Strike England, and strike home[3]

Just as the war split opinion at home, it also produced divisions among poets. Although in general believing the conflict to be necessary, or at least unavoidable, great writers like Thomas Hardy and A.E. Housman had a keen perception of the suffering of the ordinary soldier, far from home and often bewildered by the turn of events and the daily task of survival. It was Hardy, always aspiring to be an even more accomplished and celebrated poet than a novelist, who encapsulated this in his brilliantly conceived 'Drummer Hodge':

> They throw in Drummer Hodge, to rest
> Uncoffined – just as found;
> His landmark is a kopje-crest
> That breaks the veldt around;
> And foreign constellations west
> Each night above his mound[4]

There was also British poetry that reflected the humanitarian, often pro-Boer point of view. William Watson, a Liberal poet, who campaigned vigorously against the war, was a powerful literary voice calling for the recognition of Boer virtues – widely perceived as pastoral, patriarchal and self-sufficient – that had been lost in urbanised, industrialised Britain. Similar in many ways to the idealisation by some British officers serving in South Africa of the Boers as sturdy, rural, blue-eyed Aryans, Watson's poetry extolled the Afrikaners as:

> Unskilled in Letters, and in Arts unversed;
> Ignorant of empire; bounded in their view
> By the lone billowing veldt, where they upgrew
> Amid great silences.[5]

This romanticised, hayseed perception of the Boers was peddled in many liberal and progressive circles; though based on a half-truth, it conveniently ignored both the industrialisation of the Transvaal and the cultural and intellectual sophistication of many Afrikaner leaders.

Pro-Boer sentiment was also fed from two other rich sources that were sometimes blended together in a murky stream – anti-Semitism, and sympathy for the plight of the common soldier allegedly ruthlessly manipulated by the sinister forces of capitalism. Dislike of Jewish entrepreneurial and financial success was not the prerogative of either the left or the right in British politics. Liberals and Conservatives could equally find it offensive. The writers G.K. Chesterton and Hilaire Belloc, though Liberals, both gave vent to open anti-Semitic prejudices. Chesterton was to write after the war:

> Leave them the gold that worked and whined for it,
> Let them that have no nation anywhere
> Be native here, and fat and full of bread;
> But we, whose sins were human, we will quit
> The land of blood. And leave these vultures there,
> Noiselessly happy, feeding on the dead[6]

A socialist, campaigning journal such as *Reynolds's Newspaper* published the following verse a few weeks after the outbreak of the war:

> Oh, Tommy, Tommy Atkins,
> My heart beats sore for you,
> To be made the bloomin' catspaw
> Of the all-pervading Jew.
> And when you're back in England
> Invalided, full of care,
> You'll find you've drawn the chestnuts
> For the multi-millionaire[7]

Left-wing perceptions of the war as simply another example of the crude manipulation and duping of the working classes by international financiers and domestic capitalists alike were wide-spread. One piece of verse provides an eerie foreboding of the slaughter in the trenches during the First World War and particularly of Wilfred Owen's great poem 'Anthem for Doomed Youth' with its opening lines: 'What passing bells for these who die like cattle?/Only the monstrous anger of the guns.' In similar vein, B. Paul Neuman wrote in the pacifist journal *Concord*:

> For brave and simple are the gathering hosts
> Who move like dumb beasts to the shambles led,
> Who hear the word and take their ordered posts,
> Nor know the cause for which their blood is shed[8]

Afrikaner poets naturally gave expression to the fears, hopes and anger of their people. Once more, the picture is complex and cross-hatched with contradictions and confusion. For instance, there were those of the Cape Afrikaner population who stayed loyal to the British crown and those – the Cape Rebels – who decided to fight for the Boer cause. Because so many of the ordinary Afrikaners who made up the commandos were from a rural, sometimes nomadic, often poorly educated background they have left comparatively little verse composed on the battlefield.

There are some exceptions, though much of it remained unpublished for decades, the secret, privately cherished archive of a defeated people. E.E. Meyer of the Transvaal, writing in Afrikaans, imagined a girl's thoughts as she faced the possibilities of her lover's death:

> Were it to happen that you should die,
> They will sing in praise of you;
> They will pick flowers on the hills
> To plant round your still dust[9]

Interestingly, some of the best Afrikaner poetry was written and published in English, yet further proof of the complex, interwoven identities and fates of the two white groups in South Africa. Ex-President F.W. Reitz of the Orange Free State had five sons who fought in the war; three of them subsequently wrote about their experiences. The Reitz family was highly cultured and their home full of books – mostly in English. One son, Joubert Reitz, almost always wrote verse in English. One poem of his that was eagerly read by Boer prisoners of war is 'The Searchlight':

> And I think of things that have been
> And happiness that's past
> And only then I realise
> How much my freedom meant,
> When the searchlight from the gunboat
> Casts its rays upon my tent.[10]

Boer soldiers did of course sing songs, including hymns, and enjoyed setting some of their own ditties to English music-hall tunes like 'Daisy, Daisy'. As the war drew to a close and so many of them became prisoners of war, the need to keep up morale and to celebrate and mark their battered identities led to a profusion of verse and song. Particularly galling was the fact that several thousand Boer prisoners were deported to places like Bermuda, southern India or Ceylon – all highly sought after and up-market holiday destinations a hundred years later! One poignant poem is 'On New Years' Day 1901', which sums up the feeling of one group of prisoners who mistakenly believed they were going to be released:

> We thought we were going home,
> So we tied our bundles across our backs.
> At one o'clock we went to the gate;
> I thought the men were going crazy:
> They laughed, chattered, wept all at once.
> My heart ached, it was too terrible.[11]

Gradually they realised that they were being marched to the docks for transportation, and their disappointment and humiliation was compounded by Cape coloured onlookers taunting them with shouts of, 'Boers, where's your pass?' Once on board ship and bound for exile, some groups of prisoners tried to keep their spirits up with sprightly songs satirising their conditions:

> As far as the food is concerned,
> If you really want to know:
> Curried rice and troops' sweat,

> Bitter coffee and sour bread;
> Only a Jew can stomach the meat.[12]

British sympathisers and British subjects like the Cape Afrikaners also wrote verse supporting the Boer cause or drawing attention to the cruelties of Kitchener's scorched-earth and concentration camp policies. Olive Schreiner was one such powerful voice, but there were also women like Alice Greene, Betty Molteno and Anna Purcell. As the British determination to make an example of at least some of the 'Cape Rebels' led to trial and execution, Alice Greene wrote scathingly of the British:

> And their answer is still the prison grim
> And the scaffold ghastly high,
> And the red, red blood which soaks the ground
> Where 'rebels' calmly die[13]

Verse critical of British policy in South Africa was also written and published in other parts of the world, especially in the United States, Germany, France, and the Netherlands. In these countries stories of British atrocities were often gleefully but irresponsibly embroidered, and accounts of imperial military successes ignored or underestimated.

Despite the friendly, inclusive tone of Kipling's 1898 poem 'Take up the White Man's Burden', written in the immediate aftermath of the United States' triumph in the recent war with Spain and welcoming them to the unenviable though necessary task of imperial administration, anti-British feeling in America ran high during the Boer War. Typical of an American poem admiringly extolling the virtues of the Boer commandos is 'Rebel of the Veldt' by Bernard Shadwell:

> Saddle and bridle and girth,
> Stirrup and cropper and bit:
> Man on top of a little horse,
> Shaggy and strong and fit:
> Rugged and bearded face,
> Ragged old hat of felt,
> Rifle that kills at a thousand yards,
> And a tight-crammed cartridge belt.[14]

Perhaps more understandably, German and French poets had a field day attacking and mocking the British war effort in South Africa. One French poem, entitled 'Courage, Boers!', glorified the stoical qualities of Afrikaner womenfolk:

> It is the Boer woman, the heroine of olden times!
> She has seen her village gutted by shrapnel
> And her son shot dead in his cradle,
> But her heart desires its tragic revenge[15]

In many of the poems written in Western Europe, the themes were those of sympathy for Boer suffering and admiration for their collective bravery. There was also much recycling of the myths cherished by many British pro-Boers, depicting the Afrikaners as peaceful, sturdy pastoralists assaulted by both British imperialism and international – often Jewish – financiers and capitalists. A Dutch poem puts it plainly:

> The usurious race which lives off the Boers
> Knows, with its starved host of servants,
> How to lay its table opulently in the paved city . . .
> Behold the Dutch family
> At a clean, well filled table,
> Peaceful and pious.[16]

Finally, it might be expected that Rudyard Kipling, poet of Empire, friend of the foot-slogging British Tommy, ironic observer of 'lesser breeds without the law', would have produced a set of tub-thumping, jangling patriotic ballads espousing the justice of the imperial cause.

Kipling, however, was far too shrewd an imperialist and far too fine a poet to fall into so crude a trap. His best known Boer War poems, 'No End of a Lesson' and 'The Absent Minded Beggar' are in fact cogent and thoughtful criticisms of aspects of British policy and military tactics. They were written in the hope that lessons could be learned and the Empire better defended and promoted as a result.

So often concerned with looking ahead to discern obstacles to the national self-interest and to suggest appropriate remedies, Kipling had no doubt about what was best once South Africa had been brought under British rule. Like so many of his contemporaries he desired an accommodation, at best a reconciliation with the

Afrikaner people. Nowhere does he articulate this ambition with greater power than in his poem 'Piet'.

Piet is the archetypal Boer fighter; defeated but unbowed. He is also shrewd, daring and brave, and in the end comes off at least as well as his victorious British opponents. Kipling paints a final picture of Piet revelling in the new agricultural equipment and facilities provided free by the British taxpayer – but, since Kitchener's armies had burnt Piet's farm to the ground to begin with, this seems fair enough. The overriding theme of the poem is respect for a gallant defeated foe and the desire for future friendship, laced with a flash of bitter contempt for 'all that foreign lot' – the Germans, Russians, French, Americans and so forth of the international units who only joined the fight against the British Empire 'for spite'. The poem's plea for mutual respect, and its plain desire for reconstruction and reconciliation, are the very qualities that, after the peace settlement in 1902, were being harnessed to the service of the creation of greater South Africa:

> I do not love my Empire's foes,
> Nor call 'em angels; still,
> What is the sense of 'ating those
> 'Oom you are sent to kill?
> So, barrin' all that foreign lot
> Which only joined for spite,
> Myself, I'd just as soon as not
> Respect the man I fight.

> Ah, there, Piet! With your brand-new English plough,
> Your gratis tents an' cattle, an' your most ungrateful frow,
> You've made the British taxpayer rebuild your country seat –
> I've known some pet battalions charge a dam' sight more than Piet.

> From Plewman's to Marabastad
> From Ookiep to De Aar,
> Me an' my trusty friend 'ave 'ad,
> As you might say, a war;
> But seein' what both parties done
> Before 'e owned defeat,
> I ain't more proud of 'aving won
> Than I am pleased with Piet.[17]

Part V

The Peace

2 1

The Talks Begin

IN APRIL 1902 the British and the Boers resumed negotiations that had fallen into abeyance the year before. During that time the war had become more bitter and more devastating, consuming the resources of both sides in ever growing amounts. This time the talks would not collapse and would conclude at the end of May with the peace treaty that would finally bring the war to an end.

By April 1902 the Transvaal's Commandant General, Louis Botha, began to question whether the Boers should sacrifice everything to preserve their independence. By then their land had been devastated and their women and children were dying in the concentration camps. For Botha and his men, the Boers had sacrificed enough and it was time to negotiate, not to save their precious independence, but to preserve the Boer people themselves. This more realistic attitude did not, however, find complete favour. The leaders of the Orange Free State, President Steyn and his Chief Commandant, Christiaan de Wet, believed the British would compromise on independence if the guerrilla war could be kept alive. Steyn, the earlier man of peace, had become the man of war who would never surrender save on his own terms. The split between the leaders of the Transvaal and the Orange Free State, already evident from the earlier attempts to negotiate, would become palpable in 1902.

On the British side, the divisions between the civil and military authorities, represented by Lord Milner and Lord Kitchener respectively, would reveal themselves once again. Milner still wanted the Boers to surrender unconditionally and leave him free to rebuild South Africa in such a way that the British element would be forever dominant. His aims had remained undimmed, in spite of the ongoing war, and he continued fervently to hope that the Boer leadership would be discredited, that new Boer collaborators would emerge, and that British colonists would settle in the Boer heartlands and ensure that the Boers would never trouble the Empire again.

On the other hand, Kitchener felt that the Boer leaders had to be accommodated once they had accepted that the independence of the republics had gone forever. This had been his plan during the abortive talks with Botha in March 1901. To Kitchener, the realist, South Africa would always be dominated by the Boers and it would be better if Britain's former enemies accepted their fate and became willing partners in the imperial enterprise. Thus for Kitchener the military and political aspects were intimately tied together and he was determined to stamp his own authority on the peace process. This he could do while the war lasted because he was in supreme command, a fact that Milner found hard to accept and one which meant that the Boers would first go through him should they ask to negotiate. There was also a more basic reason why Kitchener would be present at any talks: the Boers detested Milner, the architect of their misfortunes, and they preferred that his presence be diluted.

The negotiations that finally led to what became known as the peace of Vereeniging were riddled with ironies. Instead of a simple Boer versus Britain dichotomy, the talks became complicated by divisions on both sides; the double irony was that those who would have been considered the aggressive and obdurate voices at such talks – the representatives of the British army and the Transvaal – were in fact the parties most determined to reach a settlement acceptable to all concerned. Such are the vagaries of war.

During 1901, as we have seen, the war had steadily become one of blockhouses, wire fences, burnt farms and concentration camps. With the Boers being deprived of food, information and space, the British began to hope that the end of the war was near. Lieutenant Colonel David Henderson, the head of British military intelligence in South Africa – whose efforts ensured the British enjoyed an excellent field intelligence network which enabled them, at long last, to match and catch the Boers on the veld – reported to London in growingly optimistic terms. At times he sounded too hopeful, but there was an increasing sense that the Boers were being worn down by the continual harassment from British columns. As early as

August 1901 Henderson reported that the Boers 'are more uppish than ever in public, but in private they admit that they are sick of their present life and wish the Government would give in'. By December, his reports were more upbeat: 'It is possible that De Wet means to have a try at one of the unfinished blockhouse lines. These are worrying the Boers terribly, as they now find their movements cramped and can foresee how much worse it will be when they are completed.' Even better news arrived in January 1902 when one of his intelligence officers, Baird of the Gordons, visited one of the Boer laagers (the British and Boers were in contact throughout the guerrilla war, sometimes unofficially) and found 'that the great majority of the men were satisfied that the game was up; they are individually ripe for surrender, but the collective surrender does not yet seem imminent. This exactly agrees with the sentiments of the men I met when I went out from Belfast a few weeks ago.' And to cap it all, he was pleased to announce that the recruitment of the National Scouts, those Boers prepared to join the British as scouts and soldiers, was thriving and that they had had some recent success against the enemy. All in all, 'This movement is having a depressing effect on the Boers still on commando.'[1]

Henderson's prognostications were in the main correct by the beginning of 1902. Although few Boers would admit outwardly that their cause might be lost, inwardly deep misgivings emerged as the prospects for the coming year were pondered. Before them, of course, lay the trials and tribulations of another winter, this time made infinitely worse by the enclosure of the land and its continuing devastation. Now was added another burden: since December Kitchener had ordered that no more civilians be taken into the camps; farms were still to be destroyed but their inhabitants would now have to fend for themselves on the veld or be taken in by the commandos. Ironically, this measure ensured that conditions in the concentration camps were improved, but it did nothing for those cast adrift at the mercy of the elements and hostile tribespeople. By now the tribes of the Transvaal, particularly the Pedi, were in revolt, taking advantage of British encouragement and the breakdown of Boer authority to settle old scores and deny the Boers access to their lands.

Nevertheless, certain Boers could still show defiance. Jan Smuts, by now conducting an increasingly marginalised campaign in the

Cape Colony, having failed to incite a major rebellion, attempted to reinvigorate the propaganda war by sending an open letter to W.T. Stead in which he stated that the Boers still felt their cause to be just and that they were honourable foes, not 'brigands and ruffians' as described recently by Chamberlain. To the Boers, Smuts argued, their cause 'has become a Boer religion'. At the same time Smuts wrote to Abraham Fischer, a member of the Boer delegation in Europe, and admitted that the prospect of famine was real and frightened him; he wondered just how long the struggle could continue, 'so we must not lose sight of a reasonable settlement on the basis of our independence'.

By 1902 the Boers were becoming desperately short of arms and ammunition, especially the commandos in the Transvaal, which led Viljoen to inform Botha that he would have to run rather than fight. Everywhere the Boers looked, the position was increasingly hopeless. The National Scouts were becoming more numerous and were giving incalculable help to the British. There was growing demoralisation in the prisoner of war camps and public appeals were being made by Boers to the leadership exhorting them to give in. Yet, as Smuts's letter showed, for the leadership the desire to retain some form of independence still drove them on and the occasional military success, like that of De la Rey at Tweebosch on 7 March 1902, when Lord Methuen was wounded and captured, managed to revive Boer spirits a bit longer. But all around them the evidence was mounting that the people and the country could not endure; it would be only a matter of time before the signs became irrefutable and could not be ignored by the leadership or anyone else.[2]

For the British the expectation of success brought its own complications – what sort of peace should be concluded when the time came? As yet there was no clear policy, except the idea of unconditional surrender. This, more or less, was reiterated in a speech given by Milner to the Johannesburg business community on 8 January 1902. The speech was also an endorsement of the loyalists and those Boers who had surrendered earlier, whose interests Milner thought had been too often ignored. Not for him would there be any accommodation with the commandos. Indeed, Milner was already thinking ahead regarding the return to South Africa of the Boer prisoners of war. Before that should happen, he explained to Chamberlain, the Uitlander refugees should return to Johannesburg, then 'reconciled'

Boers and finally the irreconcilables 'should be allowed to return only when [the] country is partially occupied by these safe elements'.[3]

Yet Chamberlain had at that very moment revealed that the government might not be so intransigent after all. A Reuters telegram reporting the contents of Chamberlain's speech in the House of Commons on the evening of 20 January 1902, announced that the British authorities were prepared to grant a general amnesty to those rebels who had not committed any particular crimes, although they would still be liable to disenfranchisement. Kitchener and some of his officers latched on to this information immediately. To Kitchener, it might lead to the rebels deserting the Boers and removing the main impediment to peace. However, Kitchener soon realised that the report was not totally correct, but he said nevertheless that the amnesty question was 'the crux of the situation at present' and that in the Transvaal the leaders only kept their men in the field because it was a 'point of honour' not to desert the rebels. 'For instance, De la Rey had a meeting a few days ago and spoke of peace, but the Cape rebels with him abused the Boers for thinking of leaving them to their fate, so nothing came of the meeting.'

Brodrick indeed confirmed that Chamberlain's reported speech was incorrect and that only after peace would an amnesty be granted and only then once British interests had been taken into consideration. Even so, Brodrick reiterated that it was for the Boers to make the first move and that they must approach Kitchener. At first glance it seems odd that Kitchener should still regard an amnesty as the most vital determinant of peace. One can only assume that Kitchener had taken for granted that the Boers would give up their independence and the main bargaining element after that remained the amnesty question. Kitchener had said too often before that the independence issue was the all-important one; negotiations, therefore, would revolve around the concessions the British government was willing to make.[4]

In spite of the false hopes generated by the reporter's attempts to distil the politician's speech, moves towards peace moved on inexorably but slowly. On 5 February 1902 Kitchener reported an interview with captured General Ben Viljoen, in which he claimed the Transvaal was eager for peace and that Schalk Burgers, the Acting President, was going to see Steyn and De Wet to discuss peace proposals. Nothing came of this, even if it were true.

Methuen's defeat at Tweebosch profoundly shook Kitchener's iron resolve. This was, however, a temporary setback in every sense: it made no real difference to the military situation, and it did not deflect the peace process. Three days before Methuen's defeat, Kitchener had sent to Schalk Burgers a note from the Dutch government offering its services as mediator and requesting that Kruger and the other exiles, who were based in the Netherlands, be allowed to return to South Africa with complete powers to make peace. Replying for the British, Lord Lansdowne thanked the Dutch for their concern, politely refused their offer and also refused to acknowledge that the delegation held any influence over those still in the field, who he believed held the requisite powers to negotiate. This was to ensure that those who had not suffered the hardships of the war and did not appreciate fully the state of their former republics, should have no power over those who had. This was basically an invitation to the commandos to come forward with proposals. Schalk Burgers replied that he was willing to make peace proposals but only after he had discussed the matter with Steyn, and that he must be allowed safe passage through the British lines. The action at Tweebosch had not weakened the British will to persist with the war. The Dutch note would have been passed on whether Tweebosch had happened or not. The crucial point is that Tweebosch did not strengthen the Boer will to resist. Burgers's swift reply to Kitchener indicated plainly the realisation that De la Rey's victory had not altered the military situation in any significant way. The Boers were now taking up what had been since mid-1901 a standing British offer to come forward with their proposals.

The British government agreed to Burgers's request for safe passage and messengers were sent across the veld to find Steyn and De la Rey. Eventually, on 9 April 1902, the two Boer governments came together at Klerksdorp under the watchful eyes of the British garrison and Kitchener's representatives, to thrash out the details of their terms.[5]

The representatives from the Transvaal included Schalk Burgers, Botha, De la Rey and Reitz, the former State Secretary, who was identified quite erroneously by Kitchener as 'the ruling spirit' who would 'probably put forward impossible terms'. From the Orange Free State the leading lights were Steyn, and Generals de Wet, Hertzog, and Olivier; altogether the two delegations numbered seventeen. Burgers was elected chairman of the proceedings, a capacity in which he acted for the remainder of the talks and negotiations. The three generals, Botha, De la Rey and De Wet were asked to review the military situation. Botha's tale was one of woe: in his area, the eastern Transvaal, there was little food, dwindling space, and armed Zulus to contend with. Hostilities with the Zulu had begun to escalate because the Boers were raiding Zulu territory for supplies. This led, naturally enough, to Zulu retaliation, which was encouraged by the British. De la Rey, speaking for the western Transvaal, painted a gloomy picture that gave substance to the success of the blockhouses; crucially, they were denying him access to those districts where food could be obtained. Nevertheless, he still felt the war could be continued. De Wet, on the other hand, was more optimistic, the outlook as far as he was concerned was far brighter than that in Botha's area.

Steyn spoke out immediately, saying that the Boers should hold out for their independence and if the British refused to grant this then the war should continue, as this was what the Boer governments had agreed in June 1901. He then made an interesting remark which Kitchener became aware of and used often to justify his desire for terms (it would seem that some of the British officers detailed to accompany the Boers were chosen because of their ability to understand Afrikaans). Steyn evidently indicated that if he were to give in at all he would 'submit unconditionally' rather than make terms. He was to reiterate this as the peace talks developed and by it he meant that he would not feel bound by any British terms and would remain free to choose whether he accepted British rule or not. Such a position would give him the moral right to take up arms again later.

After an adjournment the delegates met again the following day and the discussions continued in much the same vein. The Transvaal's General Lukas Meyer, an opponent of Kruger before the war, felt there was little hope and if Britain would not countenance Boer independence then 'the time would have arrived for the matter to be laid before the people'. De Wet, though, continued to spit defiance: he could get recruits from the Cape to fill his depleted ranks; he had enough food and ammunition for another year; and in a telling remark he said that 'Before he conceded an iota of their independence he would allow himself to be banished for ever.' This sort of discussion illuminated the viewpoints of the delegates but did not get them very far, so on Hertzog's suggestion it was decided to approach Kitchener with an offer of certain proposals 'which can serve as a basis for further negotiations with the object of establishing the desired peace'. A commission consisting of Steyn, Burgers, Reitz and Hertzog then formulated a series of proposals, which were accepted by the rest of the delegates. These proposals, unsurprisingly, did not mention the loss of independence but instead offered: a treaty of friendship; the dismantling of all the Boer forts; a procedure for the arbitration of all future differences; equal educational rights for the use of English and Dutch; and a mutual amnesty. So armed, the delegates went to meet Kitchener the following day.

The Free Staters in particular were trying to convince themselves that the British position was not as rosy as might be supposed. Hertzog especially felt that the British might not be so willing to carry on: the Boers only heard news of the outside world from British newspapers, and Britain could not recruit troops and borrow money indefinitely. Basically, until they knew much more of the outside world there was room for optimism. Whereas this seemed to comfort the likes of Steyn and De Wet, the Transvaalers did not openly endorse this reasoning.[6]

Meanwhile, the British camp, both in Britain and South Africa, had been stirred by the meeting of the Boer delegates and hopes and fears were expressed in equal measure. Within the government, divisions resurfaced that had emerged the previous year over the costs of the war and of army reform, particularly between the Chancellor of the Exchequer, Sir Michael Hicks Beach, and Chamberlain, to which the service ministers had been a party. In a note to Lord Salisbury, Hicks Beach was determined to ensure that any Boer proposals would be discussed by the Cabinet as a whole, and wished they had been in 1899, a clear dig at Chamberlain's handling of that particular crisis, to which Chamberlain reacted with undisguised hostility. He also felt that the King, who hankered for peace, was being too readily influenced by the former Liberal leader Lord Rosebery, who had possibly suggested that peace was obtainable if both Milner and Chamberlain were dismissed! On the back of this criticism, Chamberlain briefed Milner on the government's position. Although he had not shifted his own stance, in that he stood by the idea of 'unconditional surrender', his letter reflected his own realisation that the mood within the Cabinet had changed, with some ministers now prepared to be more lenient. He advised Milner that he should be flexible in his approach and not too rigid. Clearly, Chamberlain appreciated that the climate of opinion in Britain would brook no failure if the talks with the Boers should collapse on issues that were not considered fundamental; hence his conversion to a more liberal approach towards the questions of amnesty and the financing of Boer reconstruction. A date for self-government, however, remained non-negotiable.

For Milner, Chamberlain's more flexible attitude was not one that he shared and was not appreciated because it signalled a considerable and unwelcome shift in the government's approach. Although regularly appraised of public opinion in Britain by his friends and ministers, he seemed still to think that the Boers were on the brink of collapse and that obstinacy on the part of the British would ensure their total capitulation. But before he had time to digest Chamberlain's unwelcome news, matters took a turn for the worse when he heard from Kitchener that the Boers had requested an interview. This, he feared, was 'a commencement of negotiations'. To Milner, Kitchener was no judge of the political effects of any proposals; he was too eager to get away and too lax on the matter of setting a date for Boer self-government.

Milner's initial fears about Kitchener were unfounded however. On receipt of the Boer request for a meeting, Kitchener had telegraphed immediately to Brodrick informing him of this and asking for instructions as soon as possible, not wishing to keep the Boers lingering at Klerksdorp any longer than necessary. At the government's behest he also informed Milner of what was transpiring and arranged to see the delegates only to hear their proposals without offering anything in return. With the proviso that Kitchener should have witnesses present the government agreed that he could meet the Boer delegates. However, the government would issue no instructions until the Boers had forwarded their proposals upon which, he was told, neither he nor Milner should offer any opinion.[7]

The best source for the meeting between Kitchener and the delegates remains the unofficial account provided by the Reverend J.D. Kestell, chaplain to Steyn and De Wet, and D.E. van Velden, who were appointed secretaries to the Orange Free State and Transvaal delegations respectively, despite their being excluded from the meeting by Kitchener who wanted to make it more informal.

Lieutenant Colonel Hubert Hamilton, Kitchener's military secretary, took notes for the Commander-in-Chief and told one of his colleagues afterwards that 'K. did the business extraordinarily well, they were all afraid of him and respected him tremendously'. Another colleague, Captain R.J. Marker, described the Boers to his father as follows: 'if you were to go to a market ... especially in the South of Scotland, & pick the first half dozen farmers you meet you would get a very excellent idea of what the bulk of the representatives of both governments are like.'[8]

From Kestell's notes, dictated to him by Hertzog and corrected by Steyn and Brebner, the Acting State Secretary, the terms were relayed to Kitchener with Reitz acting as interpreter. Steyn said that they had come to gain 'that for which the People had fought until this moment'. This remark astonished Kitchener and he asked, somewhat bewildered, 'Must I understand from what you say that you wish to retain your independence?' Steyn confirmed this was so and then said it was a matter of the people's self-respect, that they 'must not feel themselves humiliated in the eyes of the British'. Kitchener then spent the rest of the meeting trying to convince the delegates that surrendering and obtaining terms 'as regards self-government' were the best options. Becoming British subjects was no humiliation since other colonists were 'proud of their nationality'. In spite of his best urging Kitchener could make no headway and so, reluctantly, he helped the Boers draw up a telegram incorporating their proposals to be sent to the British government. In his telegram to Brodrick afterwards, Kitchener explained that the Boers would not give up their independence 'without reference to the people' and that Schalk Burgers had said 'We must have something to give to the people instead of independence. What shall we be able to offer them?'[9]

Two days later, on 14 April 1902, Kitchener, this time with Milner in attendance, met the delegates to appraise them of the British reply. With Milner in the room the mood evidently changed; all the burghers it seems 'held him in abhorrence'. Steyn was reluctant to talk to Milner but the others were prepared to put up with their mortal enemy and so Milner remained an integral part of the proceedings.

Milner had been briefed by Chamberlain, his note seen only by Hicks Beach and Brodrick because the rest of the Cabinet were away for the weekend. This time Chamberlain was more explicit in his view that some conciliation was necessary even if it meant diverging from his speech of 20 January, which formed the basis of Milner's instructions. Hicks Beach was pleased with Chamberlain's moderation and that Milner had been ordered to adopt a flexible attitude. As he told Chamberlain, public opinion would not tolerate any failures on 'minor grounds': 'If I am right in this, Milner might see, more than I imagine he does now, that Kitchener's desire to get away from S. Africa is not the only reason for not being too stiff on the present occasion.'[10]

Once the meeting got underway Milner immediately caused irritation by refusing to address Steyn and Burgers as 'president', although he did try to allay any fears that he was ill-disposed towards the Boers. Then the delegates were given copies of Brodrick's telegram to Kitchener that rejected the idea of Boer independence and requested that they make fresh proposals. This the Boers did after a short adjournment, but requested that they be allowed to consult the Boer representatives in Europe and also that an armistice be declared to enable them to consult the people, namely those still in the field. Kitchener refused the first point because it would be 'an exceptional mode of proceeding' and then suggested that the British government be asked for compensation in return for their independence. This was agreed and messages were sent off to London.

Kitchener informed Brodrick that the Boer delegates had no constitutional authority to surrender their independence and so wanted the government to state its terms so that the Boers could be offered something in return for the loss of their freedom. Although the British authorities were surprised at this turn of events, ministers were nonetheless concerned 'to spare the effusion of further blood' and so gave permission to Kitchener and Milner to refer once again to the terms discussed at Middelburg in 1901. This return to Middelburg had actually been suggested by Milner on 14 April. He had begun his telegram by stating unequivocally:

Personally, I distrust all negotiations and should regard the future with more hope if the war ended by a continuance of captures and surrenders which despite our constantly recurring mishaps continue to take place at a satisfactory rate. This feeling is shared by all our friends in South Africa. But as public feeling at home evidently favours negotiations we must do the best we can. I am strongly of opinion that we should not retreat an inch from the position taken up by you in speech of January 20th. I think that in reply to Boer message of today H.M.G. would do well to refer to the offer made to Botha in Kitchener's letter of March 7th [1901].

Such a move, according to Milner, would indicate British clemency considering the lives lost and money spent since then, but, as Chamberlain then replied, any concessions would 'represent I think the extreme limit' and the Boers had to give something in return.[11] Milner's suggestion that the Middelburg terms form the basis of future negotiations shows a distinct shift in his attitude. Apart from endorsing Kitchener's military strategy, which beforehand he had condemned as slow and bereft of results, Milner now realised that he could not scupper the talks, but that a line had to be drawn which British concession-giving could not cross. From this point on, Milner was conducting a strategic withdrawal, prepared to concede certain basic points in order to retain the substance of his aims.

Brodrick's reply to Kitchener, outlining the British concessions, was shown to the Boers on 17 April. However, they still insisted on the return of the delegation in Europe and on an armistice to enable them to consult the people. Kitchener refused both requests and assured them 'on his word of honour' that they could expect no military help from Europe. In the end it was decided that facilities would be given to the Boers in order for them to assemble the burghers at various points so they could elect delegates for a general conference. Each republic would bring thirty representatives. Each commando would send two burghers after voting by ballot, but foreigners serving with the commandos, both Cape rebels and the few non-South Africans still remaining, were denied this privilege. These matters were worked out by Kitchener, Botha, De Wet and De la Rey, with Kitchener promising to suspend operations near where the meetings would take place; nor would any attack be made on the commandos whose leaders had been elected and notification given to Kitchener. It was agreed that the elected delegates and the governments would meet at Vereeniging, a town south of Johannesburg, on 15 May 1902.[12]

22

Taking Stock

ONCE THE BOER governments parted to go and visit their commandos, the British took stock of the situation. Writing to Chamberlain, Milner could still find no grounds for optimism or satisfaction, believing the Boers would not reach a 'straightforward decision'. He felt they would give up their independence but would do so only after demanding 'unacceptable conditions and we shall be no further advanced than we are today'.

Milner had identified the Free Staters as the difficult ones and believed that Hertzog was irreconcilable and had undue influence over Steyn, whose own obstinacy was vitiated by his poor health. De Wet was 'a good fighter but is a low fellow and will put his own interests first'. This meant securing an amnesty, a reference to the fact that De Wet was considered to have murdered Morgendaal, the Boer peace emissary sent by the British. Surprisingly perhaps Milner was ready to guarantee his personal safety in the interests of peace but only if it could be done 'privately'. But at the heart of Milner's pessimism was Kitchener, who he did not trust and resented his 'opportunities of influencing the Boers which I have not'. As for the talks themselves, Kitchener 'held all the strings throughout . . . and steered them [the Boers] into the paths he chose'. Letting the Boers go without any commitments being made was, as far as he was concerned, a mistake and Kitchener's eagerness to get them gone led merely to the 'farcicality of our formal proceedings'. He was certain the Boers would continue to procrastinate even after they had made up their minds whether to surrender or not. 'They are past masters in the "Kaffir bargain".' He warned he was determined to ensure the

Boers would not gain from any 'thoughtless generosity' and if this meant his being 'represented as the evil genius, who always prevents peace and conciliation I can't help it. I know I am right.'

Milner was troubled about the loyalists and how they would receive a negotiated peace. How would they regard an amnesty for rebels, even if coupled with disenfranchisement, which he was determined to secure? He felt the loyalists 'could be made to swallow it', but a general amnesty for the Boer leaders, who were technically outlaws and liable for banishment, still haunted him. If they were to be forgiven, which was likely under the circumstances, then the postwar authorities would have to deal with the likes of Steyn and Smuts, whom he classed as Britain's inveterate enemies. This, however, was preferable to running a government handicapped by political pledges made beforehand. It was at this moment that Milner referred to the possible, or perhaps probable, fate of the National Scouts – their abandonment by the British authorities. Until now they had played no part in the negotiations, but Milner surprisingly rejected offhand their right to be heard. He had been reminded of these men by J.G. Fraser, an Englishman long resident in the Orange Free State, who had reached high office in the administration of that republic. Milner's remarks on this knotty problem were curt: 'Of course it is the vice of all negotiations with the men who have stuck out, that it to some extent gives away the men who have already come in. That can't be helped, but Fraser was most insistent that we shd. bear this in mind & minimise it as much as possible.'

Two lines suggest themselves here: either Milner had recognised that the National Scouts were to have no say in the peace process, which is in marked contrast to earlier pronouncements he made, particularly in his Johannesburg speech in January; or he was being disingenuous and trying to bring the National Scouts and *hensoppers* into the equation while feigning disinterestedness. It was probably the latter because Milner hated the idea of negotiating with the irreconcilables. He was aware that surrendered Boers were being sidelined and generally forgotten, and it was these who were to be part of his new South Africa, alongside the loyalists and the expected British immigrants. For Kitchener the collaborators were never going to influence the peace negotiations because they were too few, were detested by the Boers, and London offered no opinion on their fate whatsoever. Milner, while realising the advantageous position gained by the *bittereinders*, nevertheless attempted to ensure the input of his favoured constituency at some point or other. For Milner, the game was not up yet.

In any case, Milner was more concerned about the loyalists and how they would interpret any terms given to the Boers. At the time, while he thought the question of an amnesty might not be the sticking point he had first supposed, that of financial compensation to the Boers was an issue that might cause difficulties. After some reconsideration he was not, as he had said earlier, prepared to be too liberal in this regard. The loyalists he felt would not agree to help finance the rebuilding of what he called 'half-pauper' Boer farms. It would mean the Boers receiving better treatment than the loyalists and 'the point is, & everybody sees it, that all our liberality is necessarily out of the pockets of our friends'. Milner would rather pay for the development of the country than give money away to individuals; South Africa was 'out & away the finest "undeveloped estate" in the Empire'. This issue of financial compensation would ultimately become a contentious issue when talks with the Boers resumed.[1]

For the leading loyalists themselves, particularly the men of Johannesburg, the onset of talks and the forthcoming negotiations were anathema. Percy FitzPatrick, the Uitlander spokesman, explained to one correspondent that he was worried, his uneasiness made worse by having little official information and being dependent partly on Boer informants. He believed the Boers would hold out for civil government to be restored by a specific date; for the equality of Dutch with English; and an amnesty for rebels. Basically, FitzPatrick was against the granting of any of these concessions and according to his friend and colleague Aubrey Woolls-Sampson, the Boers, especially Botha's forces, were on the point of collapse and required only some military persuasion to give in altogether. Six months more and the Boers would surrender.

FitzPatrick knew that Milner too was worried and he knew the cause of his anxiety – Kitchener. FitzPatrick echoed Milner's sentiments in almost every way, writing that Kitchener was 'so little the statesman that he really does not care and perhaps does not really appreciate what the terms should be'. FitzPatrick knew that Kitchener wanted to keep secret the fact that Natal had annexed the Vryheid and Utrecht areas of the Transvaal. Although announcements had been made in the press, Kitchener apparently tried to throw doubts on their validity and had actually tried to get the Natal government to drop the announcement until after peace had been assured. Milner was also incensed by Kitchener's actions, which smacked of underhand diplomacy. This was of course rich coming from two men whose own diplomacy before the war had not exactly been above suspicion. Moreover, this 'holier than thou' attitude was rather disingenuous because they had everything to gain from an early announcement of Natal's territorial aggrandisement: it might lead to the Boers breaking off negotiations. FitzPatrick was also dumbstruck by a note from Kitchener outlining his views about recent developments in which he reiterated his desire that the Boers should not accept 'unconditional surrender' as defined by Steyn earlier. To FitzPatrick, such an idea was 'rot' and as he told Julius Wernher, 'One can hardly credit that a man in his position should seriously defend and explain such a policy.' Obviously, FitzPatrick's informants had not been so informative on this issue because Steyn was quite serious.

FitzPatrick's views and those of thirty-nine 'leading residents' of the Rand were incorporated in a document, which Milner described as 'temperate' and 'able'. These eminent citizens wanted to see the interests of the *hensoppers* given due consideration and believed that no concessions should be granted in a hasty and unconsidered manner. This view was more or less endorsed by the governments of the Cape Colony and Natal, who welcomed the disenfranchisement of rebels and also wanted to see them tried before the colonial courts for treason. McCallum, the Prime Minister of Natal, later informed Milner that his stance was backed by the visiting New Zealand premier, Richard Seddon, who was 'bellicose' and believed as they all did on 'unconditional surrender first and concessions afterwards'; Seddon was adamant that his views were shared by the Australians. Thus by the time the Boers came to Vereeniging, Milner had drawn up his array: behind him he had the leading Uitlanders alongside the cooperative governments of the Cape Colony and Natal, and possibly some of the colonies of settlement as well, even if the last had no official position in the negotiations.[2]

For Kitchener and many of his officers there was a strong sense of optimism, blighted only by their fear that somehow Milner would scupper the talks, or the extreme *bittereinders* would persuade the other Boers to carry on. Just after the talks at Klerksdorp finished,

Kitchener reported to Lady Cranborne that 'things have gone off fairly well', but 'the Boers have a deadly loathing for Milner which makes it difficult at times, as he hardly recognizes how much they detest him. It is quite exciting to think that by the 20th of next month we may have peace.' For the time being, however, all Kitchener could do was wait, under instructions not to give away any concessions that might restrict in any way the post-war administration.[3]

As the British authorities pondered the situation and tried to envisage all the possibilities, the Boers had gone back to their commandos and had begun the process of electing delegates for the conference at Vereeniging.

In the Orange Free State, the meetings to elect the representatives were conducted by De Wet and Hertzog and each was unanimous that the independence of the republic should not be surrendered. De Wet informed Kitchener that all the leading officers of his commandos had been elected and therefore under the agreement reached at Klerksdorp these commandos were exempt from future attack while their leaders were away at Vereeniging. In fact, this meant that the Orange Free State was to enjoy an armistice for the duration of the peace conference. However, according to De Wet, it was agreed initially that the armistice should commence on 11 May but, when this agreement came to be finalised, Kitchener changed the date to 13 May and even then British forces acted against the commandos the day after. De Wet wrote later: 'Such a misunderstanding was very regrettable, and all the more so because we were never indemnified for the damage thus done.'

It would appear that the unanimity of the Free Staters was not prevalent among the Transvaal commandos, where there was a greater desire to end the war owing to the appalling conditions in which they lived and fought. Roland Schikkerling confided to his diary how the men of his commando discussed politics and wondered if the British would offer terms and what they would be. Yet certain misgivings were evident: 'We fear that if no peace comes great numbers will abandon the struggle and we dread to think of the dark prospects of the coming winter in the field.'

Elsewhere, the Transvaal government desired that its State Attorney, Jan Christiaan Smuts, be present at the talks. He was eventually found conducting the siege of O'Okiep in far-off Namaqualand, the desert area of the Cape Colony – an action that would have been labelled a 'side-show' in Great War terms. The officer who escorted Smuts, Colonel Douglas Haig, thought that as Smuts had been at Cambridge he was 'more or less civilised'. Smuts embarked at Port Nolloth on a British warship on 24 April, from whence he was taken to Simonstown and then placed on a train to the north. He left behind a commando convinced that the British were asking for terms and that independence had been won. On reaching Kroonstad, Smuts was met by Kitchener who told him what was what: the Boers would be treated with generosity once they surrendered and would under special circumstances be allowed to keep their arms and horses; there would be no immediate self-government and that only when this was granted would blacks be liable for the franchise. Kitchener also warned against the idea of unconditional surrender, because it would show Boer determination to fight again and no prisoners of war would ever return if the fighting continued, unless they joined the British. It was clear that Kitchener was undertaking some unofficial lobbying, indicating perhaps that he too felt like Milner that Smuts, owing to his pre-war stance, was an irreconcilable similar to Steyn and De Wet. If, however, Smuts and his men, including Deneys Reitz, wanted any indication of the condition of the Transvaal burghers then it was provided by men from the eastern areas of the country under Louis Botha, who they met before the talks. Later, Reitz wrote that:

> nothing could have proved more clearly how nearly the Boer cause was spent than these starving, ragged men, clad in skins or sacking, their bodies covered with sores, from lack of salt and food, and their appearance was a great shock to us, who came from the better conditioned forces in the Cape. Their spirit was undaunted, but they had reached the limit of physical endurance, and we realized that, if these haggard, emaciated men were the pick of the Transvaal Commandos, then the war must be irretrievably lost.

According to Reitz, the outcome of the peace conference was a 'foregone conclusion'.[4]

23

Peace at Last

ON 15 MAY 1902 the sixty delegates from the Transvaal and the Orange Free State came together for the meeting at Vereeniging that would decide the fate of the republics. They had been separated on arrival, each delegation being housed at different ends of the town, a device, no doubt, to ensure that the more pacific Transvaalers were not unduly influenced by the diehards of the Orange Free State. Not that Kitchener needed to worry too much: Steyn's health was deteriorating badly and his morale had been affected by the sight of the local concentration camp, the condition of which had quite stunned him. Steyn would take little part in the forthcoming deliberations, his illness forcing his confinement to his own tent.

The initial meeting began at eleven o'clock in the morning, with the delegates swearing an oath to be faithful to the people, country and government. Thereafter they began arguing whether they were free to reach a decision on matters themselves or whether they were beholden to the dictates of their electors. Eventually Hertzog's opinion won the day; he stated that the delegates were plenipotentiaries, were not the mouthpieces of their constituents, and that they could act if they were convinced that a fully appraised electorate would reach the same conclusions if informed of all the facts. Backed by the equally astute legal mind of Smuts, Hertzog's judgement was fully accepted. Botha's Assistant Commandant General, Christiaan Beyers, was then made chairman and the real business of the day could begin.

This consisted of a series of statements made by various

delegates about the condition of their men, resources and country-side, similar to those made at Klerksdorp in April. Basically, the same line was taken again with the Transvaalers recounting tales of woe and horror, with Botha, this time, informing the assembly of the many families on the veld, which gave the delegates a new statistic to ponder. The Free Staters admitted to scarcities and other problems but said they could carry on. Once the meeting had been informed of the conditions in the countryside it adjourned until the following day.

The second day continued much like the first until Schalk Burgers made another impassioned speech during which he asked the assembly: 'Can we let the people be annihilated for the sake of honour and fame for ourselves?' He then suggested a 'proper' peace proposal be prepared which would concede much but not independence. This broke the impasse because the meeting had become fixed with one group saying they could not go on, while the other said they could. Each side's attempts to convince the other was not working. As a result Burgers's motion was accepted by the assembly and a committee, consisting of Smuts, Hertzog, Steyn and Burgers was formed to draft a resolution. There then followed more impassioned speeches during which those who favoured peace tried to convey the hope-lessness of their cause: the hunger, and the threat posed to the people not only by armed blacks – the Zulu victory over Veldkornet J.A. Potgieter's men at Holkrantz on 6 May was still fresh in their minds – but perhaps worst of all, by the escalating civil war among the Boers themselves, as the number of National Scouts serving the British continued to grow. On this second day, De la Rey's words stand out as some of the most memorable. He picked up on Botha's remarks about fighting to the bitter end, but as yet no one had said when the bitter end would be reached. The words of De la Rey, who was considered to be a most irreconcilable Boer, revealed just how desperate the cause was in the Transvaal and gave added credence to Botha's position:

I think each one must decide for himself. It must be borne in mind that everything – cattle, goods, money, man, woman and child – has been sacrificed. In my division many people go almost naked. There are men and women who wear nothing more than plain skins on the naked body. Is this not the bitter end?

Fine words indeed and heartfelt, but they still made little impression on those who believed that the bitter end was still some way off. They too could use equally fine words to rebut the opinions of Botha and De la Rey. Harking back to a previous time when the *volk* was in mortal danger, De Wet urged the assembly to 'Let us again renew our covenant with God' and would not countenance the surrender of Boer independence.

In spite of the pleas and defiant gestures, an agreement was reached on a set of four proposals to present to the British. These were: surrender of relations with foreign powers; the establishment of a British protectorate; the surrender to Britain of Swaziland and the Witwatersrand ('that cancer in our country' according to Botha because of the goldfields it contained); and a defensive treaty with Britain. A commission was then appointed, consisting of Botha, De Wet, De la Rey, Smuts and Hertzog, empowered to meet with Kitchener (Milner was not mentioned) and conclude a peace settlement subject to the approval of the assembly.

After having travelled to Pretoria on Saturday 17 May, the commission finally faced Kitchener and Milner across the conference table on Monday 19 May 1902.[1]

The progress of the talks was eagerly followed by the British, though the Cabinet had broken up for the Whitsun holidays. Even so, Kitchener informed Brodrick that although the Free Staters had improved their tone, a split between them and the Transvaalers 'would be the best result'. Kitchener also mentioned, and refrained from recording any satisfaction, that Steyn was too ill to carry on and had asked to spend what everybody thought would be his last days with his family. This was granted and a major impediment to peace was about to leave the scene.

Milner's waiting was not relieved by notes from the likes of Lady Violet Cecil, who told him that her father-in-law, Lord Salisbury, 'is saying openly and to gossips (therefore on purpose) that K. would make any peace to get out of the country ... K. is of course the danger, he is offering the Government what seventeen of them want'. Forewarned and forearmed, Milner joined Kitchener to face the greatest stumbling blocks to his plans for a British South Africa.[2]

The meeting between Kitchener and Milner and the Boer commission began at 10 a.m. in Melrose House, Kitchener's Pretoria headquarters. It commenced ominously with the Boer proposals being read out and then rejected immediately by Kitchener and Milner, who reminded the Boers that the annexation of the republics was non-negotiable and that they had gone against the Middelburg terms. Despite Kitchener's attempts to lighten proceedings with some off-hand humour, the talks had bogged down before they had really begun. Both Kitchener and Milner were angry that the Boers were offering new proposals and had not considered those of the British government. The Boer suggestion that by surrendering their foreign relations to Britain they were technically surrendering their independence received short shrift from the British side. After further talks, which achieved nothing, the meeting was adjourned until 4 p.m. Nevertheless, Kitchener and Milner, following a discussion with Smuts, drafted their own proposals, which when shown to the Boers elicited some amazement. Botha enquired whether the Boer proposals had been rejected and was met with a curt 'yes'. De Wet protested vehemently, especially as the Boers would have to recognise Edward VII as their king. Famously, Kitchener intervened and managed to get De Wet, Botha and himself away from the discussions to allow the 'civil' element to draft terms. Consequently it was agreed that a sub-committee – consisting of Milner, advised by Sir Richard Solomon, Kitchener's legal adviser and the Attorney General of the Cape Colony, Hertzog and Smuts – would draft new terms based on those discussed at Middelburg, for further consideration on Wednesday 21 May.

Kitchener later informed Brodrick that things were proceeding well and that even Milner seemed pleased. However, when the two sides met again things did not go as well as Kitchener had hoped. On the whole the new terms, twelve altogether, followed the Middelburg proposals: Clauses one to four covered such matters as the surrender of the Boer forces; the return of those outside the old republican frontiers, meaning those fighting in the Cape; the return of prisoners of war once they had sworn an oath of allegiance to the king; and a guarantee of freedom and property. Clause five gave an amnesty to surrendered Boers 'for any action of theirs in connexion with the carrying on of the war'. Clause six allowed the teaching of English and Dutch in schools and its use in the courts; Clause seven allowed the retention of rifles under special licence, something Kitchener had already cleared with Brodrick; Clause eight promised the return of self-government 'as soon as circumstances permit it'; Clause nine stipulated that the black franchise would be discussed only when the former republics received a 'representative constitution'; Clause ten promised that there would be no tax on 'landed property' to help pay for the war; Clause eleven provided for the payment of the former republics' banknotes and official receipts issued in the field; Clause twelve made provision for the establishment of a commission to assist the return of farmers and help them re-establish themselves.[3]

These terms, however, differed from those issued at Middelburg on three points: the treatment of rebels; the question of black rights; and the issue of financial compensation. Rebels would suffer penalties imposed by the colonial governments, which meant that in the Cape Colony ordinary rebels would only lose their right to vote, while their leaders might face imprisonment; rebels in Natal, of whom there were very few, would be tried by due process of the law. The black franchise question had first been mooted at Middelburg and then altered by Chamberlain, who had insisted that blacks have a limited right to vote. Now black South Africans were to be thrown over again. And finally, under the Middelburg terms, consideration was given to unofficial receipts, those issued by commandants during the guerrilla war for goods requisitioned from civilians, but this time they were not included. This was not accepted by the Boers and led to a palpable disagreement between Kitchener and Milner.

Botha was very concerned about Clause 11 because if the debts owed to the people could be paid this would in his view 'strengthen our hands by enabling us honourably to terminate this matter'. Kitchener openly supported Botha's request and agreed 'that the honour of every officer is affected by these documents'. Milner, however, remained obdurate: while willing to take over pre-war debts, he steadfastly refused to consider paying 'every debt incurred by every officer of both armies for the purpose of fighting us'. This, he believed, would embarrass the British authorities with (though not in so many words) the loyalists. The discussion then boiled down to whether Milner's refusal went against the Middelburg terms, until Milner suggested that the matter be referred to the British government. Kitchener tried to dampen the dispute by drawing out from the Boers an amount of money that might cover these debts incurred by their officers. When Botha refused an initial offer of one million pounds, Kitchener asked whether two or three million would suffice. On his suggestion, the Boers discussed the matter among themselves and accepted the figure of three million. Accordingly, it was agreed that receipts could be presented for assessment of their validity up to three million pounds. This became the basis of the redrafted Clause 11.

Both Kitchener and Milner reported back to their respective political masters, each trying to impress their views on the Cabinet, which took the next week to hammer out an acceptable set of proposals to offer the Boers.

The financial issue had become the main bone of contention between Kitchener and Milner and each felt the matter vital enough to make their case immediately. In fact, for them it seemed that the success or failure of the talks would depend on the government's decision on this prickly question. After setting out the nature of the problem, Kitchener wanted Clause 11 accepted because it was 'vital to peace' since the Boers were adamant on this. Milner, on the other hand, was more forthright in the way he denounced Kitchener's stance, which weakened his own position. Milner told Chamberlain that Clause 11 was 'detestable' and 'an audacious try-on' and it would mean Britain, or as he put it, the British Transvaal, paying for the Boers' war effort. In a further note, which was printed for the Cabinet, Milner reaffirmed his distaste for the whole idea of negotiating with the Boers. 'My own conviction is that [the] Boers are done for, and that if the assembly at Vereeniging breaks up without peace they will surrender right and left.'

If Milner was hoping for a soothing response from Chamberlain then he was mistaken. Chamberlain's immediate reply about Clause 11 was anything but supportive: 'I do not think a mere question of money should prevent termination of war, which costs more than a million per week ... There should be some argument more cogent than money cost to justify risking a failure on this point. Can you supply it, and would you go so far as to wreck agreement at this stage upon this one question?'

Milner apparently was ready to do it and argued that money itself was not the issue, but the way it was to be given out. While disposing of Kitchener's view that it was vital to peace because he had 'used the same argument with regard to every other Boer demand to which I have specially objected', it would be better for the commission mentioned in Clause 12 to give the money away as grants. Milner argued that this would prevent swindling and ensure that the money went to the right people, but this was a smokescreen. His real objection was that the money would be paid out by the former Boer governments and generals and would cement their leadership in post-war South Africa. He was correct in his assertion that money had nothing to do with his objections; but politics did, and Milner saw that Clause 11 would have political repercussions that he was not willing to accept.[4]

Unfortunately for Milner it was not for him to decide; the final responsibility lay with the Cabinet, which met on 23 May 1902. Both Milner and Kitchener were informed that Clause 11 was the main difficulty and that while accepting that money should not lead to the collapse of the talks, they felt they should not offend loyalist interests by being too generous to the Boers. As Chamberlain remarked: 'It can hardly be justifiable to compensate an enemy for supplies which he may have been willingly offered, and to leave a loyal man whose goods have been forcibly confiscated without redress.'

In a similar vein, Brodrick informed Kitchener that 'we must find a way, if possible, to put it [Clause 11] which will be less crude & offensive to loyalist sentiment both here & in S. Africa than that originally sketched out'. With these reservations in mind Kitchener and Milner met immediately to try to reach some sort of agreement over the money issue. The point was thoroughly discussed and although we do not know how it developed, we know that in the end both Clauses 11 and 12 were combined into a new clause, which was shown to Hertzog and Smuts, who eventually accepted it. Kitchener reported to Brodrick that Milner was still unhappy but had nevertheless informed Chamberlain of the new clause. For good measure, and to inject a degree of urgency into Cabinet discussions, Kitchener finished his report by hoping that a decision would soon be reached, 'as the present state of suspense here and among the delegates at Vereeniging is not at all satisfactory'. Kitchener was certainly accurate in his belief that Milner was unhappy with the modifications made to Clauses 11 and 12 and he wasted no time in telling Chamberlain of his objections. Three million pounds was to him excessive because there were not enough notes and receipts 'wh[ich] can pass muster, even those cleverly forged'. Again, he argued that the British would pay for everything the Boers had commandeered, from their own people, neutrals and loyalists.

The new clause desired that notes and receipts be delivered to a judicial commission within six months, which would then pay cash or kind to cover these debts. If accepted debts exceeded three million pounds, then 'there would be a *pro rata* diminution' of all individual payments. Any other monies advanced for the reconstruction of farms by the British government would be in the form of interest-free loans repayable over a given number of years. 'No foreigners or rebels will be entitled to the benefit of this clause.' The one point on which Milner and Kitchener agreed was that once the British government delivered its terms the Boers would be given a take-it-or-leave-it ultimatum. There was to be no more haggling, for as Milner said, 'finality is everything'.

The Cabinet met again on 27 May finally to decide the terms to be offered the Boers. The final version was telegraphed to Milner and Kitchener that same day. In all, only minor changes were made: Clauses 2 and 3 were amalgamated; while to Clause 5 (now 4) an addition was made which excepted any one found guilty of acts 'contrary to the usages of war' from the general amnesty. The new Clause 10 (formally 11 and 12) virtually followed the earlier draft except that no time limit for the presentation of debts was announced and that government loans would be interest free for two years, after which a rate of three per cent would be levied. Furthermore, the clause applied to everyone – irreconcilables, *hensoppers* and National Scouts – and was aimed specifically at those whose property had been destroyed. In reporting to the King, Salisbury revealed that the question of the black franchise had been discussed and it had been the Cabinet's decision to avoid a quarrel with the Boers. A breakdown over this issue was considered more dangerous 'than the danger to which the natives would be exposed by the maintained supremacy of the Boers'.

On 28 May 1902 the Boers were handed the government's terms and to Botha's question whether the delegates could alter any of the clauses, Milner replied emphatically that there was to be no alterations, just a yes or no answer. The Boers had three days to decide whether to accept the terms or carry on the war.[5]

The concluding phase of the peace talks now switched to the assembled delegates at Vereeniging. Schalk Burgers opened the meeting by stating that the Boers now had three choices: to continue the struggle; to accept the British terms; or to surrender unconditionally, meaning that they would reserve to themselves the moral right to fight again when the opportunity presented itself (and thus making a nonsense of FitzPatrick's criticisms of Kitchener mentioned earlier). From then on, the Boers traversed the same ground they had covered during the earlier meetings. Steyn, still defiant, could only last through that day's meeting and resigned in order to seek medical help, leaving De Wet as Acting President and the delegates with his last words on the subject:

> If the Transvaalers should decide to make peace and if you should find it futile to resist any further – then give in. We cannot continue the war with a handful of Free Staters. So we are not to blame. We have fulfilled to the letter our agreement with the sister Republic. Without the Transvaal it would be folly for us to continue the struggle on our own.

But De Wet and Hertzog remained obdurate, although Hertzog's obduracy was tempered by a realisation that the morale of the Boer delegates had been seriously weakened by Botha's revelations about conditions and losses. The leaders from the Transvaal were now set against continuation. To many Boers several inescapable facts had now been revealed and were instrumental in shifting the mood of the assembly: the lack of food; the black threat; and the growing number of women and children adrift on the veld because the British would no longer take them to the camps. It is estimated that about 13,000 women and children had been left to the mercy of the elements and vengeful tribespeople, the vast bulk, some 10,000, in the Transvaal. This fact was doubly demoralising when the casualty list from the camps became known. The fighting ability of the Boers was also severely hampered by the loss of horses, which left many Boers as useless infantry. These facts of war were embodied in a resolution by Hertzog and Smuts, which declared to the world why the Boers would have to give up:

> This meeting is therefore of the opinion that there is no reasonable ground to expect that by carrying on the war the People will be able to retain their independence, and considers that, under the circumstances, the People are not justified in proceeding with the war, since such can only tend to the social and material ruin, not only of ourselves, but also our posterity.

At 2 p.m. on 31 May 1902 the meeting at Vereeniging, after a short adjournment, gathered to vote on the resolution, to decide whether it would be the end of the republics or continued war. Fifty-six voted for acceptance, six (three from each republic) voted against. To the tearful gathering Schalk Burgers spoke a funeral oration telling the delegates that 'We stand at the graveside of two Republics.' He urged the assembled throng to succour the people and to forgive those Boers who had fought against them. It was left to Botha, amidst a 'death-like' silence to inform Kitchener's aides that the peace proposals had been accepted. That night at 11 p.m. the final document was signed at Kitchener's headquarters in Pretoria by the representatives of the two governments. Each Boer delegate signed the document but Reitz declared he did so only as a government official; personally, he refused to accept it. After the Boers had signed, Kitchener signed his name, followed, last of all, by Milner. In the words of the Boer secretaries, Kestell and Van Velden: 'As the members of the Governments of the now late republics stood up, as men stupefied, to leave the apartment, Lord Kitchener rose and, going up to each of them, offered his hand, saying "We are good friends now".' De la Rey allegedly broke the Boer silence by remarking in his poor English, 'We are a bloody cheerful looking lot of British subjects!'

The news of the surrender was received with incredulity by some Boer commandos, a sign that self-delusion was still widespread. De la Rey's own commando thought that the republics had retained their independence, while his daughters danced a jig of delight wrapped in the *vierkleur* flag of the Transvaal. This sort of response was not uncommon; at least two commandos partied the night away after they had heard that peace had been signed, again in the mistaken belief that Boer independence had been won. For others, the news was a shattering blow, often received in silence and with copious tears afterwards. In Smuts's commando, which had no real idea of conditions outside the Cape Colony, some, incredulous at the news, got roaring drunk and became violent. A few refused to accept the new order altogether and were given help to ride to German South West Africa. Some questioned their religious faith, feeling they had been abandoned by God; others accepted God's judgement; others still just shrugged their shoulders and got ready to go home. 'To me,' wrote Roland Schikkerling, 'everything in which hope was, seems gone and I feel as if our liberty has been buried alive and our future stillborn. Our opportunities seem forever past and gone.'

Nevertheless, the thought of at last going home sustained many men in their grief.

For most British troops the thought of going home was paramount, although one or two had a different emotion; Major General J.F.C. Fuller, then a subaltern, recorded that on being told that peace had just been signed he exclaimed, '"Well, I *am* sorry" – and so I was.' Higher up the scale Kitchener basked in a mass of congratulations, some from unlikely quarters. An arch critic, Sir Henry Campbell-Bannerman, supported the parliamentary motion to award Kitchener £50,000 and in a fulsome speech praised the conquering hero as a great soldier and one who 'has shown himself to be a great administrator, a master of the art of organisation, a tactful negotiator and a large-minded man'. It was well known that Kitchener had been the more liberal of the two British negotiators and it was Kitchener the magnanimous who collected the most plaudits. Milner, on the other hand, never accepted the peace and felt his task unfulfilled. A year later, Milner remained unrepentant and for him the war remained unfinished. As he told the journalist H. Spenser Wilkinson: 'It has changed its character: it is no longer war with bullets, but war it still is. It is quite true we hold the winning cards, but it is not true we have won the game, and we cannot afford to lose a single trick.'[6]

The Aftermath: Winners and Losers

THUS IN MAY 1902, after lengthy negotiations with Kitchener and the British authorities, the Boer guerrilla leaders surrendered. They were not, however, a beaten army. They had kept at bay a force vastly superior in numbers and equipment. The peace treaty was a negotiated settlement which, although it incorporated the fallen republics within the Empire, also contained important concessions: generous financial assistance was granted in the form of £3,000,000 to restore families to their homes and work and to repair much of the collateral war damage; interest-free loans were made available for two years; more significant, especially to the long-term development of South Africa, was the shelving of proposals to enfranchise 'non-Europeans' until the Transvaal and Orange Free State were once more self governing. In effect, this guaranteed that in these two territories blacks, Indians and coloureds would remain voteless and underprivileged.

Despite its triumphal passages and its victorious conclusion, the war had exposed a daunting number of British weaknesses. Among the lessons learnt was that the leadership and exercise of British arms was barely adequate – or at least inadequate for too much of the time and too often when it really mattered. The generalship of commanders like the hapless Buller, and others, had been exposed as outmoded, indecisive and over-cautious.

There had been other scandals, perhaps less likely to catch the headlines, but equally symptomatic of low morale, disorderliness and a cynicism not generally associated with the high idealism of Empire promoted by the *Daily Mail* and much of the Tory press. The trial of

'Breaker' Morant and several Australian serving officers had been acutely embarrassing to the British. So were W.T. Stead's assertions that Boer women had been raped during Kitchener's scorched-earth campaign. After the Boer surrender, as the Butler Committee of Inquiry revealed in 1905, enormous quantities of military supplies no longer needed by the army had been sold off in South Africa and it became clear that certain British officers had defrauded the government and pocketed the proceeds. The Liberal opposition claimed that, as a result, the government had been robbed of something like £7,000,000.[1] Joseph Chamberlain had also been publicly accused of profiting from the war.[2] All of this compounded incompetence and a dubious *casus belli* with sleaze and more than a whiff of corruption.

The revealed inadequacies of British arms at least prompted an avalanche of reform. The Committee of Imperial Defence was established in the aftermath of the war. The Elgin Commission, and the War Office (Reconstitution) Committee, recommended sweeping military and organisational reforms. Conscious of her isolated diplomatic position during the conflict, Britain took immediate steps to restructure her foreign policy. Between 1902 and 1904 she concluded an alliance with Japan, and an entente with France. In these ways, at least on paper, Britain emerged from the humiliations of the Boer War in a stronger position than after many of her previous victories.

Within South Africa itself, the aftermath of war was less encouraging and productive. Although the victorious Milner was able to persuade the four British-dominated colonies (which now included of course the Transvaal and the renamed Orange River Colony) and Northern and Southern Rhodesia to join a customs union in 1903, he had not achieved the federation of South Africa by the time he resigned as Governor of the Cape and High Commissioner in 1905.

More significantly, the overall aims of 'Milnerism' failed. As a result of this, permanent British supremacy was not established in South Africa. The wider use of English did not relegate Afrikaans to the status of a second-class language. Indeed there is much evidence to show that Afrikaners, mocked at school and elsewhere as 'donkeys' if they refused to use English, reacted by clinging all the more determinedly to their language and sense of identity.

As a result of the arrogance of post-war Milnerism and the programme of Anglicisation, Afrikaner nationalism was not swamped by the rising tide of Anglo-Saxon cultural influence, constitutional practice and business dominance. Indeed it is arguable that the war and its aftermath refined and subtly strengthened Afrikaner nationalism, which, embittered by defeat and the experience of the concentration camps, became much more difficult to browbeat and subvert. It is worth noting that every Prime Minister of the Union of South Africa, from 1910 to 1961, and every Prime Minister and State President from the establishment of the Republic of South Africa to the election of Nelson Mandela in 1994, was an Afrikaner.

British control of the Rand's industries was now, however, guaranteed. In the Transvaal the English-speaking Uitlanders became full citizens, thus fulfilling one of the chief justifications for the war. The regulations applying to African workers, especially mine workers, were to some extent improved and liberalised, although their conditions of work remained shameful by European standards. A somewhat more humanitarian approach characterised the official attitude towards indigenous people. The Simonstown naval base could expect decades of security, both as a safe harbour for the Royal Navy and later for the warships of NATO. These were all substantial achievements for the British government and for British policy.

A further achievement, though not one which Balfour's outgoing Unionist government welcomed, was the restoration of the Transvaal and the Orange Free State's autonomy by Campbell-Bannerman's Liberal administration in 1906. By 1907 elections to install the first responsible governments of the Transvaal and the Free State had resulted in a dramatic comeback for the defeated Afrikaners. The whites of the Free State returned a large Afrikaner majority. Even in the Transvaal, with its large English-speaking population, Afrikaner solidarity triumphed with the election of the Het Volk party, led by the ex-generals Botha and Smuts, over the divided political allegiances of the English-speaking Transvaalers. Some contemporaries ruefully noticed that the Uitlanders were apparently as unreliable in victory as they had previously been in adversity.

The victory of Het Volk in the Transvaal in practice brought Britain substantial benefits. Botha and Smuts were Afrikaner leaders of broader vision and more urbane sympathies than the departed Krugerite hierarchy. The old alliance between Afrikaner moderates and English-speaking South Africans, which had served Cecil Rhodes so well but so briefly in the Cape, was revived within a wider political framework. This alliance dominated the first years of the

Union of South Africa after 1910, and in 1914 Botha and Smuts led their people, despite the protests of a dissident minority, into the First World War at Britain's side. By 1914 it appeared, therefore, that all of the old goals of British policy had been achieved: federation, a suitable political and economic climate within which local and international businesses could thrive, the incorporation of the Boer Republics into the Empire and, at the same time, a working accommodation with the Afrikaner people. The greater South Africa, for which so many had yearned in the years before 1899, had apparently arrived.

It is therefore debatable who won and who lost the great Boer War. Technically and constitutionally Britain won, yet the future could not be considered safe for British business and English-speaking settlers without reaching an accommodation with the Afrikaner majority. It was the Union of 1910 which provided the framework for the cooperation, sometimes wary, sometimes grudging, but always necessary between the two dominant white groups. The historic compromises of 1902 and 1906–10 paved the way for a greater South Africa that was merely to be given its hard ideological edge, and, in a way, its more honest identity with the construction of the apartheid state after 1948.

In this sense, the Boer War served as an essential, though bloody and tragic, rite of passage between one confused and sometimes counterproductive stage of white supremacy and another that was far more secure and far more acceptable to the bulk of European South Africans. Hardly less ambitious in its long-term aims than Hitler's Thousand Year Reich, the Union of South Africa lasted for the best part of the twentieth century.

The system of Apartheid ultimately failed not simply because of its essential inhumanity, or because of the belated economic pressure brought to bear on the regime by the United States and other Western powers. What fatally undermined it was the ideology at its core – its lack of inclusiveness, though of course this also carried a moral dimension. While blacks, Indians and coloureds remained outside the privileged structure, no whites could ever really feel that their long-term future was guaranteed or that they could sleep safely in their beds.

The makers of the post-1902 greater South Africa had displayed more wisdom than this when they sought, behind the rhetoric of both victory and defeat, to bind up the white nation's wounds and thus to guarantee its relative security in a predominantly black country set within an overwhelmingly black continent. In this sense the Boer War was, in the end, a healing process, an undeniably violent episode, but one that achieved a narrowly-based but perfectly feasible objective. If the spirit that had animated the white founding fathers of the 1910 Union could only have been pressed into the service of all South Africans, the country's history would have unfolded in an infinitely more stable and creative fashion.

APPENDIX I

Chronology

1814   Britain annexes the Cape Colony from the Dutch.

1820   Arrival of British immigrants.

1834   Beginning of the Great Trek; many Boers leave the Cape Colony and move inland.

1838   Boers defeat Zulus at the battle of Blood River.

1840   Boers establish republic of Natalia (Natal).

1843   Britain annexes Natal.

1848   Britain annexes Boer republic of Transorangia.

1852   Britain recognises autonomy of Boer republic of Transvaal following the Sand River Convention.

1854   Britain recognises autonomy of the Orange Free State following the Bloemfontein Convention.

1867   Diamonds discovered in Griqualand West, north of the Orange River.

1871   Griqualand West annexed by the Cape Colony on Britain's behalf.

1872   Britain grants full self-government to the Cape Colony.

1877   Britain annexes the Transvaal.

1879   Anglo-Zulu War; Britain defeats Zulu kingdom, after early Zulu victory at Isandlwana.

1880   Transvaal rebels against the British.

1881   Boers defeat the British at the battle of Majuba Hill.
Pretoria Convention brings war to an end.

1884   London Convention re-establishes Transvaal independence. Britain exercises 'suzerainty'.

1886   The main gold-bearing reef discovered on the Witwatersrand in the Transvaal.

1888   Cecil Rhodes forms the British South Africa Company.

1896   Boers defeat Jameson and his raiders at Doornkop.

1897   Milner appointed High Commissioner for South Africa and Governor of the Cape Colony.

1899   May–June: Bloemfontein Conference.
9 October: Kruger sends Britain an ultimatum to withdraw recent re-inforcements sent to South Africa.
11 October: Ultimatum expires.

WAR BEGINS: 1899

12 October	Boers invade Natal.
14 October	Siege of Mafeking begins.
15 October	Kimberley besieged.
20 October	Battle of Talana, outside Dundee in Natal; British victory.
21 October	Battle of Elandslaagte; British victory.
23 October	British forced to retreat from Dundee.
24 October	Battle of Rietfontein; inconclusive, but covers withdrawal from Dundee.
30 October	Battle of Ladysmith; General White defeated; many British troops captured at Nicholson's Nek; also known by the British as 'mournful Monday'.
31 October	Sir Redvers Buller arrives in Cape Town.
1 November	Boers from the Orange Free State invade the Cape Colony.
2 November	Siege of Ladysmith begins.
12 November	Lord Methuen assumes command at the Orange River.
14 November	Boers take Colesberg in the Cape Colony.
15 November	Boers capture Winston Churchill.
22 November	Buller leaves the Cape Colony for Natal.
23 November	Methuen outmanoeuvres Boers at Belmont. Boer success at Willow Grange in Natal.
25 November	Methuen achieves another minor success at Graspan.
28 November	Methuen's army checked at battle of Modder River.
10 December	Gatacre defeated at battle of Stormberg by Boers; beginning of Black Week.
11 December	Methuen defeated at battle of Magersfontein.
15 December	Buller repulsed at battle of Colenso.
18 December	Lord Roberts supersedes Buller as Commander-in-Chief in South Africa; Lord Kitchener appointed as Chief of Staff to Lord Roberts.

1900

10 January	Roberts and Kitchener arrive at Cape Town. Buller begins attempt to outflank Boer positions at Colenso.
24 January	British defeated attempting to hold Spion Kop.
25 January	Buller retreats back across the Tugela River.
5–7 February	Buller's forces capture and withdraw from Vaal Krantz.
8 February	Roberts takes command of army at Modder River.
11 February	Roberts's flank march begins.
14 February	Buller begins his fourth attempt to relieve Ladysmith.
15 February	General French relieves Kimberley.

Chronology

17 February	Cronje's retreating army trapped at Paardeberg.
27 February	Cronje surrenders at Paardeberg.
28 February	Ladysmith relieved.
7 March	Battle of Poplar Grove; Boers retreat.
13 March	British occupy Bloemfontein.
15 March	Roberts's proclamation calling on Boers to surrender.
17 March	Boer meeting at Kroonstad; they decide to launch guerrilla warfare.
27 March	Death of Boer Commandant General Joubert; succeeded by Louis Botha.
31 March	Action at Sannah's Post; De Wet defeats Brigadier General Broadwood.
5 April	Minor battle at Boshof; Boers defeated and their French commander, Villebois-Mareuil killed.
17 May	Relief of Mafeking.
28 May	The Orange Free State annexed by Britain; renamed the Orange River Colony.
31 May	Johannesburg occupied by the British.
5 June	Pretoria occupied by the British.
12 June	Battle of Diamond Hill; Botha forced to retreat.
13 June	Resignation of Schreiner's government in the Cape Colony.
18 June	The Progressive Party under Sir Gordon Sprigg succeeds Schreiner's ministry.
4 July	Armies of Roberts and Buller meet at Vlakfontein.
15 July	Steyn and De Wet escape encirclement at Brandwater Basin.
30 July	Prinsloo surrenders his forces to the British in Brandwater Basin.
27 August	British victory at Bergendal; last conventional battle.
25 September	British occupy Komati Poort; Boers now cut off from outside world. General election called in Britain.
19 October	Kruger sails for Europe; Schalk Burgers remains as Acting President.
25 October	Britain formally annexes the Transvaal.
29 November	Kitchener succeeds Roberts as Commander-in-Chief in South Africa.
10 December	Roberts leaves South Africa to succeed Wolseley as Britain's Commander-in-Chief.

16 December	Boers under Kritzinger and Hertzog launch second invasion of the Cape Colony.
27 December	Emily Hobhouse arrives in Cape Town.

1901

17 January	The Cape Colony comes under martial law except in the ports and 'native' territories.
10 February	De Wet invades the Cape Colony.
24 February	De Wet withdraws from the Cape Colony.
28 February	Kitchener and Botha talk peace at Middelburg. Milner leaves Cape Town to take up duties as administrator of new colonies. Milner is now High Commissioner and Governor of the Transvaal. Sir Walter Hely-Hutchinson, former Governor of Natal, succeeds him in the Cape Colony. Sir H. McCallum will become Governor of Natal on 13 May.
16 March	Botha rejects the British government's peace terms.
10 April	British begin first drive in Orange River Colony.
8 May	Milner leaves for a holiday in Britain.
16 May	Kritzinger invades the Cape Colony for the second time.
11 July	Steyn escapes capture when his commando is surprised at Reitz by Broadwood.
18 July	First drive in the Cape Colony.
7 August	Kitchener proclaims that if Boer leaders do not surrender by 15 September, they will be banished.
10 August	Milner leaves Britain for South Africa.
3 September	Smuts invades the Cape Colony.
5 September	Commandant Lötter captured by the British under Scobell.
7 September	Botha invades Natal.
17 September	Botha defeats Gough at Blood River Poort. In the Cape Colony Smuts defeats 17th Lancers at Modderfontein.
6 October	Botha retreats from Natal.
12 October	Lötter executed by the British; Commandant Gideon Scheepers captured by the British.
30 October	Botha's victory over Benson, who is killed at Bakenlaagte.
7 November	Sir Ian Hamilton appointed Kitchener's Chief of Staff.

7 December	National Scouts formed.
11 December	Kritzinger's third invasion of the Cape Colony.
16 December	Kritzinger captured by the British.
25 December	De Wet defeats the British at Tweefontein.

1902

13–15 January	Boers under Maritz attack Baster (Cape coloured) community at Leliefontein in the Cape Colony, and destroy the settlement.
18 January	Scheepers executed by the British.
25 January	Ben Viljoen captured by the British.
5 February	Commencement of nearly month-long drives against De Wet.
24 February	De la Rey ambushes the British force at Yzer Spruit.
27 February	Lieutenants Morant and Handcock executed for killing Boer prisoners.
7 March	Methuen defeated at Tweebosch by De la Rey.
24 March	First drive begins in western Transvaal against De la Rey.
26 March	Death of Cecil Rhodes.
9 April	Boer delegates meet at Klerksdorp to discuss peace terms.
11 April	Boers defeated at Rooiwal.
12–18 April	Boer delegates discuss peace terms with Kitchener and Milner in Pretoria.
18 April	Boer delegates leave Pretoria to consult burghers.
24 April	Commandos discuss question of peace.
6 May	Boers defeated by Zulus at Holkrantz.
15 May	Boer conference at Vereeniging begins.
18 May	Boer delegates resume talks with Kitchener and Milner in Pretoria.
29–31 May	Final meeting between Boer delegates to decide on peace.
31 May	Peace of Vereeniging signed in Pretoria.

APPENDIX 2

Some Leading Figures

1. Politicians
Prime Minister and Foreign Secretary: Lord Salisbury
Foreign Secretary from October 1900: Lord Lansdowne
Chancellor of the Exchequer: Sir M. Hicks Beach
First Lord of the Treasury, and Leader of the House: Arthur James Balfour
Secretary of State for War:
   1895–1900 – Lord Lansdowne
   October 1900 – Hon. St John Brodrick
Colonial Secretary: Joseph Chamberlain
Under Secretary of State for the Colonies: 1895–1900 – Lord Selborne
High Commissioner for South Africa and Governor of the Cape Colony:
   1895–7 – Sir H. Robinson
   1897–1905 – Lord Milner (relinquished Cape governorship in 1901)
Governor of the Cape Colony:
   1901–10 – Sir W. Hely-Hutchinson
Prime Minister of the Cape Colony:
   1890–6 – Cecil John Rhodes
   1896–8 – Sir G. Sprigg
   1898–1900 – William P. Schreiner
   1900–4 – Sir G. Sprigg
Governor of Natal:
   1893–1901 – Sir W. Hely-Hutchinson
   1901–7 – Sir H. McCallum

2. Soldiers
Commander-in-Chief in Britain:
   1895–1900 – Lord Wolseley
   1900–5 – Lord Roberts

Commander-in-Chief in South Africa:
    October–December 1899 – Sir Redvers Buller
    1900 – Lord Roberts
    1900–2 – Lord Kitchener

Other leading officers
Natal, 1899–1900:
    Sir George White
    Sir William Penn Symons
    Major General the Hon. N. Lyttleton
    Sir Charles Warren
The Cape Colony, 1899–1900:
    Lord Methuen
    Sir William Gatacre
In Mafeking: Colonel R. Baden-Powell
In Kimberley:
    Colonel R. Kekewich
With Roberts:
    Sir Ian Hamilton
    Sir John French

3. Businessmen, industrialists etc.
    Cecil John Rhodes
    Alfred Beit
    Sammy Marks
    Joseph Robinson
    Julius Wernher

BOERS

1. South African Republic (Transvaal)
President: S.J.P. (Paul) Kruger
Acting President (1900–2): Schalk Burgers
State Attorney: Jan Christiaan Smuts
Commandant General:
    Petrus (Piet) J. Joubert
    1900–2: Louis Botha
State Secretary: F.W. Reitz
Leading officers:
    General J.H. (Koos) De la Rey
    General C. Beyers
    General Piet Cronje (commanded Boer forces facing Methuen in 1899–1900)
    General J.P. Snyman (commanded Boer forces at Mafeking after Cronje)
    General B.J. (Ben) Viljoen
    General Lucas Meyer

2. Orange Free State
President: M.T. Steyn
Chief Commandant: Christiaan de Wet
Vice Chief Commandant: Judge J.B.M. Hertzog
State Secretary: W.J.C. Brebner
Leading officers:
   Assistant Chief Commandant P.H. Kritzinger
   Commandant Gideon Scheepers
   General C.H. Olivier
   Major F.W.R. Albrecht

OTHER POLITICIANS IN THE CAPE COLONY AND THE TRANSVAAL

John X. Merriman
Dr Leander Starr Jameson
Percy FitzPatrick (leading Uitlander spokesman)
Jan Hofmeyr (leader of the Afrikaner Bond party)

APPENDIX 3

Abbreviations

BL	British Library
BVC	Bushveldt Carbineers
CAB	Cabinet papers
CIV	City Imperial Volunteers
CMR	Cape Mounted Rifles
CO	Colonial Office papers
IY	Imperial Yeomanry
ILH	Imperial Light Horse
JC	Joseph Chamberlain papers
LC	Lady Cranborne papers
LP	Lansdowne papers
MCP	Marker papers
MP	Milner papers
OFS	Orange Free State
PP	Parliamentary papers
PRO	Public Record Office
RAMC	Royal Army Medical Corps
RP	Roberts papers
SACC	South African Conciliation Committee
SP	Salisbury papers
UCT	University of Cape Town
VC	Victoria Cross
VSC	Volunteer Service Companies
WO	War Office papers
WOCT	War Office confidential telegrams
WP	Wolseley papers

Notes

INTRODUCTION: AN IRREPRESSIBLE CONFLICT?

1. R. Kipling, *The Definitive Edition of Rudyard Kipling's Verse* (1949), 'No End of a Lesson', pp.229–30
2. J. Wilson, *C-B: A Life of Sir Henry Campbell-Bannerman* (1973), p. 349
3. D.P. McCracken, *MacBride's Brigade* (1999), p. 9
4. I. Uys, *Heidelbergers of the Boer War* (1981), pp. 10–13
5. Mary Kingsley, *Travels in West Africa* (1993), from the introduction by Elspeth Huxley, p. 9
6. J. Meintjes, *President Paul Kruger* (1974), p. 209; and R. Mendelsohn, *Sammy Marks* (1991), pp. 88–9
7. D. Judd, *Palmerston* (1975), pp. 93–4
8. A. Conan Doyle, *The Great Boer War* (1900), p. 25
9. J. Ramsay MacDonald, *What I Saw in South Africa* (1902), pp. 1–30
10. D. Reitz, *Commando* (1929), pp. 11–15
11. T. Pakenham, *The Boer War* (1979), pp. 62–310.
12. D. Judd, *Empire* (1996), p. 139
13. D. Bates, *The Fashoda Incident of 1898* (1984), pp. 180–1; and P.M. Holt, *A Modern History of the Sudan* (1961), pp. 109–12
14. Kipling, *Rudyard Kipling's Verse*, 'The Absent Minded Beggar', p. 459
15. Wilson, *Campbell-Bannerman*, p. 349
16. W.T. Stead, *'Methods of Barbarism'; the Case for Intervention*, pp. 3–4
17. *The Times*, 23 January 1901; C.F.G. Masterman et al., *The Heart of the Empire* (1902), p. vii; and R.D. Blumenfeld, *Diary 1887–1914* (1930), pp. 191–2
18. Donald Read (ed.), *Edwardian England* (1971), pp. 241–6

CHAPTER 1: BRITISH RULE, CONFRONTATION AND COMPROMISE, 1815–1886

1. A. Sparks, *The Mind of South Africa* (1997 edition), chapter 3
2. Sparks, *Mind of South Africa*, chapter 5

3. D. Harrison, *The White Tribe of Africa* (1981), pp. 14–20
4. I.D. MacCrone, *Race Relations in South Africa* (1937), p. 126, quoted in R. Hyam, *Britain's Imperial Century* (1993), pp. 47–8
5. N. Parsons, *A New History of South Africa* (1982), pp. 109–23
6. N. Mansergh, *The Commonwealth Experience*, II, (1982 edition), p. 69
7. A. Porter, 'Britain, the Cape Colony and Natal, 1870–1914: capital, shipping and the colonial connection', *Econ. Hist. Review*, 2nd ser. (1981), p. xxxiv
8. Freda Troup, *South Africa: An Historical Introduction* (1975), p. 148
9. See J. Guy, *The Destruction of the Zulu Kingdom* (1979)
10. BL, Add. Mss. 4464, Gladstone to Kruger, 15 June 1880; see also J. Lehmann, *The First Boer War* (1972)
11. J.P. FitzPatrick, *The Transvaal from Within* (1899), Appendix B

CHAPTER 2: THE DESCENT TO WAR, 1886–1899

1. R. Mendelsohn, *Sammy Marks* (1991), pp. 97–100
2. Bodleian Library, Selborne papers, Selborne to Joseph Chamberlain, 18 October 1896
3. See E. Longford, *Jameson's Raid* (1982 edition)
4. T. Pakenham, *The Boer War* (1979), p. 22
5. D. Judd, *Radical Joe: A Life of Joseph Chamberlain* (1993 edition), p. 199
6. UCT, W.P. Schreiner papers, A.J.L. Hofmeyr to W.P. Schreiner, 17 March 1897
7. UCT, Sibbert papers, 'Cecil Rhodes', a lecture by Cecil. C. Sibbert, Rotary Club of London, 10 August 1935
8. UCT, Schreiner papers, P. FitzPatrick to A. Beit, 10 December 1896
9. UCT, Schreiner papers, FitzPatrick to Beit, 10 December 1896
10. UCT, Schreiner papers, FitzPatrick to Beit, 10 December 1896
11. UCT, Schreiner papers, Schreiner to Joseph Chamberlain, 12 March 1897
12. UCT, Schreiner papers, Schreiner to Chamberlain, 12 March 1897
13. UCT, Miss W. de Villiers papers, BC 30
14. W.R. Nasson, *The South African War, 1899–1902* (1999), p. 84
15. UCT, Schreiner papers, Alfred Milner to Schreiner, 8 December 1898
16. UCT, Schreiner papers, John X. Merriman to Schreiner, 6 March 1899
17. UCT, Schreiner papers, Merriman to Schreiner, 6 March 1899
18. UCT, Schreiner papers, Milner to Schreiner, 12 June 1900
19. PRO, Cabinet papers, CAB. 37/49/29
20. J.S. Marais, *The Fall of Kruger's Republic* (1961), p. 318
21. P.J. Cain & A.G. Hopkins, *British Imperialism*, I, (1993), p. 273
22. S. Marks, interviewed in 'A White Man's War?', BBC Radio 4 programme, September 1999
23. UCT, Schreiner papers, Milner to Schreiner, 15 April 1899
24. UCT, Schreiner papers, Milner to Schreiner, 20 June 1899
25. UCT, Schreiner papers, Milner to Schreiner, 17 June 1899
26. UCT, Schreiner papers, Merriman to W.E.T Hargrove, 19 April 1899
27. UCT, Schreiner papers, J.S. Moffat to Schreiner, 11 July 1899
28. UCT, Schreiner papers, Moffat to Schreiner, 11 July 1899

CHAPTER 3: THE BRITISH ARMY

1. JC 5/51/89
2. G.F.R. Henderson, *The Science of War* (1908), p. 371
3. Henderson, *Science of War*, p. 385
4. D.G. Boyce (ed.), *The Crisis of British Power* (1990), p. 95
5. H.W. Wilson, *With the Flag to Pretoria*, I, (1900), pp. 18–9; R. Blatchford quoted in P. Ward, *Red Flag and Union Jack* (1998), p. 60.
6. WP 28/61; W. Mackail & G. Wyndham (eds.), *Life and Letters of George Wyndham*, I, (1925), p. 361
7. Quoted in H. Kochanski, *Sir Garnet Wolseley* (1999), p. 223
8. M.S. Stone, 'The Victorian army' (1993), pp. 143–71
9. R. Schikkerling, *Commando Courageous* (1964), p. 10
10. LP (5)/58
11. Quoted in E.M. Spiers, *The Late-Victorian Army* (1992), p. 252
12. Quoted in Beckett in J. Gooch (ed.), *The Boer War* (2000), p. 45
13. Wilson, *Flag to Pretoria*, I, p. 17
14. Wilson, *Flag to Pretoria*, I, p. 230; PP (1904), xl, Cd. 1789, pp. 63–4
15. WO 32/7887
16. Quoted in W. Bennett, *Absent-Minded Beggars* (1999), pp. 9–10
17. PP (1904), xl, Cd. 1789, pp. 66–7
18. PP (1904), xl, Cd. 1789, p. 67
19. S. Peel, *Trooper 8008 I.Y.* (1901), p. 1; Buller quoted in T. Pakenham, *The Boer War* (1979), p. 252
20. Mackail & Wyndham, *George Wyndham*, I, p. 382
21. Marquess of Anglesey, *A History of the British Cavalry 1816–1919*, IV, (1986), pp. 90–4
22. WO 32/7866
23. Anglesey, *British Cavalry*, IV, p. 93; Jeffrey in Gooch, *Boer War*, p. 147
24. Peel, *Trooper 8008*, pp. 3–5
25. 'Report on the Imperial Yeomanry', WO 108/263
26. PP (1904), xl, Cd. 1789, pp. 72–5; Anglesey, *British Cavalry*, IV, p. 87

CHAPTER 4: RALLYING THE EMPIRE

1. LP (5)/40; C. Miller, *Painting the Map Red: Canada and the South African War 1899–1902* (1993), pp. 1–64
2. H.W. Wilson, *With the Flag to Pretoria*, I, (1900), p. 228
3. F. Wilkinson, *Australia at the Front* (1901), p. 2
4. P. Lewsen (ed.), *Selections from the Correspondence of John X. Merriman 1899–1905* (1966), p. 139
5. Trollope quoted in K. Sinclair, *A History of New Zealand* (1969), p. 213; see also pp. 220-1
6. Quoted in Wilson, I, *Flag to Pretoria*, p. 29
7. L.S. Amery (gen. ed.), *The Times History of the War in South Africa 1899–1902*, III, p. 38; D.O.W. Hall, *The New Zealanders in South Africa 1899–1902* (1949), p. 82

8. D. Cammack, *The Rand at War 1899–1902* (1990), pp. 118–9
9. Quoted in Makhura in E. Carruthers (ed.), *The Jameson Raid* (1996), pp. 114–6
10. Marquess of Anglesey, *A History of the British Cavalry 1816–1919*, IV, (1986), p. 48
11. L. March Phillipps, *With Rimington* (1901), pp. 4–5
12. Quoted in J. Stirling, *The Colonials in South Africa 1899–1902* (1907 & 1990), pp. 100–1
13. H. Gough, *Soldiering On* (1954), p. 66
14. Quoted in Chandramohan in D. Lowry (ed.), *The South African War Reappraised* (2000), p. 153; Quoted in P. Tichmann in *Soldiers of the Queen*, 87, (1996); M.K. Gandhi, *An Autobiography* (1982), pp. 203–5
15. Cronje's letter in P. Warwick, *Black People and the South African War 1899–1902* (1983), p. 34; see also pp. 42–4

CHAPTER 5: THE BOERS

1. R. Schikkerling, *Commando Courageous* (1964), pp. 7–8; W.K. Hancock, *Smuts*, I, (1962), p. 104
2. H. Hillegas, *With the Boer Forces* (1900), pp. 50–1
3. J. Taitz, K. Gillings, & A. Davey (eds.), *The War Memoirs of Commandant Ludwig Krause 1899–1900* (1996), pp. 1–5
4. Hillegas, *With the Boer Forces*, pp. 90–1
5. W.K. Hancock & J. van der Poel (eds.), *Selections from the Smuts Papers*, I, (1966), pp. 322–9
6. D. Reitz, *Commando* (1929), p. 17; J. Meintjes, *The Commandant-General* (1971), pp. 165–9; A. Conan Doyle, *The Great Boer War* (1900), p. 80
7. Conan Doyle, *Great Boer War*, pp. 79, 85–6
8. Taitz, Gillings & Davey, *Ludwig Krause*, pp. 6–17
9. O.J.O. Ferreira (ed.), *Memoirs of General Ben Bouwer* (1980), pp. 37–40
10. D. van Warmelo, *On Commando* (1902 & 1977), pp. 11–2; Reitz, *Commando*, pp. 20–2
11. B. Viljoen, *My Reminiscences of the Anglo-Boer War* (1903 & 1973), pp. 24–7
12. Grundlingh, in P. Warwick (ed.), *The South African War* (1980), pp. 264–74
13. J.P. Brits (ed.), *Diary of a National Scout* (1974), pp. 14–5, 51–2, 54–5
14. Viljoen, *Reminiscences*, pp. 23; Schikkerling, *Commando Courageous*, pp. 375–6
15. I. Uys, *Heidelbergers of the Boer War* (1981), pp. 10–13
16. G.W. Steevens, *From Cape Town to Ladysmith* (1900), pp. 22, 31–3
17. CO 48/542/30666/f. 928
18. P. Lewsen (ed.), *Selections from the Correspondence of John X. Merriman 1899–1905* (1966), pp. 97, 100–3
19. See Wessels in J. Gooch (ed.), *The Boer War* (2000), pp. 103, 264, fn. p. 129; F. Pretorius, *Life on Commando During the Anglo-Boer War 1899–1902* (1999), pp. 282–99

CHAPTER 6: THE OPENING BATTLES

1. H.J. May, *Music of the Guns* (1970), p. 18
2. May, *Music*, p. 18
3. May, *Music*, p. 23
4 May, *Music*, p. 25
5. May, *Music*, pp. 23–5
6. May, *Music*, pp. 19–20
7. J.L. Comoroff (ed.), *The Boer War Diary of Sol T. Plaatje* (1973), p. 12
8. Comoroff, *Sol T. Plaatje*, p. 13

CHAPTER 7: THE DISASTERS OF BLACK WEEK

1. D. Judd, *Someone Has Blundered: Calamities of the British Army in the Victorian Age* (1999), p. 152
2. H.J. May, *Music of the Guns* (1970), p. 41
3. W.S. Churchill, *My Early Life: A Roving Commission, 1874–1908* (1959 edition), p. 316
4. Salisbury papers, A.J. Balfour to Violet Cecil, 19 December 1899
5. R. Kipling, *The Definitive Edition of Rudyard Kipling's Verse* (1949), p. 395

CHAPTER 8: HUMILIATION

1. BL, Balfour papers, Sir A. Bigge to A.J. Balfour, 2 January 1900
2. H.J. May, *Music of the Guns* (1970), p. 51

CHAPTER 9: 'I THANK GOD WE HAVE KEPT THE FLAG FLYING'

1. J. Selby, *The Boer War* (1969), pp. 132–3
2. H.J. May, *Music of the Guns* (1970), p. 42
3. May, *Music*, p. 43
4. May, *Music*, pp. 58–9
5. PRO 105.14, 9 February 1900
6. *Diamond Fields Advertiser*, 10 February 1900
7. W.A.J. O'Meara, *Kekewich in Kimberley* (1926), p. 115
8. O'Meara, *Kekewich*, p. 116
9. J.L. Comoroff (ed.), *The Boer War Diary of Sol T. Plaatje* (1973), pp. 4–6
10. Selby, *Boer War*, p. 162
11. Selby, *Boer War*, p. 160
12. Comoroff, *Sol T. Plaatje*, p. 129

CHAPTER 10: THE TURN OF THE TIDE

1. B. Gardner, *The Lion's Cage* (1969), p. 176; also L.S. Amery (gen. ed.), *The Times History of the War in South Africa*, III, p. 371
2. *Daily Mail*, 17 February 1900
3. *New York Tribune*, 18 February 1900
4. Gardner, *Lion's Cage*, p. 184
5. F. Young, *The Relief of Mafeking* (1900), pp. 92–4
6. R. Kruger, *Good-bye Dolly Gray* (1959), pp. 251–2
7. D. Reitz, *Commando* (1929), p. 87
8. Kruger, *Dolly Gray*, p. 257
9. H.J. May, *Music of the Guns* (1970), p. 63

CHAPTER 11: MARCHING TO PRETORIA (AND JOHANNESBURG)

1. C.R. de Wet, *Three Years' War* (1902), p. 88
2. De Wet, *Three Years' War*, p. 89
3. Kruger, *Good-bye Dolly Gray* (1959), p. 290
4. Kruger, *Dolly Gray*, p. 298
5. De Wet, *Three Years' War*, p. 164

CHAPTER 12: METHODS OF BARBARISM?

1. C.R. de Wet, *Three Years' War* (1902), p. 231
2. De Wet, *Three Years' War*, p. 237
3. De Wet, *Three Years' War*, p. 321
4. De Wet, *Three Years' War*, p. 366
5. J. Selby, *The Boer War* (1969), p. 210
6. R. Kipling, *The Definitive Edition of Rudyard Kipling's Verse* (1949) 'Ubique', p. 484
7. Selby, *Boer War*, p. 217
8. L.M. Phillipps, *With Rimington* (1901), p. 187
9. De Wet, *Three Years' War*, p. 241
10. H.J. May, *Music of the Guns*, p. 161

CHAPTER 13: SEEKING PEACE

1. J. Taitz, K. Gillings, & A. Davey (eds.), *The War Memoirs of Commandant Ludwig Krause 1899–1900* (1996), p. 139
2. Quoted in A. Roberts, *Lord Salisbury* (1999), pp. 746, 758, 766
3. PP (1901), xlvii, Cd. 547, p. 12
4. LC, 11 January 1900; PRO 30/57/22/Y18
5. WO 108/399/ 475A, 479A; PRO 30/57/22/Y26
6. WO 108/399/480D; CAB 41/26/3

7. WO 108/399/ 438A
8. WO 108/399/ 487B
9. Quoted in T. Pakenham, *The Boer War* (1979), pp. 488–9
10. MP IV/B/226/ff.12–17
11. CAB 37/57/34; PRO 30/57/22/Y30; LC 8/3/1901
12. WO 108/399/ 498A & B; JC 11/8/17; C. Headlam (ed.), *The Milner Papers*, II, (1935), p. 215
13. 'Address of Louis Botha to the burghers', in PP (1901), xlvii, Cd. 663, p. 3; quoted in F. Pretorius, *Life on Commando During the Anglo-Boer War 1899–1902* (1999), pp. 329, 330–1; D. van Warmelo, *On Commando* (1902 & 1977), p. 115
14. PRO 30/57/22/Y33–6; see also 15 April 1901, WO 108/399/ 526
15. PRO 30/57/22/Y32; WO 108/399/ 528A
16. PRO 30/57/22/Y48, Y62; WO 108/399/ 555A
17. WO 108/399/ 537A, B, C, D, 563, 565, 570

14. THE FINAL BATTLES

1. Headlam, *Milner Papers*, II, p. 245
2. CAB 37/57/62; PRO 30/57/22/Y68
3. D. Reitz, *Commando* (1929), p. 231
4. RP 7101/23/122/2/ff. 149–50
5. JC 11/18/10
6. PRO 30/57/22/Y100
7. JC 13/1/191; JC 11/30/216
8. J. Selby, *The Boer War* (1969), p. 218
9. Selby, *Boer War*, p. 219–20
10. Selby, *Boer War*, p. 221
11. Quoted in G. Arthur, *Life of Lord Kitchener*, II, (1920), pp. 67, 71

CHAPTER 15: BIG BUSINESS, CAPITALISM AND THE WAR

1. A. Mawby, *Gold Mining and Politics: Johannesburg 1900–07* (2000), pp. 267–83, 344–9
2. Iain R. Smith, draft chapter 'Capitalism and the War', in D. Omissi & A.S. Thompson (eds.), *The Impact of the South African War* (2002)
3. See J.A. Hobson, *The War in South Africa* (1900)
4. Eric Hobsbawm, *The Age of Empire, 1875–1914* (1987), p. 66
5. Iain R. Smith, 'A century of controversy over origins', in D. Lowry (ed.), *The South African War Reappraised* (2000), p. 33
6. W.R. Nasson, *The South African War, 1899–1902* (1999), pp. 36–7
7. PRO, Cabinet papers, CAB 37/49/29
8. See D. Judd, *Radical Joe: A Life of Joseph Chamberlain* (1993 edition), chapter 11
9. Nasson, *South African War*, p. 38

CHAPTER 16: THE LAST OF THE GENTLEMEN'S WARS?

1. PP (1905), IX, Cd. 2435, p. 13
2. H. de Watteville, *Lord Kitchener* (1939), p. 78
3. WO 108/399/456, 462
4. WO 132/13/257
5. WO 108/399/933, 940, 954, 958
6. A. Davey (ed.), *Breaker Morant and the Bushveldt Carbineers* (1987), pp. xxxii–lxv.
7. WO 108/399/516A, 524; CO 48/564/ff. 115–26; CO 48/568/ff. 631–4
8. CO 48/553/27883/ff. 84–5; 289/44/f. 590; quoted in SB. Spies, *Methods of Barbarism?* (1977), p. 240
9. WO 108/399/541A, B, 546, 581A, B, 549, 627, 629, 631, 653, 655; Lord Carver, *The National Army Museum Book of the Boer War* (2000), pp. 242–3
10. WO 108/399/725B, 765
11. WO 108/399/813, 815; WO 108/405
12. WO 108/399/927–8, 938, 947–9, 957, 975, 985, 996, 1007, 1048, 1052, 1054; PRO 30/57/22/Y129; CO 879/74/681/43, 46, 54
13. I. Uys, *Heidelbergers of the Boer War* (1981), pp. 172–5, 231–2

CHAPTER 17: THE PRO-BOERS

1. G.P. Gooch, *Life of Lord Courtney* (1920), pp. 368–71, 376–8, 381–2, 390
2. J.W. Bicknell (ed.), *Selected Letters of Leslie Stephen*, II, (1996), p. 509, fn.3
3. N. & J. Mackenzie (eds.), *The Diary of Beatrice Webb*, II, (1983), p. 179
4. Mackenzie, *Beatrice Webb*, II, p. 166
5. N. Mackenzie (ed.), *The Letters of Sidney and Beatrice Webb*, II, (1978), p. 124
6. P. Ward, *Red Flag and Union Jack* (1998), pp. 71–5
7. J. Vincent (ed.), *The Crawford Papers* (1984), p. 62
8. J.A. Hobson, *The War in South Africa* (1900), pp. 11–13, 189–97, 313
9. Quotes from Surridge in *History*, 82, (1997) pp. 268, 589, 591, 597; E.S. May, *A Retrospect on the South African War* (1901), pp. 8–9
10. B. Roberts, *Those Bloody Women* (1991), pp. 122–3, 133–49, 166–228; CO 48/555/41513
11. E.B. Mackerness (ed.), *The Journals of George Sturt, 1890–1927*, I, (1967), pp. 321–2

CHAPTER 18: FOREIGNERS AND THE WAR

1. Quoted in A. Davidson & I. Filatova, *The Russians and the Anglo-Boer War* (1998), p. 209
2. R. Schikkerling, *Commando Courageous* (1964) p. 27
3. H. Hillegas, *With the Boer Forces* (1900), p. 257
4. Hillegas, *Boer Forces*, p. 248
5. Schikkerling, *Commando Courageous*, p. 27
6. Davidson & Filatova, *Russians*, p. 29

CHAPTER 19: THE PRESS AND THE WAR

1. E.B. Mackerness (ed.), *The Journals of George Sturt, 1890–1927*, I, (1967), p. 302
2. P. Lewsen (ed.), *Selections from the Correspondence of John X. Merriman 1899–1905* (1966), p. 196
3. Potter in C. Wilcox (ed.), *Recording the South African War* (1999), pp. 20–1; Badsey in P. Dennis & J. Grey (eds.), *The Boer War* (2000), p. 75; Beaumont Hughes in *The Historian*, 61, (1999), pp. 10–15
4. K.T. Surridge, *Managing the South African War 1899–1902* (1998), pp. 61–2
5. E. Wallace, *Unofficial Despatches* (1901), pp. 283–4
6. RP 7101/23/33/f. 58
7. Badsey in J. Gooch (ed.), *The Boer War* (2000), p. 201

CHAPTER 20: THE LITERATURE OF THE WAR

1. Quoted in M. van Wyk Smith, 'The Poetry of the War', in P. Warwick (ed.), *The South African War* (1980), p. 292
2. *Literary World*, 6 July 1900
3. Van Wyk Smith, *South African War*, p. 294
4. Thomas Hardy, 'Drummer Hodge', quoted in M. van Wyk Smith, *Drummer Hodge: Poetry of the Anglo-Boer War 1899–1902*, p. 147
5. Van Wyk Smith, *South African War*, p. 299
6. G.K. Chesterton, 'Africa', quoted in Van Wyk Smith, *Drummer Hodge*, p.124
7. *Reynold's Newspaper*, 12 November 1899
8. Van Wyk Smith, *Drummer Hodge*, p.140
9. Van Wyk Smith, *Drummer Hodge*, pp. 204 –5
10. Van Wyk Smith, *Drummer Hodge*, pp. 209–10
11. Van Wyk Smith, *Drummer Hodge*, pp. 212–13
12. Van Wyk Smith, *Drummer Hodge*, pp. 212–13
13. Alice Greene, 'A Song of Freedom', quoted in *Drummer Hodge*, p. 240
14. Van Wyk Smith, *Drummer Hodge*, p. 253
15. Van Wyk Smith, *Drummer Hodge*, p. 270
16. Van Wyk Smith, *Drummer Hodge*, p. 300
17. R. Kipling, *The Definitive Edition of Rudyard Kipling's Verse* (1949), pp. 479–81

CHAPTER 21: THE TALKS BEGIN

1. CO 417/334/f. 470; 360/ff. 272–4; 353–8; 385–8
2. W.K. Hancock & J. van der Poel (eds.), *Selections from the Smuts Papers*, I, (1966), pp. 461–95; W.K. Hancock, *Smuts*, I, (1962), pp. 148–9; F. Pretorius, *Life on Commando During the Anglo-Boer War 1899–1902* (1999) p. 341; G.H. le May, *British Supremacy in South Africa 1899–1907* (1965), p. 126
3. CO 879/74/681/no. 17, 29
4. WO 108/399/ 850, 861; PRO 30/57/22/Y121
5. WO 108/399/ 880, 1009A, B, C, 1033, 1041A, 1045, 1046, 1055, 1058, 1059;

Le May, *British Supremacy*, p. 130; J.D. Kestell & D.E. van Velden, *The Peace Negotiations Between Boer and Briton in South Africa* (1912), pp. 1–19

6. Kestell & Van Velden, *Peace Negotiations*, pp. 19–32; C.R. de Wet, *Three Years' War* (1902), pp. 373–6; Le May, *British Supremacy*, pp. 131–3
7. SP, Hicks Beach corr., ff. 284–5; JC 11/30/226; JC 13/1/219; WO 108/399/ 1065–71; 1074.
8. Quoted in J. Pollock, *Kitchener: The Road to Omdurman* (1998), p. 210; MCP 6804/4/4/34
9. Kestell & Van Velden, *Peace Negotiations*, pp. 33–8; WO 108/399/ 1075–77; 'Notes on meeting with Boer representatives at Pretoria', WO 32/8103
10. J. Meintjes, *General Louis Botha* (1970), p. 98; J. Meintjes *President Steyn* (1969), p. 171; JC 11/18/20
11. Kestell & Van Velden, *Peace Negotiations*, pp. 39–41; Kitchener to Brodrick, 14 April 1902, Brodrick to Kitchener, 16 April 1902, WOCT, 1083, 1090, pp. 436 & 438; Milner to Chamberlain, 14 April 1902, JC 13/1/225; Chamberlain to Milner, 16 April 1902, JC 13/1/226 & 227
12. Kestell & Van Velden, *Peace Negotiations*, pp. 42–5; WO 108/399/ 1097–8, 1100–2

CHAPTER 22: TAKING STOCK

1. JC 13/1/228, 235 and 244
2. A.H. Duminy & W.R. Guest (eds.), *FitzPatrick* (1976), pp. 314–22; CO 879/74/681/f. 112; MP IV/A/172/18/ff. 242–5
3. LC, 20 April 1902; WO 108/399/ 1109
4. C.R. de Wet, *Three Years' War* (1902), pp. 380–84; R. Schikkerling, *Commando Courageous* (1964), pp. 381–6; W.K. Hancock, *Smuts*, I, (1962) p. 155; G.J. de Groot, *Douglas Haig 1861–1928* (1988), pp. 91–2; D. Reitz, *Commando* (1929), pp. 315, 319–22

CHAPTER 23: PEACE AT LAST

1. J.D. Kestell & D.E. van Velden, *The Peace Negotiations Between Boer and Briton in South Africa* (1912), pp. 46–97; J. Meintjes, *President Steyn* (1969), pp. 172–3; J. Meintjes, *General Louis Botha* (1970), pp. 99–102; C.R. de Wet, *Three Years' War* (1902) pp. 387–8
2. WO 108/399/ 1144, 1152, 1156; C. Headlam (ed.), *The Milner Papers*, II, (1935), p. 342; MP, IV/A/172/18/ff. 242–5
3. Kestell & Van Velden, *Peace Negotiations*, pp. 98–126; De Wet, *Three Years' War*, pp. 451–3; M. Marix Evans, *Encyclopedia of the Boer War* (2000), pp. 381–3; G.H. le May, *British Supremacy in South Africa 1899–1907* (1965), pp. 147–8; T. Pakenham, *The Boer War* (1979), p. 563; G. Arthur, *Life of Lord Kitchener*, II, (1920), pp. 99–101; Kitchener to Brodrick, 19 and 20 May 1902, WOCT, 1160–61, 1163, pp. 457–8; Minutes of meeting, 19 and 21 May 1902, WO 32/8108

4. WO 108/399/1165; Headlam, *Milner Papers*, pp. 352–4
5. Headlam, *Milner Papers*, pp. 355–61; PRO 30/57/22/Y151; WO 108/399/1170–3, 1178; CAB 41/27/19; Kestell & Van Velden, *Peace Negotiations*, pp. 132–6
6. Kestell & Van Velden, *Peace Negotiations*, pp. 140–207; Meintjes, *Steyn*, pp. 176–8; J. Meintjes, *De la Rey* (1966), p. 67; F. Pretorius, *Life on Commando During the Anglo-Boer War 1899–1902* (1999), pp. 338–43; O.J.O. Ferreira (ed.), *Memoirs of General Ben Bouwer* (1980), pp. 284–5; R. Schikkerling, *Commando Courageous* (1964), pp. 388–90; J.F.C. Fuller, *The Last of the Gentlemen's Wars* (1937), p. 263; J.A. Spender, *The Life of the Right-Honourable Sir Henry Campbell-Bannerman G.C.B.*, II, (n.d.), pp. 41–2; Milner to Spenser Wilkinson, quoted in K.T. Surridge, *Managing the South African War 1899–1902* (1998), p. 174

THE AFTERMATH: WINNERS AND LOSERS

1. Hansard Parliamentary Debates, 4th ser., vol. 148, 26 June 1905, cols. 191–202
2. D. Judd, *Lord Reading* (1982), pp. 42–3

Bibliography

I. MANUSCRIPT SOURCES

Birmingham University Library:
    Joseph Chamberlain papers
Bodleian Library, Oxford:
    Asquith papers
    Lord Selborne papers
    Lord Milner papers
British Library:
    Balfour papers
    Campbell-Bannerman papers
    Fifth Marquess of Lansdowne papers
    Morley papers
Hatfield House:
    Lady Cranborne papers
    Third Marquess of Salisbury papers
House of Lords Record Office:
    Lloyd George papers
Hove Central Library:
    Lord Wolseley papers
National Army Museum:
    Lord Roberts papers
    Marker papers
Public Record Office, Kew:
    Buller papers
    Cabinet records
    Colonial Office Files
    Lord Kitchener papers
    War Office Files
University of Cape Town:
    Miss W. de Villiers papers

323

Sibbert papers
W.P. Schreiner papers

2. PARLIAMENTARY PAPERS AND OFFICIAL DOCUMENTS

Vol. xlvii (1901):
  Cd. 528, 'Papers relating to negotiations between Commandant Louis Botha and Lord Kitchener'.
  Cd. 546, 'Letter from Commandant Louis Botha to Lord Kitchener, dated 13th February 1901'.
  Cd. 663, Further papers relating to negotiations between Commandant Louis Botha and Lord Kitchener'.
Vol. xl (1904):
  Cd. 1789, 'Report of His Majesty's Commissioners appointed to inquire into the military preparations, and other matters connected with the war in South Africa'.
  Cd. 1790, 'Minutes of evidence taken before the Royal Commission on the war in South Africa', vol. i.
Vol. xli (1904):
  Cd. 1791, 'Minutes of evidence taken before the Royal Commission on the war in South Africa', vol. ii.
Vol. xlii (1904):
  Cd. 1792, 'Appendices to the minutes of evidence taken before the Royal Commission on the war in South Africa'.
Vol. ix (1905):
  Cd. 1932, 1968, 2002, 'Report of the War Office (reconstitution) Committee, P.P 1906.
  Cd. 2435, 'Report of the committee appointed by the army council to consider the question of sales and refunds to contractors in South Africa together with appendices'.

Hansard, Fourth Series, Parliamentary Debates

3. NEWSPAPERS AND JOURNALS

Daily Mail
Diamonds Fields Advertiser
Mafeking Mail
Manchester Guardian
Morning Post
National Review
Punch
Reynolds's Newspaper
Standard and Digger News
The Times

Bibliography

4. SELECTED BOOKS AND ARTICLES

Books

Ally, R., *Gold and Empire: The Bank of England and South Africa's Gold Producers, 1886–1926*, Johannesburg 1994.

Amery, L.S. (gen. ed.), *The Times History of the War in South Africa 1899–1902*, London, 1900–9.

Anglesey, The Marquess of, *A History of the British Cavalry 1816–1919*, London, 1986.

Arthur, Sir G., *Life of Lord Kitchener*, London, 1920.

Ashe, E.O., *Besieged by the Boers*, London, 1900.

Baden-Powell, R.S.S., *Sketches in Mafeking and East Africa*, London, 1907.

Baker, A., *The Battles and Battlefields of the Anglo-Boer War 1899–1902*, Milton Keynes, 1999.

Barnes, J., *Filming the Boer War*, London, 1990.

Bassett, J., *Guns and Brooches: Australian Army Nursing from the Boer War to the Gulf War*, Melbourne & Oxford, 1992.

Bateman, P., *Generals of the Anglo-Boer War*, Cape Town, 1977.

Beckett, I.F.W., *Riflemen Form: A Study of the Rifle Volunteer Movement 1859–1908*, Aldershot, 1982.

Beinhart, W. & Dubow, S. (eds.), *Segregation and Apartheid in Twentieth Century South Africa*, London, 1995.

Benn, C., *Keir Hardie*, London, 1992.

Bennett, W., *Absent-Minded Beggars: Volunteers in the Boer War*, London, 1999.

Bester, R., *Boer Rifles & Carbines of the Anglo-Boer War*, Bloemfontein, 1994.

Bicknell, J.W. (ed.), *Selected Letters of Leslie Stephen*, Basingstoke, 1996.

Biggar, E.B., *The Boer War: Its Causes and Its Interest to Canadians*, Toronto & Montreal, 1899.

Bond, B., *The Victorian Army and the Staff College 1854–1914*, London, 1972.

Boyce, D. George (ed.), *The Crisis of British Power: The Imperial and Naval Papers of the Second Earl of Selborne, 1895–1910*, London, 1990.

Brits, J.P. (ed.), *Diary of a National Scout: P.J. Du Toit 1900–1902*, Pretoria, 1974.

Bron, A., *Diary of a Nurse in South Africa*, London, 1901.

Brown, J. & Louis, W.R. (eds.), *The Oxford History of the British Empire, Vol. 4, The Twentieth Century*, Oxford, 1999.

Burdett-Coutts, W., *The Sick and Wounded in South Africa*, London, 1900.

Bush, J., *Edwardian Ladies and Imperial Power*, Leicester, 2000.

Cain, P.J. & Hopkins, A.G., *British Imperialism, Vol. 1 1688–1914*, London, 1993.

Cammack, D., *The Rand at War 1899–1902*, London, 1990.

Campbell, R.G., *Neutral Rights & Obligations in the Anglo–Boer War*, Baltimore, 1908.

Carruthers, E. (ed.), *The Jameson Raid: A Centennial Perspective*, Johannesburg, 1996.

Carver, Field-Marshal Lord, *The National Army Museum Book of the Boer War*, London, 2000.

Chattan, K. & others, *Valour and Victory*, London, 1903.

Churchill, W.S., *The Boer War*, London, 1989 edition.

——, *My Early Life: A Roving Commission, 1874–1908*, London, 1930 and 1959.

Coetzer, O., *The Road to Infamy 1899–1900*, Johannesburg, 1996.

Comoroff, J.L. (ed.), *The Boer War Diary of Sol T. Plaatje: An African at Mafeking*, London, 1973.

Creswicke, L., *South Africa and the Transvaal War*, Edinburgh, 1900.

Cunningham, H., *The Volunteer Force*, London, 1975.

Curtis, L., *With Milner in South Africa*, London, 1951.

Davenport, T.R.H., *South Africa: A Modern History*, London, 1991.

Davey, A., *The British Pro-Boers*, London, 1978.

——, (ed.), *Breaker Morant and the Bushveldt Carbineers*, Cape Town, 1987.

Davidson, A. & Filatova, I., *The Russians and the Anglo-Boer War*, Cape Town, 1998.

De Groot, G.J., *Douglas Haig 1861–1928*, London, 1988.

Dennis, P. & Grey, J. (eds.), *The Boer War: Army, Nation and Empire*, Canberra, 2000.

De la Rey, J.E., *A Woman's Wanderings and Trials During the Boer War*, London, 1903.

Denoon, D., *A Grand Illusion: The Failure of Imperial Policy in the Transvaal Colony During the Period of Reconstruction 1900–1905*, London, 1973.

De Watteville, Lt. Col. H., *Lord Kitchener*, London, 1939.

De Wet, C.R., *Three Years' War*, London, 1902.

Dixon, N.F., *On the Psychology of Military Incompetence*, London, 1979.

Doyle, A. Conan, *The Great Boer War*, London, 1900.

Duminy, A.H. & Guest, W.R. (eds.), *FitzPatrick: South African Politician. Selected Papers 1888–1906*, Johannesburg, 1976.

Evans, M. Marix, *Encyclopaedia of the Boer War*, Oxford, 2000.

Farwell, B., *The Great Boer War*, New York, 1976.

Ferguson, J.H., *American Diplomacy and the Boer War*, Philadelphia, 1939.

Ferreira, O.J.O. (ed.), *Memoirs of General Ben Bouwer*, Pretoria, 1980.

Field, L., *The Forgotten War: Australia and the Boer War*, Melbourne, 1995.

Fisher, J., *That Miss Hobhouse: The Life of a Great Feminist*, London, 1971.

FitzPatrick, J.P., *South African Memories*, London, 1932.

Foden, G., *Ladysmith*, London, 1999.

Fuller, Major General J.F.C., *The Last of the Gentlemen's Wars: A Subaltern's Journal of the War in South Africa 1899–1902*, London, 1937.

Gandhi, M.K., *An Autobiography*, London, 1982.

Gardner, B., *The Lion's Cage*, London, 1969.

——, *Mafeking: a Victorian Legend*, London, 1966.

Gilmour, D., *The Long Recessional: The Imperial Life of Rudyard Kipling*, London, 2002.

Gleichen, Major General Lord E., *A Guardsman's Memories: A Book of Recollections*, Edinburgh & London, 1932.

Gooch, G.P., *Life of Lord Courtney*, London, 1920.

Gooch, J. (ed.), *The Boer War: Direction, Experience and Image*, London, 2000.

Gough, General Sir H., *Soldering On*, London, 1954.

Greenwall, R., *Artists and Illustrators of the Anglo-Boer War*, Cape Town, 1992.

Grierson, J.M., *Scarlet into Khaki: The British Army on the Eve of the Boer War*, London, 1899; 1988 edition.

Griffiths, K., *Thank God We Kept the Flag Flying*, London, 1974.

Hall, D., *The Hall Handbook of the Anglo-Boer War*, Natal, 1999.

Hall, D.O.W., *The New Zealanders in South Africa 1899–1902*, Wellington, 1949.

Hamilton, I.B.M., *The Happy Warrior: A Life of General Sir Ian Hamilton*, London, 1966.

Hancock, W.K., *Smuts: Vol. 1, The Sanguine Years, 1870–1919*, Cambridge, 1962.

——, & Van der Poel, J. (eds.), *Selections from the Smuts Papers*, Cambridge, 1966.

Harrison, D., *The White Tribe of Africa: South Africa in Perspective*, London, 1981.

Haycock, R. & Neilson, K. (eds.), *Men, Machines and War*, Ontario, 1988.

Headlam, C. (ed.), *The Milner Papers: South Africa 1899–1905*, London, 1931 & 1935.

Henderson, Colonel G.F.R., *The Science of War: A Collection of Essays and Lectures 1891–1903*, London, 1908.

Hewison, H.H., *Hedge of Wild Almonds: South Africa, the Pro-Boers & the Quaker Conscience*, London, 1989.

Hillegas, H., *With the Boer Forces*, London, 1900.

Hobhouse, E., *The Brunt of the War and Where it Fell*, London, 1902

Hobson, J.A., *The War in South Africa: Its Causes and Effects*, London, 1900.

——, *Imperialism: A Study*, London, 1988 edition.

Hyam, R., *Britain's Imperial Century, 1815–1914*, London, 1993 edition.

Intelligence Officer, The, *On the Heels of De Wet*, Edinburgh & London, 1903.

Jackson, T., *The White Man's War*, London, 1999.

James, D., *Lord Roberts*, London, 1954.

Jeal, T., *Baden-Powell*, London, 1989.

Johnson, D.F. & O'Leary, B.E., *The South African War, 1899–1902: New Brunswick Men at War*, n.p.,1989.

Judd, D., *Balfour and the British Empire*, London, 1968.

——, *Empire: The British Imperial Experience from 1765 to the Present*, London, 2001 edition.

——, *Radical Joe: A Life of Joseph Chamberlain*, London, 1977.

Kandyba-Foxcroft, E., *Russia and the Anglo-Boer War, 1899–1902*, Roodepoort, South Africa, 1981.

Keegan, T., *Colonial South Africa and the Origins of the Racial Order*, London, 1996.

Keppel-Jones, A., *South Africa*, London, 1975 edition.

Kestell, J.D., *Through Shot and Flame*, London, 1903.

——, & Van Velden, D.E., *The Peace Negotiations Between Boer and Briton in South Africa*, London, 1912.

Kipling, R., *The Definitive Edition of Rudyard Kipling's Verse*, London, 1949.

Knight, I., *Colenso, 1899: The Boer War in Natal*, London, 1995.

Kochanski, H., *Sir Garnet Wolseley: Victorian Hero*, London, 1999.

Koss, S., *The Rise and Fall of the Political Press*, London, 1981 & 1984.

——, (ed.), *The Pro-Boers: The Anatomy of an Antiwar Movement*, Chicago, 1973.

Krikler, J., *Revolution from Above, Rebellion from Below: The Agrarian Transvaal at the Turn of the Century*, Oxford, 1993.

Kruger, R., *Good-bye Dolly Gray: The Story of the Boer War*, London, 1983 edition.

Lee, E., *To the Bitter End: A Photographic History of the Boer War*, Harmondsworth, 1985.

Le May, G.H., *British Supremacy in South Africa 1899–1907*, Oxford, 1965.

Lewsen, P. (ed.), *Selections from the Correspondence of John X. Merriman 1899–1905*, Cape Town, 1966.

Longford, E., *Jameson's Raid: The Prelude to the Boer War*, London, revised edition 1982.

Lowry, D. (ed.), *The South African War Reappraised*, London, 2000.

MacDonald, R.H., *The Language of Empire: Myths and Metaphors of Popular Imperialism, 1880–1918*, Manchester, 1994.

Mackail, W. & Wyndham, G. (eds.), *Life and Letters of George Wyndham*, London, 1925.

Mackenzie, J.M., *Popular Imperialism and the Military, 1850–1950*, Manchester, 1992.

Mackenzie, N. (ed.), *The Letters of Sidney and Beatrice Webb*, Cambridge, 1978.

——, & J. (eds.), *The Diary of Beatrice Webb*, London, 1983.

Mackerness, E.B. (ed.), *The Journals of George Sturt, 1890–1927*, Cambridge, 1967.

MacKinnon, H.V., *War Sketches: Reminiscences of the Boer War in South Africa, 1899–1902*, n.p., 1900.

Macnab, R., *The French Colonel: Villebois-Mareuil and the Boers 1899–1900*, Cape Town, 1975.

Marais, J.S., *The Fall of Kruger's Republic*, Oxford, 1961.

Marks, S. & Atmore, A. (eds.), *Economy and Society in Pre-industrial South Africa*, London, 1980.

Marlowe, J., *Milner: Apostle of Empire*, London, 1976.

Marsh, P., *Joseph Chamberlain: Entrepreneur in Politics*, New Haven, 1994.

May, Lt. Col. E.S., *A Retrospect on the South African War*, London, 1901.

May, H.J., *Music of the Guns*, London, 1970.

McCourt, E., *Remember Butler: The Story of Sir William Butler*, London, 1967.

McCracken, D.P., *The Irish Pro-Boers, 1877–1902*, Johannesburg, 1989.

——, *MacBride's Brigade: Irish Commandos in the Anglo-Boer War*, Dublin, 1999.

McDonald, I., *The Boer War in Postcards*, n.p., 1990.

Meintjes, J., *The Anglo-Boer War, 1899–1902*, Cape Town, 1976.

——, *The Commandant-General: The Life and Times of Petrus Jacobus Joubert of the South African Republic 1831–1900*, Cape Town, 1971.

——, *De la Rey: Lion of the West*, Johannesburg, 1966.

——, *General Louis Botha: A Biography*, London, 1970.

——, *President Paul Kruger*, London, 1974.

——, *President Steyn: A Biography*, Cape Town, 1969.

——, *Stormberg: A Lost Opportunity*, Cape Town, 1969.

Mendelsohn, R., *Sammy Marks: The Uncrowned King of the Transvaal*, Cape Town, 1991.

Methuen, A.M.S., *Peace or War in South Africa*, London, 1901.

Mileham, P. (ed.), *Clearly My Duty: Letters of Sir John Gilmour from the Boer War 1900–01*, East Linton, 1996.

Miller, C., *Painting the Map Red: Canada and the South African War 1899–1902*, Montreal, 1993.

Miller, S.M., *Lord Methuen and the British Army*, London, 1999.

Nasson, W.R., *Abraham Esau's War: A Black South African War in the Cape 1899–1902*, Cape Town, 1991.

——, *The South African War, 1899–1902*, London, 1999.

Nattrass, G. & Spies, S.B. (eds.), *Memoirs of the Boer War: Jan Smuts*, Johannesburg, 1994.

Nimocks, W., *Milner's Young Men: The Kindergarten in Edwardian Imperial Affairs*, Durham, NC, 1968.

O'Brien, T.H., *Milner*, London, 1974.

Odendaal, A., *Vukani Bantu! The Beginnings of Black Protest Politics in South Africa to 1912*, Cape Town, 1984.

Omissi, D. & Thompson, A.S. (eds.), *The Impact of the South African War*, Basingstoke, 2002.

Pakenham, T., *The Boer War*, London, 1979, 1982, 1999.

Parsons, N., *A New History of South Africa*, London, 1982.

Peel, Hon. S., *Trooper 8008 I.Y.*, London, 1901.

Pemberton, W.B., *Battles of the Boer War*, London, 1964.

Phillipps, L. March, *With Rimington*, London, 1901.

Piennar, P., *With Steyn and De Wet*, London, 1902.

Pillay, B., *British Indians in the Transvaal: Trade, Politics and Imperial Relations 1885–1906*, London, 1976.

Pirow, O., *James Barry Munnik Hertzog*, Cape Town, 1957.

Pollock, J., *Kitchener: The Road to Omdurman*, London, 1998.

Porter, A.N., *The Origins of the South African War: Joseph Chamberlain and the Diplomacy of Imperialism, 1895–99*, Manchester, 1980.

—— (ed.), *The Oxford History of the British Empire, Vol. 3, The Nineteenth Century*, Oxford, 1999.

Porter, B., *Critics of Empire: British Radical Attitudes to Colonialism in Africa 1895–1914*, London, 1968.

——, *The Lion's Share: A Short History of British Imperialism, 1850–1983*, London, 1984.

Powell, G., *Buller: A Scapegoat? A life of General Sir Redvers Buller VC*, London, 1994.

Pretorius, F., *The Anglo-Boer War, 1899–1902*, Cape Town, 1985.

——, *Life on Commando During the Anglo-Boer War 1899–1902*, Pretoria, 1999.

Price, R., *An Imperial War and the British Working-Class: Working-Class Attitudes and Reactions to the Boer War 1899–1902*, London, 1972.

Pyrah, G., *Imperial Policy and South Africa, 1902–10*, Oxford, 1955.

Ransford, O., *The Battle of Spion Kop*, London, 1969.

Reitz, D., *Commando: A Boer Journal of the Boer War*, London, 1929 & 1983.

Roberts, A., *Lord Salisbury: Victorian Titan*, London, 1999.

Roberts, B., *Those Bloody Women: Three Heroines of the Boer War*, London, 1991.

Sampson, V. & Hamilton, I., *Anti-commando*, London, 1931.

Sandys, C., *Churchill: Wanted Dead or Alive*, London, 1999.

Schikkerling, R., *Commando Courageous: A Boer's Diary*, Johannesburg, 1964.

Schreiner, O., *Thoughts on South Africa*, London, 1923.

Shearing, T. & D., *Commandant Johannes Lötter and His Rebels*, Sedgefield, South Africa, 1998.

Sibbald, R., *The War Correspondents: The Boer War*, Johannesburg, 1993.

Sinclair, K., *A History of New Zealand*, Harmondsworth, 1969.

Smith, I., *The Origins of the South African War, 1899–1902*, London, 1996.

—— (ed.), *The Siege of Mafeking*, Houghton, South Africa, 2001.

Sparks, A., *The Mind of South Africa*, London, 1990.

Spender, J.A., *The Life of the Right-Honourable Sir Henry Campbell-Bannerman G.C.B.*, London, n.d.

Spiers, E.M., *The Late-Victorian Army*, Manchester, 1992.

Spies, S.B., *Methods of Barbarism? Roberts and Kitchener and Civilians in the Boer Republics: January 1900 – May 1902*, Cape Town, 1977.

Bibliography

Stead, W.T., *The War in South Africa: Methods of Barbarism*, London, 1901.

Steevens, G.W., *From Cape Town to Ladysmith*, Edinburgh & London, 1900.

Stirling, J., *The Colonials in South Africa 1899–1902*, Edinburgh, London & Polstead, 1907 & 1990.

Surridge, K.T., *Managing the South African War 1899–1902: Politicians Versus Generals*, Woodbridge, 1998.

Symons, J., *Buller's Campaign*, London, 1963.

Taitz, J., Gillings, K. & Davey, A. (eds.), *The War Memoirs of Commandant Ludwig Krause, 1899–1900*, Cape Town, 1996.

Thomas, A., *Rhodes: The Race for Africa*, London, 1998.

Thompson, L.M., *The Unification of South Africa, 1902–1910*, Oxford, 1960.

Todd, P. & Fordham, D. (eds.), *Private Tucker's Boer War Diary: The Transvaal War of 1899–1902, with the Natal Field Forces*, London, 1980.

Torlage, G., *The Battle of Colenso*, Johannesburg, 1999.

Uncovered Editions, *The Boer War: Ladysmith & Mafeking*, 1900, London, 1999.

Uys, I., *Heidelbergers of the Boer War*, Heidelberg, South Africa, 1981.

Van Reenen, R. (ed.), *Emily Hobhouse: Boer War Letters*, Cape Town & Pretoria, 1984.

Van Warmelo, D., *On Commando*, London & Johannesburg, 1902 & 1977.

Van Wyk Smith, M., *Drummer Hodge: The Poetry of the Anglo-Boer War 1899–1902*, Oxford, 1978.

Viljoen, General Ben, *My Reminiscences of the Anglo-Boer War*, London & Cape Town, 1903 & 1973.

Vincent, J. (ed.), *The Crawford Papers: The Journals of David Lindsay, Twenty-seventh Earl of Crawford and Tenth Earl of Balcarres 1871-1940*, Manchester, 1984.

Walker, E.A., *W.P. Schreiner: A South African*, Oxford, 1937.

Wallace, E., *Unofficial Despatches*, London & Cape Town, 1901 & 1975.

Wallace, R.L., *The Australians at the Boer War*, Canberra, 1976.

Ward, P., *Red Flag and Union Jack: Englishness, Patriotism and the British Left, 1881–1924*, Woodbridge, 1998.

Warwick, P., *Black People and the South African War 1899–1902*, Cambridge, 1983.

—— (ed.), *The South African War: The Anglo-Boer War 1899–1902*, Harlow, 1980.

Watkins-Pitchford, H., *Besieged in Ladysmith*, Durban, 1964.

Watt, S., *The Siege of Ladysmith*, Johannesburg, 1999.

Wheatcroft, G., *The Randlords: The Men who Made South Africa*, London, 1985.

Wilcox, C. (ed.), *Recording the South African War: Journalism and Official History*, London, 1999.

Wilkinson, F., *Australia at the Front: A Colonial View of the Boer War*, London, 1901.

Williams, C., *Hushed Up*, London, 1902.

Wilson, H.W., *With the Flag to Pretoria*, London, 1900.

Wilson, J., *C-B: A Life of Sir Henry Campbell-Bannerman*, London, 1973.

Witton, Lt. G., *Scapegoats of Empire: The True Story of Breaker Morant's Bushveldt Carbineers*, London & Sydney, 1907 & 1982.

Worsfold, B., *Lord Milner's Work in South Africa*, London, 1906.

Articles

Boyd, K., 'Exemplars and ingrates: imperialism and the Boys' story paper, 1880–1930', *Historical Research*, 67, (1994).

Grundlingh, A.W., 'The bitter legacy of the Boer War', *History Today*, November (1999).

Hughes, J. Beaumont, 'The press and the public during the Boer War 1899–1902', *The Historian*, 61, (1999).

Lowry, D., 'When the world loved the Boers', *History Today*, May (1999).

McCracken, D.P., 'MacBride's brigade in the Anglo-Boer War', *History Ireland*, 8, (2000).

Pelletier, J.-G., 'France and the Boer War', *Historia* 33/1, 1988.

Porter, A.N., 'Sir Alfred Milner and the press, 1897–1899', *Historical Journal*, 16, (1973).

Surridge, K.T., '"All you soldiers are what we call pro-Boer": the military critique of the South African War 1899–1902', *History*, 82, (1997).

——, 'Rebellion, martial law and British civil-military relations: the war in Cape Colony, 1899–1902', *Small Wars and Insurgencies*, 8, (1997).

Tamarkin, M., 'Milner, the Cape Afrikaners, and the outbreak of the South African War: from a point of no return to a dead end', *Journal of Imperial and Commonwealth History*, 25, (1997).

Tichmann, P., '"We are sons of the Empire after all": the Indian ambulance corps during the South African War, 1899–1902', *Soldiers of the Queen: The Journal of the Victorian Military Society*, 87, (1996).

5. UNPUBLISHED THESES

Stone, M.S., 'The Victorian Army: health, hospitals and social conditions as encountered by British troops during the South African War, 1899–1902', unpublished. Ph.D. thesis, London, 1993.

Index

Ranks and titles are generally the highest applying within the period covered.

no

Selborne writes to on public
attitude to war, 57; mistrusts
Cape Afrikaners, 98; and Boer
invasion of Cape, 99; message
from Rhodes in Kimberley, 147;
wishes to suspend Cape
constitution, 185; and peace
proposals, 199, 202, 204–5,
276–84; appointed Governor of
Transvaal, 201; plan for post-war
South Africa, 202–3, 208–9,
212–13, 269–70, 299; peerage,
208; visits Britain (May 1901),
208–9; advocates removing
Kitchener, 213; and outbreak of
war, 223, 225; pro-Boer
opposition to, 239; allows Emily
Hobhouse to travel north, 245;
and press coverage, 252; demands
unconditional surrender, 269,
272; detested by Boers, 270, 278,
285; Rosebery suggests dismissal
of, 276; relations with Kitchener,
281, 283–4, 289, 291; view of
Smuts, 286; negotiates at
Vereeniging, 289–94; signs peace
terms, 296; dissatisfaction with
peace agreement, 297; forms
customs union, 299; resigns
posts, 299
Minski, Paul, 4
missionaries: influence on colonial
policy, 19
Modder River, 118–21, 125, 146,
160–1, 164, 176–7
Modder Spruit, 112–13
Modderfontein, 211
Moffat, J.S., 49
Möller, Colonel Bernhard Drusdale,
108
Molteno, 122–3
Molteno, Betty, 263

Mont Blanc, 119
Montmorency, Captain H., 5
Morant, Lieutenant H.H.
('Breaker'), 229–32, 299
Morgan, Colonel, 228
Morgan, Frank, 228
Morgendaal, J.J. (executed Boer),
200, 281
Morley, John, 239
Morning Leader, 240
Morning Post, 128, 252–3
Mostert's Hoek, 179
Mountain Battery, 10th, 112
Mounted Brigade, 126
'Mournful Monday' (30 October
1899), 112, 115
Mozambique, 45, 226
Munger's Farm, 136

Natal: annexed (1843), 21; British
rule in, 24; non-European
franchise in, 24; support for
Rhodes, 37; opposes use of
armed natives, 48; army
volunteers from, 56, 83–4; Asians
(Indians) raise ambulance corps,
84–5; Boer strategy in, 93; Boers
invade, 95, 105; Boer successes
in, 116; Buller's forces in, 131–2;
Boer offensive broken, 173;
concentration camps in, 194;
annexes Vryheid and Utrecht,
283–4; and peace terms, 284, 291
Natal Mounted Rifles, 109
Natal Volunteer Field Battery, 108,
112
Natal Volunteers, 83
National Scouts (*joiners*), 6, 95–7,
271–2, 282, 288, 294
naval brigades, 114–16
Ndebele rebellion (1896), 36
Nel, Commandant, 177